"Hamilton has done his homework—and numerous footnotes reveal his scholarship—but he keeps the plot moving as he focuses on the pastoral duty of preaching the book. When exegeting difficult texts he presents the best case for differing viewpoints and then argues persuasively for his, all with an eye on preaching. Pastors will find here an inspiring foundation to craft their own sermons (and check their work), and laypeople will discover a pastoral guide through the minefield that is Revelation. Do you have a question about a passage in Revelation? Look here first."

Michael Wittmer, Professor of Systematic and Historical Theology, Cornerstone University

"In a day when most preachers appear to be terrified by the prospects of preaching any text beyond the third chapter of the Apocalypse, I find Dr. James Hamilton's *Revelation: The Spirit Speaks to the Churches* to be an oasis in the wilderness. Though my own interpretation of the book is light years removed from that of Professor Hamilton, the purity of his love for Christ, for his church, and for the Word of God makes every page a delight to read regardless of his eschatological position."

Paige Patterson, President, Southwestern Baptist Theological Seminary

REVELATION

PREACHING THE WORD
Edited by R. Kent Hughes

Unless otherwise indicated, all volumes are by R. Kent Hughes

(((PREACHING *the* WORD)))

REVELATION

The SPIRIT SPEAKS
to the CHURCHES

JAMES M. HAMILTON JR.

R. Kent Hughes
Series Editor

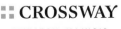 CROSSWAY

WHEATON, ILLINOIS

Cover design: Simplicated Studio

Cover illustration: Adam Greene

First printing 2012

Printed in the United States of America

Italics in biblical quotes indicate emphasis added.

Unless otherwise indicated, Scripture quotations are from the ESV® Bible (*The Holy Bible, English Standard Version*®), copyright © 2001 by Crossway. Used by permission. All rights reserved.

Scripture quotations marked HCSB have been taken from *The Holman Christian Standard Bible*®. Copyright © 1999, 2000, 2002, 2003 by Holman Bible Publishers. Used by permission.

Scripture quotations marked NASB are from *The New American Standard Bible*®. Copyright © The Lockman Foundation 1960, 1962, 1963, 1968, 1971, 1972, 1973, 1975, 1977, 1995. Used by permission.

Scripture quotations marked NIV are from *The Holy Bible, New International Version*®, NIV® Copyright © 1973, 1978, 1984, 2010 by Biblica, Inc. Used by permission. All rights reserved worldwide.

ISBN-13: 978-1-4335-0541-6
ISBN-10: 1-4335-0541-X
PDF ISBN: 978-1-4335-0542-3
Mobipocket ISBN: 978-1-4335-0543-0
ePub ISBN: 978-1-4335-2307-6

Library of Congress Cataloging-in-Publication Data
Hamilton, James M., 1974–
   Revelation : the Spirit speaks to the churches / James M. Hamilton, Jr.
      p. cm. (Preaching the Word)
   Includes bibliographical references and index.
   ISBN 978-1-4335-0541-6 (hc)
   1. Bible. N.T. Revelation—Commentaries. I. Title. II. Series.
BS2825.53.H36   2011
228'.07—dc22   2011006216

Crossway is a publishing ministry of Good News Publishers.

TS		24	23	22	21	20	19	18	17	16	15	14	13
16	15	14	13	12	11	10	9	8	7	6	5	4	3	2

For Jake, Jed, and Luke
May the High King on the white horse
capture your imagination
and lay claim to your allegiance

To him who loves us and has freed us from our sins
by his blood.
REVELATION 1:5b

Behold, the Lion of the tribe of Judah, the Root of David,
has conquered. . . . I saw a Lamb standing,
as though it had been slain.
REVELATION 5:5b, 6b

And they have conquered him by the blood of the Lamb
and by the word of their testimony,
for they loved not their lives even unto death.
REVELATION 12:11

Let us rejoice and exult and give him the glory,
for the marriage of the Lamb has come,
and his Bride has made herself ready.
REVELATION 19:7

. . . and behold, a white horse!
The one sitting on it is called Faithful and True,
and in righteousness he judges and makes war.
REVELATION 19:11

They will see his face,
and his name will be on their foreheads.
REVELATION 22:4

"Behold, I am coming soon, bringing my recompense with me,
to repay everyone for what he has done.
I am the Alpha and the Omega, the first and the last,
the beginning and the end."
REVELATION 22:12, 13

The Spirit and the Bride say, "Come."
And let the one who hears say, "Come." And let the one
who is thirsty come; let the one who desires
take the water of life without price.
REVELATION 22:17

Contents

List of Tables

A Word to Those Who
Preach the Word

There are times when I am preaching that I have especially sensed the pleasure of God. I usually become aware of it through the unnatural silence. The ever-present coughing ceases, and the pews stop creaking, bringing an almost physical quiet to the sanctuary—through which my words sail like arrows. I experience a heightened eloquence, so that the cadence and volume of my voice intensify the truth I am preaching.

There is nothing quite like it—the Holy Spirit filling one's sails, the sense of his pleasure, and the awareness that something is happening among one's hearers. This experience is, of course, not unique, for thousands of preachers have similar experiences, even greater ones.

What has happened when this takes place? How do we account for this sense of his smile? The answer for me has come from the ancient rhetorical categories of *logos*, *ethos*, and *pathos*.

The first reason for his smile is the *logos*—in terms of preaching, God's Word. This means that as we stand before God's people to proclaim his Word, we have done our homework. We have exegeted the passage, mined the significance of its words in their context, and applied sound hermeneutical principles in interpreting the text so that we understand what its words meant to its hearers. And it means that we have labored long until we can express in a sentence what the theme of the text is—so that our outline springs from the text. Then our preparation will be such that as we preach, we will not be preaching our own thoughts about God's Word, but God's actual Word, his *logos*. This is fundamental to pleasing him in preaching.

The second element in knowing God's smile in preaching is *ethos*—what you are as a person. There is a danger endemic to preaching, which is having your hands and heart cauterized by holy things. Phillips Brooks illustrated it by the analogy of a train conductor who comes to believe that he has been to the places he announces because of his long and loud heralding of them. And that is why Brooks insisted that preaching must be "the bringing of truth through personality." Though we can never perfectly embody the truth we preach, we must be subject to it, long for it, and make it as much a part of our ethos as possible. As the Puritan William Ames said, "Next to the Scriptures,

13

nothing makes a sermon more to pierce, than when it comes out of the inward affection of the heart without any affectation." When a preacher's *ethos* backs up his *logos*, there will be the pleasure of God.

Last, there is *pathos*—personal passion and conviction. David Hume, the Scottish philosopher and skeptic, was once challenged as he was seen going to hear George Whitefield preach: "I thought you do not believe in the gospel." Hume replied, "I don't, but he does." Just so! When a preacher believes what he preaches, there will be passion. And this belief and requisite passion will know the smile of God.

The pleasure of God is a matter of *logos* (the Word), *ethos* (what you are), and *pathos* (your passion). As you preach the Word may you experience his smile—the Holy Spirit in your sails!

R. Kent Hughes

Preface

Jesus is Lord—crucified, risen, ascended, reigning, and returning. All Scripture is God-breathed and profitable—including John's Apocalypse. It was my privilege to preach the book of Revelation to the saints at Baptist Church of the Redeemer in Houston, Texas, from March 12 to August 14, 2005. I did not manuscript those sermons, and as the church plant was at that time in its infancy, the sermons were not recorded. At that time the congregation consisted of twenty to thirty people (including children!), and the church had no sound system. We were small, but the Word of God is big. I went through the book then in larger units of text than I have done so in the sermons in this volume. There is more than one way to preach through a book. The sermons in this book were preached at Kenwood Baptist Church in Louisville, Kentucky, from April 5, 2009 to April 4, 2010. I chose smaller units of text for the sermons in this volume so that more detail could be included, but the book of Revelation has by no means been exhausted, nor can it ever be.

The sermons in this volume have a straightforward structure: Introduction, Body, Conclusion. In the *introduction* I seek to do five things: (1) Grab attention. (2) Raise awareness of a real need that people have, a need that is addressed by the teaching of the text. The goal is to make people feel that they need to listen closely. Ideally, the need we have will be connected somehow to the opening attention-grabber. (3) State the main point of the text. The main idea of the text is the main idea of the sermon. This main idea seeks to meet the need that has just been raised. (4) Preview the structure of the text that will be preached. The structure of the text will then become the structure of the sermon. (5) Give the wider context of the passage at hand. Depending on the details of the text, the discussion of the wider context will focus on either the book of Revelation or the whole canon of Scripture, and relevant information from the historical background might be introduced here as well.

The *body* of the sermon then proceeds through the structure of the text. There are as many points in the sermon as there are sections in the text being preached. In addition to expositing the meaning of each section of the passage, I seek (1) to connect the main ideas in this section to the main point of the passage, and (2) to apply the teaching of this section of text to the congregation. In thinking about how to apply texts, I have benefited from Mark Dever's "Application Grid."[1]

The *conclusion* of the sermon seeks to restate the key ideas in the sections of the text, which should naturally lead to a restatement of the main idea of the passage. A sermon might also conclude with some poignant example or illustration that communicates the burden of the sermon.

Expository preaching happens when the main point of the text is the main point of the sermon and the structure of the text is the structure of the sermon. More gifted expositors may be able to exposit texts in a variety of ways. The rest of us are helped by "cookie-cutter" structures like the one I have just outlined.

I wish to thank Kent Hughes for inviting me to contribute this volume to the Preaching the Word series, along with Justin Taylor and the others at Crossway. Tom Schreiner discussed the details of the book of Revelation with me at many points, and my gratitude for his friendship goes beyond what I can put into words. Several of my PhD students were kind enough to work carefully through the manuscript, saving me from many errors and improving the project in many ways. Hearty thanks to Mitch Chase, Cameron Jungels, Nick Moore, and Dieudonne Tamfu. My parents heard many of these sermons, and my father's encouragement and my mother's love plant joy's roots way down deep.

If marriage is about the relationship between Christ and the church (cf. Ephesians 5:21–33), the epic task of my life is to love my sweet wife as Christ has loved his bride. No undertaking could be more thrilling to me. In Marilynne Robinson's *Gilead*, John Ames remarks, "In eternity this world will be Troy, I believe, and all that has passed here will be the epic of the universe, the ballad they sing in the streets." The good gift of my wife makes our song sweeter than I can say. It is our nightly prayer that God would be pleased to extend his mercy to our sons, that their eyes would be opened to the glory and trustworthiness of the one who redeemed us from our sins by his blood (Revelation 1:5). I dedicate this book to Jake, Jed, and Luke, with the prayer that they will swear fealty to Jesus the great King, Lord of the world, the Conqueror coming on the white horse.

Praise God for the Bible! And thanks be to God for sending his angel to his servant John, to show his servants what must soon take place. What a blessing to study and proclaim this revelation of Jesus the Messiah, to love God and his people by expositing the riches of this portion of holy writ, and to say with John, the Spirit, and the Bride, "Come, Lord Jesus!" (Revelation 22:17, 20). May ours be the blessing on those who read, hear, and keep the words of the prophecy of this book of Revelation (Revelation 1:3; 22:7).

Jim Hamilton, Easter 2010

1

The Revelation of the Glory of God's Justice and Mercy

REVELATION 1—22

WE ALL KNOW WHAT TOOK PLACE September 11, 2001. Nineteen terrorists. Four planes. Two towers of the World Trade Center. The Pentagon. An open field. Nearly three thousand people dead.

What if you had known about all that with absolute certainty on September 10, 2001? What if you had gotten information on the afternoon of September 10, 2001, about what was going to happen the next morning? What if your wife or your son or your mother or your brother-in-law was going to be on one of those planes? Would you not do absolutely everything in your power to use the information you had received to help people avoid the fiery destruction that was coming?

Something is coming that is going to be infinitely worse than 9/11, eternally worse—the judgment of God.

God has given information in the past that has helped people escape the coming conflagration, and there have been times when people have made powerful use of what God revealed about the future. Why couldn't something like that happen today? What would your life look like if you made use of what God has revealed about what is to come?

In Moses' day the Lord revealed himself to Israel, creating them as a nation, reshaping their lives around his word. We have the Bible. Why not today?

Samuel faithfully proclaimed the word of God for twenty years, and then revival came. We have the Bible. Why not today?

The Bible was rediscovered in Josiah's day. The priest Hilkiah found the Book of the Law in the house of the Lord, and once again society was reshaped around the Word of God. We have the Bible. Why not today?

In Ezra's day he faithfully proclaimed the word of God for thirteen years. Nehemiah came on the scene, and the people turned their hearts to the word of the Lord proclaimed by Ezra. The society was reshaped around the word of God. We have the Bible. Why not today?

We could go on and on giving examples of times when things were awful, and then people got serious about God's revelation of himself, and so many lives were changed that society was transformed. It happened in Luther's day, in Whitefield's day, and in some places it is happening today. Why not here? Why not today?

What would it look like for this to happen today? What would it look like for God to become the dominant reality in your life, in my life? What would it look like for the things in the Bible to be more real to you than the things on television or the things on the Internet?

God has revealed himself to accomplish this very thing. God reveals himself so that we will know reality. In the book of Revelation, God unveils the world as it really is.

Need

We have been lulled to sleep by the ordinariness of our lives. Our senses have been dulled by the humdrum of one day after another. We need to see God as he is. We need to be convinced that Jesus is reigning as the risen King. We need to have him speak to the situation in our churches. We need to know that God is right now on his throne, in control in Heaven, worshiped by myriads upon myriads of the heavenly host. We need to see the way that God will pulverize wickedness, obliterate those who oppose him, and set up his kingdom. The book of Revelation has exactly what we need.

Main Point

The Lord gives us this "*revelation* of Jesus Christ" and of what will "soon take place" (1:1) so that we can know and enjoy him by living in light of reality and in light of the way history will be brought to its consummation. More specifically, God wants us to know the glory of his mercy and his justice, and that is what we see in Revelation: history culminates in climactic demonstrations of the glory of God in salvation through judgment.[1]

To say it another way, God has given us the book of Revelation so we can know him in his glorious justice and mercy and live worshipfully by faith.

Structure

Broadly speaking, we can break the whole book of Revelation down into three parts:

Revelation 1:1–8	The Opening: the Apocalyptic Prophecy's Epistolary Opening
Revelation 1:9–22:9	The Vision: John's Vision on the Lord's Day
Revelation 22:10–21	The Closing: the Apocalyptic Prophecy's Epistolary Closing

We can also break the body of the book, John's Vision (1:9–22:9), down into three large sections:

1:9–3:22	Jesus and the Letters
4:1–16:21	The Throne and the Judgments
17:1–22:9	The Harlot, the King, and the Bride

Context

The book of the Revelation of Jesus Christ is appropriately placed at the end of the canon. This book catches up and weaves together all the Bible's lines of prophetic revelation. John writes in such a way that his book is the capstone of all the prophecy in the Bible.[2]

Table 1.1: The Structure of Revelation

1:1–8, Revelation, Blessing, and Epistolary Opening

1:9–22:9, John's Vision on the Lord's Day

    1:9–3:22, The Risen Christ to the Seven Churches

    4:1–16:21, The Throne and the Judgments

        4:1–5:14, The Throne Room Vision

        6:1–17, Six Seals

        7:1–17, The Sealing of the Saints and Their Worship

        8:1–5, The Seventh Seal

        8:6–9:21, Six Trumpets

        10:1–11:14, Prophetic Witness

        11:15–19, The Seventh Trumpet

        12:1–14:20, Conflict Between the Seed of the Woman and the Seed of the Serpent

        15:1–16:21, Seven Bowls

    17:1–22:9, The Fall of the Harlot, the Return of the King, and the Descent of the Bride

22:10–21, Revelation, Blessing, and Epistolary Closing

In this chapter we will overview the book of Revelation in order to prepare us for the immediate future, the distant future, and the eternal future. We want to get the weight and balance of the whole book.[3] We want to understand the book's flow of thought, its structure, and the main points made in each section. This will help us rightly understand the smaller units of the book in context when we study them in coming chapters. So we'll look at the Opening (1:1–8), the Vision (1:9–22:9), and the Closing (22:10–21).

As we begin, let's ask the Lord to use this book to fire us with the same urgency we would have if it were September 10, 2001, and we had just learned what was going to happen the next morning. You would not rest with that information. So may it be with this information.

Revelation 1:1–8: The Apocalyptic Prophecy's Epistolary Opening

One of the most important things to do when trying to understand any piece of writing is to understand the genre of what it is we are reading. We know what to expect from comic strips, blogs, novels, and nonfiction books. So it's important to understand the genre of Revelation to know what to expect.

The opening words of the book identify it, literally, as an "Apocalypse of Jesus Christ" (1:1). An *apocalypse* typically concerns itself with what will take place at the end of history, whereas *prophecy* usually deals with what will take place in the flow of history before it reaches its consummation.[4] That the book of Revelation is an apocalypse, then, leads us to expect that it will "unveil"—which is the etymological meaning of the term "apocalypse"—what will take place at the end of history.[5] This Bible book claims to "uncover" how history will be concluded.

John also pronounces a blessing in 1:3 on those who read, hear, and keep what is written in "this prophecy." So John not only describes his book as an apocalypse, he also tells us that it is a prophecy. Revelation, then, is an apocalyptic prophecy.

And there is more. Beginning in 1:4 John takes up the same format that we see in Paul's letters: the author identifies himself, identifies the recipients of the letter, and wishes them grace. The book also ends in a way that is similar to the way many New Testament letters end, with the words, "The grace of the Lord Jesus be with all. Amen" (22:21). The churches mentioned as the recipients of the book in 1:4 are further identified in 1:11, and then they are directly addressed in chapters 2, 3. These churches appear to be named in the order in which a letter carrier would have gone from one church to another, starting from Ephesus.[6] What we have in Revelation, then, is "an apocalyptic prophecy in the form of a circular letter."[7]

This book is a circular letter addressed to Christians in churches. That means it is written to encourage Christians. The whole book was probably intended to be read aloud, in one sitting, in a worship gathering of the local church.[8] In writing to seven churches, seven being a number of completion and wholeness, John writes to all the churches.[9] Being an apocalyptic prophecy, this letter reveals the future to us; it pulls back the veil and lets us see the world as it truly is. The book of Revelation is meant to help us see reality. And the truth about this world is that it is a world in which the glory of God will be seen in his justice, which in turn will highlight the gracious and free character of his mercy. Knowing that it is God's purpose to display his glory in these ways is one of the blessings of reading and studying this book.

Revelation 1:9–22:9: John's Vision on the Lord's Day

John has tipped us off as to the structure of the book of Revelation by using the phrase "in the Spirit" near the beginning of the major sections of the body of the book (1:10; 4:2; 17:3; 21:10).[10] Beginning in 1:9, John recounts the way that Jesus appeared to him in glory (1:9–20), dictated to him specific letters addressing the seven churches (2:1–3:22), and called him up into the heavenly throne room to see the worship of God there (4:1–5:14). In the throne room, John sees Jesus take a scroll from the Father, and from what happens when the scroll is opened, we know that the writing on the scroll describes the events that will bring history to its appointed consummation. Jesus opens the seals on the scroll (6:1–8:1); then seven angels blow seven trumpets (8:2–11:19).

John describes the conflict between the seed of the woman and the seed of the serpent in cosmic terms in chapters 12—14. Then the final seven bowls of God's wrath are poured out in chapters 15, 16.

In chapters 17—22 we have a harlot, the King, and his bride. Revelation 17:1–19:10 personifies the wicked world system as a prostitute named Babylon, and the outpouring of God's wrath results in her fall. King Jesus then comes and sets up his kingdom in 19:11–21:8. His coming is followed by the description of the people of God personified as the pure bride of the Lamb, the new Jerusalem, descending from Heaven for the marriage supper of the Lamb (21:9–22:9).

Let's look more closely at each of these sections to see the overarching point of each part of the body of Revelation.

Revelation 1:9–3:22: Jesus and the Letters

There is a striking contrast between the obvious glory and authority of the risen Christ in 1:9–20 and the beleaguered, persecuted, oppressed, sinful, unimpressive, insignificant state of the churches addressed in chapters 2, 3. Five of the seven churches are rebuked for some specific sin and called to repentance. The two churches that are not rebuked are opposed by the "synagogue of Satan" (2:9; 3:9) and are told that they will suffer (2:10). Jesus promises to preserve them through suffering (3:10).

Most of us are probably not facing life-threatening persecution like the church in Smyrna was facing (2:10), but we are probably all aware of plenty of reasons to be discouraged about the state of the church. Like Ephesus and Laodicea, we either know that our love is not what it was at first (2:4), or we know those in the church who are lukewarm (3:16). We don't have to look far, either, to find false teaching, idolatry, immorality, and spiritual death in churches (cf. 2:14, 20; 3:2). Until Jesus comes, as long as there are people in churches, there will be problems in churches.

We might be discouraged by the letters to the seven churches. They tell the truth about the sinful, challenged, seemingly weak state of the churches. On the other hand, the vision of the risen Christ in 1:9–20 shows that Jesus is standing among the churches, holding the angels of the churches in his right hand, attending to their well-being, and possessing all glory and power and authority. Then as Jesus addresses the churches, the opening of each letter proclaims some aspect of his glory. He shows his love for the churches by disciplining them (3:19), and then he promises breathtaking rewards to those who overcome.

When seemingly weak Christians who are unappreciated by the wider society maintain their faith and continue to proclaim the gospel in spite of every temptation and opposition, God shows his glory in his ability to preserve his people. These people also testify that Jesus is their treasure, which condemns the treasures of the world as worthless. And when the unimpressive, insignificant church is vindicated, the things that are impressive by worldly standards are condemned, and the wisdom and power of God are displayed.

As the churches are compelled by the glory of Christ (1:9–20) to obey what he calls them to (2:1–3:22), we see that in spite of the way things seem now, God is the central reality of life. He is going to save the righteous and judge the wicked. And the righteous are those who have been freed from their sins by the blood of Jesus (1:5).

If it seems to you that the church is unimpressive, may I suggest that this is the way God intended the church to seem. Jesus, too, was unimpressive by worldly standards. He has now been exalted, and the promises he makes to those who overcome guarantee that exaltation will follow humiliation. We see in 2:7 that the overcomers will eat of the tree of life; in 2:11 they will not be hurt by the second death; in 2:17 they are promised hidden manna and a new name on a white stone; in 2:26 they are promised authority over the nations; in 3:5 they are promised white garments and Jesus' acknowledgment before the Father; in 3:12 they are promised the right to a place in God's temple with the name of God and Jesus written on them; in 3:21 they are promised the right to sit with Jesus on his throne.

Are you suffering? Are you persecuted? Do you feel that Christianity ruins your reputation? My friend, as a Christian you follow Jesus, who was humiliated before he was exalted. That sequence will be your sequence: first humiliation, then exaltation. God is going to make the wisdom of the world into foolishness and will reward those who trust him; which is to say, God will display his glory when he saves his people by condemning the wicked. Endure the cross, scorning its shame, empowered by the joy set before you in these promises of future exaltation.

Revelation 4:1–16:21: The Throne and the Judgments

Just as there is a stark contrast between the exalted Christ in chapter 1 and the lowly churches in chapters 2, 3, there is a similar contrast between the lukewarm, sinful churches in chapters 2, 3 and the throne room of Heaven in chapters 4, 5. This contrast is intended to jolt the churches out of lukewarmness into the same passionate worship of God that is happening even now in Heaven. The description of the radiant glory of God in chapter 4 is meant to put the spotlight on the beauty of holiness and the wretchedness of sin, and this is meant to purify the churches.

Flowing out of the heavenly worship scene are the judgments of the seals, the trumpets, and the bowls. In 4:5 we read that "From the throne came flashes of lightning, and rumblings and peals of thunder," and then we find lightning and thunder after the seventh seal (8:5), after the seventh trumpet (11:19), and after the seventh bowl (16:18). This is one of the features in Revelation that connects the judgments of the seals, trumpets, and bowls with the throne: these judgments come from God himself. When we feel the magnetic force of temptation, we need to visualize the inescapable judgment of God described in chapters 6—16. We need to pray that God will use the revelation of his wrath to bulldoze the wickedness that is wooing us.

Interspersed through these chapters are also several sections that show God's ability to preserve his people. Between the opening of the sixth seal in 6:12–17 and the seventh seal in 8:1, chapter 7 describes the saints of God being sealed (7:1–8) and worshiping God in Heaven (7:9–17). Similarly, between the sixth trumpet in 9:13–21 and the seventh trumpet in 11:15–19,

10:1–11:14 presents the divine origin and protection of the church's prophetic witness.

God's protection of his people is also dramatically illustrated in chapters 12—14 where the cosmic conflict between Satan and the people of God is described. Satan presents a cheap imitation of the crucifixion and resurrection of the Lamb of God in the form of a seven-headed beast with one head that was mortally wounded and then healed (13:1–3). Everyone worships the beast, the fake christ (13:3)—everyone, that is, except those whose names God wrote in the Lamb's book of life before the foundation of the world (13:8). God protects his people from all Satan's schemes.

Satan then counterfeits the Trinity (cf. 12:17; 13:1, 11; 16:13). He has faked the crucifixion, and now he produces a cheap imitation of the Holy Spirit (13:11–14). This beastly fake holy spirit then produces a cheap imitation of the sealing of God's saints when he compels the world to receive the number of the beast (13:16–18). Satan is a fake. Don't be taken in by his schemes. Don't be tempted by his false offers. See him for what he is—for what Revelation reveals him to be: a perverse twister of the beauties of God.

As we proceed through chapters 6—16, the judgments get progressively worse. The seals affect one fourth of the world (6:8), the trumpets affect one third of the world (9:18), and the outpouring of the bowls will complete God's wrath as no one escapes his judgment (16:1–21).

God's justice is perfect. He is holy. All deserve to be consumed by it. But again and again in Revelation we see that God spares some, and we see them declaring in 7:10, "Salvation belongs to our God who sits on the throne, and to the Lamb!" In 5:9 we see that Jesus "ransomed people for God." In 14:4 we read that they "follow the Lamb wherever he goes" and were "redeemed from mankind." So we must ask: is it possible to join the ranks of those described in 7:3, who receive the seal of God on the forehead? Is it possible to become one who is redeemed, as 1:5 describes, one who is freed from sin by the blood of Jesus?

First, let's look at what Revelation shows us *not* to do. We should not be like those who see the outpouring of God's wrath and refuse to repent. After the sixth trumpet, we read in 9:20, "The rest of mankind, who were not killed by these plagues, did not repent." After the fourth bowl is poured out, we see in 16:9, "They did not repent and give him glory." After the fifth bowl is poured out, in 16:11, "They did not repent of their deeds." And after the seventh bowl, in 16:21, "they cursed God."

These who refused to repent failed to see the mercy God folded into his judgment. The outpouring of God's wrath is meant to condemn everything else that you trust. God's judgment is actually his kindness in disguise. He uses it, while we live, to lead us to repentance and salvation. God judges us so that he can save us.

We see a universal proclamation of the gospel in 14:6, 7: "Then I saw another angel flying directly overhead, with an eternal gospel to proclaim to those who dwell on earth, to every nation and tribe and language and people. And he said with a loud voice, 'Fear God and give him glory, because the hour of his judgment has come, and worship him who made heaven and earth, the sea and the springs of water.'"

Revelation 1:3 promises a blessing to those who "hear, and keep what is written" in the book. Through this book you are intended to *hear* of the coming judgment, *believe* what it says, and *keep* the words of this book by repenting of sin and worshiping God. And God will be glorified in your salvation, which came through the judgment of all the false things you trusted.

Have you noticed how nothing seems to last in this world? Have you noticed how nothing works out exactly the way we hoped it would? Have you noticed how all your best intentions often come to nothing? Jesus is your only hope. If you don't already trust him, turn to him now and place your faith in his ability to save you.

Revelation 17:1–22:9: The Harlot, the King, and the Bride

Chapters 17—22 tell us about the harlot, the King, and the bride. The section on the King is in the middle, and John marks off the boundaries of these three sections by using similar language at the beginning and end of the sections on the harlot and the bride.[11]

So the wording of the beginning of the section on the harlot is matched by the wording of the beginning of the section on the bride.

Table 1.2: Matching Language Opening the Sections on the Harlot and the Bride

Revelation 17:1, 3	Revelation 21:9, 10
"Then one of the seven angels who had the seven bowls came and said to me, 'Come, I will show you . . . And he carried me away in the Spirit."	"Then came one of the seven angels who had the seven bowls . . . and spoke to me saying, 'Come, I will show you . . . And he carried me away in the Spirit."

Similarly, the wording of the ending of the section on the harlot is matched by the wording of the ending of the section on the bride.

The harlot is a symbol for the world system that is opposed to God. She is called Babylon because in the Bible Babylon is the capital of those who rebel against God. Chapters 17, 18 show her debased and exposed, and all her seductive power comes to nothing.

Table 1.3: Matching Language Ending the Sections on the Harlot and the Bride

Revelation 19:9, 10	Revelation 22:6, 8, 9
"... And he said to me, 'These are the true words of God.' Then I fell down at his feet to worship him, but he said to me, 'You must not do that! I am a fellow servant with you and your brothers who hold to the testimony of Jesus. Worship God.'"	"And he said to me, 'These words are trustworthy and true.' ... I fell down to worship at the feet of the angel who showed them to me, but he said to me, 'You must not do that! I am a fellow servant with you and your brothers the prophets, and with those who keep the words of this book. Worship God.'"

Let me put that another way: the things that tempt us are exposed. They are nothing but the devil's attempt to make the bride of Christ into a harlot. We who believe are the bride of the Lord Jesus Christ. Satan wants to make us common whores. He wants to lure us into spiritual adultery with his cheap imitations of true pleasure. The book of Revelation shows us that these pleasures will not satisfy and do not last. They will be destroyed with the wicked world system ranged against God.

Then the King comes, conquers his enemies (19:11–21) and sets up his kingdom (20:1–21:8), and his glorious bride descends from Heaven (21:9–22:9). The bride is a symbol of the people of God, the redeemed, those who trust in Jesus. She is called the new Jerusalem because Jerusalem was the dwelling place of God in the Old Testament, the city where the Lord chose to put his name, and in the new covenant God's *people* are his dwelling place.[12]

We would do well to take to heart the splendor of the wedding of the Lord Jesus Christ and his pure bride. Jesus cleanses his bride with the water of the Word. He laid down his life for his bride (cf. Ephesians 5:22–33). Fix your heart on the glory of that wedding day. Point your whole life toward that glorious consummation, and let everything you do between now and then be informed by that moment when Jesus will come. Live for him now so that you will enjoy him then. Meditate on these texts until the blazing purity of the Lord Jesus is more desirable to you than the filthy pleasures that are nothing more than twisted parodies of his good gifts. And do everything you can to make sure that your day-to-day activities are done in a way that honors the King. God has given the book of Revelation to us so that we will live in light of the punishing and rewarding Jesus will do when he comes.

We want everyone we know to enjoy Jesus with us. We want everyone we know to escape the judgment of God. We want everyone we know to realize that "the day of the Lord will come like a thief in the night" (1 Thessalonians 5:2). Something worse than 9/11 could happen to them at any moment. Is your heart hardened to what could happen to people you know? If it was September 10, 2001, and someone you knew worked at the World Trade Center or was scheduled to be on one of those planes, you would communicate with them, wouldn't you? Any minute now something worse could happen to every unbelieving person you know.

Revelation 22:10–21: The Apocalyptic Prophecy's Epistolary Closing

The future has been unveiled. This book is "The revelation of Jesus Christ" (1:1). And it is given to us because the angel speaking to John told him what we read in 22:10, "Do not seal up the words of the prophecy of this book, for the time is near."

Why could that not happen today? Why not thousands converted? Why not the Bible preached and the gospel cherished and the churches full to bursting? Why not so many people in so many gospel churches that the whole society is reshaped around God's Word? Why not today? God's arm is not too short to save.

Is your imagination too small? Is your love too little? Is your Bible reading too infrequent? Are your evangelistic efforts too seldom? Are your prayers too self-centered? God's arm is not too short to save!

Jesus your Savior and Lord? Why not today?

The power of sin broken in your life? Why not today?

Devoted to prayer and Bible study? Why not today?

Eager to tell others about God's work in salvation and their need to respond in faith? Why not today?

Hell is real, and it never ends. The Savior has been slain, and he rose from the dead. God warns you of judgment to come. Faith in Christ saves. Jesus is King.

Our task is to live in a way that matches what the unveiling, the book of Revelation, has shown us about the way things really are. Jesus is coming quickly, bringing his recompense (22:12).

"Every eye will see him, even those who pierced him" (1:7). Every knee will bow and every tongue confess him as Lord (Philippians 2:10, 11). Every action, word, and thought will be measured by the standard of God's glory. Every transgression or disobedience will receive just retribution (cf. Hebrews 2:2). You will either be among those praising God for saving you from his wrath through the judgment of Jesus on the cross, or you will be judged to display the eternal, almighty justice of God. Trust in Jesus. He is humanity's only hope. If you trust him, live for him. He asserts in 22:20 that he is coming soon.

May you know him in his saving and judging glory, in his awful wrath that highlights his tender mercy. May you abide in this Revelation, and may "The grace of the Lord Jesus be with all. Amen" (22:21).

2

The Blessing of the
Revelation of Jesus Christ

REVELATION 1:1–8

THE ANCIENT ROMAN HISTORIAN Suetonius writes of the emperor Domitian (A.D. 51–96), "after making free with the wives of many men, he went so far as to marry Domitia Longina, who was the wife of Aelius Lamia."[1] Suetonius also relates that when his brother Titus "was seized with a dangerous illness," Domitian "ordered that he be left for dead, before he had actually drawn his last breath."[2] When Cornelia, the chief vestal virgin, was found guilty of having a lover, Domitian had her "buried alive; and her lovers were beaten to death with rods."[3] Domitian "slew Aelius Lamia for joking remarks, which were reflections on him, it is true, but made long before and harmless."[4] He seduced his niece, who was married, and eventually "became the cause of her death by compelling her to get rid of a child of his by abortion."[5]

Domitian was a moral catastrophe of a man, and he was also physically unimpressive. There is an account of him vigorously scratching a festered wart on his forehead and drawing blood.[6] He is described as being "sensitive about his baldness" and as having "a protruding belly, and spindling legs."[7] This weak and wicked Caesar insisted on being addressed as "Lord and God" (*Dominus et deus*).[8]

And we complain about our government!

The Roman Caesars were pictures of human depravity. Roman culture lacked the benefit of the restraining influence of Christianity. The nature of Roman virtue and what Roman culture valued presents a stark contrast with Christian virtues and values.

Imagine living in a world ruled by a man who would leave his brother to die, seduce his own niece, kill people for making jokes about him, and then demand to be addressed as "Lord and God." Irenaeus tells us that John "beheld the apocalyptic vision . . . towards the end of Domitian's reign."[9] From what we see in Revelation, it appears that Christians were facing persecution, and John himself had been exiled to Patmos.

As we read Revelation, it helps to know that the first audience's culture was uninfluenced by Christianity. It is also important to recognize the obvious: persecuted people tend to feel persecuted. Persecuted people are not *normally* inclined to feel that God has blessed them, and persecuted people are not *normally* inclined to praise God. So when persecuted people claim to be blessed and when persecuted people praise God, they are behaving in *abnormal* ways.

Need

At this point in our experience most of us are probably not facing exile, like John experienced (1:9), and while there are martyrs today, like Antipas (2:13), most of us are not facing the threat of being killed for the faith. But this does not mean that we face *no* persecution for our faith. Have you ever had family members resent your presence—even if you haven't said anything—because they know what you believe? Have you ever been accused of being judgmental? Have you ever been called "narrow-minded," "arrogant," "self-righteous," "intolerant," "bigoted," or "unenlightened" because you believe that the only way to be right with God is to trust in Jesus?

Even if these mild forms of persecution have not resulted in exile or physical violence, our culture communicates to us that our ideas about religion will not be tolerated. Strange how intolerant the champions of tolerance can be!

The churches that received the book of Revelation needed to know *how* God had blessed them—because by the world's standards they did not seem blessed. We too need to know how God has blessed us.

The churches that received the book of Revelation also needed to know *why* they should praise God—because by the world's way of reckoning, God had not made them the most influential, most successful, most impressive, most wealthy, most healthy people. We too need to know why we should praise God.

Main Point

As we look at 1:1–8, we see that God reveals himself so that those who know him are blessed and praise him regardless of their circumstances.

Preview

These first eight verses of Revelation fall into two sections:

1:1–3   The Blessing of the Apocalyptic Prophecy
1:4–8   The Doxology of the Epistolary Opening

Don't let those big words bother you. If you prefer, drop the big words and simply think of verses 1–3 as "Blessing" and verses 4–8 as "Doxology."

Context

The book of Revelation stands at the end of the canon. So these first eight verses of the book introduce the exclamation point at the end of the sentence that is the Bible. The first eight verses of Revelation introduce the rest of the book, and so these verses are sometimes referred to as a prologue. Similarly, the last twelve verses (22:10–21) are sometimes referred to as an epilogue. Everything in between, 1:9–22:9, constitutes the body of the book—the visionary experience John had on the Lord's day (1:10). What we see in 1:1–8 sets up the body of the book.

Revelation 1:1–3: The Blessing of the Apocalyptic Prophecy

The opening words of the book of Revelation tell us what this book is. It is "The revelation of Jesus Christ" (1:1). The term "revelation" is sometimes rendered "apocalypse." This book unveils Jesus. It reveals him, telling us how things really are. The book of Revelation shows us the cataclysmic events at the end of history when good will finally triumph over evil.[10]

This phrase, "The revelation of Jesus Christ" (1:1), also has wider implications. Some people today prefer to describe the Bible as a "record of God's revelation."[11] This locates God's revelation in the *events* that Scripture records. According to this way of looking at things, the record of the event in the Bible is not the revelation, the event is. This is one of the ways that people who think that the Bible has errors nevertheless claim that God's revelation is true. But this way of looking at things does not describe the Bible the way the Bible describes itself.

Notice what John tells us about his book in that first phrase: "The revelation of Jesus Christ." John claims that his book *is* the *revelation* of Jesus. John does not say that his book is a *record* of the revelation of Jesus, but that his book *is* a revelation of Jesus. John writes this book and sends it to the churches so that the churches will be blessed by what he has written to them (see 1:3), not so that they will try to get behind the book to the visionary experience that John had. John wants the churches to read and hear his book. He does not want them to set the events the book records against his inspired description of those events in the book itself. Let me encourage you to trust the words of the Bible. Insofar as a particular translation accurately renders the original, it is the very word of God.[12] Read the Bible. Search it. Mark it. Live it. Holy Scripture will never mislead you.

We also see a chain of revelatory disclosure in verse 1. There are five parties involved: (1) God gave the revelation to (2) Jesus who made it known by sending his (3) angel to his servant (4) John who wrote it down for (5) the servants of God and Christ.

Do you see from this chain of people how important this book is? What I'm getting at is this: imagine visiting England and receiving a gift from the Queen. That would be pretty special, right? But look at what 1:1 claims about itself: "The revelation of Jesus Christ, *which God gave him. . . .* " This book comes from God himself. And God didn't give it to just anyone—he gave it to Jesus, who gave it to his angel, who revealed it to the beloved disciple, the Apostle John. Let this dignified series of people involved in the production of this gift provoke your appreciation for the Bible.

Sometime around A.D. 150 an early Christian wrote a letter to a man named Diognetus, and the author of that letter stresses that Christianity has been *revealed* by God, not *invented* by humans: "This teaching of theirs has not been discovered by the thought and reflection of ingenious people, nor do they promote any human doctrine, as some do" (*Diognetus* 5:3).[13]

The revelation is given so that the servants of God and Christ will know "the things that must soon take place" (1:1). No matter how many millennia pass before these events occur, in the light of eternity they will come soon. These events could happen at any moment. Are you ready?

The servants of God receive the revelation from God's servant, John. The ancient testimony is that this John is none other than the Apostle John, the son of Zebedee, the brother of James, the beloved disciple, author of the Gospel of John and the three letters of John.[14] John tells us in verse 2 that he "bore witness to the word of God and to the testimony of Jesus Christ, even to all that he saw." This is a claim to be telling the truth, all of it that he saw. The author of this book has identified himself by name in verse 1, and he has claimed to be giving eyewitness testimony in verse 2. This is strong attestation to the author's intention to tell what he believes is the truth.[15] You can trust the Bible, and you can trust the book of Revelation. John signed his name. To reject his testimony is to call him a liar or say he got it wrong.

God gave this revelation through Jesus (1:1), John testified to everything he saw (1:2), and that leads to verse 3: "Blessed is the one who reads aloud the words of this prophecy." This statement is made in spite of the fact that

John's testimony got him exiled to Patmos (1:2, 9). John evidently thought it more blessed to proclaim the book of Revelation than to avoid the suffering that could result.

He continues in verse 3, "and blessed are those who hear. . . ." This statement is made in spite of the fact that gathering with other Christians could have adverse effects upon one's standing in the community. A person could be held guilty by association with them. Your reputation could be tarnished. You could find yourself persecuted for being a Christian, persecuted by the wretched Domitian. John evidently thought it more blessed to hear the book of Revelation than to avoid such persecution.

How good must John's experience of Christianity be for him to declare this blessing! In spite of persecution, in spite of the ways that Christianity will not advance people in Roman culture, in spite of the fact that Christianity could cost you your life, you're blessed if you hear and keep the faith revealed in this book. John must think it's better to stand right before God by faith in Christ, forgiven and free of all sin, than it is to have all Rome bow before you.

John must think there is a life after this life in which the rewards for those who belong to Jesus will be superior to all the pleasures of sin in the present world. Is your experience of Christianity like John's? Do you know the relief that comes from knowing that faith in Christ and his death on the cross makes you right before God? Do you know there is something better to live for than this world?

If you're not a Christian, let me invite you to consider your standing before God. Let me invite you to consider the fact that you will stand before him to give an account of your actions. If you trust in Jesus, God will forgive your sins because Christ paid the penalty. If you don't trust in Jesus, you'll pay that penalty for yourself. Won't you trust Jesus today?

If you're a Christian, are you like John? Are you announcing to anyone who will listen how *blessed* it is to know God? Are you calling people to taste and see that the Lord is good? Won't you feast yourself on the Lord, and won't you announce his goodness to anyone who will listen?

Long ago a brother in Christ wrote to Diognetus about Christians:

> They love everyone, and by everyone they are persecuted.
> They are unknown, yet they are condemned;
>   they are put to death, yet they are brought to life.
> They are poor, yet they make many rich;
>   they are in need of everything, yet they abound in everything.
> They are dishonored, yet they are glorified in their dishonor;
>   they are slandered, yet they are vindicated.

They are cursed, yet they bless;
 they are insulted, yet they offer respect.
When they do good, they are punished as evildoers;
 when they are punished, they rejoice as though brought to life . . .
 and so Christians when punished daily increase more and more.
                                   (*Diognetus* 5:11–16; 6:9b)

Don't miss what that quotation communicates: these Christians live in a way that says that knowing God is better than freedom from persecution. Knowing God is better than avoiding martyrdom by denying him. Knowing God is better than money. Knowing God is better than worldly fame. Knowing God is better than doing evil to avoid persecution from a criminal government. And this causes their numbers to increase. When people show by their lives that knowing God is this good, others want to know such a God!

The next phrase in 1:3 significantly qualifies the blessing on those who read and those who hear with the words, "and who keep what is written in it." This tells us that the blessing John is talking about is not some external magic formula that automatically results in what the world thinks of when they hear the word "blessed." This blessing that John is describing is the blessing of being *affected* by the reading and the hearing of the words of this prophecy. The reading and hearing of the words of Revelation *changes* those who experience it. They *believe* what it reveals, and as a result they "keep what is written in it."

John intends the book of Revelation to produce a radical change in perspective. He intends the persecuted members of these lowly and insignificant churches to feel the reality that they are blessed. In spite of the fact that they are at odds with the reigning culture of the Roman Empire, in spite of the hostility of the Emperor and, more significantly, Satan himself, they are blessed! They are blessed because of what this book reveals. It may not seem that they are blessed by worldly, fleshly standards of reckoning, but this book will make plain that the awful judgment of God is coming against those who have rebelled against God and opposed his people. Meanwhile, God's people will ultimately be delivered and will enjoy the new heavens and the new earth under the benevolent rule of King Jesus. So it may not seem like it to human perception, but those who read, hear, and keep the book of Revelation are truly blessed in reality. The pregnant words at the end of verse 3, "for the time is near," declare that reality is soon to break into this world where things are not as they seem.

In these first three verses of Revelation, then, John lays out the blessing of the apocalyptic prophecy. What is that blessing? God sent this message to his servants to tell them that those who keep the words of this book will be delivered, while those who have rebelled against God and opposed his people will answer to his justice. The blessing of Revelation is to know how things really are: God is going to be glorified when he demonstrates his mercy in the salvation of his people, and that mercy will be highlighted by the justice he visits upon his enemies. God's people are those who keep the words of this book. Are you among those blessed people who keep the words of Revelation?

God reveals himself so that those who know him are blessed and praise him regardless of their circumstances.

Revelation 1:4–8: The Doxology of the Epistolary Opening

Revelation 1:4–8 is a letter-style greeting that looks like the salutations we find at the beginnings of the letters in the New Testament (cf. also 22:21). This means that the book of Revelation is an apocalyptic prophecy in the form of a circular letter.

In verses 4–8 we have John's salutation, in which he wishes grace and peace to the churches (1:4, 5a), a doxology to Jesus (1:5b, 6), an announcement of the second coming of Jesus (1:7), and a solemn pronouncement from the Father (1:8).

John's Salutation (1:4, 5a)

John addresses "the seven churches that are in Asia" (1:4; cf. 1:11; 2—3). Obviously these are not the only seven churches in the province of Asia, but they are representative of all the churches in Asia.[16]

This section in verses 4–8 is bracketed by references at the beginning and end to the one "who is and who was and who is to come" (1:4, 8). The first of these comes when John writes in verse 4, "Grace to you and peace from him who is and who was and who is to come." The one "who is and who was and who is to come" is the Father, but the grace John wishes to the churches is not from the Father alone. He continues, "and from the seven spirits who are before his throne, and from Jesus Christ" (1:4, 5).

The reference to "the seven spirits who are before his throne" (1:4) is a reference to the Holy Spirit,[17] and so by greeting the churches with grace and peace from the Father, the Spirit, and the Son, John has greeted them with grace from all three persons of the Godhead. Following this Trinitarian formula, John identifies Jesus in three ways in 1:5. He is, first, "the faithful witness." John has identified himself as one who "bore witness" (1:2, cf. 1:9), and other Christians in the book who are described as witnesses are, like Jesus, slain—Antipas in 2:13, the two witnesses in 11:3, 7, and those on whose blood the harlot was drunk in 17:6 (cf. 6:9; 12:11; 19:10; 20:4). Jesus is "the faithful witness," and his people follow him by faithfully bearing witness.

The second way in which Jesus is identified in 1:5 is as "the firstborn of the dead." This phrase points to the way that Jesus has pioneered the resurrection from the dead. He is the first whose resurrection is not merely resuscitation of bodily life. When Jesus rose, he rose in a glorified body. Revelation 20:4 indicates that those who are faithful unto death like he was will be raised from the dead like he was.

The third description of Jesus in 1:5 is that he is "the ruler of kings on earth." However powerful Domitian or any other ruler might be, they all answer to Jesus. He will call them to account. Jesus is the King.

The Doxology to Jesus (1:5b, 6)

In the middle of verse 5 John begins a doxology that will carry through verse 6. This doxology is addressed to Jesus, and John summarizes what Jesus has done for his people in three statements; then in response to these things he ascribes glory to Jesus.

John addresses the doxology "To him who loves us" (1:5b). This is the first thing Jesus has done for his people. Notice that this statement is made in the present tense. Jesus loves his people. Jesus' love for his people led him to lay down his life, and what Jesus accomplished by laying down his life is identified in the final words of verse 5: "and has freed us from our sins by his blood." This is the second thing Jesus has done for his people. The blood of Jesus frees us from our sins in the sense that his death cancels our obligation to pay the penalty of our sins to the Father. Those who sin deserve to die. Death is separation from God. Jesus died that death so that his people could be reconciled to God and live. Jesus' death was a penal, substitutionary atonement.[18] The word *penal* points to the fact that he paid the penalty. The word *substitutionary* means he died in place of his people as their substitute. The word *atonement* means that his death reconciled men to God.

Not only does his blood free us from the penalty of our sins, it also frees us from slavery to sin, which is elaborated upon in the next phrase. After stating at the end of verse 5 that Jesus "has freed us from our sins by his blood," John states the third thing Jesus has done for his people: "and made us a kingdom, priests to his God and Father" (1:6). The statement that he "made us a kingdom" points to the fact that we now belong to King Jesus. Our obligation is no longer to the prince of the power of the air, the ruler of this age, Satan. Jesus made us his kingdom. We are his people. The blood of Jesus frees people from lust, greed, pride, anger, and every other enslaving sin. The blood of Jesus breaks the power of canceled sin. The kingdom of Jesus cannot be overcome by any worldly power.

Again I quote our brother in Christ who wrote to Diognetus about the way that no power on earth can make Christians deny Jesus:

> Do you not see how they are thrown to wild beasts to make them deny the Lord, and yet they are not conquered? Do you not see that as more of them are punished, the more others increase? These things do not look like human works; they are the power of God, they are proofs of his presence. (*Diognetus* 7:7–9)

The next phrase in 1:6, "priests to his God and Father," points to two things Christians do. First, Christians serve and worship God. Second, building on what John says in Revelation about Christians bearing witness to Jesus, our status as "priests" means that we mediate the knowledge of God to others. We proclaim the saving good news. We announce that God has put Jesus forward as a sacrifice of propitiation to be received in faith (Romans 3:25). This good news means that all who call on the name of the Lord will be saved (Romans 10:13).

John names these three things Jesus has done for his people in 1:5, 6, then responds to these things at the end of verse 6: "to him be glory and dominion forever and ever." We see here the pattern of all worship: God reveals himself, and his people respond with the praise due him. Glory and dominion belong to Jesus because 1) he "loves us," 2) he "freed us from our sins by his blood," and 3) he made us a kingdom and priests. He made the kingdom; so dominion over that kingdom belongs to him. He loves and frees; so those loved and freed give him glory.

Are you living like you belong to the kingdom of Jesus? Does your life attest that dominion belongs to Jesus? Do you live like he is your Lord? Is he Lord over your Internet usage? Is he Lord over your money? Is he Lord over your ambitions for your children? Is he Lord over your conversations?

Are you living like a priest, worshiping God and helping others know God? Does your life announce that glory belongs to Jesus? The one flows from the other: those who know God most have the most reason to worship, for worship is our response to what God reveals of himself. And from there, those who see God and enjoy him in worship will also have most reason to serve as ambassadors of Christ, urging all to be reconciled to God through faith in Christ (cf. 2 Corinthians 5:20, 21).

Have you been freed from your sins by the blood of Jesus? Do you belong to the kingdom of Satan, or are you now part of Jesus' kingdom? If you are not sure, call on the name of the Lord and you will be saved (Romans 10:13). Trust him. His blood can free you from your sins.

The Coming of Jesus (1:7)

The urgency of the need to be reconciled to God through faith in Christ is announced in verse 7 when John proclaims, "Behold, he is coming with the clouds, and every eye will see him, even those who pierced him, and all tribes of the earth will wail on account of him. Even so. Amen."

In this verse John has masterfully brought together two statements that comprise major features of the Old Testament's teaching on the coming Messiah. The first statement, "Behold, he is coming with the clouds," picks up the Old Testament's indications of a conquering Messiah by quoting Daniel 7:13. Daniel 7 portrays the Messiah's receiving an everlasting kingdom, and this was the accepted messianic expectation in Jesus' day.

The part that was not accepted is articulated in the next phrases of 1:7 in the words, "and every eye will see him, even those who pierced him, and all tribes of the earth will wail on account of him." Here John quotes Zechariah 12:10 in order to put the idea of a suffering Messiah side by side with the idea of a conquering and ruling Messiah. This part of the Old Testament's messianic proclamation seems to have been overlooked in Jesus' day, and it seems from some things that Paul wrote that the dying and rising Messiah was a "mystery hidden for ages and generations but now revealed to his saints" (Colossians 1:26).

Many Jews no doubt rejected Jesus precisely because they believed that the crucifixion proved he was not the Messiah, but John quotes these two texts in order to prove that what happened with Jesus is exactly what was predicted in the Old Testament. John proclaims that those who rejected him "will wail on account of him," but John announces this in the hope that some will repent in response to this announcement of Jesus' coming. You can be sure that he will come. And you can be sure that if you are his enemy, you will wail. Repent and believe on the Lord Christ!

The Father's Solemn Pronouncement (1:8)

The words of the Father in verse 8 function as a solemn verification of what John has written to this point in the letter. The revelation of Jesus (1:1), the testimony of John (1:2), the blessing on those who read, hear, and keep this prophecy (1:3), John's wish of grace and peace for the churches (1:4), the doxology to Jesus (1:5, 6), and the warning of the coming of Jesus (1:7) are all attested to by the one who has always been and will always be.

The fact that he is "the Alpha and the Omega" means that he is the beginning and the end, the first and the last, and this is explicitly reiterated when he identifies himself as the one "who is and who was and who is to come, the Almighty" (1:8). God is always and eternal, everlasting and almighty, and there is no escaping him. By giving his solemn self-attestation to what John has written, the Father is verifying its truthfulness. Nothing has been overlooked or unexamined by him. Nothing was before him, and nothing will outlast him. What he declares to be true is certain to be inerrant, infallible, authoritative, reliable, totally true and trustworthy. You can trust the book of Revelation, and you can trust the Bible.

Let me suggest a way that you can grow in Christ and enable yourself to meditate on the Law of the Lord day and night. This is also something that parents can do with their children at the breakfast table or in the car or at bedtime, as Deuteronomy 6 describes. Memorize passages that grab you. Of course, it would be great to memorize the whole book of Revelation! But if you want one verse to memorize from these first eight verses of the book, I suggest you commit 1:8 to memory: "'I am the Alpha and the Omega,' says the Lord God, 'who is and who was and who is to come, the Almighty.'" If you have children, don't think they can't do it. They'll probably learn it faster than you will. That's a short verse, so if you want a head start for later studies, why not memorize 1:14–16?

God reveals himself so that those who know him are blessed and praise him regardless of their circumstances.

Conclusion

Suetonius tells us that Domitian "became an object of terror and hatred to all, but he was overthrown at last by a conspiracy of his friends and favorite freedmen, to which his wife was also privy."[19]

Domitian tried to take unto himself titles that belong rightly to Jesus— Lord and God. No matter how successful the enemies of God may seem in the short term, the book of Revelation shows how things really are.

Domitian, by worldly standards, had everything, and he sought to keep his life and make himself god. But he lost everything, betrayed even by his wife and friends.

Jesus, by worldly standards, had nothing and lost everything when he laid down his life for his friends (John 15:13). Paradoxically, he gained every-thing, vindicated by his Father, who raised him from the dead by the power of the Spirit and gave him the name that is above every name (Philippians 2:9).

3

John's Vision of the Risen Christ

REVELATION 1:9–20

BECAUSE OF THE RESURRECTION OF JESUS, we must not allow anything to crowd out our first love for God (cf. 2:4). We must love God first so that we can rise to love him forever.

Because of the resurrection of Jesus, we can face suffering, imprisonment, testing, and tribulation without fear. Because of the resurrection of Jesus, we can be faithful unto death (cf. 2:10). The resurrection of Jesus guarantees that though we suffer we will not be crushed, though we are tested we will not fail, though we face tribulation we will be preserved, though we die we will rise.

Because of the resurrection of Jesus, we do not worship idols and we do not engage in sexual immorality (cf. 2:14, 20). The resurrection of Jesus guarantees that our God will provide for us, so we need no idols, and the resurrection of Jesus provides an intimacy with our Lord Christ, so we have what people seek when they engage in sexual immorality.

Because of the resurrection of Jesus, we can be wakened from death and made alive (cf. 3:1, 2). The power of his indestructible life has broken the back of death itself.

Because of the resurrection of Jesus, he can put before us an open door that no one can shut, keep us through trials that come upon us, and call us to hold fast so that no one seizes our crown (cf. 3:8–11). Jesus has triumphed. Not even death stopped him. So nothing can stop his church.

Because of the resurrection of Jesus, lukewarmness is not tolerated. We are offered gold that we might be rich, garments to clothe our nakedness, and anointing for our eyes that we might see (cf. 3:15–18).

Everything that I have just mentioned is empowered by the resurrection of Jesus, and all these things are found in the letters to the seven churches in chapters 2, 3. Jesus describes himself at the beginning of each of the seven letters. He describes his own *risen* glory. Jesus does not describe himself using things he did before he was crucified. He describes himself as the *risen* Lord.

Jesus appeared to John in *risen* glory, and then as he addressed the seven churches he described his own *risen* majesty. This is very important: the risen Christ summons his churches to obedience.

Need

We need to love God first and not be lukewarm. We need to be faithful unto death and go through the open door of gospel proclamation Jesus sets before us. We need to reject false teaching, refuse idolatry, and flee sexual immorality.

The royal majesty of the *risen* King fires our hearts with passion, holds us faithful through flame and sword, and compels us to herald the good news of his salvation, for he has freed us from our sins by his blood.

In 1:9–20 the risen Christ appears to John to commission him to write this prophecy of Revelation. John sees Jesus in the full splendor of his majesty. John has been exiled to the island of Patmos because of his testimony to Jesus, and he writes to churches facing tribulation and persecution. The message that Jesus communicates through John is that they are to endure faithfully, and that message is made compelling by the glory of the risen Christ.

Main Point

The risen Christ in glory summons forth obedience from his churches. The incomparable glory of the risen Christ motivates John's audience to heed what John has been commissioned to write. The matchless splendor of Heaven's King attracts the attention and compels the obedience of the churches John addresses.

Preview

This passage falls into three parts:

1:9–11   John's Situation and Commission to Write
1:12–16   John's Description of the Risen Jesus
1:17–20   Jesus Asserts His Authority and Commissions John to Write

Context

We have seen the chain of revelatory disclosure God gave in 1:1, 2 and the blessing on those who read and hear this revelation in 1:3. After that came a greeting that looks like the greetings that accompany other letters in the New

Testament (1:4–8). The book of Revelation is an apocalyptic (1:1, 2) prophecy (1:3) in the form of a circular letter (1:4, 5; 22:21).[1]

The opening of Revelation (1:1–8) is followed by John's vision of the risen Christ in 1:9–20. In this passage Jesus reveals his authority, and then on the basis of that authority he will address the seven churches in chapters 2, 3. John will then be invited into Heaven to behold the throne of God and the Lamb in chapters 4, 5. John sees the Lamb take a scroll, sealed with seven seals, and the opening of the seals is followed by the seven trumpet blasts, which are followed by the outpouring of the seven bowls of God's wrath. All this is recounted in chapters 6—16. The outpouring of the wrath of God has results for two cities, each of which is depicted as a woman. The harlot Babylon falls in chapters 17—19, and the return of the King in chapter 19 is followed by his setting up his thousand-year kingdom, which is followed by the great white throne judgment in chapter 20. With the harlot Babylon destroyed, the new Jerusalem descends from Heaven as the bride of the Lamb in chapters 21, 22.

In 1:9–20, the risen Christ appears in glory to capture the imagination and constrain the obedience of John's audience, and we are part of that audience. The risen Christ in glory summons forth obedience from his churches.

Revelation 1:9–11: John's Situation and Commission to Write

In verse 9, John identifies himself with his audience as their "brother." This reflects the teaching of the New Testament that everyone who is born again is now part of the family of God. Not only does John identify himself as a "brother" to his audience, he also states in the rest of the verse that he is their "partner in the tribulation and the kingdom and the patient endurance that are in Jesus." John is their partner in tribulation because the kingdom of Jesus is one that is entered through the patient endurance of suffering.

- Matthew 24:9: "Then they will deliver you up to *tribulation* and put you to death, and you will be hated by all nations for my name's sake."
- Acts 14:22: ". . . through many *tribulations* we must enter the kingdom of God."
- Romans 12:12: "Rejoice in hope, be patient in *tribulation*, be constant in prayer."
- 1 Thessalonians 3:2, 3: "We sent Timothy . . . to establish and exhort you in your faith, that no one be moved by these *afflictions*. For you yourselves know that *we are destined for this*."

Unlike the Roman Empire, which promised peace but delivered brutality and fear, the kingdom of God promises tribulation and delivers peace and confidence and eternal salvation to those who patiently endure. Jesus will bring hope and change.

Make no mistake about it: your best life is not now. Your best life will begin when the skies are split by the shout of the archangel. When you patiently endure whatever afflictions you face in your life, you follow in the footsteps of the Old Testament prophets, the Lord Jesus, and his disciples.

John writes in verse 9 that he is on the island of Patmos[2] "on account of the word of God and the testimony of Jesus." This makes it clear that John is not on Patmos because he did something wrong, but for the sake of the gospel.[3] John has been proclaiming God's word and testifying to Jesus, and as a result he has been exiled to Patmos.[4]

If we are to suffer affliction, we must heed the exhortation of 1 Peter 4:15, 16: "But let none of you suffer as a murderer or a thief or an evildoer or as a meddler. Yet if anyone suffers as a Christian, let him not be ashamed, but let him glorify God in that name."

John wrote to churches facing persecution and tribulation, and he identifies with them as one who also endured persecution and tribulation. The glory of the Lord Christ kept John through the tribulation he faced. He recounts one of his experiences of that glory for us in these verses.

John writes in 1:10 that he was "in the Spirit on the Lord's day." There are four places in Revelation where John records that he was "in the Spirit"—here in 1:10, in 4:2, in 17:3, and in 21:10. Each marks the beginning of a signifi-cant movement in John's visionary experience. Here in 1:10 John is about to see the risen Christ. In 4:2 John sees the heavenly court. In 17:3 John is car-ried away in the Spirit at the beginning of his vision of the fall of the harlot Babylon, and in 21:10 John is carried away in the Spirit to see the descent of the bride of the Lamb, the new Jerusalem.[5]

The reference to "the Lord's day" in verse 10 most likely refers to Sunday, which became "the Lord's day" because on that day Jesus rose from the dead.

John hears a "voice like a trumpet" behind him. The voice tells John in 1:11 to "Write what you see in a book and send it to the seven churches, to Ephesus and to Smyrna and to Pergamum and to Thyatira and to Sardis and to Philadelphia and to Laodicea."

The churches appear to be named in the order that they would be vis-ited on a circular route beginning from Patmos and moving around Asia.[6] It seems that these cities were "the natural centres of communication for an itinerant Christian messenger" and that "the seven focal cities . . . had acquired a special importance as organizational and distributive centres for the church of the area."[7] It is also significant that "All but Thyatira had temples dedicated to the emperors, and all but Philadelphia and Laodicea had imperial priests and altars."[8]

Before we move to John's description of Jesus, let me invite you to contemplate the fact that John's apostolic status did not mean that he would not be persecuted and suffer tribulation (1:9). With John, we are servants of the Most High God, and with John we will suffer affliction—he is our "brother and partner" in these things.

Note also that in verse 11 John states the reason he wrote the book of Revelation: because the risen Christ told him to do so! John is not fashioning some imaginative fantasy about how he wants things to turn out. No, John is obeying the Lord Jesus. Jesus said to write, so John wrote.[9] Revelation exists because Jesus called John to write. The Church exists because Jesus is the Good Shepherd who calls his sheep by name, and they follow him.

Missionaries go to the ends of the earth because Jesus said, "Go . . . make disciples" (Matthew 28:19). Christians are faithful in marriage because Jesus said, "What . . . God has joined together, let not man separate" (Matthew 19:6). Christians love one another because Jesus said, "This is my commandment, that you love one another as I have loved you" (John 15:12). People repent of their sins and trust in Jesus because he said, "I am the resurrection and the life. Whoever believes in me, though he die, yet shall he live" (John 11:25). Do you realize that if you refuse to do these things—believe in Jesus, love one another, be faithful to your spouse, make disciples—you are rejecting the word of the risen Christ? He is the one who speaks and it is so. To oppose him is as futile as the universe trying to resist his word when he says, "Let there be light!" The light will shine. Let's respond to the word of Christ the way the elements did when he summoned them by his word to do his bidding.

The incomparable glory of the risen Christ is meant to motivate John's audience to heed what John has been commissioned to write. The matchless splendor of Heaven's King will attract the attention and compel the obedience of the churches John addresses. The risen Christ in glory summons forth obedience from his churches.

Revelation 1:12–16: John's Description of the Risen Jesus

Notice the startling statement in 1:12—John "turned to *see* the *voice*." John heard "a loud voice like a trumpet" (1:10), and he turned to see who was speaking. On turning, John states first that he "saw seven golden lampstands" (1:12). In order to understand this passage, it is important to understand the Old Testament background. Most of the references to lampstands in the Old Testament are references to the lampstand in the tabernacle or the ten lampstands that Solomon prepared for the temple.[10] But the most important background for what John relates here about Jesus in the midst of the seven lampstands is what Zechariah saw as stated in Zechariah 4:1–14. John's experience of Jesus in 1:9–20 fulfills Zechariah 4 in significant ways.[11]

Zechariah saw a lampstand with seven lamps flanked by "two olive trees" (4:2, 3). Zechariah 4 presents an angel explaining the meaning of the lampstand and the two olive trees to Zechariah. John sees Jesus standing in the midst of seven lampstands, and in 1:20 Jesus interprets the meaning of the lampstands for John.

The lampstand Zechariah saw points to the successful rebuilding of the temple and the renewal of God's presence among his people (4:4–10).[12] The two olive trees are explained as "the two anointed ones [lit., 'two sons of oil'] who stand by the Lord of the whole earth" (4:11–14). In Zechariah these two anointed ones are the anointed priest, Joshua (cf. 3:1–10), and the descendant of David, Zerubbabel (4:1–14).[13] This text and others like it seem to have given rise to the expectation of two messiahs, one priestly and one royal, as seen in the documents found at Qumran (cf. e.g., 1QS 9:11). In Zechariah the vision means that God will accomplish his purpose in the rebuilding of the temple: "Not by might, nor by power, but by my Spirit, says the LORD of hosts" (4:6). The "two olive trees," anointed and empowered, will be the means God uses to bring this about.

This scenario now finds its fulfillment in what John sees in Revelation. The Lord is not building a temple in which he will dwell but a church (cf. Matthew 16:18)! The Church is not a building but believers who are "living stones" (cf. 1 Peter 2:5). Zechariah's lampstand, which symbolized the presence of God in the temple, is fulfilled by the seven lampstands of Revelation, which symbolizes God's presence in the seven churches to whom John writes (1:20; cf. 2:5). Zechariah's "two sons of oil," Joshua the high priest and Zerubbabel the royal descendant of David, are fulfilled in Jesus, who stands among the lampstands as God's presence in his church. Jesus himself fills the offices of High Priest and High King of Israel. The vision of the lampstand and the two olive trees in Zechariah guaranteed that God would empower the rebuilding of the temple. Similarly, John's vision of Jesus among the lampstands guarantees that God will accomplish his purpose in the building of the Church.

In verse 13 John's description of what he saw continues: "and in the midst of the lampstands one like a son of man, clothed with a long robe and with a golden sash around his chest." A number of Old Testament texts refer to a "son of man," but John's description here of "one like a son of man" points to Daniel 7:13, 14:

I saw in the night visions, and behold, with the clouds of heaven there came one like a son of man, and he came to the Ancient of Days and was present-ed before him. And to him was given dominion and glory and a kingdom, that all peoples, nations, and languages should serve him; his dominion is an everlasting dominion, which shall not pass away, and his kingdom one that shall not be destroyed.

From the context of chapter 1 it is clear that this passage has influenced John's thinking about Jesus—look back at 1:7, where the phrase "Behold, he is coming with the clouds" alludes to Daniel 7:13, ". . . and behold, with the clouds of heaven there came one like a son of man."

The "son of man" in Daniel 7:13, 14 receives an eternal kingdom, which means that by alluding to this passage John is describing Jesus in royal terms. John also presents Jesus in priestly terms because he stands among the lamp-stands, which were part of the furniture of the temple, and it was the job of the Levitical priests to tend and maintain the lampstands in the temple. Jesus will tend and maintain the lampstands by calling the churches to repentance.[14] Jesus' clothes in 1:13 should probably be interpreted as the robe and golden sash of the heavenly high priest (cf. Daniel 10:5).

Daniel's visions have to do with the son of man who receives an eternal kingdom, and in Daniel 10:14 Daniel encountered a man from Heaven who told him that he "came to make you understand what is to happen to your people in the latter days. For the vision is for days yet to come."

John's vision of Jesus is shaped, it seems, by two major influences. First, the phrases John employs in his descriptions of Jesus seem to derive from the letters that Jesus dictates to John in chapters 2, 3. This influence can be seen from the chart "Revelation 1 and the Salutations of the Seven Letters," which draws attention to the way that Jesus announces something about himself at the beginning of each letter, and these things are all drawn from Revelation 1:

Table 3.1: Revelation 1 and the Salutations of the Seven Letters

Revelation 1	Description of Jesus	Revelation 2, 3
1:13; 1:16, 20	Among the lampstands; holding seven stars	2:1
1:17, 18	First and last, died and came to life	2:8
1:16	Two-edged sword from his mouth	2:12 (cf. 2:16)
1:14, 15	Eyes of flame, feet like burnished bronze	2:18
1:4, 16, 20	Seven spirits, seven stars	3:1
1:18	Holder of the key	3:7
1:5, 17	Faithful and true witness, beginning	3:14

The way that Jesus described himself at the beginning of each of the seven letters seems to have had a decisive influence on the way John describes Jesus in chapter 1, so that even though chapter 1 comes before chapters 2, 3 in literary terms, John's experience of Jesus announcing these things about himself shaped the way that John later described the risen Christ in glory.

The second major influence on the way John described his initial encounter with the risen Jesus appears to have been Daniel 10. John seems to have understood that just as Daniel's vision concerned "the latter days" (10:14) but Daniel was instructed to "shut up the words and seal the book, until the time of the end" (12:4), so now he, John, was receiving a vision that concerned "the things that must soon take place" (1:1). Unlike Daniel, John was told, "Do not seal up the words of the prophecy of this book, for the time is near" (22:10). Thus, what was prophesied by Daniel is fulfilled in Revelation. The relationship between Daniel 10 and Revelation 1:12–20 can be seen in the sequence of events in the two chapters and in the descriptions of those revealed in the two chapters:

Table 3.2: The Sequence of Events in Daniel 10 and Revelation 1

Daniel 10	Event	Revelation 1
10:5a	Seer looks	1:12a
10:5b, 6	Description of "a man" in Daniel, "one like a son of man" in Revelation	1:13–16
10:8, 9 (cf. "deep sleep" in Genesis 2:21; 15:12; 1 Samuel 26:12; Daniel 8:18)	Seer undone: Daniel — no strength, deep sleep; John fell as though dead	1:17a
10:10–14 10:15–21 note 10:16, "one in the likeness of the children of man"	The one revealed touches the seer and explains the vision	1:17–20

In 1:14 John unfurls the banner of the divinity of Jesus. He does this by describing Jesus in terms that match the description of the Ancient of Days in Daniel 7:9, where we read that "the hair of his head [was] like pure wool." When John writes of Jesus that "The hairs of his head were white, like white wool, like snow," he is describing Jesus in the same terms used to describe the Ancient of days in Daniel 7:9.[15]

That Jesus is God is a fact! To insist on this is not to impose our opinions on others but to tell them the truth about reality.[16] The Church has the responsibility of serving the world at large as "a pillar and buttress of the truth" (1 Timothy 3:15). Local churches must endeavor to uphold the truth as a pillar supports a building, and we must be a strong foundation, a ground, on which a true understanding of the world can be built. That's our role.

Table 3.3: The Descriptions of the Ones Revealed in Daniel 10
         and Revelation 1

Daniel 10	Revelation 1
10:5, "clothed in linen, with a belt of fine gold"	1:13, "clothed with a long robe and with a golden sash around his chest"
7:9, "the hair of his head like pure wool"	1:14a, "the hairs of his head were white, like white wool"
10:6c, "his eyes like flaming torches"	1:14b, "His eyes were like a flame of fire" (description also found in 2:18)
10:6d, "his arms and legs like the gleam of burnished bronze"	1:15a, "his feet were like burnished bronze, refined in a furnace" (description also found in 2:18)
10:6e, "and the sound of his words like the sound of a multitude"	1:15b, "and his voice was like the roar of many waters"
10:6b, "his face like the appearance of lightning"	1:16c, "and his face was like the sun shining in full strength"

When John describes Jesus in 1:14 as one whose "eyes were like a flame of fire" (cf. 19:12; Daniel 10:6), he is declaring the reality that nothing escapes the all-searching, pure gaze of Jesus. This has at least three implications: 1) no sin that we commit will escape his notice, 2) he will see every faithful thing his people do, and 3) he will note every injustice done to his people by their enemies.

The statement in 1:15 that "his feet were like burnished bronze, refined in a furnace" points to the absolute purity of Jesus (cf. Daniel 10:6).[17] And not only is the voice loud like a trumpet (1:10), which recalls the voice at Mount Sinai (Exodus 19:16, 19, 20), the voice was also "like the roar of many waters" (1:15; cf. 14:2; 19:6; Ezekiel 1:24; 43:2). These descriptions of the powerful voice of the risen Christ are arresting, communicating his authority, which is to be obeyed. The trumpet and the roar of the waters of Jesus' voice are to drown out the other voices that would call Christians away from the true faith and holiness that marks those who know God. Are you inclining your ear to the blasting roar of Jesus' voice in the Scriptures? Or are you listening for the siren songs of the enemies of God and his people?

John tells us three more things about Jesus in 1:16. First, "In his right hand he held seven stars." The stars will be explained in verse 20. Second, "from his mouth came a sharp two-edged sword." I don't think we are to imagine that Jesus has a literal sword coming out of his mouth. This is a colorful way to say that Jesus will speak decisive words of judgment (cf. Isaiah

11:4; 49:2; Ephesians 6:17; Hebrews 4:12; Revelation 2:12; 19:15, 21). And third, John tells us that "his face was like the sun shining in full strength." This description points to the painful brightness of the sun, on which we cannot fix our eyes. As we see in verses 17–20, this appearance of the risen Christ, in blazing splendor like the sun shining in full strength, produced in John a sensory overload that left him "as though dead" (v. 17).

The incomparable glory of the risen Christ motivates John's audience to heed what John has been commissioned to write. The matchless splendor of Heaven's King attracts the attention and compels the obedience of the churches John addresses. The risen Christ in glory summons forth obedience from his churches.

Revelation 1:17–20: Jesus Asserts His Authority and Commissions John to Write

John relates, "When I saw him, I fell at his feet as though dead" (1:17). The glory of Jesus overpowered John in a way that no Roman emperor could imitate. John's audience is thus encouraged by the fact that they serve one whose glory surpasses that of mere human power. This Jesus will address them directly in the letters he dictates to John in chapters 2, 3, and his authoritative word is validated by his overwhelming glory.

Jesus doesn't leave John. "But he laid his right hand on me, saying, 'Fear not'" (1:17). We pause in the middle of this statement to observe that Jesus is about to tell John why he shouldn't be afraid—and the reason that John shouldn't be afraid is not that Jesus isn't scary. The glory of the risen Christ is terrifying!

Jesus tells John that he shouldn't be afraid because "I am the first and the last" (1:17). This is a declaration from Jesus that he is what God is—before all things and after all things. This matches God the Father's announcement in 1:8, "I am the Alpha and the Omega" (cf. 2:8; 21:6; 22:13). But the fact that Jesus is first and last isn't the only reason John shouldn't fear: Jesus goes on to say, ". . . and the living one. I died, and behold I am alive forevermore, and I have the keys of Death and Hades" (1:18). Jesus is the living one—death has no power to hold him (cf. Acts 2:24). And the statement that he died and is now alive forevermore is an unmistakable reference to Jesus' death and resurrection. Moreover, having died on the cross to pay the penalty for sin and having been raised from the dead, Jesus has "the keys of Death and Hades," which means that he is in control of who gets locked up and who gets liberated. This is why Jesus tells John not to be afraid.

Though Jesus is terrifying in his holiness to all sinners, he died to pay the penalty for sin, and by virtue of his resurrection he now holds the keys of death and Hell. Thus, if Jesus tells John not to fear, this points to John's sins being forgiven.[18] Jesus has the keys! He can loose all bonds. John need not fear. The glorious good news is that all those who trust in Jesus have their sins forgiven. The death of Jesus saves all who trust in him. If you do not know God, which is to say, if you do not trust Jesus, let me assure you of his trustworthiness, and let me urge you to trust him right now!

The voice that arrested John's attention commanded him to write (1:10, 11), and now that John has seen Jesus in his glory, Jesus says again in 1:19, "Write therefore," and the "therefore" places this command to write on the ground of Jesus' glory that John has seen (1:12–16) and on Jesus' ability to tell John not to fear because he, Jesus, has conquered sin, death, and Hell (1:17, 18).

What Jesus tells John to write in 1:19 is "the things that you have seen," which probably refers to the vision that John has just recorded (1:9–20), "those that are," which probably refers to the present state of the churches that Jesus will describe and address in chapters 2, 3, "and those that are to take place after this," which probably refers to the events John records in chapters 4—22. Revelation 1:19, then, serves as a preview of the overarching structure of the book of Revelation.

Finally, in 1:20, Jesus explains to John "the mystery of the seven stars . . . and the seven golden lampstands," saying that the stars "are the angels of the seven churches, and the seven lampstands are the seven churches." These are angelic beings that represent each church. I do not think the reference to "the angels of the seven churches" is a reference to the senior pastor of each individual church, with "angel" meaning something more like messenger, for several reasons. First, pastors are not called "angels" elsewhere in Revelation or the New Testament; second, the book of Revelation is full of heavenly beings called "angels," which makes it likely that these angels are also heavenly beings; and third, John distinguishes between heavenly beings and human beings elsewhere in Revelation, so if these were human beings it would probably be more clearly stated that human pastors are in view.

That Jesus holds the seven stars in his right hand means that he is in control of the churches, and that he is among the lampstands means that he is present with the churches.

The incomparable glory of the risen Christ motivates John's audience to heed what John has been commissioned to write. The matchless splendor of Heaven's King attracts the attention and compels the obedience of the churches John addresses. The risen Christ in glory summons forth obedience from his churches.

Conclusion

In Revelation 1:9–20, we see John's situation and commission to write in 1:9–11, John's description of the risen Jesus in 1:12–16, and Jesus asserts his authority and again commissions John to write in 1:17–20. The most significant feature of this passage is the overwhelming glory of Jesus. The grabbing description of the sovereign Lord Christ, the King Messiah, assures John's audience, which includes us, that Jesus is to be worshiped and obeyed because of his surpassing worth and power. His authority is such, as the one who holds the keys of death and Hades, that he controls the earthly and the eternal destiny of every man, woman, and child. Your response to Jesus as he is revealed in this passage determines whether you will rule with him or will be slain by the sword that comes from his mouth. He is risen. He is indestructible. He is unconquerable. He is Lord.

On Sunday, March 8, 2009, Pastor Fred Winters was shot in his pulpit. When she was interviewed in the following week, his widow, Cindy, expressed forgiveness for the man who murdered her husband and said she was praying that her husband's killer would trust Jesus. That forgiveness and desire to see the man who murdered her husband saved is only possible because death is not the end. Death is not the end because Jesus rose from the dead. Because of the resurrection of Jesus, Cindy Winters could forgive the man who murdered her husband and pray for his salvation.

Jesus reveals himself to John the way he does to compel John's audience to heed the seven letters he is about to dictate to John and to convince them of the truth of what John will then recount of the events of the end of history in chapters 4–22. "He who has an ear, let him hear what the Spirit says to the churches" (2:7).

4

The Risen Christ to the Seven Churches

REVELATION 2, 3

IF JESUS WERE TO WRITE A LETTER to your local church, what do you think he would say? Think of it: the Risen Christ himself, dictating a message addressing the strengths and weaknesses of your local church, prefaced by a description of some aspect of his own glory, containing important information for the immediate future of the church, and concluded by a promised reward offered to those who heed his word.

Wouldn't we want to hear what he has to say to us?

Need

The greatest need of a local church is not to be more impressive by worldly standards of measurement—whether that means having a bigger crowd, a better building, or being more able to boast about all the great things we do.

The greatest need of a local church is to be faithful to Jesus, to hold fast to the gospel, and to live lives that are pleasing to him. And I have good news for us: In the Bible, God has given us everything that we need to know to be right with God through Jesus and live in a way that pleases him.

Main Point

As we look at the letters to the seven churches in chapters 2, 3, we are going to see that the main point of these seven letters goes like this: For the glory of God, Jesus charges the churches to be zealous for the gospel, reject false teaching, and live in a manner that corresponds to the gospel.

Preview

In this chapter we will examine an overview of the seven letters. Then we will look at them each in more detail, but the benefits of looking at them all together will (hopefully) be obvious. First we will examine the structure of the seven letters, then the contents of the seven letters.

Part of the reason we are doing this overview of the seven letters to the churches is because there is truth in the ancient opinion expressed in the Muratorian Canon: "John also in the Revelation writes indeed to seven churches yet speaks to all."[1] There is a sense in which by addressing these seven churches, John has representatively addressed all churches. This impression is strengthened by the refrain that concludes each of the seven letters: "He who has an ear, let him hear what the Spirit says to the churches" (2:7, 11, 17, 29; 3:6, 13, 22).[2] Jesus speaks *to the churches* in these letters. We should also keep in mind that John probably wrote Revelation to be read aloud to the gathered congregation, and John almost certainly expected Revelation to be read to congregations other than the seven Jesus addresses directly in chapters 2, 3. John might have intended for the whole book to be read aloud during a worship service. Reading the whole book at one sitting is a valuable thing for all of us to do, and it would probably take a little over an hour to do so.

Context

After John introduces the book of Revelation (1:1–8), he recounts the experience he had when the risen Christ appeared to him and commissioned him to write Revelation (1:9–20). We are now looking at seven letters that Jesus dictated to John in chapters 2, 3. In chapters 4, 5 John recounts his vision of the throne room of God, and flowing out of that vision are the judgments that come in chapters 6—16. These judgments conclude with the fall of Babylon and the descent of the new Jerusalem in chapters 17—22.

As we look at the seven letters in chapters 2, 3, it is important to keep in mind that they are preceded by the overwhelming glory of Christ described in chapter 1 and backed up by the onrush of images of the power and mercy of God in judgment and final salvation described in chapters 4—22.

As we look at the structure and contents of the seven letters to the churches, John's point will be clear: For the glory of God, the churches are to be zealous for the gospel, reject false teachers, and live in a manner that corresponds to the gospel.

The Structure of the Seven Letters

We'll look more carefully at the contents of these letters in a moment; for now I want to suggest to you that the seven letters balance one another to form a chiasm.[3] The term *chiasm* refers to the Greek letter *chi*, which is shaped like an X. If you're not familiar with this term, think of a picture frame. A picture frame has an outer wooden piece, and inside that you'll often find a mat. Inside the mat is the picture. Just as a nice frame and a well-chosen mat complement whatever is in the frame, so also chiasms often highlight whatever is at the center of the chiasm.

If we examine what Jesus says about the condition of the churches, we see that the first and last church have a similar problem—the loss of the first love in Ephesus is like the lukewarm state of Laodicea. Similarly, the second church addressed is like the next to last church addressed in that the churches in both Smyrna and Philadelphia are commended, not reproved, and neither church is called to repent. The three churches in the middle seem to progress from bad to worse: the letters to both Pergamum and Thyatira mention false teaching, idolatry, and immorality, and Thyatira seems to be in a worse state than Pergamum, while Jesus says that the church in Sardis is dead!

So here's how our chiasm, or picture frame, falls out:

Table 4.1: The Seven Letters as a Chiasm

A. **Revelation 2:1–7**, to the church in **Ephesus**, which has lost its first love. Think of the letter to Ephesus as the wooden border of the frame on one side.

    B. **Revelation 2:8–11**, to the church in **Smyrna**, which is commended for its faithfulness, not reproved, and not called to repentance. Think of the letter to Smyrna as the mat on one side of the frame.

        C1. **Revelation 2:12–17**, to the church in **Pergamum**, which has people who hold to false teaching, eat food sacrificed to idols, and practice sexual immorality. Think of the letter to Pergamum as one side of the picture that is matted and framed.

        C2. **Revelation 2:18–29**, to the church in **Thyatira**, which seems worse off than the church in Pergamum because it tolerates a false prophetess who seduces people to practice sexual immorality, eat food sacrificed to idols, and is unrepentant! Think of the letter to Thyatira as the middle of the picture that is matted and framed.

        C3. **Revelation 3:1–6**, to the church in **Sardis**, which is worse than both Pergamum and Thyatira because it is dead. Think of the letter to Sardis as the other side of the framed and matted picture.

    B`. **Revelation 3:7–13**, to the church in **Philadelphia**, which like the church in Smyrna is commended for its faithfulness, not reproved, and not called to repentance. Think of the letter to Philadelphia as the other side of the mat.

A`. **Revelation 3:14–22**, to the church in **Laodicea**, which like Ephesus has lost its first love and is now lukewarm. Think of the letter to Laodicea as the other wooden border on the far side of the frame.

In coming chapters we will look at each of these letters one by one. In this chapter we want to feel the cumulative effect of what Christ says to his churches. Again, Jesus charges the churches to be zealous for the gospel, reject false teaching, and live in a manner that corresponds to the gospel.

It is informative for us to reflect on the state of these seven churches. Only two of the seven were not reproved, and when this letter was written, the apostolic age had not yet closed! The church has never really had a "golden age" when everything was right. From the beginning there were problems—think of the dispute over the neglected widows described in Acts 6, or the problems with Gentiles and circumcision in Acts 10, 11, and 15. It seems to me that the sorry state of these churches Jesus addresses in chapters 2, 3, churches that were receiving apostolic ministry firsthand from John, gives us unexpected encouragement today. We struggle with many of the same problems. We need not be excessively discouraged, much less despair, however, because just as Jesus loved these churches enough to reprove and discipline them (3:19), so also he loves us enough to reprove and discipline us. Then as now, the healthy churches are in the minority.[4] Then as now, though, Jesus is committed to building his Church! As we consider these passages, ask the Lord to reprove and discipline you. Ask God to give you ears to hear what the Spirit is even now saying to the churches through this Word he inspired.

The main problem with the first and last churches addressed, Ephesus and Laodicea, seems to be complacency. Jesus does not want this. He wants Ephesus to return to its first love, and Laodicea to be zealous and repent.

The problems with the three churches in the middle of the chiasm, the picture in the frame, if you will, progresses from bad to worse. When we look at the description of the problems in Pergamum (2:12–17), we see that they are tolerating the false teaching of the Nicolaitans (2:15). This teaching is likened to the teaching of Balaam (2:14a), and John points out that Balaam's teaching led to Israel's eating food sacrificed to idols and engaging in sexual immorality (2:14b). But notice that while verse 15 says some in Pergamum are holding to the teaching of the Nicolaitans, it does not say that members of the church in Pergamum are eating food sacrificed to idols and engaging in sexual immorality. The implication seems to be, however, that the teaching of the Nicolaitans could very well lead to idolatry and immorality, just as Balaam's teaching did.

We can contrast this with Jesus' description of the church in Thyatira (2:18–29). The church is not only tolerating a false teacher, the false prophetess whom John calls Jezebel (2:20), but this false prophetess "is teaching and seducing my servants to practice sexual immorality and to eat food sacrificed to idols" (2:20b). So whereas the false teaching of the Nicolaitans could lead to this in Pergamum, the false teaching in Thyatira seems to have already borne its sordid fruit. When Jesus says in 2:21a, "I gave her time to repent," this may mean that the process of church discipline outlined by Jesus in Matthew 18:15–18 was initiated. The attempted discipline, however, does not appear to have been successful: "but she refuses to repent"

(2:21b). The rest of Jesus' comments seem meant to compel the church to carry out the needed discipline.

Worse off than the churches in either Pergamum or Thyatira is the church in Sardis, which is dead (3:1). This is where false teaching leads—death. This is where idolatry and immorality lead—death. No exceptions! For the glory of God, Jesus calls these churches to reject this false teaching, hold fast to the gospel, and live in a way that corresponds with the gospel rather than in ways that correspond with false teaching.

Is your first love still flaming, or are you lukewarm? Are you ready to be faithful unto death like those in Smyrna, holding fast and not denying the name of Jesus, like those in Philadelphia? Or are you more like the churches in Pergamum and Thyatira, not so concerned about sound doctrine, with the result that idolatry and immorality have come? If you're not at all concerned with these things, it might be that you're most like Sardis: dead. Where are you?

We can be sure of what Jesus has promised: "all the churches will know that I am he who searches mind and heart, and I will give to each of you according to your works" (2:23). Jesus is going to make himself known, and from what we see of him when he makes himself known to John, we know that he is worthy of our patiently enduring whatever we might face in this life. We know that he is worthy of our singular devotion, to the exclusion of idols. We know that walking in purity, avoiding sexual immorality of the spiritual and physical kinds, will repay us with greater pleasures and rewards than anything that sin promises with its forked tongue. We can all stand to hear again the word of 2:5, "Repent!" 2:16, "Repent!" 2:22, "Repent!" 3:3, "Repent!" and 3:19, "Repent!" As we will see in coming chapters when we look more closely at these letters individually, Jesus intends the whole church to repent, and given his teaching in Matthew 18:15–18, the repentance needs to take shape in the church's practice of corrective discipline.

A church can honor Christ and be zealous for the gospel by practicing church discipline, or they can risk Jesus' taking their lampstand away (2:5) and waging war on them with the sword of his mouth (2:16).

For the glory of God, Jesus charges the churches to be zealous for the gospel, reject false teaching, and live in a manner that corresponds to the gospel.

The Contents of the Seven Letters

Think again of the opening words of the book (1:1–8), which are followed by John's encounter with the risen Christ on the Lord's day (1:9–20). Chapter 1 is important for understanding chapters 2, 3 because Jesus identifies himself in ways that John described him in chapter 1 at the beginning of each of the seven letters in chapters 2. 3. Perhaps as John experienced the vision of Jesus and heard Jesus describe himself in these ways, Jesus' self-descriptions influenced the way John described Jesus in Revelation 1 (see Table 3.1 in chapter 3 of this book).

As Jesus introduces himself in these ways, he is both proclaiming his own matchless glory and authority and announcing the truths of the gospel. If we look only at the message Jesus gives to each church, we might be tempted to think these letters are concerned more with behavior than with theology. But that would be a false conclusion. There is high Christology in these seven letters, and it comes in the way that Jesus describes himself and what he has accomplished. Each introductory statement Jesus makes also relates to some aspect of the message to that church.

Jesus holds the seven stars and walks among the *lampstands* (2:1), which means that he is in control of these churches—because he told John in 1:20 that the stars are the angels of the churches and the lampstands are the churches. Later in the letter to Ephesus he warns them that if they do not repent, he will take away their *lampstand* (2:5).

He is "the first and the last" (2:8b), which means he is God because God identified himself as "the Alpha and the Omega" in 1:8. He *died* and came to life (2:8c), which reminds the audience of these letters of his death and resurrection. Just as Jesus died, he calls the faithful church in Smyrna "to be faithful *unto death*" (2:10).

He has "the sharp *two-edged sword*" (2:12), and he warns the church in Pergamum that he will use the *sword* for judgment against them if they do not repent (2:16). These references to the sword that comes from Jesus' mouth (cf. 1:16) are a colorful way to say that Jesus is going to speak decisive words of judgment.

He has "*eyes* like a flame of fire" (2:18b), and he *searches* minds and hearts (2:23). His *feet* are "like burnished bronze" (2:18c), pointing to his absolute purity.

He has "the *seven spirits* of God" (3:1), meaning that he is fully endowed with the Spirit of God (cf. Isaiah 11:2). What he calls the dead church of Sardis to do—waking, strengthening, remembering (3:2, 3)—results from *the life-giving power of God's Spirit* (cf. John 3:3–8; 6:63).[5]

He has the *key* of David, and what he opens no one can shut, and what he closes no one can open (3:7). He then proclaims to the church in Philadelphia that no one can shut the *open door* he has put before them (3:8).

He is "the Amen, the *faithful and true* witness" (3:14). So his word should be believed. The church in Laodicea should do what he *counsels* them to do (3:18a). It is by believing his testimony that their shame will be covered (3:18b). They should heed his reproving discipline (3:19).

So when we look at these ways that Jesus identifies himself, we see that he identifies himself as God, as the one who died and rose again, and as the one whose word is to be believed by the power of the Spirit. Believing his word will result in the covering of our shame, the forgiveness of our sins.

Perhaps someone reading this chapter has not believed Jesus' word. Let me say to you that he is the one who searches minds and hearts—he knows what you have done. He is also the one who is going to speak the decisive judgment that will decide your eternal destiny. Your only hope is to trust him. And he deserves your trust! He is faithful and true, and he will never disappoint you. Trust him today!

For believers, the fullness of this theology and the clear articulation of the gospel informs the behavioral instructions that follow in the body of the letters. These churches are called to be zealous for the gospel for the glory of Christ, as announced in these salutations that Jesus speaks in these seven letters.

Just as the beginning of each of the seven letters proclaims the gospel and points us back to the glory of Jesus as John described him in chapter 1, so also the body of each letter introduces themes that will echo through the rest of the book of Revelation.

Table 4.2: The Body of the Letters and the Body of the Letter

Revelation 2, 3	Themes Introduced	Revelation 4—20
2:2, 3, 19; 3:8, 10	Patient endurance, even unto death, for the honor of Christ through sufferings and tribulations	6:11; 7:1–8, 14; 8:3–4; 11:2, 3; 12:11, 17; 13:5–10, 15; 14:13
2:16, 22, 23	Judgments on the wicked: war with the sword of his mouth, sickness and death	6:8; 9:5, 6, 15, 18; 16–18; 19:21
2:23	Recompense according to works	18:6; 20:12, 13

The opening words of each letter announce the gospel and the greatness of Jesus. The body of each letter calls the churches to live in a way that corresponds to the gospel and images the purity and holiness of Jesus. This makes John's main point: For the glory of God the churches are to be zealous for the gospel, reject false teaching, and live according to the gospel.

The opening words of each letter in chapters 2, 3 point us back to chapter 1, the contents of the letter portend what will be described in chapters 4—20, and the conclusion of each letter promises blessings that the faithful enjoy in chapters 20—22.

Table 4.3: To Those Who Overcome: Promises and Fulfillment

Revelation 2, 3	Promised Blessing	Revelation 20—22
2:7	Eat from the tree of life	22:2
2:11	No harm from the second death	20:6; 21:7, 8
2:17, 28	A bright stone and the morning star	21:11, 18—21, 23; 22:5, 16
2:26, 27; 3:21	Reign with Christ	22:5
3:5	Name in the book of life	21:27
3:5	Clothed in white	21:2; cf. 19:7, 8
3:12	Made a pillar in the temple	21:3, 22
3:12	Identification with an eternal city	21:2, 10
3:12	A great name	22:4

At the end of the first three letters, the statement "He who has an ear, let him hear what the Spirit says to the churches" comes before the promises made "To the one who conquers" (2:7, 11, 17). At the end of the last four letters, the promises made "To the one who conquers" come before the statement "He who has an ear, let him hear what the Spirit says to the churches" (2:26–29; 3:5, 6; 3:12, 13; 3:21, 22). The reversal of the order of the statements in the last four letters makes the call to hear what the Spirit says to the churches the final word of the seventh letter, calling all churches who hear these letters to reflect upon their contents.

The contents of these letters, then, begin with the gospel and the greatness of Christ, call the churches to reject false teaching and live in a way that corresponds to the gospel, and then promise astonishing rewards to those who hear what the Spirit says and overcome temptation and affliction by holding fast to the gospel even unto death. And these letters proclaim these things not only to the members of the seven churches that are directly addressed but also proclaim these glorious things to "those who hear, and who keep what is written in" this prophecy of Revelation (1:3). That includes us.

For the glory of God, Jesus wants these churches to hold fast to the gospel, reject false teaching, and live in a way that matches the gospel. And he wants the same from our churches today.

Conclusion

Let us pursue the steadfast faithfulness to the gospel for which the churches in Smyrna and Philadelphia are commended. Let us be diligent about sound doctrine, that we might be able to discern truth from error. Let us live in pure devotion to Jesus, avoiding the idolatry and immorality that grow from false teaching. Let us practice church discipline when necessary. And let us heed the word of Jesus to the church in Smyrna to "be faithful unto death" (2:10).

In his book *Democratic Religion*, Greg Wills gives an inspiring example of a pastor willing to be faithful unto death for the purity of the church:

> Churches sometimes intensified the shame by a practice called "publishing." Presbyterian courts conducted judicial proceedings in private but announced before the church and world all excommunications and some suspensions. . . . So great was the dread of publishing that when Benjamin Morgan Palmer, pastor of New Orleans First Presbyterian Church, intended to publish a member suspended for drunkenness, the offender warned Palmer to desist: "I will arm myself and take a seat in the gallery over the pulpit, and if you attempt to read that paper I shall fire upon you." Palmer, unruffled, read the suspension without incident.[6]

For the glory of God, Jesus charges the churches to be zealous for the gospel, reject false teaching, and live in a manner that corresponds to the gospel.

5

First Love

WHAT IS IT THAT HAPPENS TO PEOPLE between the wedding day, so joyous, so earnest, so sincere, and the day the divorce papers are signed? What happens to parents between the day the child is born and the day they complain about that bothersome, frustrating brat? What happens to us between the day a loved one is diagnosed with some awful condition and the day that loved one, whom we cherish, becomes a burden?

In each case—divorced spouses, frustrated parents, burdened family members—what happens is a loss of first love. Gradually, almost imperceptibly what was once done from passionate fervor becomes little more than a duty, a chore.

Need

Maybe this is how some of us feel right now about Christianity. Perhaps you're just trudging through, hanging on, doing your duty.

Main Point

Revelation 2:1–7 teaches us that the great commandment matters to God. Jesus identified our greatest obligation as wholehearted love for God (Matthew 22:36–38), which declares to us that God is not pleased by dutiful obedience that does not flow from genuine love. In 2:1–7 Jesus mercifully reveals his glory to the church in Ephesus to summon forth from them the first love that he requires.

Preview

As we look at these individual letters to the seven churches, we'll see a regular pattern:

- First, each letter is addressed "to the angel" of the particular church.
- Second, Jesus announces what he has to say and describes himself in terms of the vision John had of Jesus, which he described in chapter 1.
- Third, Jesus tells the church that he knows them, and he describes what he knows about them in particular. Sometimes this includes words of commendation.
- Fourth, in most of the letters Jesus says, "but I have this against you," and then he tells the church where they have gone wrong.
- Fifth, having announced to the church what he has against them, he calls them to repentance.
- Sixth, having called the church to repentance, Jesus threatens the church with the consequences that will follow if they do not repent.
- Seventh, the letters are concluded with a command for those with ears to hear what the Spirit says to the churches.
- Eighth, the churches are motivated to heed the contents of the letter by the promises made to those who overcome.

Most of these elements are present in each letter, though there is some variation both in what is included and in the order of these elements.[1]

Here in Revelation 2:1–7, we will see:

2:1	The Authority of Jesus
2:2–6	The Address to the Church at Ephesus
2:7	The Call to Hear and Heed the Promises

Context

After the opening of the book of Revelation (1:1–8), John experiences an overpowering vision of Jesus in 1:9–20. There is no break in the action between the end of chapter 1 and the letters to the seven churches in chapters 2, 3. Jesus is talking to John at the end of chapter 1, explaining the meaning of the stars and the lampstands (1:12, 13, 16, 20), and he keeps right on talking through the end of chapter 3. We should read the letters to the churches, then, in light of the glory of Jesus that John described for us in the second half of chapter 1. After Jesus dictated the letters to the churches that John records in chapters 2, 3, John has a throne room vision that he recounts in chapters 4, 5. Flowing out of that throne room vision are a series of judgments that are described in chapters 6—16, and the book of Revelation is then concluded with the fall of Babylon in chapters 17, 18, the return of King Jesus in chapters 19, 20, and the coming of the new Jerusalem in chapters 21, 22.

The Authority of Jesus (2:1)

Revelation 2:1 opens with the words, "To the angel of the church in Ephesus write . . . " The first church that Jesus addresses in these letters in chapters 2, 3 is the church at Ephesus. Ephesus was a significant city in early Christianity. Paul's ministry in Ephesus is summarized in Acts 19, 20. The letter to the Ephesians was sent there, as were 1 and 2 Timothy, and 1 Corinthians was written from Ephesus. Early church tradition indicates that the Apostle John ministered there; so the letters of John may have been addressed to issues in the churches in and around Ephesus. The isle of Patmos is about sixty miles southwest of Ephesus.[2] We might also observe that there were probably a number of house churches in Ephesus. The early church seems to have met in homes (cf. Acts 2:46; 8:1, 3; 12:12).[3] Still, though there were probably a number of individual churches meeting in different homes in Ephesus, Jesus writes to "the church" in that city.

Having told John who to write to in the first part of 2:1, the rest of the verse states, "'The words of him who holds the seven stars in his right hand, who walks among the seven golden lampstands.'" That Jesus holds the seven stars in his right hand means that he has authority over the angels of the seven churches, because 1:20 identified those stars as the angels of the churches. That Jesus walks among the lampstands means that Jesus is present with his people, because 1:20 identifies the lampstands as the churches. Jesus is present, and he is in control right now.

How would your demeanor in worship be different if the governor of your state visited your church this Sunday? We would all be more attentive, more responsive—in appropriate ways. We would be more deliberate and more careful about what we are doing. Someone infinitely more significant, with infinitely more authority than any governor, is with us as we worship every Lord's day.

Revelation 2:1 reminds us of two ways that Jesus was described in 1:9–20, so that the terrible majesty of Jesus will make the Ephesian church attentive to what Jesus says to them.

The Address to the Church at Ephesus (2:2–6)

As Jesus addresses the church in Ephesus, he presents them with nine positive statements connected by "and" in 2:2, 3;[4] then a sudden "but" introduces the one negative mark he has against them in 2:4. They are summoned to repent, and a final positive remark about how they are doing in 2:6 encourages them before they are commanded to hear and the promise to those who overcome closes the letter.

Revelation 2:2, 3 present one sentence in which Jesus states nine positive things he knows about the church in Ephesus:

1. Jesus tells them: "I know your works" (2:2). Jesus knows the good things they have done. Are you ever discouraged that your neighbor didn't seem to notice that you raked his lawn because you love Jesus and wanted to bless your neighbor? Jesus knows your works.
2. Jesus also says he knows their "toil" and . . .
3. their "patient endurance" (2:2). These first three characteristics Jesus knows about them have a similar ring—"works," "toil," "endurance." The church in Ephesus was persevering.
4. Jesus also states that he knows that they "cannot bear with those who are evil" (2:2). The church in Ephesus was not able to tolerate evildoers. That's a good thing. Even if the world thinks we are intolerant, we dare not win the world's approval by harboring those whom Jesus identifies as evil.
5. Jesus knows that the church in Ephesus "tested those who call themselves apostles and are not" (2:2) . . .
6. and "found them to be false" (2:2). This testing and finding false these who claimed to be apostles seems to indicate that some people were going around to churches claiming to be messengers of other churches,[5] but those claims were false. It may be that the Ephesian church was directly obeying the instructions in 2 John 7, 10 in this testing and refusal of these false messengers.[6] There are false messengers today just as there were false messengers in the Ephesian church. We must know the gospel, know our Bibles, and know Christian theology so that we can tell the difference between someone who increases our faith in Jesus by telling us the truth about his greatness and someone who makes us feel good about ourselves by giving us pep talks and "encouragement" to rely on our own resources.
7. Jesus has commended the church for its endurance at the beginning of 2:2, and he returns to their endurance at the beginning of 2:3.
8. They are "bearing up" for his "name's sake" (2:3).
9. And they "have not grown weary" (2:3).

We can summarize these nine good things that the Ephesian church is doing by grouping them into two categories: 1) deeds and 2) theology. Everything said about their deeds is good: they're working, toiling, patiently enduring—stated in both 2:2 and 2:3, and they are bearing up for Jesus' name. And everything said about their theology is good, too: they are recognizing the difference between good and evil, testing those who claim to be messengers of other churches, and refusing to recognize liars.

But the one thing that the church lacks, which Jesus will identify in 2:4, seems to indicate that the Ephesian church is muddling through without much joy, holding out with steadfastness but with faded fervor. It may be that they are slipping into a pattern of just going through the motions.

All this seems to be indicated by what Jesus says to the Ephesian church in Revelation 2:4, "but"—the string of nine things linked by "and" is now broken with this one word. Jesus says, "But I have this against you, that you have abandoned the love you had at first."

Jesus doesn't merely state what he has against the church in Ephesus—the abandonment of their first love, he gives them a plan of action to address this situation. In 2:5 we find the three-step program Jesus has for the church: "Remember therefore from where you have fallen; repent, and do the works you did at first."

The first thing Jesus tells the church in Ephesus to do is, "Remember" (v. 5).

I remember what it was like when my wife and I met and fell in love eleven years ago. We were students together, and I could not wait for class to end so I could bolt to the door of the class she was in, so I could spend every second of the ten-minute break between classes by her side. On other days I had a class that started at 7:45 A.M., and she didn't have class until later in the day. I would get up early in the morning so I could go by her apartment on my way to school, just so I could see her for a moment before going to class. I was zealous for her. That first love was passionate, fervent, diligent, disciplined, furious, all-consuming.

How long has it been since you felt that way about Jesus? Do you "remember" what it was that made you feel that first desperate, "sell every-thing and follow Jesus" kind of love? Do you remember what made you ready to throw your life away, to sell it cheap to follow the Galilean King?

How long has it been since you felt the holiness of God exposing all your selfishness and all the moral filth in your soul? Perhaps someone has recently been upset with you for something that seems trivial. Do you know that what God has against you is anything but trivial? Do you see the way that you have been proud more times than you can count? Can you number the times you have acted out of greed or lust or failed to act because of sloth or a lack of faith?

Have you sensed the weight of divine displeasure? Omnipotent divine displeasure? Divine displeasure that is altogether righteous, pure, unquestion-ably just, infinite in scope, and eternal in duration, matching the indescribable worth of the God whom you have offended?

And how long has it been since you felt the weight of all your guilt, real-ized anew that you had no deals to make, no appeasement to offer, nowhere to flee, and no hope that God might forget what you have done, only to experi-ence anew the wonder of God's mercy in Christ Jesus?

Because you trust Christ, all your guilt is freely pardoned. It is separated from you as far as the east is from the west. The steadfast love of the Lord toward you reaches to the heavens above, places a rock under your feet, and upholds that rock with a foundation that will never be shaken. You stand by faith in Christ fully forgiven, cleansed, sanctified, adopted, justified, welcomed, in a word, mercied.

Perhaps you have never experienced this. Let me encourage you to think on your sin. How do you propose to cleanse yourself from the stain? How do you plan to propitiate God's justice against your misdeeds? There is only one mediator between God and man, and his name is Jesus. He died to pay the penalty for sin. If you trust him, God will forgive your sin and make you part of his family. I urge you to trust him today. He is your only hope.

This line of thought—from God's holiness to our sin to God's justice against sin to the provision God made for our salvation in Christ and the mercy he shows to those who trust him—this thinking on the gospel is what will fire anew our first love. And John has already heralded these truths in 1:5 when he described Jesus as the one who "has freed us from our sins by his blood."

Just as thinking on your need for Jesus will fan the flames of your love for him, so also thinking on God's mercy in giving you a spouse you don't deserve will refresh your zeal for your spouse, and the same goes for our children and friends. Do you remember how you felt on your wedding day? Do you recall what you felt the day your child was born? What a privilege—that God would give us people to whom we can show the self-sacrificial love of Christ!

Maybe you feel that the things your church needs from you are a burden. Your turn in the nursery comes around so often. You keep waiting for someone else to wipe up the tables after the potluck lunch, but no one else steps forward.

The solution for these "problems" is not for the church to hire nursery workers so we don't have to be bothered with that problem. Nor, in my opinion, is it for us to stop doing those troublesome potluck lunches. The solution is for us to think on the gospel. When we meditate on the gospel, we become people who want to lay down our lives for others the way Jesus laid down his life for us. We become people who want to serve others the way the King served us. The gospel makes us want to love other people the way we have been loved.

Someday we will wish we had served others more. Someday we will wish we had rejoiced at every opportunity to make sacrifices for the church's needs. The church is the discipleship program that God has given to his people. When the church meets, discipleship is happening as those who are farther along in Christlikeness act like Jesus on behalf of those who have farther to go. We all have a long way to go; so we should look around and observe the way other people are acting like Jesus, then imitate them. He didn't come to be served but to serve (Mark 10:45). He was the greatest, and he was the servant (Matthew 23:11). The idea is for all of us to be living out Christlikeness for the benefit of others, so other people will see what it means to look not only to your own interests but also to the interests of others (Philippians 2:4). The church lives out discipleship, and Christ is glorified.

Let's rejoice in opportunities to display Christlikeness. Let's "outdo one another in showing honor" (Romans 12:10). Let's be glad that we have a nursery that needs workers. Let's be glad that we have a potluck lunch that gives us the opportunity to love other people by listening to them, to serve other people by helping them to their seats, by helping parents get food for their kids, by helping to clean up.

Meditate on the gospel. Do what Jesus says in 2:5: "Remember." The gospel will make you want to serve others.

The second action step that Jesus gives the church in Ephesus is for them to "repent" (2:5). Turn away from the way of thinking that makes you presume on Jesus. Turn away from the things that make you lose sight of his worth. Turn away from the things that dull your appetite for the Bible. Turn away from the things that steal the time you have for prayer. Turn away from the pride and self-reliance that keeps you from the Bible and prayer and your need for Jesus. Repent!

What is it that keeps you from Bible study, prayer, reliance on Christ? Your soul depends on your ability to repent of those things so that you might cultivate the first love that Jesus wants.

My sons don't want me to agree reluctantly to read books to them or play ball with them. My wife doesn't want me to reluctantly agree to spend time with her. Your spouse and your children can tell whether you are going through the motions, plodding along, persevering in doing your duty for them. They would rather have you joyfully delighting in loving them by seeking their happiness in what is best for their souls. They want you to love them, and Jesus wants no less.

The great commandment matters to the Lord Jesus Christ. He is not honored by joyless obedience that plods along, proclaiming that other things are more exciting than he is, more rewarding, more intriguing, more stimulating. That kind of perseverance does not please him, and you won't be able to keep it up for long. You will satisfy yourself on what you are convinced is most pleasurable.

The truth is that nothing is more satisfying than knowing God, and nothing will make you happier than following Jesus—which is to say, nothing will make you happier than treating other people the way Jesus treats you.

The third thing that Jesus calls the church in Ephesus to do is to "do the works you did at first" (2:5). These works done "at first" are probably the kinds of things people do when their minds and hearts are dominated by overwhelming devotion. Evidently this devotion had faded in the church in Ephesus, and here Jesus calls them to "remember" how things used to be, to "repent" of the things that have drawn them away from that devotion, and to "do the works" they did "at first" (2:5).

The seriousness with which Jesus takes "first love" can be seen in the way he threatens the church in Ephesus at the end of 2:5. Having called them to "remember," "repent," and "do" what they did at first, he then says, "If not, I will come to you and remove your lampstand from its place, unless you repent." The lampstands symbolize the churches (1:20), so this is nothing less than a promise to un-church the church.[7] If they do not repent, Jesus says that he will take away their standing as a church. The last words of 2:5 point to the only hope they have of maintaining their lampstand: "unless you repent."

Why does Jesus take this so seriously? Why is he ready to remove the lampstand of the church in Ephesus? Because they have forsaken the *first* and *greatest* commandment.

The final positive characteristic that Jesus names about the church in Ephesus is found in 2:6, where Jesus says, "Yet this you have: you hate the works of the Nicolaitans, which I also hate." We don't know who these Nicolaitans are. The only other place they are mentioned in the Bible is in 2:15. Because 2:14 mentions idolatry and sexual immorality, it might be that the teaching of the Nicolaitans inclined in those directions. The important thing for us to see, though, is that some ideas that get floated in churches—note that some in the church in Pergamum "hold the teaching of the Nicolaitans" (2:15)—Jesus *hates*.

Do you hate what Jesus hates and love what he loves? Do you know what kinds of things Jesus loves? There is one book in the world that will tell you all about those things. How interested are you in knowing the contents of that book?

So the church in Ephesus is doing nine things right and one thing wrong. But that one thing they have abandoned, the love they had at first (2:4), threatens to nullify everything that they are doing right. Loving God is the first and greatest commandment. Do you love him?

Believer or unbeliever, one sure way to grow in your love for God is to think on the gospel—God's holiness and justice against sin, the peril of your condition, the provision made in Christ, and your need to trust in Jesus.

A Call to Hear and Heed the Promises (2:7)

This first letter now concludes with a command for those with ears to hear: "He who has an ear, let him hear what the Spirit says to the churches" (2:7).

Jesus speaks this way in the Gospels (Matthew 11:15; 13:9, 43; Mark 4:9, 23; Luke 8:8; 14:35).[8] Notice that Jesus has been speaking, dictating this letter to John (2:1), but it is the Spirit who has been speaking (2:7). Notice also that while the church in Ephesus has been addressed (2:1), these words are addressed "to the churches" (2:7).

This letter to Ephesus closes with a promise at the end of 2:7: "To the one who conquers I will grant to eat of the tree of life, which is in the paradise of God." This promise declares that those who conquer will enjoy privileges lost when Adam and Eve were expelled from the Garden of Eden.

In 5:5, 6 Jesus is heralded as the conquering one. He conquers as the Lamb, standing as though slain. This points to Jesus conquering by faithfully doing what God called him to do. His conquest enables us to conquer, and in Revelation the saints conquer in the same way that Jesus conquered, through faithfulness to God even unto death. This is exactly what we see in 12:11, where the saints triumph over Satan: "And they have conquered him by the blood of the Lamb and by the word of their testimony, for they loved not their lives even unto death."

Those who conquer will eat from "the tree of life." The tree of life will be infinitely satisfying, and those who fail to conquer because they prized other things over Jesus will feel infinite remorse. And that remorse will never end.

Conclusion

If you look at your frustrating spouse and see the bride or groom of the wedding day, if you look at your "brats" and see the newborn babe, if you look at your ill or afflicted loved one and see someone you have loved, someone you will miss when he or she is gone, if you look at your needy church and see those for whom Christ died, first love will awaken in your heart.

Look at Jesus, the one who died in your place, showing you steadfast mercy, everlasting loving-kindness. Remember the way you felt when you first loved the one who first loved us. Repent, and do the works you did at first.

John Newton wrote:

In evil long I took delight,
Unawed by shame or fear,
Till a new object struck my sight,
And stopped my wild career.

I saw One hanging on a tree,
In agony and blood,
Who fixed His languid eyes on me,
As near His cross I stood.

Sure, never to my latest breath,
Can I forget that look;
It seemed to charge me with His death,
Though not a word He spoke.

My conscience felt and owned the guilt,
And plunged me in despair,
I saw my sins His blood had spilt,
And helped to nail Him there.

A second look He gave, which said,
"I freely all forgive;
This blood is for thy ransom paid;
I die that thou mayst live."

Thus, while His death my sin displays
In all its blackest hue,
Such is the mystery of grace,
It seals my pardon too.

6

Faithful unto Death

REVELATION 2:8–11

IN A.D. 177 PHOTINUS, bishop of Lyons, was martyred along with many Christians of his city. The Christians were accused of incest, probably a result of their referring to one another as "brother" and "sister," and cannibalism, probably resulting from misunderstandings of what happened during the Lord's Supper. Christians were arrested, tortured, and then brought into the arena to serve as public entertainment. Two by two they were brought out for the gawking, bloodthirsty crowd. They were tortured and then thrown to the beasts.[1]

Eusebius describes the suffering of one young female slave named Blandina:

> . . . her human mistress, who was herself one of the contenders among the martyrs, was in distress lest she should not be able, through the weakness of her body, to be bold enough even to make confession. Blandina was filled with such power that she was released and rescued from those who took turns in torturing her in every way from morning until evening, and they themselves confessed that they were beaten, for they had nothing left to do to her, and they marveled that she still remained alive, seeing that her whole body was broken and opened, and they testified that any one of these tortures was sufficient to destroy life, even when they had not been magnified and multiplied. But the blessed woman, like a noble athlete, kept gaining in vigour in her confession, and found comfort and rest and freedom from pain from what was done to her by saying, "I am a Christian woman and nothing wicked happens among us."[2]

When Blandina finally perished, Eusebius describes her as:

... glad at her departure as though invited to a marriage feast rather than cast to the beasts. . . . and the heathen themselves confessed that never before among them had a woman suffered so much and so long.[3]

Why do people persist when surrendering would save their lives? What keeps people, like this weak young woman Blandina, faithful unto death? How do they remain faithful unto death?

Need

We need to understand what it is that keeps people faithful unto death, so that we can live and die well ourselves.

Main Point

In order to be faithful unto death, the knowledge of Jesus must be bigger to us than the reality of death itself. Jesus is the First and the Last, the Conqueror over death, the Giver of the crown of life to those who are faithful unto death. Jesus must be bigger to us than death itself.

Preview

This letter to the church in Smyrna is all about Jesus. It may seem like the letter is about the suffering and persecution that the church in Smyrna is about to undergo, but from what Jesus says about that, it becomes clear that the suffering and persecution are just a stage built for the enactment of the drama that displays the worth of Christ.

So in Revelation 2:8–11 we will see:

2:8	Jesus Is Bigger than Death
2:9	Jesus Knows His People in Their Suffering
2:10	Jesus Calls His People to Be Faithful unto Death
2:11	Jesus Promises His People Life

Context

We can summarize the whole book of Revelation by thinking of it in three parts: Jesus and the letters, the throne and the judgments, and Babylon, Jesus, and the bride. In chapters 1—3 we see Jesus in chapter 1, then Jesus speaks the seven letters to the churches in chapters 2, 3. Chapters 4—5 show us God and Christ on the throne; then chapters 6—16 show us the judgments that issue from God's throne. Babylon falls in chapters 17—19; then Jesus comes and sets up his kingdom in chapters 19, 20, and the bride descends from Heaven in chapters 21, 22. Jesus and the letters. The throne and the judgments. Babylon, Jesus, and the bride. That's the book of Revelation.

This is the second of the seven letters in chapters 2, 3. This letter and the second to last letter match each other in that they are the only two letters in which Jesus neither rebukes the church nor calls it to repentance. The second and second to last letters are also the only two letters that make mention of the "synagogue of Satan" (2:9; 3:9). The first and last letters also match each other, with the first addressing "first love" and the last addressing lukewarmness. The middle three letters also match each other in that they deal with sexual immorality, idolatry, and spiritual death. So the outer two letters, the first and last and the second and second to last, are in a sense framing the inner three letters.

These letters are preceded by the opening of Revelation (1:1–8), and they are introduced by the stupendous glory of Jesus that knocks John down in 1:9–20. Immediately after Jesus dictates these letters to John (chapters 2, 3), he calls John up into Heaven, where John beholds the worship going on there (chapters 4, 5). So the situation in the church that we see in chapters 2, 3 is framed by the reality of the glory of Christ seen in John's vision of Jesus in chapter 1 and in John's description of the worship in Heaven in chapters 4, 5. And then the judgments of God that will bring history to its consummation come streaming out of that vision of worship in chapters 4, 5 as the seals, trumpets, and bowls of God's wrath are unleashed on the world in chapters 6—16. Babylon, the wicked world system, is demolished in chapters 17, 18, the King sets up his kingdom in chapters 19, 20, and the new Jerusalem descends from Heaven in chapters 21, 22.

This is reality: Jesus is glorious (chapter 1). The church must be faithful (chapters 2, 3). God and Jesus are being worshiped in Heaven as they deserve right now (chapters 4, 5). God's wrath is going to be let loose with fury when the Lamb breaks the seals (chapters 6—16). The enemies of God will be smashed (chapters 17, 18). Jesus will reign (chapters 19, 20). We will someday be home (chapters 21, 22).

It is easy to lose sight of this reality, so we should study what Jesus says to these churches because he means to help them live in light of it—that's why God gave "The Revelation"—so that his people would know "the things that must soon take place" (1:1).

Revelation 2:8: Jesus Is Bigger than Death

In 2:8 Jesus tells John to write "to the angel of the church in Smyrna." The "thus says" type of statement at the beginning of each of the seven letters recalls an aspect of the description of Jesus in glory in 1:9–20, and in each case the aspect of Jesus' glory that is mentioned is relevant for the contents of the rest of that particular letter.

In this case Jesus identifies himself as "the first and the last, who died and came to life" (2:8). There is depth here that cannot be plumbed. Think as far back as your mind can go, and Jesus was there before all that. He is "the first," before all else that is. He cannot be preempted. Be careful because thinking about him as "the first and the last" will tax your mental capacity to the breaking point. Jesus is bigger than our ability to understand.

He is also "the last." Nothing will endure longer than Jesus. He is before and after everything. By identifying himself in this way, as "the first and the last," Jesus is explicitly claiming divinity. This is equivalent to God the Father identifying himself as "the Alpha and the Omega" in 1:8. There are also important connections with the way that God makes exclusive claims to divinity based upon his unique status as "the first and the last" in Isaiah 40—48 (cf. 41:4; 43:10; 44:6; 48:12). Jesus here identifies himself with the Father. This is what scholars refer to as "high Christology." It is so high that the air is not only so thin it makes us dizzy, the atmospheric pressure at this height crushes lungs. Jesus is God!

Jesus goes on in 2:8 to say that he is the one "who died and came to life." This will blow your mind. How does "the first and the last" die? Who would have imagined that God could, or would, die? He is before and after all that is, and yet he entered into the progress of history, was killed, and rose from the dead. There are no categories for these kinds of claims in the religions and philosophies of the world. Being "the first and the last" makes Jesus eternal. How can one who is eternal die? I do not know *how* it happened, but I do know *that* it happened.

The death and resurrection of Jesus mean that death has no power over him. He is bigger than death itself, and given what the church in Smyrna faces, that reality is one they must keep in their minds if they are to be faithful.

When you think about the end of your life, do you apply to your contemplation the fact that Jesus has conquered death? When you think about dangerous situations you might face—the noise in the night that means an intruder might be in your home, the thought that someone you love could fall into a rushing river or be in some other situation that, if you try to help, might end your own life—when you think of life-threatening danger, do you apply to your thinking the triumph of Jesus over death? My friends, this is what it means to make connections between the good news of Jesus Christ, crucified and risen, and all of life. Applying to our fears the knowledge that Jesus is bigger than death will make us courageous.

Courage is a great thing, but we must keep in mind that courage is not our ultimate goal. Our ultimate goal is to live in ways that show our confidence in Jesus. When we are courageous because we know that Jesus is bigger than death, we honor Jesus. And when we put ourselves in harm's way in order to protect others, or even to save their lives, because we love Jesus and know that he is in control and trust him to take care of us—even if we die—we are following Jesus.

If you do not know Jesus, you cannot follow him. If you do not know Jesus, you do not know the one who has conquered death and freed us from the fear of it. Perhaps you realize that you don't know Jesus, and you wonder what it means to know him. I would simply invite you to behold his glory. Think about the way that he died to protect others, to deliver those who would trust him from the power of sin and death, and know, indeed fully trust, that he can deliver you. He is *able* to save, and he is *mighty* to save. Believe that. Know him as Savior. Trust him. And continue to think on his power to save. If you trust him, he will save you. He is the only hope you have to be delivered from the power of sin and death. Don't you feel your need for him? Don't you want "the first and the last, who died and came to life" to stand between you and the awful forces of sin and death?

Let's hide these truths in our hearts. Jesus is the first and the last. He died and came to life. He is bigger than death. He has conquered death. And let's be courageous because we trust Jesus and follow him by laying down our lives for others just as he laid down his life for us.

Revelation 2:9: Jesus Knows His People in Their Suffering

After Jesus announces himself in 2:8, he says in 2:9 that he knows three things: 1) their "tribulation," 2) their "poverty," and 3) the "slander" made against them.

What could be more comforting to the church in Smyrna than Jesus saying to them, "I know your tribulation"? Tribulation is painful and wearisome. It pecks away at us little by little, chipping away at our joy, taking the wind out of our perseverance, and things only worsen as tribulation drags on. Jesus does not trivialize their suffering by telling them it isn't really that bad. He doesn't demean them by telling them that if they were stronger it wouldn't bother them so much. And he doesn't cheapen their experience by offering unsympathetic advice. Rather, Jesus ennobles their suffering with the simple and comforting words, "I know your tribulation."

One of the most discouraging effects of suffering is that we feel alone. When Jesus tells the church in Smyrna that he knows their tribulation, he is reminding them of his presence with them.

The second thing Jesus knows is their "poverty." The church was poor. The tribulation probably resulted from the people of influence in Smyrna opposing Christianity because they perceived that this new religion was not going to appease the gods of the Greco-Roman pantheon, it was not going to make Caesar happy, and it was not going to raise the city of Smyrna to new heights of prominence in the Roman Empire. In fact, the values of this new faith were at odds with the values of the Roman Empire.

So the little church in Smyrna was opposed by the power structures in the Empire and had no financial resources and no influence in society. Or so it seemed.

Jesus says to them, "I know your tribulation and your poverty" (2:9). This means that the true Lord of lords, the real King of kings, the one to whom Caesar will bow the knee, knows them, knows their need, and he adds, "but you are rich" (2:9). This is the same paradox expressed by Paul when he described himself "as poor, yet making many rich; as having nothing, yet possessing everything" (2 Corinthians 6:10). Though we do not have what the world counts as wealth, we have what is *in reality* wealth. By telling the church in Smyrna that they are rich, Jesus is redirecting their perspective away from worldly standards of evaluation and reminding them of what matters.

We who have the wealth of which Jesus speaks are like a poor man boarding the *Titanic*. We watch all the bejeweled people of wealth and fashion and etiquette and connection pass us by with never so much as a nod of courtesy, because all we brought on board the ship that will sink in the night is a small, seemingly worthless lifeboat.

Brothers and sisters, we are rich because we have what will save life unto eternity. When Jesus comes on that white horse, outdated clothes, beat-up cars, and houses where the appliances have not been updated will cease to be indications that we are unwealthy. The only thing that will matter is whether or not you have the gospel. And if you have the gospel, you are rich indeed. This wealth is yours if you will trust Christ. But you should not trust him to have a paradoxical version of wealth; you should trust him so you can be reconciled to God, so you can treasure God.

Here is another point of application—another point where we apply the gospel of Jesus to all of life: How do you measure your economic standing? By the kind of cell phone or cell phone plan you can afford? By the amount of your income you can throw away on entertainment or travel? Or do you measure your economic standing by the fact that Jesus has reconciled you to God and made it so that you are a child of God your Father, who owns the cattle on a thousand hills and has promised you the world and life and all things as your inheritance (1 Corinthians 3:21–23)?

Those who are fabulously wealthy often display a careless nonchalance about all they have. We Christians ought to feel something similar—not that we disregard the goodness of the things that God has promised. But we will, I think, feel a certain freedom from all that God has promised to give us, so long as he gives us the one thing we cannot do without: himself.

The third thing that Jesus tells the church in Smyrna that he knows is "the slander of those who say that they are Jews and are not, but are a synagogue of Satan" (2:9). The Romans had granted the Jews an exemption from required participation in the Roman Imperial Cult. In other words, the Jews did not have to take part in Roman idolatry. Everyone else was required to participate. Obviously Christians would not want to participate with the Romans in their idolatrous festivals and celebrations. The Jewish slander in view here probably has to do with Jews denouncing Christians to the Romans,[4] and we get a glimpse of something like this in Acts 18:12–17. As long as Christianity was under the Jewish umbrella, Christians were also exempt from required participation in the growing Roman Imperial Cult. If the Jews began denouncing Christians to the Romans—arguing that they were not Jews at all—Christians who refused to participate in Roman idolatry could face retribution.

Something like this seems to be going on in Smyrna, and Jesus says that he knows "the slander of those who say that they are Jews and are not, but are a synagogue of Satan" (2:9). Jesus denies the status of "Jew" to those who do not serve the Jewish King, Jesus himself. He identifies their true allegiance: they are those who gather in synagogues to celebrate Satan's kingdom, not God's. God's kingdom is advancing with King Jesus at its head. All who oppose King Jesus are allied with the dark power in service to a rebel kingdom whose lord is a liar and murderer who hates those who serve Jesus. Our Lord said that those who are not for him are against him (Matthew 12:30). And in language similar to the reference in Revelation to these Jews being a "synagogue of Satan" (2:9; cf. 3:9), in John 8:44 Jesus told his Jewish opponents that they were of their father the Devil.[5]

Whose side are you on?

Revelation 2:10: Jesus Calls His People to Be Faithful unto Death

Having stated that he knows what they are facing, Jesus tells the church in Smyrna, "Do not fear what you are about to suffer. Behold, the devil is about to throw some of you into prison, that you may be tested, and for ten days you will have tribulation" (2:10).

We should note several things here before we read the rest of this verse. First, he tells them not to fear what they are about to suffer. The only thing that will keep the Smyrnan Christians from fearing what they are about to suffer is their living on what Jesus has said to them thus far. He has announced himself as "the first and the last, who died and came to life" (2:8), and he has assured them that he knows what they suffer and knows who their enemies are (2:9). Because of who he is, and because he will be with them through the suffering, they can be free from fear.

Second, he identifies who is at work in their suffering—"the devil is about to throw some of you into prison" (2:10). There is no question here about who is in the right and who is in the wrong. There is no suggestion from Jesus that a change in strategy might palliate the adversaries of the church. There is none of this namby-pamby nonsense suggesting that maybe if the Christians were less dogmatic, or maybe if they were more open to the possibility of there being more than one right way, they would not be suffering. None of that garbage from Jesus. He recognizes who the enemy is, and it is clear that those who oppose his people are diabolical. The devil is about to have them arrested.

Notice, though, third, that there is a purpose statement following the announcement that the opposition comes from Satan—"that you may be tested" (2:10). I don't think this is a satanic purpose. It seems that, like 17:17, this is one of those texts in Revelation that indicates that God is using Satan to accomplish his purposes. God is using the devil's persecution to test and prove his people. And when his people come through the test, they make God look good, for only God could preserve them.

Fourth, Jesus tells them that "for ten days you will have tribulation" (2:10). It seems that "ten days" here points to a full but limited amount of time. I don't think we should read this as a literal reference to ten twenty-four-hour periods of time. What if they wind up imprisoned for longer than ten days? I don't think that's the point. The point is to communicate to these Christians that Jesus knows how long their suffering is going to last, and in comparison with other periods of time in Revelation—for instance, the thousand years we read of in chapter 20—the ten days of their suffering is relatively short. They can hold on to the end because it is a relatively short period of time, and Jesus knows how long it will last.

And then we get the audacious command, "Be faithful unto death" (2:10). Only Jesus could make this kind of demand. Only Jesus has the authority necessary to place this kind of obligation upon people. Only Jesus has the ability to recompense those who would obey this injunction. The command to "be faithful unto death" proclaims that it is more important to be faithful to Jesus than it is to go on living. Philip Doddridge (1702–1751) once wrote, "I am more afraid of doing what is wrong than of dying."[6]

Jesus is worth dying for. And if he is worth dying for, then he is worth living for. Only those who are gripped by something worth more to them than life can be truly courageous. And courage is precisely what Jesus calls the church in Smyrna to in this command. He is proclaiming to them that he is better than life.

Those who experience his goodness, who know him this way, know the truth that Jesus spoke: "For whoever would save his life will lose it, but whoever loses his life for my sake and the gospel's will save it" (Mark 8:35). Jesus promises life to those who are faithful unto death. He says, "Be faithful unto death, and I will give you the crown of life" (2:10). This is the only way to life: death. Death to self. Death to sin. Then you will be dead to the world and dead to fear. You will also be alive by the power of the Spirit and through faith in Jesus.

Revelation 2:11: Jesus Promises His People Life

Revelation 2:11 closes the letter to the church at Smyrna by calling those who have ears to hear, and then the promise of life in verse 10 is restated in different language. At the end of 2:11 we read, "The one who conquers will not be hurt by the second death." In this context, conquering clearly means remaining faithful to Jesus even unto death, and it means the same thing in 12:11. Those who conquer in this way "will not be hurt by the second death" (2:11). We see what the second death is in 20:14: "This is the second death, the lake of fire." The second death is a death that those who are thrown into the lake of fire will experience forever.

The only way to avoid it is to believe in Jesus and to live like you believe in Jesus, being faithful unto death (2:10, 11).

Conclusion

In the fall of 1997 I trained for and ran the Dallas White Rock Marathon. Leading up to the race, and even during the race, I was not absolutely sure that I was going to be able to finish. My plan was to start running and keep running as long as I possibly could. Hopefully that would take me through the 26.2 miles, but as I watched people's bodies fail on them as the race wore on—as people literally collapsed—I wondered if I would make it to the end.

Perhaps as you think about faithfulness unto death, you wonder, as I did regarding the marathon, whether you will hold up all the way through. Perhaps you know of accounts where people have broken under torture or extreme psychological strain, and perhaps you are uncertain as to whether you would be able to "be faithful unto death" (2:10).

We can all be encouraged by the story of Thomas Cranmer.[7] In the spring of 1556, Thomas Cranmer's "consistent and careful preservation of his integrity over two and a half years of mental assault began to crumble."[8]

He had been arrested in 1553. Talented Spanish scholars had been brought in to dispute with Cranmer. On January 1, 1556, Cranmer admitted that he had not seen certain implications in texts from Augustine. Cranmer had always placed the authority of councils over the authority of popes, and having seen his dear friends Latimer and Ridley burn at the stake, having endured exhausting mental exercise, he finally conceded that if he could be shown that the first ecumenical council of Nicaea in 325 had been called by a pope, "I will indeed openly affirm the Pope to have been and to be now head of the Church."[9] Texts were produced. Cranmer alleged that they were corrupted, "which resulted in an ill-tempered contest leafing through piles of various editions, and a systematic search in the college libraries throughout the University. None of them proved his contention. It was a bad moment, and he had been trapped."[10] Cranmer, an intellectual powerhouse who had studied the fathers of the church all his life, who had been able to withstand the barrage from a team of the finest Spanish scholars, was cornered on a point that he could not disprove.

His biographer writes, "he was under terrible emotional strain: he had always relied much on a small intimate circle of trusted friends, and they had all been taken from him. Not surprisingly, his health was now frail."[11] By the end of January he had capitulated. Then he drew back from the surrender. On February 14, 1556, he appealed for a General Council. He reasserted his rejection of papal authority and reaffirmed his Protestant views of the Eucharist.

On February 26, however, he signed a recantation. The sixty-seven-year old Cranmer was exhausted—mentally, emotionally, physically. Some suggest he was suffering from a heart condition , and his biographer writes, "After the miserable history of brain-washing and interrogation in the twentieth century, we are better placed . . . to understand the sort of pressures to which Cranmer had been subjected."[12] He acknowledged the Pope, transubstantiation, seven sacraments, and purgatory and repented of previous belief. He heard the Mass. In all he signed six recantations.

On March 21, 1556, just before being taken to the University Church, he stated to a Roman Catholic friend who had used Cranmer's need for friendship against him that "God would finish what he had begun. It was a statement which could be taken in two ways, as became apparent in what happened next."[13]

Cranmer was taken to the University Church, where Dr. Henry Cole first preached a sermon seeking to explain "why a repentant sinner should still be burnt at the stake for heresy."[14] Cranmer then stood at a specially prepared pulpit, where he was to read a manuscript. The authorities had the manuscript, so they knew what was coming.

Cranmer was supposed to explain "the great thing, which so much troubleth my conscience . . . the untrue books and writings, contrary to the truth of God's word . . . which I wrote against the sacrament of the altar since the death of King Henry the eight." But instead he denounced what he had written "contrary to the truth which I thought in my heart, and written for fear of death . . . all such bills and papers which I have written or signed with my hand since my degradation."[15]

There was uproar in the church—joy and rage. Cranmer shouted, "And as for the Pope, I refuse him, as Christ's enemy, and Antichrist, with all his false doctrine. . . . and as for the sacrament, I believe as I have taught in my book against the Bishop of Winchester."[16]

He was dragged from the pulpit, through the streets, with the Spanish scholar Villagarcia following him dazedly repeating, "You didn't do it?" Villagarcia said Cranmer would have acknowledged the Pope to save his life. Cranmer agreed. Villagarcia pointed out that that very day he had confessed to a priest. Cranmer retorted contemptuously, "What if the confession is no good?"[17]

In the church Cranmer had shouted, "Forasmuch as my hand offended, writing contrary to my heart, my hand shall first be punished there-for." At the stake Cranmer stretched his right hand into the heart of the fire, and for as long as he could he repeated the words, "my unworthy right hand," "this hand hath offended," and "Lord Jesus, receive my spirit . . . I see the heavens open and Jesus standing at the right hand of God."[18]

The only explanation for Thomas Cranmer's life and death is to be found in the words of Philippians 1:6, which he quoted on the morning of his death: "God, who began a good work . . . will bring it to completion."

Thus, the main point of this study is that the knowledge of Jesus must be bigger than life to us. Consider the following key Scriptures:

- 1 Corinthians 1:9: "God is faithful, by whom you were called into the fellowship of his Son, Jesus Christ our Lord."
- 2 Corinthians 1:9: "Indeed, we felt that we had received the sentence of death. But that was to make us rely not on ourselves but on God who raises the dead."
- 1 Thessalonians 5:23, 24: "Now may the God of peace himself sanctify you completely, and may your whole spirit and soul and body be kept blameless at the coming of our Lord Jesus Christ. He who calls you is faithful; he will surely do it."
- Revelation 12:11: "And they have conquered him by the blood of the Lamb and by the word of their testimony, for they loved not their lives even unto death."

God gets the glory for martyrs because he is the one who has convinced them that his love is better than life (Psalm 63:3). He is the one whose worth their deaths declare. He is the one who has so satisfied their hearts that they *cannot* deny him—they *are not able to do so*—they *do not want to do so* because they want to be faithful to him.

God's word is true. If we know Jesus we know he is bigger than life, better than life. God gets the glory as people who know him declare that it is better to die than to live without him.

We need this. Not just because some of us might die as martyrs, but because all of us live. The death of the martyrs points to the life worth living, to the life worth dying for—the life that is lived to and through and for God through Jesus Christ in the power of the Holy Spirit.

7

Repent of Nicolaitan Teaching

REVELATION 2:12–17

IN EDMUND SPENSER'S ALLEGORICAL POEM *The Faerie Queene*, Spenser depicts the church as a lovely lady who is accompanied by the Knight of the Redcrosse, who corresponds in many ways to the individual Christian. At one point an evil enchanter deceives the Redcrosse knight into thinking that the fair lady, the church, has been unfaithful to him. So he leaves her and strikes out on his own. As he makes his way, he finds another lovely young lady, with whom he comes to a quiet, secluded repose under a foreboding tree. The Redcrosse knight then hears someone shout a cry of warning, telling him that he should flee lest he should buy pleasures from a lurking lady at the cost of his life. At first the Redcrosse knight is frightened by this cry, but then he is overcome by the beauty of the lady, who is a witch in disguise.

Then the tree speaks to him, telling him that he was formerly a man, but a witch disguised as a beautiful young maid transformed him into a tree. The tree tells him that though he is a tree, the heat and the cold pain him, and he relates how one day he happened to see the witch as she really was:

A filthy foule old woman I did vew [view],
That ever to have toucht [touched] her, I did deadly rew [rue].

When he recoiled from the witch in horror, she turned him into a tree.

The point that Spenser is making is simple: sin always promises, but it never pays. Sin disguises itself as something attractive, refreshing, rewarding. But underneath the false exterior, sin is filthy and foul, and those who sport with it know only regret.

Need

We need to be convinced that we must never flirt with evil. We need to have the false exterior of sin pulled back so that we see it as it is.

Main Point

The main point of the letter to the church in Pergamum is that they must repent of Nicolaitan teaching.

Preview

Revelation 2:12	Jesus Has the Sword of Judgment
Revelation 2:13	Faithfulness in Pergamum
Revelation 2:14–16	A Call to Repent of Nicolaitan Teaching
Revelation 2:17	The Promise of Hidden Manna and a White Stone

Context

There seems to be a progression in these middle three letters. The first of the three, to Pergamum, addresses a church that holds to false teaching, but they are not explicitly rebuked for false teaching and sexual immorality. The second of the three, to Thyatira, rebukes the church for tolerating Jezebel, who teaches the Lord's servants to commit sexual immorality and to eat food offered to idols. The third letter, to Sardis, addresses a church that is dead. Do you want to know how a church dies? I would suggest that we have a hint here. It starts with false teaching, which leads to idolatry and immorality, which kills the church.

Just as these three churches seem to be at different points on the spectrum, so today there are churches at different points of the spectrum. As Jesus addresses the church at Pergamum, the believers there seem to be flirting with evil. They are not openly embracing immorality and idolatry but are not closing the door to it either. Jesus calls them to repent of the teaching of the Nicolaitans, which is false teaching, before it is too late.

Revelation 2:12: Jesus Has the Sword of Judgment

In this letter Jesus introduces himself to the church in Pergamum as the one "who has the sharp two-edged sword" (2:12). Back in 1:16 John had seen Jesus in glory, and "from his mouth came a sharp two-edged sword." When Jesus returns in glory in chapter 19, we read that "From his mouth comes a sharp sword with which to strike down the nations" (v. 15). So we know that this "sharp two-edged sword" is probably an image of judgment. Rather than envisioning Jesus with a sword-shaped tongue, we should probably understand this to mean that Jesus will speak decisive words of judgment. The sword was certainly used in judgment in the Roman world, so this introduction contains a threatening image. John's audience knows that Rome wields the sword of judgment, but the authority of Jesus and the sword of judgment that comes from his mouth will strike down the idolatry of Rome.

Whose judgment do you fear? The Christians in John's audience could avoid the sword of Rome by doing things that would put them in danger of the sword of Jesus. We will all face situations where what the world judges to be right conflicts with what Jesus judges to be right. Whose sword do you respect in that moment? The sword of the world and the judgment the world might inflict, or the sharp two-edged sword in the mouth of the Son of man?

Revelation 2:13: Faithfulness in Pergamum

Jesus begins his address to the church in Pergamum with a strong commendation of the church. This commendation is made even stronger by the way it is presented. What the church has done right is framed by statements acknowledging that the church is in a very bad neighborhood. Revelation 2:13 opens with the words, "I know where you dwell, where Satan's throne is," and the last words of that verse are, "among you, where Satan dwells."

Between these references to Satan's throne and dwelling in Pergamum, Jesus commends the church because, in spite of the bad influence of their neighborhood, he says, "Yet you hold fast my name, and you did not deny my faith even in the days of Antipas my faithful witness, who was killed among you" (2:13).[1] So in spite of their proximity to Satan's throne, they "hold fast" to the name of Jesus. That they hold fast to Jesus' name means that they are conducting themselves for Jesus' glory. We can see that Jesus' own glory matters to him by the way he mentions it over and over to these churches:

- 2:3, "you are enduring patiently and bearing up for my name's sake."
- 2:13, "you hold fast my name."
- 3:8, "you have kept my word and have not denied my name."
- 3:12, "I will write on him the name of my God . . . and my own new name."

Jesus cares about his reputation. In what ways does your life indicate that you don't?

The church in Pergamum has held fast to the name of Jesus, and they have not denied the faith, even though the "faithful witness," Antipas, was killed, apparently for the faith (2:13). To deny the faith in the face of death would be to declare that one believes life in the here and now is better than Jesus, better than having the life he promises, which cannot be defeated by death. By holding to Jesus' name and not denying the faith, even when Antipas was killed for the faith, the Christians in Pergamum declare that Jesus is better than life.

The references at the beginning and end of this verse to "Satan's throne" and the place "where Satan dwells" seem to reflect the status of Pergamum as "the religious capital of the province of Asia."[2] Even if other cities were more prominent, and some suggest Ephesus was, Pergamum was "the site of the first and most important temple to the deified Augustus."[3] There was a strong rivalry between Ephesus, Smyrna, and Pergamum, and Pergamum seems to have become the most important city in Asia as far as the Roman Imperial Cult was concerned.[4] In the Roman Empire we see "a ruler cult which was a permanent institution, created and organized by the subjects of a great empire in order to represent to themselves the ruling power."[5]

These Christians in Pergamum were holding up well in the satanic stronghold in which they lived, but as we see from ensuing verses, they needed to repent of their toleration of false teaching.

Revelation 2:14–16: A Call to Repent of Nicolaitan Teaching

In 2:14, 15 John records what seems to be an instance of Jesus engaging in typological interpretation and application of the Old Testament to the situation of the church in Pergamum. The key features of typological interpretation are (1) historical correspondence and (2) escalation.

In this case Jesus says, "But I have a few things against you: you have some there who hold the teaching of Balaam" (2:14). But before we look at the brief recap of what Balaam taught in the rest of verse 14, notice that the phrasing of verse 15 parallels the first part of verse 14 exactly: "So also you have some who hold the teaching of the Nicolaitans." The "so also" that begins verse 15 introduces the comparison between what happened in history when Balaam introduced idolatry and immorality in Israel and the way that the teaching of the Nicolaitans will introduce idolatry and immorality in the church in Pergamum.

The incident referenced in the mention of Balaam is explained in the rest of 2:14: ". . . Balaam, who taught Balak to put a stumbling block before the sons of Israel, so that they might eat food sacrificed to idols and practice sexual immorality." So it seems that whoever the Nicolaitans were (and we saw in 2:6 that the Ephesian church was commended for hating their teaching), and whatever the particular nuances of their teaching were, their teaching would lead to sexual immorality and idolatry, just like Balaam's.

We can also observe that this idolatry and immorality threatening the church in Pergamum is probably connected to the references to "Satan's throne" and the place "where Satan dwells" in 2:13. The church was probably facing pressure from the Roman Imperial Cult in Asia Minor. This cult included homage paid to the emperor and the gods that would be inescapably idolatrous,[6] and there is no shortage of evidence that Roman celebrations could degenerate into drunken orgies. So the teaching of the Nicolaitans probably validated a certain level of participation in civic life, the celebrations of the city of Pergamum, which would have been idolatrous and immoral in nature.

Are ideas circulating in our culture that we could liken to "the teaching of the Nicolaitans" (2:15)? Ideas that would result in our thinking it right to gratify our sinful desires? Ideas that would result in our thinking it right to give worship to something other than God alone? And more specifically in line with what this text is teaching, are there people who put themselves forward as Christian teachers, pastors, or authors of Christian books who advocate a lifestyle that results in idolatry and immorality?

As a body of believers, we have to be theologically and culturally sensitive enough to recognize when someone is teaching us to minimize sin, to avoid too much talk about who God is or what the Bible says, and to enjoy the good life here in America. This kind of thing is not what we need.

We need to be taught to value Christ, to honor God, to celebrate God's mercy in Christ's death on the cross for our sins, to celebrate even the teaching of human sinfulness because it highlights God's grace in sending Jesus to die for us "while we were still sinners" (Romans 5:8). We hate sin, but we love the Bible's telling us the truth, and we love to see that "where sin increased, grace abounded all the more" (Romans 5:20). We have to be able to recognize the difference between faithful preachers, teachers, and authors who help us boast in God and glory in the cross and so-called preachers, teachers, and authors who teach us to minimize human sinfulness, avoid talking too much about God, and all the while are teaching us to value what Americans value, to love what the world loves, to measure success the way the world measures success. Where you have false teaching, idolatry and immorality are close behind.

Let me observe at this point that often what drives sexual immorality and idolatry is not *only* the sinful appeal of idolatry and immoral behavior. The illicit appeal of objects of lust and of false gods is combined with the fact that these objects and behaviors provide what we might call love-substitutes. Often what is really at the root of idolatry is the mistaken conclusion that this false god is going to provide for me. Similarly, what might be at the root of sexual immorality is a longing for intimacy. False thinking about what will provide for us and give us the intimacy we desire leads to immorality and idolatry.

When we come to verse 16, I think the typology with the incident involving Balaam continues. So far the typology looks like this:

Table 7.1: Balaam False Teaching Typology

1) the false teaching of Balaam (cf. Numbers 25:1; 31:16)	corresponds to	the false teaching of the Nicolaitans
2) the immorality and idolatry in Israel (Numbers 25:1–4)	corresponds to	the immorality and idolatry tempting the church in Pergamum

In 2:16 we have another correspondence that also contributes escalation. Jesus says, "Therefore repent. If not, I will come to you soon and war against them with the sword of my mouth." So this last correspondence looks like this:

Table 7.2: Judgment of False Teaching Typology

3) the judgment of Israel's sin and idolatry (cf. Numbers 25:3, 9)	corresponds to	the threatened greater judgment Jesus will bring against the church's immorality and idolatry

The judgment that Jesus threatens has to do with the sword that comes from his mouth, which he announced in the opening of this letter to the church in Pergamum (2:12; cf. 2:16). Just as the Lord struck down those who yoked themselves to the Baal of Peor, and 24,000 died (Numbers 25:9), so Jesus threatens to "war against them"—apparently those holding to the teaching of the Nicolaitans.

It is interesting to observe that the command to "repent" is in the second person singular, as in, "you must repent," and the address is representatively made to the angel who represents the church. But if the church does not repent, Jesus threatens to make war on "them." This seems to indicate that repentance is to take the form of the church pursuing a process of discipline with those who are holding to the teaching of the Nicolaitans. And this process of discipline is motivated by a desire to keep Jesus from making war on those who are holding to the false teaching. We call people to repent because we love them and want to keep them from judgment. And if they do not repent, we are to follow the steps prescribed in Matthew 18:15–18 because we love them and want to keep them from judgment.

Revelation 2:17: The Promise of Hidden Manna and a White Stone

This letter closes with the call for those who have an ear to "hear what the Spirit says to the churches" (2:17). Again I would observe that "churches" is in the plural, even though it is the church in Pergamum that has been addressed in this letter. We are not the church in Pergamum, but Jesus is speaking to us by the Holy Spirit. We can also observe that there is a tension between the singular and the plural in this call and in the promised reward. "He who has an ear, let him hear" is singular—individuals are called to hear and respond. The tension comes in the next phrase, "what the Spirit says to the churches." "Churches" is plural, and a church is a group of believers.

Then there are the promises made to him who conquers. Notice that "the one who conquers" is in the singular. It seems to me that the back and forth between the singular and the plural points to the way that as members of the church we have *both* individual responsibility for ourselves and a corporate responsibility for the other members of the body.

Why would Jesus promise "hidden manna" and "a white stone, with a new name written on the stone that no one knows except the one who receives it" (2:17) at the conclusion of this letter to the church in Pergamum? I think these promises are meant to meet the needs that people seek to meet through idolatry and sexual immorality. I suggested earlier that idolatry arises from the desire to have our needs met. Jesus promises to meet those needs. Jesus offers the provision of "hidden manna," which is a better provision than any idol offers. He tells us we don't need to go to other gods.

Similarly, I suggested that sexual immorality arises from a longing for intimacy. The promise of "a white stone, with a new name written on the stone that no one knows except the one who receives it" is a promise of intimacy. Whatever else it means, this promises that there will be a private communication between God and the one who overcomes. Surely God knows the name on the stone, and the one who receives the stone knows the name. And that exclusive knowledge, that private interaction that no one else shares, is the essence of intimacy. Jesus is arming us with weapons for the war on lust.

Conclusion

In *The Faerie Queene*, the lady, who is the symbol of the church, does not abandon the Redcrosse knight. In the poem she meets a lion, who, rather than being a threat to her, is her protector and champion. With the lion, the lady sets out to find the knight.

In God's great mercy, the Lion of the tribe of Judah is indeed the protector and champion of the Church. Do not flirt with the teaching of the Nicolaitans. Sin makes promises it does not keep. The words of Jesus are meant to remove the false beauty of the witch, so that we see sin as it is. It is ugly, vile, disgusting. It promises nourishment and intimacy, but what it delivers is only a cheap imitation of real blessings. Sin never satisfies.

Do you have ears to hear what the Spirit says to the churches? Fight the good fight. Overcome. Feed your soul on the manna Jesus gives. Enjoy the intimacy he promises. He knows you as you are, and he loves you. There is no love better than his.

8

King Jesus versus Jezebel

REVELATION 2:18–29

IN HIS BOOK *Founding Brothers*, Joseph J. Ellis writes:

> In 1780 Maj. John André was captured while attempting to serve as a British spy in league with Benedict Arnold to produce a major strategic debacle on the Hudson River at West Point. By all accounts, André was a model British officer with impeccable manners, who had the misfortune to be caught doing his duty. Several members of Washington's staff, including Hamilton, pleaded that André's life be spared because of his exceptional character. Washington dismissed the requests as sentimental, pointing out that if André had succeeded in his mission, it might very well have turned the tide of the war. The staff then supported André's gallant request that he be shot like an officer rather than hanged as a spy. Washington also rejected this request, explaining that André, regardless of his personal attractiveness, was no more and no less than a spy. He was hanged the next day.[1]

In this example from history, we see that George Washington was a man who understood what was at stake in the conflict, had a clear vision of right and wrong, and acted in accord with what he knew to be right. The rightness or wrongness of the hanging of Major John André had nothing to do with his appearance, his polite manner, or any affection his character might generate. He deserved to be hanged, so Washington had him hanged.

Need

There is a great need in our time for men and women like George Washington—people who are gripped by the truth of God's Word such that the arbiter of right and wrong is what God has spoken. We need people who understand what God calls the church to do and who do that with no favoritism shown for those who, from the world's perspective, are wealthy, influential, or significant.

Main Point

The main point of the letter to the church in Thyatira is that they need to exclude the unrepentant Jezebel. This passage indicates that this Jezebel has been called to repentance but has refused to repent, and now the church is tolerating her in her unrepentant state. Jesus promises to judge her and her children, and he threatens those who do not belong to her but who commit adultery with her with the same judgment that he will bring upon Jezebel.

It seems, then, that the church in Thyatira should have excluded Jezebel but is instead tolerating her. Jesus announces to the church that he is going to judge her, and he will not show any favoritism to her or to those who have indulged in evil with her.

The church in Thyatira needs to exclude Jezebel. They should not fail to do so because she is attractive, eloquent, or influential or because she claims to be a prophet. They must do what they know to be right.

Preview

Revelation 2:18–29 can be broken down into three main sections:

2:18   Jesus Is the Searching and Pure Davidic King
2:19–25   The Church Needs to Exclude Jezebel
    2:19   Commendation of the Church in Thyatira
    2:20–23   Jezebel and Her Children
    2:24, 25   Hold What You Have
2:26–29   Hear the Promises

In the first section Jesus will be identified as the Davidic king in terms that are reminiscent of passages such as 2 Samuel 7 and Psalm 2. In the second section we will see that those who are leading the church in Thyatira have failed to exercise justice against Jezebel. And in the third section Jesus promises that those who keep his commands will rule the fulfillment of the Davidic kingdom with Jesus.

Context

Chapters 1—3 shows us Jesus and the letters to the seven churches. Chapters 4—16 will show us the throne and the judgments. And chapters 17—22 will show us the harlot, the King, and the bride.

In the letters we have looked at, Ephesus had abandoned their first love.

Smyrna was not reproved, but they were facing tribulation. Pergamum had people holding the teaching of the Nicolaitans. Thyatira, the subject under consideration now, is tolerating Jezebel. We will see that Sardis seemed alive but was dead. Philadelphia had an open door. Laodicea was lukewarm.

The church doesn't look great in these letters, but Jesus is magnificent! We see his glory before the letters in 1:9–20, and we see God and Christ being worshiped in Heaven after the letters in chapters 4, 5. We see the certain triumph of God's justice in chapters 6—16. Then Babylon falls (chapters 17—19). Then the King comes (chapter 20), and the bride descends from Heaven (chapters 21, 22). The book of Revelation is an unveiling of reality, and the letters to the churches summon the churches to live in the reality unveiled in this book.

Revelation 2:18: Jesus Is the Searching and Pure Davidic King

Jesus introduces himself to the church in Thyatira in terms that are reminiscent of the covenant God made with David in 2 Samuel 7. In that chapter the Lord said to David, "I will raise up your offspring after you, who shall come from your body, and I will establish his kingdom. . . . I will be to him a father, and he shall be to me a son" (vv. 12, 14). This "father-son" language is picked up in Psalm 2, where we read, "The LORD said to me, 'You are my Son; today I have begotten you'" (v. 7). As we go through this passage in Revelation, we will see more allusions to Psalm 2 at the end of this letter. It is important to see here, though, that in identifying himself as "the Son of God" (2:18), Jesus announces himself to the church in Thyatira as the Davidic King.

In addition to the Old Testament overtones of Jesus identifying himself as "the Son of God" here, there is probably also some degree of polemic against the claims of Caesar. David Aune writes:

> Roman emperors characteristically claimed in their titulature introducing official letters and decrees that they were "sons of god" in the special sense that they were sons or adopted sons of their deified predecessors. A letter from Augustus to Ephesus begins this way: Αυτοκρ τωρ κα σαρ θεο 'Ιουλ ου υἱς; "Emperor Caesar, son of the god Julius."[2]

Jesus continues to describe himself as the one "who has eyes like a flame of fire, and whose feet are like burnished bronze" (2:18; cf. Daniel 10:6: "his eyes like flaming torches, his arms and legs like the gleam of burnished bronze"). The reference to "eyes like a flame of fire" seems to point to Jesus' searching gaze, from which nothing escapes (cf. 2:23). And the phrase "feet . . . like burnished bronze" seems to point to Jesus' absolute purity.

Jesus is King. Jesus sees all. Jesus is pure. This is a King worthy of your worship. These Christians in Thyatira would be inspired to worship Jesus because of who he is, and they would be encouraged that God has faithfully kept the promises he made in 2 Samuel 7 and Psalm 2. The one whose eyes are "like a flame of fire" will not overlook anything, and there is no blemish in him "whose feet are like burnished bronze"! He comes to the church in Thyatira announcing himself as the Son of God, the Davidic King, and I herald him to you as the searching and pure Son of David. Bow the knee to the Lord of the universe! Worship him!

Revelation 2:19–25: The Church That Needs to Exclude Jezebel

In 2:19–25, Jesus faults the church in Thyatira for tolerating Jezebel. This section can be broken down into three parts as follows:

2:19	Commendation of the Church in Thyatira
2:20–23	Jezebel and Her Children
2:24, 25	Hold What You Have

Revelation 2:19: Commendation of the Church in Thyatira

Jesus commends the church in Thyatira for five good things: (1) "works," (2) "love," (3) "faith," (4) "service," and (5) "patient endurance." And what's more, he tells them, "your latter works exceed the first" (2:19). They are doing good things, and they're apparently growing in doing good things.

It is important to recognize that Jesus knows and acknowledges the good in each of these churches, even when he is going to address serious problems in the churches. Sometimes when we go to address problems, even ones that are not so serious, we fail to see and acknowledge the good things that may be happening. Jesus is encouraging this church. They have problems, but those problems don't keep him from seeing and commending the fruits of the Spirit in their lives. Let's cultivate an ability to see and commend the fruits of the Spirit in each other's lives, even if we do have serious things we need to go on to address, as Jesus does here.

Revelation 2:20–23: Jezebel and Her Children

Having commended the church, Jesus says to them, "But I have this against you, that you tolerate that woman Jezebel, who calls herself a prophetess and is teaching and seducing my servants to practice sexual immorality and to eat food sacrificed to idols. I gave her time to repent, but she refuses to repent of her sexual immorality" (2:20, 21).

Jesus identifies the problem in the church in Thyatira as their toleration of this "Jezebel," whom he "gave . . . time to repent," but who "refuses to repent."

This seems to indicate that Jezebel has been called to repentance, which would perhaps indicate that the process of church discipline outlined in Matthew 18:15–18 had been started. But she did not repent, even though she was given time to do so. Jesus is now faulting the church in Thyatira for continuing to tolerate Jezebel; so it seems that they should have excluded her by now.

We are told two things about Jezebel: (1) she "calls herself a prophetess," and (2) she is "teaching and seducing my servants to practice sexual immorality and to eat food sacrificed to idols" (2:20). Jesus addresses the problem of impostors at several points in these letters. In Ephesus they are dealing with "those who call themselves apostles and are not" (2:2). In Smyrna they are dealing with "those who say that they are Jews and are not, but are a synagogue of Satan" (2:9). And in Thyatira they have this woman "who calls herself a prophetess" (2:20). Fakes cannot fool the one whose eyes are as "a flame of fire" (2:18). We can trust Jesus, and we can trust his word to tell us the truth. We should measure those who make claims for themselves against the Word of God.

As for what she does, let's note that whereas in the previous letter to Pergamum some in the church were holding to the teaching of the Nicolaitans (2:15), in Thyatira they have this self-proclaimed prophetess who is seducing those who belong to Jesus with her false teaching. As a result of her false teaching, the servants of Jesus are engaging in sexual immorality and idolatry. This woman might have been justifying participation in the Roman Imperial Cult, with the result that the Christians in Thyatira engaged in idolatrous, immoral activities that accompanied pagan celebrations. This teaching overlaps with the teaching of the Nicolaitans, which some held in Pergamum (2:15), and which was hated in Ephesus (2:6), because it resulted in the same activities—idolatry and immorality (2:14, 20). We don't know if Jezebel was a Nicolaitan, but she might have been.

It seems to me that the kind of typological interpretation we saw in 2:12–17, where the teaching of the Nicolaitans is likened to the teaching of Balaam, is likely in view here in 2:18–29. That is, this woman's name is probably not *literally* Jezebel. This false prophetess is probably identified with Jezebel because of the points of correspondence between herself and the Jezebel of Old Testament times. Jezebel was a foreigner who taught her idolatry to the Israelite king who married her. She was thus one who did not belong to the people of God, who infiltrated the people of God, and who led the people of God into idolatry. Jezebel married Ahab, king of the northern kingdom of Israel, the kingdom that broke away from the Davidic king in Jerusalem.

Identifying this false prophetess as Jezebel identifies her as a usurper of Jesus, who identified himself as the Davidic king in the opening of this letter (2:18; cf. 2:20). It also seems significant that Jesus makes a distinction between Jezebel and his own servants when he says that she "is teaching and seducing my servants" (2:20). This seems to mean that the impostor, claiming to be a prophetess, has not fooled the one whose eyes are "like a flame of fire." He sees right through her, and he identifies her as one who does not belong among his servants. She has infiltrated the people of God, and she is teaching them idolatry and immorality. She has been called to repentance, but she has refused to repent (2:21).

Those who belong to Jesus repent of sin. The refusal to repent of sin identifies someone as unregenerate.

How do you respond when you are confronted with your sin? Does it make you angry? Or does it make you humble, contrite, and more grateful that Jesus died to pay the penalty for sin? Does it make you more zealous to turn away from sin in the future? Or does it make you feel like you need to be more careful not to be caught in the future?

If you get angry when people call you to repentance, or if you feel yourself scheming about how to avoid being caught in the future when you plan to commit those same sins again, you are not acting like one who has been born again by the power of God's Spirit.

When a person hears the news that God is holy, that God calls people to account for the ways they offend his holiness, that the punishment for sin is infinite and eternal, but that Jesus took that punishment when he died on the cross, if the Spirit gives life, they hear this news and are simultaneously born again and believe in Jesus. If you believe this news and you repent of your sin—that is, you want to confess your sin and turn away from it so that you never do those evil things again—you have been born again. If you claim to believe this news, but you do not want to turn away from sin but want to keep right on committing those same sins, you should call on the Lord to send his Spirit to give you life. "Everyone who calls on the name of the Lord will be saved" (Romans 10:13).

By refusing to repent, Jezebel declared that she did not belong to the people of God. Once she made this plain, the church in Thyatira had a responsibility to tell her the truth—she was not right with God. They had a responsibility to protect the flock. They had a responsibility to exclude her from the church. Instead they were tolerating her, and as a result of the church's failure to act, she was leading the servants of Jesus into sin.

It would be like George Washington setting Major John André loose to go help Benedict Arnold. George Washington would be partly responsible for the defeat of his forces—the loss of life and the loss of battles and perhaps the war—that would ensue.

In the same way, when churches fail to exclude the unrepentant, they bear part of the responsibility for the sins provoked by the Jezebels in their midst. Jesus holds the fact that the Thyatiran church tolerates Jezebel against them (2:20). Is he holding the fact that we are tolerating someone like Jezebel against our church? If we are tolerating someone like Jezebel, we can be sure that he is holding it against us as a church.

Jesus declares what he will do to Jezebel and his servants who indulge in sin with her in 2:22, 23: "Behold, I will throw her onto a sickbed, and those who commit adultery with her I will throw into great tribulation, unless they repent of her works, and I will strike her children dead." Before we continue with the rest of verse 23, we should observe that Jesus is in effect calling his servants, who are sinning with Jezebel, to repentance. That is, Jesus is announcing judgment, and he is stating that those who sin with Jezebel will be judged unless they repent. Those who belong to Jesus will repent; those who do not belong to Jesus will not repent. Those who refuse to repent identify themselves with Jezebel rather than with the followers of Jesus. Those who refuse to repent identify themselves as Jezebel's children rather than God's children, and Jesus promises that he will kill the children of Jezebel.

So it is not that Jezebel's children are treated more harshly than Jezebel herself, as some commentators think.[3] Rather, the sickbed onto which Jezebel is thrown and the "great tribulation" (cf. Matthew 24:21; Acts 7:11; Revelation 7:14) that comes on those who sin with her should be understood as a process of purging by which Jesus means to bring his own to repentance. Those who refuse to repent show themselves to be seed of the serpent, children of Jezebel, and they will be killed by the conquering Davidic King.

The result of this is that "all the churches will know that I am he who searches mind and heart" (2:23), which seems to apply the fact that Jesus is the one "who has eyes like a flame of fire" (2:18). Then Jesus continues in verse 23, "and I will give to each of you according to your works."[4] Jesus will judge justly.

That is a frightful thought. Let me encourage you to apply what Jesus says here to any fellow believers whom you feel have wronged you and gotten away with it. Jesus will give to them as their works deserve. That's enough. Knowing that Jesus will judge them should enable you to pray for them that they will repent and avoid the treatment they deserve.

Revelation 2:24, 25: Hold What You Have

Jesus now addresses the members of the church in Thyatira who have not indulged in sin with Jezebel. He says, "But to the rest of you in Thyatira, who do not hold this teaching, who have not learned what some call the deep things of Satan, to you I say, I do not lay on you any other burden" (2:24). So clearly this group has not indulged in either the teaching or the practice of Jezebel, but they do have a "burden" on them. I think the "burden," to which Jesus does not add, is what Jesus said he was holding against them back in 2:20—"I have this against you, that you tolerate that woman Jezebel." The "burden" on them that Jesus does not add to is the simple fact that they are wrong to put up with this false prophetess, and they should exclude her from the church to protect the flock from her seduction. I think this is confirmed by what Jesus says in 2:25: "Only hold fast what you have until I come." What they have is the gospel, and holding it fast means living it out. Part of living out the gospel is drawing a line between those who believe the gospel and repent of their sin and those who by refusing to repent of their sin show that they do not believe the gospel. The church in Thyatira must hold fast to the gospel. They need to exclude Jezebel and her children.

Before we pass on to the next section, allow me to make two observations on the fact that Jezebel's teaching is described by Jesus as "the deep things of Satan" in 2:24. First, I think this substantiates the identification of the children of Jezebel, mentioned in 2:23, with the seed of the serpent, introduced into biblical theology in Genesis 3:15. Second, notice Jesus' willingness to unequivocally denounce Jezebel's teaching as evil. He doesn't explain it. He doesn't make excuses for it. He doesn't try to give it the benefit of the doubt. He simply identifies it as satanic. And he is not afraid to say what he thinks. We need more Christlikeness in our day. We need more people willing to call evil what it is.

Revelation 2:26–29: Hear the Promises

The first three of these seven letters put the statement, "He who has an ear, let him hear what the Spirit says to the churches" before the promises made "to the one who conquers" (2:7, 11, 17). But in this fourth letter, the promises made "to the one who conquers" are placed before the call to hear what the Spirit says to the churches (2:26, 29), and it will be this way in the next three letters as well—which means that the last word at the end of the seventh letter is, "He who has an ear, let him hear what the Spirit says to the churches" (cf. 3:5–6, 12–13, 21–22).

Even in this statement of promise to "the one who conquers," I think we continue to hear a call to exclude Jezebel from the church. Jesus says to the church in Thyatira, "The one who conquers and who keeps my works until the end . . . " (2:26). One of the "works" Jesus called his followers to "keep" and to "teach" (Matthew 28:18–20) was the process of church discipline he outlined in Matthew 18:15–18. One of the ways that we conquer is by keeping what Jesus commanded "until the end." The church in Thyatira needed to cease and desist their toleration of Jezebel.

And then Jesus makes astonishing promises. He continues in 2:26, 27, "to him I will give authority over the nations, and he will rule them with a rod of iron, as when earthen pots are broken in pieces, even as I myself have received authority from my Father." This string of phrases comes right out of Psalm 2:8, 9[5] and reflects the authority the Father gave to the Son in Psalm 2:6, 7. Jesus promises the ones who conquer that they will rule with him.

If we want to rule with Jesus in the future, we have to be faithful to him in the present. One of the ways that the church in Thyatira needed to be faithful to Jesus was by excluding Jezebel. The process of church discipline is preparation for ruling in the age to come.

In 2:28 Jesus promises, "And I will give him the morning star." This promise seems to reflect Numbers 24:17,[6] which prophesied that a star would arise in Israel, and Luke 1:78, which describes the coming of Jesus in terms of the "sunrise." Like the previous verses, the promise of the morning star is a promise that the overcomers will be identified with Jesus and share in his rule.

Conclusion

Jesus is the Davidic King who is searching and pure. He is opposed to the false prophetess who does not belong to his people, who like Jezebel of old seduces his people and leads them into idolatry and immorality. Jesus calls his own to repent of sin, and he brings affliction to lead people to repentance.

Jezebel refuses to repent, and others who claim to be Christians but who do not repent show themselves to be Jezebel's children, the seed of the serpent. Jesus forgives his own, who repent, and he spares them from judgment (2:22). The church is called to purity and should no longer tolerate Jezebel. And those who overcome will reign with Jesus. "He who has an ear, let him hear what the Spirit says to the churches" (2:29).

9

Wake Up!

REVELATION 3:1-6

IN BOOK I OF *The Persian War*, Herodotus recounts the taking of the city of Sardis by Cyrus the Persian—an event that was so surprising that it became proverbial in the ancient world.[1]

> The following is the way in which Sardis was taken. On the fourteenth day of the siege Cyrus bade some horsemen ride about his lines, and make proclamation to the whole army that he would give a reward to the man who should first mount the wall. After this he made an assault, but without success. His troops retired, but a certain Mardian, Hyroeades by name, resolved to approach the citadel and attempt it at a place where *no guards were ever set. On this side the rock was so precipitous, and the citadel (as it seemed) so impregnable, that no fear was entertained of its being carried in this place.* Here was the only portion of the circuit round which their old king Meles did not carry the lion which his leman bore to him. For when the Telmessians had declared that if the lion were taken round the defences, Sardis would be impregnable, and Meles, in consequence, carried it round the rest of the fortress where the citadel seemed open to attack, he scorned to take it round this side, which he looked on as a sheer precipice, and therefore *absolutely secure.* It is on that side of the city which faces Mount Tmolus. Hyroeades, however, having the day before observed a Lydian soldier descend the rock after a helmet that had rolled down from the top, and having seen him pick it up and carry it back, thought over what he had witnessed, and formed his plan. He climbed the rock himself, and other Persians followed in his track, until a large number had mounted to the top. Thus was Sardis taken, and given up entirely to pillage.[2]

Another Greek historian, Polybius, relates a very similar account in Book VII of his *Histories*. Polybius tells how a soldier in Antiochus's army found a place on the wall of Sardis that was altogether unguarded because of the extreme precipice near it. While the army mounted an attack on the gate of the city, this soldier and his comrades mounted ladders at the unguarded point, entered the city, and opened the gates for the army of Antiochus.[3]

These two famous events make it clear that Sardis was a place known for being twice captured at precisely the place where the supposed strength of the city due to the imposing precipice made the besieged forces so confident that no guards were posted.

Need

We have a great need for vigilance. Satan "prowls around like a roaring lion" (1 Peter 5:8). He disguises himself as "an angel of light" (2 Corinthians 11:14). He knows where we are unguarded, and it is his desire to destroy us.

Main Point

Jesus, the one who has the seven spirits of God and the seven stars that seem to symbolize God's watchful and empowering presence, calls the church in Sardis to wake up and strengthen what remains.

Preview

3:1a   The One Who Has the Seven Spirits and Seven Stars
3:1b–4   Jesus Knows the Weakness and Strength of the Church in Sardis
3:5, 6   Hear the Promises

Context

In Ephesus the church was slipping from its first love. In Smyrna the church was facing persecution. In Pergamum the church had some who held to the teaching of the Nicolaitans. In Thyatira the church was tolerating Jezebel. In Sardis, though the church seemed to be doing well, in reality it was dead. Philadelphia had an open door, and Laodicea was lukewarm.

The letters to Pergamum and Thyatira both mention sexual immorality and idolatry, and that may indicate there was some connection between the teaching of Jezebel and the teaching of the Nicolaitans. It may be that Sardis's supposed strength was that they had avoided the teaching of the Nicolaitans, which may have led some line to justify participation in the Roman Imperial Cult. Perhaps the appearance of life in the believers in Sardis is due to their avoidance of one error, but the gates are unguarded at another point. At that unguarded point, it is as though the enemy has swarmed into the church and killed much of it.

Revelation 3:1a: The One Who Has the Seven Spirits and Seven Stars

Jesus announces himself to the church in Sardis in 3:1 as the one "who has the seven spirits of God and the seven stars." The "seven spirits of God" seem to be "the seven spirits who are before" God's throne in 1:4. The "seven spirits of God" are also mentioned in 4:5, and in 5:6 we read that John saw "a Lamb standing, as though it had been slain, with seven horns and with seven eyes, which are the seven spirits of God sent out into all the earth."[4] The fact that the "seven eyes . . . are the seven spirits of God sent out into all the earth" in 5:6 seems to point to Jesus as the one who has a full report given by the Spirit of God, who patrols the earth and is fully (indicated by the word "seven") apprised of all that takes place. This would also seem to be what the reference to "the seven stars" is getting at. The seven stars were identified as "the angels of the seven churches" in 1:20. I take these angels of the churches to be angelic representatives who report to Jesus. So unlike the city of Sardis, and apparently unlike the church in Sardis, Jesus is fully alert, fully informed, and completely aware of all that takes place in Heaven and on earth. As the one who has the seven spirits and the seven stars, nothing escapes his notice. He calls his people to wake up and be strong.

Revelation 3:1b–4: Jesus Knows the Weakness and Strength of the Church in Sardis

Because Jesus is fully apprised of all that happens, he sees past the veneer of health in the church at Sardis. When Jesus says to them, "I know your works" (3:1), he means that he knows the good, the bad, and the incomplete. Jesus then says, "You have the reputation of being alive" (3:1), and this reputation may be related to the fact that neither the Nicolaitans, nor Jezebel, nor the attendant sexual immorality and idolatry are mentioned in the letter to Sardis. It seems that the problems with the Nicolaitans and with Jezebel may have arisen from compromise with Rome. So perhaps the church in Sardis was avoiding any compromise arising from interaction with the Roman Imperial Cult.

Jesus' next words to them, however, show that the church in Sardis did have problems. He says to them, "but you are dead" (3:1). The promise Jesus makes at the close of this letter to Sardis may help us identify the problem in Sardis. In 3:5 Jesus says of the one who conquers, "I will confess his name before my Father and before his angels." This promise reflects what Jesus said in Matthew 10:32, 33: "So everyone who acknowledges me before men, I also will acknowledge before my Father who is in heaven, but whoever denies me before men, I also will deny before my Father who is in heaven." This matches the kind of conquering that we see in 12:11, and it may be that

Jesus makes this promise because the church in Sardis was tempted to avoid confessing Jesus before men.

Why would the church in Sardis not want to confess Jesus? The churches in these letters seem to face temptation and trouble on two fronts: Rome and the Jews. We cannot be certain of this, but archaeological remains from Sardis point to a thriving Jewish community there. The synagogue excavated in Sardis is the largest that has been found from the ancient world. It is large enough to have held a thousand people.[5] So this letter is silent about sexual immorality and idolatry, and there are no references to the teachings of the Nicolaitans or the false prophetess Jezebel. This silence may indicate that the church in Sardis was not compromising with Rome. But perhaps the promise Jesus makes about acknowledging those who conquer before the Father (3:5) points to the church in Sardis being tempted to avoid confessing Jesus so that they would not be distinguished from Judaism.[6] If they were not distinguished from Judaism, they would be exempt from mandatory participation in the Roman Imperial Cult.

The text does not tell us that this indeed was the scenario in Sardis, but other background indications fit with this picture. At some point "the curse of the Minim" was added to the *18 Benedictions* prayed daily by Jews in the ancient world. "The curse of the Minim" reads, "May the Nazarenes and the Minim suddenly perish, and may they be blotted out of the book of Life and not enrolled along with the righteous."[7] Perhaps another part of the promise that Jesus makes to those who overcome in Sardis relates directly to this as well. Jesus promises, "I will never blot his name out of the book of life" (3:5). Perhaps, and it must be emphasized that this is only a hypothetical reconstruction of the situation in Sardis, those Christians who openly confessed Jesus had their names blotted out of the synagogue register, removing those who confessed Jesus from the protection from Rome found in the synagogue.[8]

This reconstruction of the situation would seem to explain how the church in Sardis could have a reputation of being alive—they are not compromising with Rome by committing idolatry and sexual immorality—even though they are dead. The death in this case would result from the fact that they were avoiding Roman persecution by refusing to confess the name of Jesus.

Jesus is not fooled by this. He speaks words that confront and call to life in 3:2: "Wake up, and strengthen what remains and is about to die, for I have not found your works complete in the sight of my God." The reference to "what remains" seems to be in line with what Jesus says in verse 4 when he refers to the few in Sardis "who have not soiled their garments." So some members of the church are undefiled, and the call to strengthen them is a call to reinforce them so that they do not give in to the pressures around them. Similarly, the call to "Wake up" seems to be a call to recognize the implications of their actions. And if the reconstruction proposed here is correct, it may be that when Jesus says, "for I have not found your works complete in the sight of my God," he is referring to the way the church has failed to confess his name.

When Jesus calls the church in Sardis to "Remember, then, what you received and heard" (3:3), he seems to be calling them to remember the way they "received and heard" the gospel of Jesus Christ, slain for sinners and risen from the dead to accomplish salvation. The language of reception is prominent in Johannine statements regarding "the beginning point of Christian faith" (cf. John 1:12; 3:11, 32, 33; 5:43; 12:48; 13:20; 17:8).[9] The language of reception is also used in the New Testament to point to the passing on of the Christian gospel (cf., e.g., 1 Corinthians 11:23; 15:1, 3).

Jesus calls the church in Sardis to remember the gospel, to "Keep it, and repent" (3:3). In this context, in view of the promise to confess them before the Father in 3:5, and in view of the way that seems to reflect what Jesus said in Matthew 10:32, keeping the gospel seems to amount to confessing Jesus before men. If this is right, repenting would be the other side of the coin. The Christians in Sardis should repent of their avoidance of confessing Jesus and should keep the gospel by confessing Jesus.

We can certainly understand this temptation, can't we? It is all too easy to stay on someone's good side—whether a family member, a coworker, a classmate, or a neighbor—by avoiding any confrontational discussions about the gospel. Confessing Jesus, proclaiming the gospel, is a divisive, confrontational thing to do. But we must do it. Jesus threatens terrible things for not doing it, and he makes remarkable promises to those who confess his name. First we will examine the threats, then the promises.

In the middle of 3:3 Jesus says to the church in Sardis, "If you will not wake up, I will come like a thief, and you will not know at what hour I will come against you." Again, the call to "wake up" in 3:2 seems to be a call to recognize the implications of refusing to confess the name of Jesus. Here Jesus mercifully seeks to help the church in Sardis understand that his coming against them will be worse than anything they might avoid by refusing to confess him before men. He will come "like a thief" (3:3)—that is, unexpected and uninvited. He will come, and they "will not know at what hour" (3:3). There will be no anticipating and preparing for the coming of Jesus; so immediate and constant vigilance is required. They must act now! Because if they do not, Jesus says, "I will come against you" (3:3). There is nothing in the world more frightening than the thought of the King of kings and Lord of lords, the conqueror of sin, death, and Hell, the everlasting Son of God, the one who has the seven spirits of God and the seven stars, the one who has a sharp two-edged sword coming out of his mouth, coming against you.

Perhaps you have not openly embraced the gospel of Jesus because you're afraid of what your family will think or you are afraid of what it will do to your reputation. Maybe you think that you'll be okay drifting through life, loosely associated with the church, avoiding an open confession of the name of Jesus. According to Jesus, that's not life, that's death. If you will not openly confess him as Lord, he will come against you, and you won't know when he's coming, and you won't be able to stop him. His coming against you is worse than whatever consequences you are trying to avoid by not confessing him. Won't you confess the name of Jesus today?

Jesus knows the bad and the incomplete in Sardis, and he also knows the good. He encourages the church with promises of rewards beginning in 3:4: "Yet you have still a few names in Sardis, people who have not soiled their garments, and they will walk with me in white, for they are worthy." This reference to not soiling one's garments points to those in the church at Sardis who are not dead. Perhaps these are the believers who have not avoided the confession of Jesus' name so as to find shelter in the synagogue. These who have not "soiled their garments" will walk with Jesus in white. Do you want to know how to keep from defiling yourself? Confess the name of Jesus. Confess your sins. Turn from them. Trust in Jesus and his death and resurrection. Embrace the mercy that God is holding out to you right now. You will be freed from your sins by the blood of Jesus (1:5). Like those who did not defile themselves in Sardis, Jesus will say that you are "worthy" (3:5).

What made those saints in Sardis worthy was their faithfulness to confess the name of Jesus, no matter what it cost them. The same faithfulness to embrace the gospel is what will make us worthy. Do you know what it means to "wake up" and be strong, which is what Jesus calls the church in Sardis to do in 3:2? It means to recognize that Jesus is bigger than anything you fear. It means recognizing that he is better than anything that pleases you. It means knowing that if you have him, you have everything you need. Won't you wake up to this? And "strengthening what remains" means confessing the name of Jesus and being bold in the life that declares that he is better than freedom from persecution, better than anything sin offers, better than life and ease without him.

Revelation 3:5, 6: Hear the Promises

Referring back to verse 4, Jesus says in 3:5, "The one who conquers will be clothed thus in white garments, and I will never blot his name out of the book of life." There is irony in these references to "conquering" at the conclusion of these letters, for in some cases conquering means being put to death because of faithfulness to Jesus. For instance, we read in 12:11, "And they have conquered him by the blood of the Lamb and by the word of their testimony, for they loved not their lives even unto death." By being faithful unto death, those who belong to Jesus follow him, for he conquered by being slain. We read in 5:5, 6, "the Root of David has conquered . . . I saw a Lamb standing, as though it had been slain."

To be faithful to confess Jesus' name, whatever it costs, is to conquer. Jesus promises white garments, and he promises that those who conquer will never have their names blotted out of the book of life. There are a number of references to the Book of Life in the Old and New Testaments (cf. Exodus 32:32; Psalm 69:28; Isaiah 4:3; Daniel 12:1, 2; Luke 10:20; Philippians 4:3; Hebrews 12:23). The value of having one's name written in the book of life is seen in what Jesus said to his disciples in Luke 10:20: "Nevertheless, do not rejoice in this, that the spirits are subject to you, but rejoice that your names are written in heaven." In the curse on the Minim, the Jews in the synagogue may call for the names of Christians to be blotted out of the book of life, but Jesus promises the church in Sardis that those who confess his name will never have their names blotted out of that book.

Jesus promises in 3:5 to confess the names of those who overcome before his Father and before the angels. We recently celebrated graduation at Southern Seminary. There before the assembled multitudes of friends and family, with the faculty in full academic regalia, the names were called as the graduating students walked across the stage to receive their reward. Imagine the horror of having that scene interrupted by the president of the seminary stopping the ceremony to say to some student, "Depart from me, I never knew you!" You don't want to hear those words on that great day when the millions of millions of all who have ever lived are gathered before the throne and the hosts of Heaven. On that day you want Jesus to confess your name and not deny you. Those who have an ear are called to hear what the Spirit says to the churches (3:6).

Conclusion

Do you have an appearance of life, while in reality you are dead? What is it about your experience that would prompt Jesus to say to you, "Wake up!"? At what place on the wall are there no guards, inviting the enemy's attack? Are there things in your life that have the appearance of godliness, which Jesus knows only result from a compromise somewhere else?

The hope for us is the same hope that Jesus offered to the church in Sardis. We must remember what we have received and heard (3:3). If you have heard the good news that there is a God who is holy, and you are sinful and under his judgment, but this holy God has made provision for your sin in the death and resurrection of Jesus the Messiah, remember this good news. Live on it. Keep it. Repent of those things you do that are not in line with the truth of God's Word.

Perhaps you feel a certain inability to live in line with the gospel, and you should. Here we have another application of the way Jesus announced himself to the church in Sardis—as the one "who has the seven spirits of God" (3:1). This refers to the fullness of the Holy Spirit. Where, you may ask, are you to find the strength to "Wake up!" (3:2)? I would suggest that this strength comes through the power of the Holy Spirit working with the words of Jesus. There is a dynamic reaction produced from the combination of the Holy Spirit's power and the word of Jesus. Jesus calls, "Wake up!" (3:2), and the Spirit he has (3:1) provides the power for people to hear his word and respond to it.

Jesus said in John 6:63, "It is the Spirit who gives life." If you sense right now that you are dead, or if you know that you are alive but you feel a creeping deadness, call on Jesus, the one "who has the seven spirits of God" (3:1), and he will give you life. We can apply this, too, to Jesus' command in 3:3 to "Remember . . . what you received and heard." Jesus promised his disciples that the Holy Spirit would bring to mind everything that he taught them (John 14:26). Jesus has the fullness of the Spirit to empower his people to remember everything that they have received (3:3).

Perhaps you find yourself timid when it comes to confessing Jesus before men, especially if it looks like unpleasant consequences might follow. Jesus said to his disciples, "And when they bring you before the synagogues and the rulers and the authorities, do not be anxious about how you should defend yourself or what you should say, for the Holy Spirit will teach you in that very hour what you ought to say" (Luke 12:11, 12).

For those who trust him, Jesus provides the power through the Holy Spirit to do everything he calls them to do. Wake up! Remember the gospel. Testify.

10

An Open Door No One Can Shut

REVELATION 3:7–13

CHARLES SIMEON PASTORED Trinity Church in Cambridge, England, for fifty-four years. He preached his first sermon there on November 10, 1782. The congregation did not want him. For five years they refused to allow him to be the Sunday afternoon lecturer, giving it instead to the assistant pastor they had wanted the church hierarchy to appoint over them. When that man left after five years, the church gave the lecture to another man for the next seven years, all the time refusing to allow Simeon to lecture on Sunday afternoons. Simeon responded by holding a Sunday evening service later than the Sunday afternoon lecture. People from the town began to come. The church wardens locked the doors, leaving people crowding in the street. Simeon had a locksmith open the doors, but when the wardens again locked the doors, he dropped the evening service. Only after twelve years did the church invite Simeon to be the Sunday afternoon lecturer.

On Sunday mornings, the pewholders refused to come to the church and locked their pew doors, refusing to allow others to sit in their personal pews. Simeon personally funded and set up seats in aisles and nooks and corners, but the church wardens removed them, throwing them out of the building. Simeon attempted to visit the members of the church, but few doors would open to him. The opposition continued for ten years, and the historical records indicate that Simeon was helped by a legal decision in 1792, to the effect that pewholders could not lock their pews and stay away indefinitely.

What sustained Charles Simeon? John Piper writes, "Simeon exerted his influence through sustained biblical preaching year after year. This was the central labor of his life. . . . Simeon preached in the same pulpit for fifty-four years. . . . through extraordinary opposition and trials."[1]

Need

We need to be so rooted and grounded that when fierce winds of opposition, rejection, and persecution blow into our lives we stand like oaks of righteousness.

Main Point

Jesus commends the church in Philadelphia for keeping his word, and their keeping of his word results in an open door and a promise that they will be kept from the coming hour of trial.

If we are to stand as oaks of righteousness, we must keep the word of Jesus.

Preview

3:7	Jesus Has the Key of David
3:8, 9	Keeping the Word: An Open Door and Subjected Enemies
3:10, 11	Keeping the Word: Kept in Tribulation and Ready for His Coming
3:12, 13	Hear the Promises: A Pillar in the Temple

Context

This is the second to last of the seven letters. Like the second letter, to Smyrna, the church is not rebuked and is not summoned to repentance but is commended by Jesus. We should recall as we think about this letter to the church in Philadelphia that Jesus called the church in Smyrna to "Be faithful unto death" (2:10). Both letters also speak of "those who say that they are Jews and are not," and in both letters these Jews are identified as a "synagogue of Satan" (2:9; 3:9). For these and other reasons, it seems that these seven letters are arranged such that the first and the last go together, the second and second to last go together, and the middle three go together.[2]

Revelation 3:7: Jesus Has the Key of David

Faith is not a vague spiritual sense. Faith is an active confidence that what one does not presently see nevertheless corresponds to reality. Our faith in Jesus does not increase because we think about faith. Our faith in Jesus increases because we are made more confident in Jesus. There is a real sense, then, in which Jesus intends every one of these introductions to these seven letters to build faith in him.

Jesus announces himself to the church in Philadelphia as "the holy one, the true one" (3:7). This is an astonishing claim. While some may have the audacity to identify themselves in this way, only Jesus is with the Father and the Spirit in being completely holy and true. The fact that he is "true" speaks to his reliability. He can be trusted. The fact that he is "holy" speaks to his purity and total consecration to God. He will not lead his people into sin. He can be followed. Those who hear Jesus announce himself as "the holy one, the true one" have their confidence in Jesus bolstered.

This confidence in Jesus, however, is not just abstract assurance. This confidence is practical and specific, and Jesus begins to articulate the practicality and specificity of faith in his holiness and truth in the next words of verse 7. He goes on to identify himself as the one "who has the key of David, who opens and no one will shut, who shuts and no one opens."

This statement is reminiscent of Isaiah 22:22, and the mention of "the key" calls to mind Jesus' words about "the keys of the kingdom of heaven" (Matthew 16:19). The point of the imagery, though, is that Jesus is unstoppable! He is "holy." He will not lead his people into moral error. He is "true." He will not lead his people into intellectual error. He opens and no one shuts, and he shuts and no one opens. He will not fail.

Revelation 3:7 is heralding the trustworthiness of Jesus for us. Do you trust him? Maybe you have consciously decided not to trust Jesus.

Let me ask you: is what you trust holy? Are you sure?

Is what you trust true? Are you sure?

Will what you trust prevail? Are you sure?

If you don't trust in Jesus, are you confident enough in what you do trust to bank your soul on it? Are you confident enough that Jesus is not to be trusted that you are ready to make the infinite, eternal wager of your everlasting destiny? Will you bet your life on your confidence that Jesus is not worthy of your trust?

Let me urge you today: bring all your questions to Jesus.

Bring all your objections to him.

Bring to Jesus all the things that you prefer to him—your wealth, your job, your entertainment.

Bring to Jesus all the things that tempt you to sin—your immorality, your theft, your lies, your gossip.

Bring to Jesus everything that you can gather in your attempt to deny him as Lord.

Do you know what you will find?

You will find that he is "holy," and everything that you prefer to him is filthy and defiled.

You will find that he is "true," and everything that you believe instead of him is false and hollow.

You will find that what he opens no one can shut, what he closes no one can open, and everything that resists him will be destroyed.

Test him with your questions! Compare the delights he offers to the paltry pleasures your sins give you! You will find him to be God, the giver of every good thing. And you will find that your myths are cheap lies, and you will find that with the idols of your heart it is all take and no give. They never satisfy.

Come to the one who is holy and true, who opens and no one can shut, who closes and no one can open. Come and trust him. Come and worship him. Come and feast yourself on the richest of fare.

Revelation 3:8, 9: Keeping the Word: An Open Door and Subjected Enemies

Jesus says to the church in Philadelphia, "I know your works" (3:8). There is a question as to how the rest of the verse should be punctuated. The NASB reads: "Behold, I have put before you an open door which no one can shut, because you have a little power, and have kept My word, and have not denied My name." The ESV reads: "Behold, I have set before you an open door, which no one is able to shut. I know that you have but little power, and yet you have kept my word and have not denied my name."

The NASB takes the little Greek word *hoti*, which can mean "that," "since," or "because" to mean "because." The ESV takes it to mean "that" and understands the phrase about the open door that no one can shut as a parenthetical remark, with the "that" outlining what Jesus knows about the works done by the church in Philadelphia.

Either way we understand the verse, it seems that Jesus has given the church in Philadelphia an open door because of their faithfulness. Jesus, then, has applied "the key of David" he has (3:7) and has opened a door for the church in Philadelphia. What is this open door? Elsewhere in the New Testament an open door refers to opportunity for ministry and evangelism (Acts 14:27; 1 Corinthians 16:9; 2 Corinthians 2:12; Colossians 4:3), and the context of 3:8 seems to point to the church's having success in evangelism and conquering their enemies. Jesus has opened the door, and no one can shut it. He is greater than all.

It seems that Jesus has given them this open door in response to the three things he says about them in the rest of the verse, and the last two things are two sides of the same coin. First, Jesus says to them, "I know that you have but little power" (3:8). This probably refers to the beleaguered position of the church in Philadelphia—small, seemingly insignificant, with an appearance, perhaps, of ineffectiveness in the eyes of those who look through the lens of the Roman Empire. And yet this is God's vehicle for advancing his purposes in the world.

Against the mounting odds and the weight of Rome, this church of little power has, second, kept Jesus' word, and third, has not denied his name (3:8; cf. 2:13). Because this church has kept the word of Jesus, they have an open door. It seems to me that the nature of the relationship between the faithfulness in the church in Philadelphia and the open door is not one of their *earning* an open door but one of the power of the word of Jesus *producing* an open door. That is, Jesus does not give the church an open door as a payment in response to the service they rendered by keeping his word. Rather, Jesus gives them his word, which is living and active, powerful, life-giving, opportunity-creating, and when they keep it the word of Jesus opens doors.

The word of Jesus is powerful. Are you keeping it?

The word of Jesus is powerful in your *personal life*. Jesus said, "If anyone thirsts, let him come to me and drink" (John 7:37). If you do that, if you go to Jesus to drink, your life will be transformed.

The word of Jesus is powerful in your *relationships*. Jesus said, "Blessed are the merciful, for they shall receive mercy" (Matthew 5:7). If you keep that word, if you show mercy, your relationships will be flavored with the very mercy of God.

The word of Jesus is powerful in the *evangelism* even of the enemies of the gospel. Jesus said, "bless those who curse you, pray for those who abuse you" (Luke 6:28). If you keep that word, you will have power. When we keep the word of Jesus, we put ourselves in position for Jesus to open doors for us.

Keeping the word of Jesus not only keeps us from denying Jesus' name (3:8), it honors Jesus' name.

This power in relationship to the enemies of the gospel that comes from keeping the word of Jesus can be seen in 3:9. "Behold," Jesus says, "I will make those of the synagogue of Satan who say that they are Jews and are not, but lie—behold, I will make them come and bow down before your feet and they will know that I have loved you."

As elsewhere in these letters, the Jewish community was causing problems for the church.[3] Anyone who has found themselves persecuted because of righteousness, opposed because of the gospel, can be encouraged by what Jesus says here to the church in Philadelphia. Jesus tells this church that keeping his word is not only the path that leads to the open door, it is also the path that leads to triumph over the enemies of the gospel.

Do you find yourself facing opposition as you pursue the health of a local church? Have you gone out to share the gospel, seeking to love and liberate people, only to be called intolerant or arrogant or to be threatened with regulations about where it is or is not permissible to share the gospel or distribute Bibles? Look at what Jesus says to the church in Philadelphia: he will make the enemies of the gospel come and bow down before the feet of those who keep the word of Jesus. The righteous conquer.

The last phrase of 3:9, "and they will learn that I have loved you," calls to mind Deuteronomy 7:8, where the Lord explained to Israel that he chose them because he loved them. Ironically, the chosen people who reject the gospel are shown that God has chosen the Gentiles who embrace the gospel.

Revelation 3:10, 11: Keeping the Word: Kept in Tribulation and Ready for His Coming

Revelation 3:10 has been debated in the modern discussion of whether the rapture of the church will take place before or after the great tribulation.[4] My purpose here is not to try to persuade you that the rapture will take place before rather than after the tribulation or vice versa. What we must see is the *reason* Jesus gives as to why his people will be protected from the tribulation. It is right there in the first phrase of 3:10: "Because you have kept my word about patient endurance . . . " We have to see this, because it was precisely this that resulted in the open door and the triumph over the enemies of the gospel in 3:8, 9. Keeping Jesus' word is what led to the open door. Keeping Jesus' word is what led to the subjugation of the enemies of the gospel.

Whether you think 3:10 means that the church will be raptured before the tribulation happens, or whether you think the verse means that the church will be preserved through the tribulation, we can all agree that Jesus says he will keep his people from the tribulation *"because you have kept my word about patient endurance."* We should also observe that the word they are keeping is a word "about patient endurance." Sometimes those who take the pre-trib rapture position can give the impression that God always keeps his people from suffering. That is not the case, and from the words that Jesus says, it has not been the case in Philadelphia—they have already "kept" the word about patient endurance, which means they have been enduring something unpleasant. We can also say that whatever Christians face in this life, the means whereby Jesus intends for his people to be kept is their keeping of his word.

It seems to me that this text refers to the church's being preserved *through* the tribulation rather than to the church being raptured *before* the tribulation. And I think that the call for the church in Smyrna to "be faithful unto death"

(2:10) goes along with this. But again the important thing for us to see and on which we can agree is the clear commendation of the way the church has kept Jesus' word. Also, we can agree that the text seems to indicate that Jesus will keep his people from/through tribulation *because* they have kept his word. Keeping the word of Jesus enables us to endure tribulation.

In 3:11 Jesus announces, "I am coming soon. Hold fast what you have, so that no one may seize your crown." Are you ready for his coming? He says it will be soon. The call to "Hold fast what you have" looks to me like a call to continue "keeping" the word of Jesus (cf. 3:8, 10). Keeping the word of Jesus will ensure that we do not lose our reward.

Revelation 3:12, 13: Hear the Promises: A Pillar in the Temple

There may be an intended contrast between the reference to the Jews who oppose the gospel, who are called "the synagogue of Satan" in 3:9, and the promise to the one who conquers that he will be "a pillar in the temple of my God" in 3:12. The Jews are only a synagogue, and it is a synagogue of Satan. Christians who are faithful to the end are the new temple, the dwelling place of God. There may also be a connection between Jesus having "the key of David," who wanted to build the temple, in 3:7 and the overcoming Christians being made into pillars of the temple in 3:12. If the key and the temple are images that should be interpreted together, Jesus has the key that gives him charge over the temple.

Jesus not only promises that the one who overcomes will be made into a pillar in the temple, he says, "Never shall he go out of it" (3:12). There will be no end to our enjoyment of God's presence. Jesus continues, "and I will write on him the name of my God, and the name of the city of my God, the new Jerusalem, which comes down from my God out of heaven, and my own new name" (3:12). Those who overcome will be fully possessed by God. Those who overcome will be his possession. He will write his name on those who overcome. Jesus too will write his new name on those who overcome. Those who overcome will enjoy new and surprisingly delightful aspects of Jesus—which I think is why he refers to his new name.

Jesus is holy. Jesus is true. Jesus is unstoppable. Jesus promises things that will be infinitely more enjoyable than anything sin, idolatry, or skepticism could ever offer.

Conclusion

The Christian church in these letters faced opposition from Rome and from the Jewish synagogue. From what Jesus says to the church in Philadelphia, it seems that their main opposition came from the synagogue. In the synagogue, the Jews were sheltered from the Roman Imperial Cult.

Note the contrast between what Jews in the synagogue have and what true believers in the Lord Jesus Christ have:

- The Jews have the synagogue. Jesus has the key of David.
- The Jews have the synagogue. Those who belong to Jesus have and keep his word.
- The Jews have the synagogue. Jesus will make the overcomers pillars in the temple.
- The Jews have the synagogue. Those who belong to Jesus and keep his word will never be made to leave God's temple, in which they themselves are pillars.
- The Jews have the synagogue. Those who belong to Jesus and keep his word will have God's name written on them.
- The Jews have the synagogue. Those who belong to Jesus and keep his word will have the name of God's city, the new Jerusalem, written on them.
- The Jews have the synagogue. Those who belong to Jesus and keep his word will have Jesus' new name written on them.

Do you see the point? What Jesus offers is better than any other place of shelter, security, confidence, or refuge. Do you want to belong to Jesus? Keep his word.

Jesus said, "Truly, truly, I say to you, whoever hears my word and believes him who sent me has eternal life. He does not come into judgment, but has passed from death to life" (John 5:24).

"He who has an ear, let him hear what the Spirit says to the churches" (3:13).

11

I Will Spit You out of My Mouth

REVELATION 3:14–22

HIERAPOLIS, WHICH IS ABOUT six miles from Laodicea, is famous for its hot springs. The waters are as hot as 95 degrees Fahrenheit. By contrast, the waters of nearby Colossae were cold and pure.[1] The site of Laodicea appears to have been chosen because it was a crossroads, not because it had its own water supply. It seems that Laodicea received water from "a remarkable aqueduct of stone pipes."[2] Archaeological evidence indicates that the waters around Laodicea were afflicted with a "calcium carbonate content" that resulted in the waters being impure and emetic—that is, they caused vomiting.[3]

Laodicea was also a wealthy banking center. After a massive earthquake in A.D. 60, Laodicea needed no help from Rome in the rebuilding of the city. In this Laodicea seems to have demonstrated a certain proud self-sufficiency.[4] There are some indications that Laodicea might have also been home to significant specialists in ophthalmology.[5] And the city of Laodicea was also something of a center of style, "promoting a fashion in black glossy fabrics from the natural fleeces of an animal developed by its own breeders."[6]

All of this wealth attracted Rome's attention, and Laodicea was abused by its Roman overlords. Colin Hemer writes, "The people were subjected to the insults of the soldiery billeted upon them, to whom their hosts were compelled to pay a daily sum. They also had to provide dinner (*dei/pnon*) for the soldiers and their guests, and clothing and daily subsidies for their officers."[7]

Bad water. Big banks. Stylish garments. Eye doctors. People demanding supper from them. Jesus speaks to them as they are, and he speaks to the needs they have.

Need

It seems that the affluence of Laodicea made the church there particularly vulnerable to self-reliance. Given the enormous affluence of our own culture, we need to hear what Jesus says to the church in Laodicea. We need to be shown that the wealth of our culture does not meet our deepest needs.

Main Point

Jesus calls the church in Laodicea to rely on him and his resources rather than on their own.

Preview

3:14	Jesus Is the True Witness
3:15–17	Laodicea's Self-reliance
3:18–20	The Counsel of the True Witness: Rely on Jesus
3:21, 22	Hear the Promises That the Spirit Speaks

Context

This is the last of the seven letters. The problem in Laodicea is similar to the problem in Ephesus. Ephesus had lost its first love, and Jesus calls them to "remember" from where they had fallen, "repent," and "do" their first works (2:5). In calling them to this he is calling them to remember their sense of need for the gospel, which would in turn refresh their appreciation of Jesus. So also in the letter to the church at Laodicea Jesus calls the church to recognize that their needs go deeper than what their resources can handle. Their problem is not physical and economic but spiritual. Their abundant physical and economic resources have dulled their sense of need for God and the gospel, and Jesus calls them to recognize the deep need they have so that they will cease to be lukewarm.

At this point we can also observe that each of these churches had its own unique problems. What Jesus said to these churches was appropriate to the needs of each, and what he said continues to be relevant to churches with these same problems today.

Revelation 3:14: Jesus Is the True Witness

The letter to the church in Laodicea is the only one of the seven in which Jesus will use the phrase, "I counsel you" (3:18). In this letter he introduces himself to the church as "the Amen, the faithful and true witness" (3:14). And in this letter "the faithful and true witness" offers counsel. His counsel can be trusted.

Are you trusting him? If you are not trusting him, it is because you are trusting some other counsel instead. When the court sits in judgment, when the books are opened, when the multitudes are assembled, and your case comes before the Judge, do you expect this counsel you are trusting to lead to your vindication? On that day, the great day, those who have rejected the counsel of Jesus for some other counsel will be damned, not vindicated. Flee the false counsel that keeps you from heeding Jesus! Your life depends upon it.

Moreover, Jesus tells them that he is "the beginning of God's creation" (3:14). This is not to be understood as though Jesus was created, for elsewhere in Revelation Jesus announces that he is "the first and the last" (1:17; 2:8), "the Alpha and the Omega, the first and the last, the beginning and the end" (22:13). The references to Jesus as "the Alpha" and "the beginning" cannot point to a time when he was created or began himself, for the same things are said about the Father, who identifies himself as "the Alpha and the Omega" (1:8) and as "the Alpha and the Omega, the beginning and the end" (21:6). Jesus and the Father are both referred to as "the Alpha" and as "the beginning" in Revelation, and the point is not that they had a point in time when they themselves came into being but rather that they *are* the beginning. As the HCSB translates it, Jesus is the "originator." That is, with the Father, Jesus began all that is. This puts Jesus in a uniquely strong position to offer counsel that the church will want to hear.

Revelation 3:15–17: Laodicea's Self-reliance

In 3:15, 16 Jesus addresses the problems in the church in Laodicea in terms that match their local setting: "'I know your works: you are neither cold nor hot. Would that you were either cold or hot! So, because you are lukewarm, and neither hot nor cold, I will spit you out of my mouth." The references to hot and cold match the temperature of the waters of Hierapolis and Colossae. Similarly, the threat that Jesus will spit them out of his mouth matches the impure waters of Laodicea that could cause vomiting.

The evidence that the water in Laodicea was of a tepid (lukewarm) temperature is disputed, however, and if the point is to match spiritual temperature to water temperature, it is unclear why Jesus would say that he would prefer them to be *either* hot *or* cold.[8] This is, after all, a church that Jesus is addressing, so the suggestion that cold opposition is better than lukewarmness does not seem to fit. Surely Jesus does not want a church to be cold to him.

We should look to what Jesus says next, in 3:17, in order to understand what exactly the Laodicean lukewarmness looked like: "For you say, I am rich, I have prospered, and I need nothing, not realizing that you are wretched, pitiable, poor, blind, and naked." This indicates that the problem of lukewarmness had to do with a deceptive sense of self-sufficiency. The Laodiceans were unaware of their true condition ("wretched, pitiable, poor, blind, and naked") and mistakenly thought they had no needs.

In your unguarded moments, how do you regard yourself? What is the default setting of your self-perception? Unless we consciously, explicitly remind ourselves of the absolute purity of God, which will provoke recognition of our impurity, we will slip into thinking that we're doing pretty well. We must remind ourselves of the gospel and its truths. We must allow the reality of the gospel to communicate to us our constant, ongoing need for Christ. If we are not reminded of our constant, ongoing need for the gospel, if we do not continually feel that Jesus is our greatest need, other "needs" will subtly but surely come to seem more urgent, more significant, more relevant. If we do not carefully and consciously oppose the growing significance of these "felt needs," which are really false needs, we will find that the world and its agenda is what is relevant to us, while for all practical purposes God and the gospel and the kingdom are irrelevant.

What needs do you most feel?

Perhaps you recognize your need for the gospel and you embrace Jesus as your hope on the last day, but when you think about overcoming sin you think about what *you* can do rather than what *Jesus* can do. We need Jesus to stand against temptation just as much as we need him to stand before God at the last judgment.

Perhaps Jesus' claim that these Laodiceans were "wretched, pitiable, poor, blind, and naked" (3:17) is shocking to you because it seems incomprehensible. Perhaps you're a person who hasn't thought much beyond your physical life, and you have not really wrestled with the idea that you could have everything and yet have nothing. Have you noticed that the wealthiest nation in the world, the USA, is also the nation with the most psychologists and psychotherapists in the world? If money made people happy, would Americans be so unhappy? More money is not what we need. Just ask someone who has more. The problem is deeper. The problem is that we were made to know and love God, but we rebel against God and worship ourselves and other created things.

If these words describe you, God is mercifully trying to bring you to the place where you understand that your sin separates you from him, but Jesus' death pays the penalty for sin. This means that everyone who trusts in Jesus can be reconciled to God. What keeps you from trusting Jesus right now? You can take him at his word. As we consider how Jesus counsels the church in Laodicea, I invite you to begin to trust Jesus right now.

Revelation 3:18–20: The Counsel of the True Witness: Rely on Jesus

Jesus has introduced himself to the church in Laodicea as "the faithful and true witness" (3:14), and he now gives them faithful and true testimony in 3:18: "I counsel you to buy from me gold refined by fire, so that you may be rich." The church in Laodicea does not need Laodicea's gold; they need the gold they can buy from Jesus—without money and without price (cf. Isaiah 55:1).

When you sense a hope, an anticipation, that your life is about to get better, what provokes that hope? Is it the thought of having more money, or is it the thought of having more of Jesus? Do you think that more cash will make you more happy, or do you think that a deeper understanding of God's character, of the humble servant way of Jesus, of the wise plan that God is infallibly bringing to pass will increase your joy? Do you want more financial security, or do you want to see more of God's splendor so that you'll be more confident in God?

Jesus continues in 3:18, "I counsel you to buy from me gold . . . and white garments so that you may clothe yourself and the shame of your nakedness may not be seen." There is a deep connection in the Bible between shame and clothing. Before they sinned, Adam and Eve were innocent, unashamed, and had nothing to hide and nothing to fear. Thus they had no need of clothing. After their sin, they sought to clothe themselves, and then the Lord provided garments of skin for them.

The church in Laodicea may have been clothed in the fine black, fashionable garments of Laodicea, but Jesus counseled them to get from him "white garments." Later in Revelation these fine white garments, "bright and pure," are identified with "the righteous deeds of the saints" (19:8). Jesus is calling the church to leave off their attempts to clothe themselves. In the physical sense, they may be wearing lavish Laodicean garments, but in their self-reliance, Jesus says in verse 17, they are "naked." Relying on Jesus, trusting in him rather than in the Laodicean economic system, will result in their being clothed in "white garments." Only Jesus can cover our shame and nakedness.

"Gold" and "garments" are about resources and adornment. Jesus offers a supply of wealth that will never be exhausted, and he gives raiment that won't go out of style, get dirty, be outgrown, or wear out. Jesus is inexhaustible. In offering "gold" he is promising to meet every need. In offering "white garments" he is promising to make those who trust him and live by what he says presentable, acceptable, even beautiful. Where will you find a better offer than this? Won't you trust him?

Finally, in 3:18 Jesus offers the church in Laodicea "salve to anoint your eyes, so that you may see." So in addition to offering them a supply of wealth and the finest fashionable attire, he now offers them the ability to see. They see themselves as rich, prosperous, needing nothing. Jesus offers them sight, that they might see themselves as they are—"wretched, pitiable, poor, blind, and naked" (3:17). The salve that Jesus offers, then, has to do with the ability to see spiritual realities.

What informs the way you see the world? Do you view the world through lenses given to you by the Holy Spirit, and have you ground those lenses in the pages of Holy Scripture? Or has the spirit of the age placed a set of lenses over your eyes that you do not even realize are there?

Here are some questions to help you evaluate the nature of the lenses on your eyes—or perhaps we could say that these questions will help you discern whether your ophthalmologist is from Laodicea or whether you have this eye salve that Jesus offers:

- Which do you view as a more pressing, more urgent activity—reading or watching the news, or reading and studying the Bible? Obviously both are valuable, but on a day-to-day basis, if you only have time to do one or the other, which gets done?
- If you only had time to do one thing or the other, and your choices were between taking the time to pray and checking your email (or Facebook or Twitter or whatever), which would you view as the more pressing activity?
- If you could choose between two things—a lottery ticket that was guaranteed to win a billion dollars or an empty bank account with the assurance that God would provide for you and meet your needs if you trust him—which would you choose? Would you choose to have more money than you could ever spend, or would you choose the opportunity to trust God?
- Which would you choose—to have your hopes and dreams realized in the American political scene by seeing all your candidates elected and all your political issues dealt with the way you want them handled or the opportunity to identify yourself as an alien and a stranger for whom this world is not home?

These questions are trying to get at four significant key questions:

- What shapes your thinking (the world or the Bible)?
- What communication do you view as non-negotiable (*horizontal* with other people or *vertical* with God)?
- What do you trust (money or Jesus)?
- With what do you ultimately identify (a political party or the kingdom of God)?

We need the "gold" that Jesus sells. We need the "white garments" he offers. We need the "salve" he offers. We need him. Apart from him all else is rubbish.

In 3:19 Jesus explains what has been driving him in everything he has said—the confrontational things and the encouraging things—in these seven letters: "Those whom I love, I reprove and discipline, so be zealous and repent." Jesus loves you enough to want you to be righteous. He loves you enough to confront your unrighteousness. He loves you enough to inspire the Bible. He loves you enough to call you to zeal and repentance.

If Jesus did not call people to repentance, he would be sending them a message. Do you know what that message would be? "Go to Hell."

But Jesus loves people, so he calls them to repent.

The believers in the church in Laodicea are self-reliant, and Jesus rebukes them. They are lukewarm, and he calls them to zeal.

The next thing Jesus says is a famous verse that has often been used in evangelistic appeals: "Behold, I stand at the door and knock. If anyone hears my voice and opens the door, I will come in to him and eat with him, and he with me" (3:20). I think that the evangelistic use of the verse matches the spirit of the verse, but I do not think the evangelistic use of the verse fits the meaning of the verse in context. This is not an evangelistic verse because Jesus is addressing a church! Churches are constituted of believers. Presumably believers have already opened the door of their hearts to Jesus; so I doubt that as Jesus says the words of 3:20 to the *church* in Laodicea he is inviting them to believe in him.

What I mean when I say that the evangelistic use of this verse matches the spirit of the verse is the way the Laodicean background might inform what Jesus says here. In the introduction to this sermon I noted the way that Roman soldiers were billeted in Laodicea—that is, the residents of Laodicea were forced to allow Roman soldiers to stay in their homes. And the Laodiceans were forced to feed and provide for those Roman soldiers.

There is a stark contrast, then, between Jesus standing at the door and knocking and the Roman soldiers forcing the Laodiceans to house and feed them. The Romans force their way in and take food from the people. Jesus knocks, waits to be invited in, and then provides the meal.

Jesus is sovereign. His will is supreme. What he wills comes to pass. He is absolutely compelling. So if he wants in, he will get in. Nevertheless, people who welcome Jesus into their lives—be it a church or an individual coming to faith—make a real choice to do so. There is a tension here between divine sovereignty and human responsibility.

When Jesus says the words of 3:20 to the church at Laodicea, he seems to be telling them that if they will "be zealous and repent" (3:19) they will know his presence. He will be *in* the church, not *outside* it. He will fellowship with them. They will sup with him. In this case, for the church to open the door to Jesus means that the church will rely on Jesus, not on their own resources, and it means that the church will do what Jesus expects it to do rather than what the world expects it to do.

In our local churches, we must commit ourselves to relying on Jesus, not on our bank account. We must trust Jesus, not our own ingenuity. We must see things the way Jesus sees them, not the way the world sees them. We must want the clothing that Jesus offers, not the styles and fashions of the world. We must want Jesus to make us beautiful, not our coolness and cleverness. Our money and savvy and ability to be hip is nothing but wretched, pitiful, poor, blind nakedness. Let's go to him for gold and garments, sight and safety. He is everything we need.

Revelation 3:21, 22: Hear the Promises That the Spirit Speaks

Each of the seven letters in chapters 2, 3 concludes with a promise to the one who overcomes. In the first three letters, the call to hear what the Spirit says to the churches comes first, then the promise is made to the one who over-comes. In the last four letters, the promise to the one who overcomes is first, and then the letter concludes with the call to hear what the Spirit says to the churches. This has the effect of making the call to hear what the Spirit says to the churches the last thing stated in the last letter.

Jesus makes the following promise to the one who overcomes at the end of the letter to the church at Laodicea: "I will grant him to sit with me on my throne, as I also conquered and sat down with my Father on his throne" (3:21). This is reminiscent of the promise Jesus made to those who overcome in Thyatira, that they will rule with him on his throne (2:26–28). Again, what Jesus promises goes beyond anything that self-reliance and worldly wealth could offer.

Favor with Rome would result in influence in the Empire, but ultimately Rome would always be in charge. They were not about sharing power but taking it. They thought it better to receive than to give. Look how different Jesus is. He promises to people that they will sit with him on his throne. He is not threatened by rivals. He is not concerned to protect his own influence, his own access to resources, and his own right to rule. He is so completely secure in his sovereignty that he can share. None can compare with him. He is matchless. Trust him. Worship him. He will never let you down.

The letters are concluded with the call to hear what the Spirit says to the churches.

Conclusion

A certain man was the adopted son of the princess, and the princess was daughter to the world's most powerful king. They knew affluence. They knew resources. They knew prestige, fine food, and stylish clothing. In worldly terms they lacked nothing. As the young man grew he was educated and cultivated. There were girls. There were privileges. There were family expectations. There were possibilities. There were the concerns of the realm. But he left it all. He had something greater, more valuable, something that would make enjoying everything he had a waste of his life. Do you know this man?

> By faith Moses, when he was grown up, refused to be called the son of Pharaoh's daughter, choosing rather to be mistreated with the people of God than to enjoy the fleeting pleasures of sin. He considered the reproach of Christ greater wealth than the treasures of Egypt, for he was looking to the reward. (Hebrews 11:24–26)

Are you rich in Christ? Clothed with the garments he provides? Enabled to see because he has been your ophthalmologist?

In his book *Don't Waste Your Life* John Piper writes about a plaque hung in his home that read:

> Only one life,
> 'Twill soon be past;
> Only what's done
> For Christ will last.[9]

"He who has an ear, let him hear what the Spirit says to the churches" (3:22).

12

The Throne Room Vision

REVELATION 4:1—5:14

CONTINUING THE STORY OF the young man mentioned at the end of the last chapter, he grew up in the palace as the son of Pharaoh and had everything anyone could ever want. He received the best education available in the world at that time. Finer food than what was served at Pharaoh's table did not exist. Any pleasure afforded by the world would have been available to him. But then everything changed.

Suddenly he was fleeing Egypt for his life. He found his way to the home of a shepherd and actually became a shepherd himself.

Then God sent Moses back to Egypt, where he saw God do awesome deeds that crushed Egypt and brought the mighty Pharaoh to his knees. God pried open Pharaoh's clenched fist with a strong hand and an outstretched arm.

Once Pharaoh let Israel go, Moses saw God provide food and water in the wilderness, but then God's people rebelled. God judged Israel, and Moses interceded with God on behalf of Israel.

Before we think about the request Moses made, answer this question in your mind: what would you ask for from God in that situation? If you were Moses and had experienced the good life, then spent forty years as a shepherd, and now you had these freed slaves to lead, what would your request be? Would you ask to be Pharaoh and have these freed slaves, Israel, immediately established in the land of promise? Would you ask to be allowed to go back to all the luxury and wealth and fine food and worldly pleasures that you formerly enjoyed? What would you ask for from God?

Do you know what Moses wanted? Moses wanted what we all need. Moses said to God in Exodus 33:18, "Please show me your glory." Just four

Hebrew words (five in English). A simple request. All he wanted was to see the glory of God.

Need

What will it take to pry you free from the world? When I ask this question, I am not talking about freedom from life in this world. I am talking about freedom from a worldly point of view.

What will it take to set you free from the world's idolatries—what will it take to keep you from trusting in things that are no gods at all? What will make you free from the world's immoralities—what will it take to make you untouched by the lust for smut that the world peddles and with which world-lings ruin their lives? What will it take to liberate you from the world's false perspective on the way things are—the perspective that assumes there is no god, there is no revelation of truth in the Bible, and there will be no judgment?

I'll tell you what it will take: it will take seeing God as he is. Beholding God will break the chains of idolatry because when you see God, you see what Deity is, and that exposes the idols as worthless and unworthy of trust. Beholding God will purify you from immorality because when you see God you see what beauty and faithfulness are, and that exposes the ugliness of adultery. Beholding God will give you new lenses through which to look at the world because God himself defines reality.

Main Point

The main point of this message is simple: God is the world's Creator and Redeemer, and those who know him worship him.

Preview

We will look more closely at chapters 4, 5 in coming studies, but in this one we want to focus on two things. First, we will look at the way that the throne room vision in chapters 4, 5 exposits Isaiah 6, Ezekiel 1, and Daniel 7. From there we will look at the ways that God and Christ are praised in chapters 4, 5 and will celebrate this vision of God as our Creator and Redeemer.

This chapter, then, falls into two parts:

1. The Exposition of Isaiah 6, Ezekiel 1, and Daniel 7 in Revelation 4, 5
2. The Worship of God and Christ in Revelation 4, 5

Context

The church is surrounded by the glory of Christ and the glory of God. That is how it is in reality, and that is how it is in the book of Revelation. The letters to the seven churches in chapters 2, 3 are preceded in 1:9–20 by John's vision of the risen Christ in glory, and they are followed by John's description of what he saw in the heavenly throne room in chapters 4, 5.

One of the main points of application of this study will be that your life is positioned in the same way that the letters to the seven churches are—you are surrounded by the glory of God. God is revealing himself in glory to you right now as we consider what chapters 4, 5 show us about the Creator and Redeemer. God reveals himself to you in his creation, which reflects his glory, and God reveals himself in a uniquely precise way in the Bible that he inspired. With the glory of God in creation all around you and with the Bible before you, you are surrounded by God's glory. Drink it in and pray that God will set you free from the world's idolatry, immorality, and godless way of interpreting life.

As we turn to the way that John interpreted what he saw, let's pay close attention to the *way* he interpreted what he saw.

The Exposition of Isaiah 6, Ezekiel 1, and Daniel 7 in Revelation 4, 5

Let me be very clear about what I am and am not suggesting about the way that the Old Testament is exposited by John in chapters 4, 5. I am *not* saying that John sat around and *invented* some things based on what the Old Testament already said. I am saying that once John saw these visions, he thought about them and carefully chose the language he would use to describe the things he saw. Not only did he carefully choose his language, he chose which details he would include in his descriptions.

So the first thing John says in 4:1—"After this I looked, and behold, a door standing open in heaven!"—is not very different from what we read in Ezekiel 1:1: ". . . the heavens were opened, and I saw visions of God."

John then tells us in 4:2 that "a throne stood in heaven, with one seated on the throne." This is reminiscent of Isaiah 6:1, "I saw the Lord sitting upon a throne, high and lifted up. . . ." Ezekiel 1:26 also describes one seated on a throne: "And above the expanse over their heads there was the likeness of a throne, in appearance like sapphire; and seated above the likeness of a throne was a likeness with a human appearance."

In 4:3 John writes that "around the throne was a rainbow that had the appearance of an emerald." Ezekiel 1:28 has a similar description: "Like the appearance of the bow that is in the cloud on the day of rain, so was the appearance of the brightness all around. Such was the appearance of the likeness of the glory of the LORD. And when I saw it, I fell on my face, and I heard the voice of one speaking."

Then John tells us in 4:4, "Around the throne were twenty-four thrones, and seated on the thrones were twenty-four elders, clothed in white garments, with golden crowns on their heads." Daniel 7:9, 10 also describes thrones surrounding the throne of God:

> As I looked, thrones were placed, and the Ancient of Days took his seat; his clothing was white as snow, and the hair of his head like pure wool; his throne was fiery flames; its wheels were burning fire. A stream of fire issued and came out from before him; a thousand thousands served him, and ten thousand times ten thousand stood before him; the court sat in judgment, and the books were opened.

Daniel's mention of the "thousand thousands" serving the Ancient of Days in 7:10 probably influenced John's statement in 5:11 that there were "myriads of myriads and thousands of thousands."

Revelation 4:5 states, "From the throne came flashes of lightning, and rumblings and peals of thunder, and before the throne were burning seven torches of fire, which are the seven spirits of God." Ezekiel 1:4 also describes "fire flashing forth continually." John mentions "torches" that are the Spirit in 4:5, and the word for s/Spirit in both Greek and Hebrew is also used to refer to "wind" or "breath." Ezekiel 1:4 also speaks of "wind" and "fire."

The next thing that John relates in 4:6 is that "before the throne there was as it were a sea of glass, like crystal." Ezekiel 1:22 describes the same thing: "Over the heads of the living creatures there was the likeness of an expanse, shining like awe-inspiring crystal, spread out above their heads."

Ezekiel 1:22 states that the expanse was "over the heads of the living creatures." John tells us in 4:6, "around the throne, on each side of the throne, are four living creatures." These four living creatures are very similar to the seraphim that Isaiah describes in Isaiah 6:2: "Above him stood the seraphim. Each had six wings: with two he covered his face, and with two he covered his feet, and with two he flew."

In 4:7 John describes the four living creatures: "the first living creature like a lion, the second living creature like an ox, the third living creature with the face of a man, and the fourth living creature like an eagle in flight." It seems that John saw either the same living creatures Ezekiel and Isaiah saw, or at least they were very similar. Ezekiel relates in Ezekiel 1:5, 6, "And from the midst of it came the likeness of four living creatures. And this was their appearance: they had a human likeness, but each had four faces, and each of them had four wings" (cf. Ezekiel 1:10[1]). John states that the living creatures were *like* a lion, an ox, a man, and an eagle, while Ezekiel states that each living creature had four faces. Either they saw different but similar living creatures, or perhaps Ezekiel had a different angle, so that where he could see four faces on each living creature, John only saw the likeness of each one to a lion, an ox, a man, and an eagle.

There is also a difference between the descriptions in that the seraphim that Isaiah saw and the living creatures that John saw had six wings (Isaiah 6:2; Revelation 4:8), but Ezekiel says that the living creatures he saw had four wings (Ezekiel 1:6). Again, either Ezekiel did not see the other two wings from the perspective he had, or perhaps these are different from and yet similar living creatures to the ones seen by Isaiah and John.

John tells us in 4:8 that the living creatures "never cease to say, 'Holy, holy, holy, is the Lord God Almighty, who was and is and is to come!'" Similarly, Isaiah 6:3 says of the seraphim, "And one called to another and said, 'Holy, holy, holy is the LORD of hosts; the whole earth is full of his glory!'"

In 5:1 John writes, "Then I saw in the right hand of him who was seated on the throne a scroll written within and on the back, sealed with seven seals." Jesus will take that scroll in 5:7, and in 6:1—8:1 Jesus opens the seals of the scroll. Then in 10:1–11 an angel brings what I think is the same scroll to John and has him eat the scroll and prophesy. The eating of the scroll seems to depict the ingestion of the message, which will result in true prophecy. Ezekiel 2:8, 9 describes a very similar sequence of events: "'But you, son of man, hear what I say to you . . . open your mouth and eat what I give you.' And when I looked . . . behold, a scroll of a book was in it. And he spread it before me. And it had writing on the front and on the back, and there were written on it words of lamentation and mourning and woe.'"

So to this point in chapters 4, 5 we have seen God seated on his throne, surrounded by his heavenly court. I have just mentioned 5:7, which describes how Jesus "went and took the scroll from the right hand of him who was seated on the throne." This reminds us of Daniel 7, where, just after the throne room scene noted above in Daniel 7:9, 10, we see in Daniel 7:13, 14,

> I saw in the night visions, and behold, with the clouds of heaven there came one like a son of man, and he came to the Ancient of Days and was presented before him. And to him was given dominion and glory and a kingdom, that all peoples, nations, and languages should serve him; his dominion is an everlasting dominion, which shall not pass away, and his kingdom one that shall not be destroyed.

Now that we have a good summary of the evidence before us, we can draw some conclusions. First, look at the way John describes what he saw. John describes what he saw in Biblical language. Now let's work back from that point: John knew the Bible, and he interpreted what he saw in light of what the Bible says. Do you know the Bible as well as John evidently did? If you saw the fantastic things that John saw, would you recognize the similarity of the things you had seen to the things that the Biblical authors described? John had to have known the Bible very well. We need to know the Bible very well also. We need to be able to look at the world, filter it through the whole Bible, and then describe the world that we have seen the way the Bible describes it. This is what it means to have a Biblical worldview. Too many Christians have a Hollywood worldview, or a Madison Avenue worldview, or a state-education system worldview. If that's your worldview, or if you don't recognize the difference between the worldview generated by the Bible and the worldview embraced by Washington, D.C., you need to spend more time reading, studying, memorizing, and meditating on the Bible.

Second, following on from the first point, you have to know the Bible in order to know God. If you don't know the Bible, how are you going to know whether what you have seen is from God or only the work of Satan disguised as an angel of light?

God reveals himself to free us from the world's idolatries, immoralities, and false worldviews. If you trust what the world trusts—the U.S. government, your bank account, your own good works, your ability to create an "image" of who you want people to think you are—if you trust these things you worship what the world worships, and the world doesn't worship the true and living Triune God of the Bible. If you worship what the world worships you don't know God. If you are unrepentant of immorality—and that word *unrepentant* is key because we all stumble in many ways—if you are unrepentant of immorality you are not a Christian.

The Worship of God and Christ in Revelation 4, 5

The cure to idolatry is seeing God as he is. The cure to immorality is seeing God as he is. The cure to a godless worldview is seeing God as he is. Revelation 4, 5 shows us God as he is. We will look at these two chapters in more detail shortly, but we turn now to examine the way that the hosts of Heaven praise God and Christ. Figure 12-1 sets the praise offered to God in Revelation 4 and to Christ in Revelation 5 side by side for easy comparison.

There are two statements of praise for God the Father in Revelation 4 and two statements of praise for Jesus in Revelation 5. Then Revelation 5 concludes with a statement of praise made to God and Christ together.

Let's look first at the first statement of praise to the Father in 4:8. Here the four living creatures say, "Holy, holy, holy, is the Lord God Almighty, who was and is and is to come!" Here God is praised simply for who he is. He is "holy," and they celebrate him for that fact. He is eternal, and they celebrate him for that fact. God is worthy of praise simply because he is God. There is no one else like him. No one else is holy. No one else is eternal. God is clearly unique, and he is worthy of praise because of who he is.

Table 12.1: The Worship of God and Christ in Revelation 4, 5

The Worship of God	The Worship of Christ
4:8, 9, "And the four living creatures . . . day and night they never cease to say, 'Holy, holy, holy, is the Lord God Almighty, who was and is and is to come!'" ". . . the living creatures give glory and honor and thanks to him who is seated on the throne, who lives forever and ever."	5:8–10, ". . . the four living creatures and the twenty-four elders fell down before the Lamb. . . . And they sang a new song, saying, 'Worthy are you to take the scroll and to open its seals, for you were slain, and by your blood you ransomed people for God from every tribe and language and people and nation, and you have made them a kingdom and priests to our God, and they shall reign on the earth.'"
4:10, 11, "the twenty-four elders fall down before him who is seated on the throne and worship him who lives forever and ever. They cast their crowns before the throne, saying, 'Worthy are you, our Lord and God, to receive glory and honor and power, for you created all things, and by your will they existed and were created.'"	5:11, 12, ". . . the voice of many angels, numbering myriads of myriads and thousands of thousands, saying with a loud voice, 'Worthy is the Lamb who was slain, to receive power and wealth and wisdom and might and honor and glory and blessing!'"

The Worship of God and Christ
5:13, 14, "And I heard every creature in heaven and on earth and under the earth and in the sea, and all that is in them, saying, 'To him who sits on the throne and to the Lamb be blessing and honor and glory and might forever and ever!' And the four living creatures said, 'Amen!' and the elders fell down and worshiped."

God's holiness means that he is altogether separated from the world that he has made. His holiness means that he is uncontaminated by sin or failure. His holiness means that he is perfectly beautiful. God is worthy to be praised for his holiness.

God's eternality—he "was and is and is to come"—means that he will never die or be defeated. Ever. No one came on the scene before him; no one can outlast him. And much as men may protest that he does not exist, *he is*. God's eternality makes him worthy of praise.

What the living creatures say in 4:8 is further explained in 4:9: "And whenever the living creatures give glory and honor and thanks to him who is seated on the throne, who lives forever and ever . . . " This is another statement of what the living creatures do—they proclaim God's holiness and eternality in 4:8, and they give glory and honor and thanks to him in 4:9.

This first statement of praise to God prompts the second. We see in 4:9, 10 that when the living creatures praise God, the twenty-four elders bow before God, cast their crowns before him, and say, "Worthy are you, our Lord and God, to receive glory and honor and power, for you created all things, and by your will they existed and were created."

Look closely at the reason the elders say that God is worthy in 4:10—he is worthy because he "created all things," and they existed and were created by his will. Nothing exists that God did not create. There is nothing in the world that God did not bring into the world. This verse also states that nothing exists apart from God's will. These truths are fundamental to a Biblical worldview.

Everything that exists was created by God—no exceptions. Everything that exists is in accordance with God's will—that's what 4:10 declares. It may be hard for us to understand how God could will some of the things we see in this world, and we may wonder why he created some of the things he created. This simply shows us that God is beyond our understanding. If he isn't beyond our understanding, he is no more worthy of worship than we are worthy of worship. But God *is* worthy of worship. He created everything, and he did it all according to his will (see also Ephesians 1:11).

In chapter 4 God is praised because of who he is and because he created the world.

In chapter 5 Jesus is praised for his work in redemption and for having taken control of the future. We see in 5:5, 6 that Jesus can take the scroll, which symbolizes his taking control of the future, Jesus can do this because he was crucified and rose from the dead.

The first statement of praise to Jesus responds to this in 5:9, 10: "And they sang a new song, saying, 'Worthy are you to take the scroll and to open its seals, for you were slain, and by your blood you ransomed people for God from every tribe and language and people and nation, and you have made them a kingdom and priests to our God, and they shall reign on the earth.'" They praise Jesus because he accomplished redemption. There is no question about it. He did it. Jesus defeated sin. Jesus overcame the devil.

Jesus conquered death. There will be no disputes. He paid the ransom. The captives are free.

Not only did he ransom them, it says in 5:10 that he made them "a kingdom and priests." This too is done. Jesus ransomed slaves of sin from the penalty, and he renovated them. They are "a kingdom and priests" to God because of what Jesus has done. Now look back at 5:9—these facts make Jesus *worthy*.

God is worthy of praise because of who he is and because he created everything by his will, and Jesus is worthy of praise because he ransomed people from the power of sin and the penalty of death and remade them into "a kingdom and priests."

Before we look at the second statement of praise to Jesus in chapter 5, let's observe a progression that goes through these chapters. It begins in 4:8, where the living creatures are declaring God's holiness and eternality. Then in 4:10 the twenty-four elders join in worship to God. Then both the four living creatures and the twenty-four elders praise Jesus in 5:8–10, and now the second statement of praise to Jesus rounds out the cast of the heavenly host. We see in 5:11, 12, "Then I looked, and I heard around the throne and the living creatures and the elders the voice of many angels numbering myriads of myriads and thousands of thousands, saying with a loud voice, 'Worthy is the Lamb who was slain, to receive power and wealth and wisdom and might and honor and glory and blessing!'"

There is a connection in 5:12 between the identification of the one who is worthy and what they say he is worthy to receive. Let me preface what I'm about to say by asking a question: what is it that makes someone *unworthy* of receiving all these things? Among the various answers we could give, think about what Jesus identified as the two greatest commandments—love for God and love for neighbor. Not loving God and not loving your neighbor would certainly disqualify you from being worthy to receive all the things listed in this verse. But the fact that Jesus is "the Lamb who was slain" means that he has perfectly loved both God and his neighbor. Jesus loved God by resisting the temptations of Satan and doing only what the Father sent him to do. Jesus loved God by ransoming people so they could know God. And simultaneously, by laying his life down for others, Jesus loved his neighbor.

By living this way, Jesus proved himself to be trustworthy. He will not abuse power. He will not spend wealth in a foolish way that helps no one. He will not use wisdom to manipulate others. He will not use might to take advantage of others. No one will regret giving him honor and glory and blessing.

You can trust Jesus. And you need to trust Jesus.

We don't worship God the way we should. All too often we trust idols.

We don't keep ourselves spiritually and morally pure. All too often we are immoral. And our worldviews are contaminated with false notions, lies of Satan. We need to be ransomed by Jesus.

The way to be ransomed by him is to repent of your sin, which means to turn away from it. You turn away from the things that you trust instead of trusting God, and you trust in God alone. You turn away from the idols. You turn away from the immorality and commit yourself to purity. You turn away from lies and embrace the truth of the Bible. Turn from your sin, and trust completely in Jesus' death and resurrection to ransom you from sin's penalty. Trust in Jesus and you will be saved!

The chorus of the living creatures was joined by the twenty-four elders, who were joined by the host of heaven, and all creation joins the song in 5:13, 14:

> And I heard every creature in heaven and on earth and under the earth and in the sea, and all that is in them, saying, "To him who sits on the throne and to the Lamb be blessing and honor and glory and might forever and ever!" And the four living creatures said, "Amen!" and the elders fell down and worshiped.

Note the way that God and Jesus are praised on equal footing here. Jesus has an unparalleled status with relation to God. Only Jesus will be praised this way with God, because Jesus is God.

Conclusion

Seeing God will change your life. When you see God as he is revealed in chapters 4, 5, you know that God is worthy of praise because of who he is. God is worthy of praise because he is holy and eternal. God is worthy of praise because he made everything according to his will. When you see God as he is, you will know that everything is accountable to God. Seeing God as he is also means seeing Jesus, the one who was slain and rose from the dead to ransom people for God.

If you see God as he is, you will worship him. He is worthy.

13

The One Seated on the Throne

REVELATION 4:1-11

CONSIDER WHAT GOD SAYS about himself:

- "I am your shield" (Genesis 15:1).
- "I am the LORD who brought you out from Ur of the Chaldeans" (Genesis 15:7).
- "I am God Almighty" (Genesis 17:1).
- "I am the God of your father, the God of Abraham, the God of Isaac, and the God of Jacob" (Exodus 3:6).
- "I Am Who I Am" (Exodus 3:14).
- "I am the LORD, and I will bring you out from under the burdens of the Egyptians" (Exodus 6:6).
- "I am the LORD in the midst of the earth" (Exodus 8:22).
- ". . . there is none like me in all the earth" (Exodus 9:14).
- "I will get glory over Pharaoh and all his host" (Exodus 14:4, 17).
- ". . . you shall know that I am the LORD your God" (Exodus 16:12).
- "I bore you on eagles' wings and brought you to myself" (Exodus 19:4).
- "I am the LORD your God, who brought you out of the land of Egypt, out of the house of slavery" (Exodus 20:2).
- "I the LORD your God am a jealous God" (Exodus 20:5).
- "I have talked with you from heaven" (Exodus 20:22).
- "I will come to you and bless you" (Exodus 20:24).
- "I will be an enemy to your enemies and an adversary to your adversaries" (Exodus 23:22).
- "I will send my terror before you . . . and I will make all your enemies turn their backs to you" (Exodus 23:27).
- "I will dwell among the people of Israel and will be their God. And they shall know that I am the LORD their God, who brought them out of the land of Egypt that I might dwell among them. I am the LORD their God" (Exodus 29:45, 46).

- "I will be gracious to whom I will be gracious, and will show mercy on whom I will show mercy" (Exodus 33:19).
- "The LORD, the LORD, a God merciful and gracious, slow to anger, and abounding in steadfast love and faithfulness, keeping steadfast love for thousands, forgiving iniquity and transgression and sin, but who will by no means clear the guilty, visiting the iniquity of the fathers on the children and the children's children, to the third and the fourth generation" (Exodus 34:6, 7).
- "Behold, I am making a covenant. Before all your people I will do marvels, such as have not been created in all the earth or in any nation. And all the people among whom you are shall see the work of the LORD, for it is an awesome thing that I will do with you" (Exodus 34:10).
- ". . . you shall worship no other god, for the LORD, whose name is Jealous, is a jealous God" (Exodus 34:14).
- "Among those who are near me I will be sanctified, and before all the people I will be glorified" (Leviticus 10:3).
- "I am the LORD who brought you up out of the land of Egypt to be your God. You shall therefore be holy, for I am holy" (Leviticus 11:45).
- "I am the LORD who sanctifies you" (Leviticus 20:8).
- "I am the LORD your God, who has separated you from the peoples" (Leviticus 20:24).
- "I the LORD, who sanctify you, am holy" (Leviticus 21:8).
- "I am the LORD your God, who brought you out of the land of Egypt to give you the land of Canaan, and to be your God" (Leviticus 25:38).
- "I will make my dwelling among you, and my soul shall not abhor you. And I will walk among you and will be your God, and you shall be my people. I am the LORD your God who brought you out of the land of Egypt, that you should not be their slaves. And I have broken the bars of your yoke and made you walk erect" (Leviticus 26:11–13).
- "And the LORD said to Moses, 'Is the LORD's hand shortened? Now you will see whether my word will come true for you or not'" (Numbers 11:23).
- ". . . as I live, and as all the earth shall be filled with the glory of the LORD, none of the men who have seen my glory and my signs that I did in Egypt and in the wilderness, and yet have put me to the test these ten times and have not obeyed my voice, shall see the land that I swore to give to their fathers" (Numbers 14:21–23).
- "And the LORD said to Aaron, ' . . . I am your portion and your inheritance among the people of Israel'" (Numbers 18:20).
- "See now that I, even I, am he, and there is no god beside me; I kill and I make alive; I wound and I heal; and there is none that can deliver out of my hand" (Deuteronomy 32:39).

That's only a sampling from the Pentateuch.

Imagine what it would be to see him.

In 4:1–11 we have eyewitness testimony to the one seated on the throne, and it is one of the fullest descriptions of God in his throne room in the Bible.

We need what this text gives us precisely because we do not see him now. We walk by faith, not by sight, and the faith we walk by is in part faith that what 4:1–11 shows us about God is true.

Need

Our need for this text is much the same as the need of the seven churches to which John sent this letter. We know from what Jesus said to them in the seven letters that they had lost their first love in Ephesus (2:4); they were about to be killed for the faith in Smyrna—husbands, wives, sons, daughters facing death (2:10); they were tempted by false teaching in Pergamum (2:14, 15); they were tolerating a false prophetess in Thyatira, and she had led some into sexual immorality and idolatry (2:20); the church was dead in Sardis (3:1), persecuted in Philadelphia (3:8, 9), and lukewarm in Laodicea (3:16).

Perhaps our spiritual state matches one of these situations: the things of God have begun to lose their luster, or maybe you're struggling with the sacrifices facing you. Or perhaps you find yourself more interested in and engaged by sinful pleasures. We need to see God as John describes him in his throne room in 4:1–11. We need the words of this passage to reach out of the page and grip our hearts with the very glory of God.

It throbs with God's majesty and power to transform your life, to give you a reason to live, to purify you from every defilement, to take you all the way home.

Main Point

The whole point of this text is to show us that right now God is on his throne being worshiped and praised as he rightly deserves.[1]

Context

John himself has been exiled to Patmos (1:9). Jesus has appeared to John in resurrection glory (1:9–20) and dictated to him the letters to the seven churches (2:1—3:22). The people in those churches are like us. Some are more faithful than others, all are challenged by temptation, all were made to know God, created to echo his greatness back to him. All are confronted with things that we can see that tempt us away from what we don't see. This text tells us about what we don't see now.

Preview

Revelation 4:1–11 falls into two parts:

4:1–6a   The One Seated on the Throne
4:6b–11   The Worship of the One Seated on the Throne

Once he enters the heavenly throne room, it is as though John starts with the throne and works out from there in 4:1–6a, and then it's as though he goes back to the throne and describes what is happening nearest the throne and works out from there again in 4:6b–11.

Revelation 4:1–6a: The One Seated on the Throne

It is interesting to observe that Jesus was standing at the door of the church of Laodicea knocking in 3:20, and in 4:1 John writes, "After this I looked, and behold, a door standing open in heaven!" It seems that the door of the church in Laodicea was closed to Jesus, but the door of Heaven was thrown wide for John.

How would Jesus find the door of the Laodicean church? I think there are churches where the deacons have locked Jesus out. I know there are. We moved recently, and as we sought a new church home, we began to visit a church that was without a pastor. I told them I would like to serve them as their pastor. They told me that they would rather see their church close its doors than have someone from Southern Seminary as their pastor. We had not had a single theological conversation, and they had not asked me a single question about the Bible. Their prejudice about what has happened at Southern Seminary in the last fifteen years caused them to ask me to find a different place to worship.[2] Are certain prejudices keeping you from loving other Christians? Jesus threatened to spew the church of Laodicea out of his mouth because they were not zealous and would not repent (3:16–19). Would he be pleased with your zeal? Would he be satisfied with your willingness to repent of your sin?

The next phrases of 4:1, 2 echo the language of Revelation 1:10. When John says in 4:1, "And the first voice, which I had heard speaking to me like a trumpet," we're reminded of 1:10, "I heard behind me a loud voice like a trumpet." That was Jesus speaking to John in 1:9–20, so you might have the next statement in 4:1 in red-letter text: "Come up here, and I will show you what must take place after this." At the words "Come up here," John is summoned by the risen Christ into the heavenly realm.

The words "I will show you what must take place" in 4:1 are very similar to 1:1, "The revelation of Jesus Christ, which God gave him to show to his servants the things that must soon take place." But here in 4:1 Jesus is going to show John "what must take place after this," and that phrase was also used in 1:19: "Write therefore the things that you have seen, those that are and those that are to take place after this."

John then tells us in the first words of 4:2, "At once I was in the Spirit," and we have noted in our studies that this phrase "in the Spirit" only occurs four times in the book, and each time it occurs it marks a turning point in the Revelation—at 1:10, 4:2, 17:3, and 21:10. The reuse of the language from chapter 1 here in 4:1, 2 (*voice speaking like a trumpet, show what must take place, take place after this*) joins with this key phrase "in the Spirit" to signal the audience of Revelation that this is a major turning point in the story.

So enter into the drama: John sees the door open, and he hears a voice like a trumpet summoning him in to see what must take place (4:1). Suddenly he is in the Spirit, and he goes on to tell us in 4:2, "and behold, a throne stood in heaven, with one seated on the throne." This throne communicates authority, and the authority of the one seated on this throne is absolute.

I would suggest that at this point, as we consider John's description of what he saw, we let our imaginations run wild. We cannot be too extravagant in our attempt to depict this for our mind's eye. The colors we imagine will not be too vibrant. The space we allot for the throne and what surrounds it will not be too large; the sights and sounds we conceive in our brains will not be too impressive, too surprising, or too overwhelming. We are talking about the glory of Almighty God, seated on his throne in Heaven. We will not overdo it in our attempt to imagine this scene.

John tells us more about the one seated on the throne in verse 3: "And he who sat there had the appearance of jasper and carnelian." Jasper is usually red, yellow, or brown in color, and it is neither transparent nor translucent, while carnelian is a reddish brown stone that can be clear to semi-translucent. So John sees something like precious stones that he can't fully see through, probably radiating hues of red and reddish brown light.

When God gave instructions for the making of the high priest's breastplate, it was to have twelve stones on it. Two of those twelve stones were jasper and carnelian (Exodus 28:17, 18, LXX). Evidently God commanded these stones to be on the high priest's breastplate because they reflect his own glory, as John sees in 4:3. John probably uses these terms to describe what he saw because his mind was saturated with Biblical terms and images. When Isaiah prophesied that the Lord would rebuild Jerusalem, he said he would build its buttresses with jasper (Isaiah 54:12, LXX). The city will show forth the glory of God. And there seems to be a connection between carnelian and jasper and the Garden of Eden in Ezekiel 28:13; so we can see that the Garden also reflected the glory of God. Revelation 21:11 describes the bride, the wife of the Lamb, the new Jerusalem, as "having the glory of God, its radiance like a most rare jewel, like a jasper, clear as crystal," and carnelian is one of the twelve stones, with jasper, on its foundations (cf. 21:18–20). The new Jerusalem will reflect God's glory. What becomes clear from this survey of

other places where we see these stones in the Bible, jasper and carnelian, is
that they are characteristic of the glory of God.

John then tells us in 4:3, "and around the throne was a rainbow that
had the appearance of an emerald." The rainbow reminds us of the sign of
God's covenant not to destroy the earth with a flood in Genesis 9. It is a
symbol of his patient mercy. The green of the emerald now adds its shades
to the radiating reddish brown light, so that what John sees when he looks at
God has the appearance of these precious stones, light emanating out from
them in red, reddish brown, and green hues, and the greens form a rainbow
that stands for God's mercy. The authoritative throne is shrouded with the
emanating colors of God's mercy. With justice and mercy in perfect balance,
God's glory shines.

Let me invite you to consider for a moment the most beautiful thing you
can imagine. Now take that beauty and multiply it by infinity, and we might
be getting close to what John saw. God created beauty. There is no defect in
him. He is perfection. He is ten thousand times more lovely than the most
compelling thing that tempts you.

So John started with "one seated on the throne" in 4:2. Verse 3 moves
to the light radiating out from the throne, and we continue outward from the
throne, in concentric circles, as it were, in verse 4: "Around the throne were
twenty-four thrones, and seated on the thrones were twenty-four elders,
clothed in white garments, with golden crowns on their heads."

Who are these twenty-four elders?

We might conclude that they are human beings, or they might be angelic
members of the heavenly court.[3] I'm not sure that we can be certain. The
twenty-four thrones are probably a symbolic number representing the twelve
tribes of Israel and the twelve apostles (cf. 21:14). They could be actual
humans who have gone to their rewards, or they could be angelic representatives of all the people of God. From the way they are described, we might
conclude that they are humans who have already received what Jesus promised to the churches in the seven letters in chapters 2, 3:

- Jesus promised the church in Laodicea in 3:21 that the one who conquers
  will sit with him on his throne. John here sees those who have what Jesus
  promised.
- Jesus promised the church in Sardis in 3:5, "The one who conquers will
  be clothed thus in white garments," and John now sees these twenty-four
  elders clothed in white garments.
- Jesus promised the church in Smyrna in 2:10, "Be faithful unto death,
  and I will give you the crown of life," and now John sees these twenty-
  four elders wearing golden crowns.

On the other hand, when we see these "elders" in the rest of the book of Revelation, they seem to be classed with angels rather than with humans (cf. 4:4, 10; 5:5, 6, 8, 11, 14; 7:11, 13; 11:16; 14:3; 19:4). If they are humans, they are those who have gone before, who have received what Jesus promised to the overcomers. If they are angelic members of the heavenly court, they testify that Jesus can make good on the promises he has made.

The vision of these twenty-four elders in 4:4, seated on thrones around the throne of God, clothed in white garments, golden crowns on their heads, declares to us that God keeps his promises. Jesus can give what he said he would give. The members of the heavenly entourage possess what Jesus promised to those who conquer.

This vision of those who have what was promised has to become more real to us than the things that would keep us from conquering.

You have to be more sure that this is real—that there are twenty-four elders seated on thrones—than you are sure of what tempted Laodicea, to whom this was promised. So what is it that keeps you from being zealous for God, with which Laodicea struggled? Are you bored with God? Do you find other things more interesting than he is? Things like television, pornography, video games? This verse, 4:4, and this chapter and this book and this Bible *exist* to convince you that God is *infinitely more interesting* than TV, porn, and video games. You were made to know God. You were not made to fritter your life away.

Maybe you're not tempted to fritter your life away with TV, porn, or video games. Maybe your problem is not lack of zeal for God so much as it is worldliness. I don't have time to go into it here,[4] but I think the problem with the church in Sardis was that they had struck a deal with the world. They had devised a way to have their cake and eat it too. They had constructed a pious front that looked good and religious, and they had avoided confessing the name of Jesus so as not to offend the world (I think that's why Jesus talks about confessing the names of those who conquer before his Father in 3:5). So what is more real to you? Are the white garments promised to those who conquer, worn by these twenty-four elders around God's throne, more precious to you than your standing in society? If you had to choose between offending worldly-minded unbelievers or forfeiting your right to these white garments, what would you choose? I'll tell you how you can know what you would choose: the next time you're tempted to compromise with the world, ask yourself whether what you will gain from the compromise is more valuable to you than being clothed in white at the throne of God.

We can say the same kind of thing about the crowns these elders wear and what tempted the church that was promised the crown of life, Smyrna. They were facing martyrdom. If they compromised, they would keep their lives in this world. If they remained faithful unto death, they would receive the crown of life beyond this life.

None of us have arrived at the point where we always resist temptation and always choose the reward over what tempts us. There is one thing we can do to move ourselves in that direction: read, study, memorize, and meditate on the Bible. One reason we give way to temptation is that we're not thinking about what we've been promised when we get tempted. If we can say to the temptation in the moment it comes to us, "You are not better to me than the crown of life, than the white garments, than the right to sit on a throne before the very throne of God!" we can stand. We can't say such things, and won't say them, if we don't know the Bible, if our world has not been absorbed by the world we see in the Bible.

To this point in John's account of what he saw in the heavenly throne room, there has been no action. The action starts in 4:5: "From the throne came flashes of lightning, and rumblings and peals of thunder." This is reminiscent of what happened when God came down on Mount Sinai after he brought Israel out of Egypt. We read in Exodus 19:16–20:

> On the morning of the third day there were thunders and lightnings and a thick cloud on the mountain and a very loud trumpet blast, so that all the people in the camp trembled. Then Moses brought the people out of the camp to meet God, and they took their stand at the foot of the mountain. Now Mount Sinai was wrapped in smoke because the LORD had descended on it in fire. The smoke of it went up like the smoke of a kiln, and the whole mountain trembled greatly. And as the sound of the trumpet grew louder and louder, Moses spoke, and God answered him in thunder. The LORD came down on Mount Sinai, to the top of the mountain. And the LORD called Moses to the top of the mountain, and Moses went up.

The cosmic disturbances, the lightning and the thunder, were not soft rumblings or weak flashes of light. We should imagine ground-shaking thunderclaps and blinding flashes—the kinds that make children cry and adults uneasy. After God came down on Mount Sinai this way, he spoke the Ten Commandments to Israel (Exodus 20:1–17).

God's mercy is seen in the emerald rainbow that encircles the throne, and his justice is depicted in the throne and in these reminders of Sinai—the lightnings, the rumblings, the peals of thunder. The book of Revelation is going to depict a lot of judgment, and John punctuates these judgments with reminders that it is God's justice that is being visited. These reminders come in the form of reports of lightnings, rumblings, and peals of thunder that come after the seven seals have been opened (8:1, 5), after the seven trumpets have been blown (11:15, 19), and after the seven bowls of God's wrath have been poured out (16:17, 18). God's justice flows from God's throne. One of the ways that John makes clear that the judgments of the seals, trumpets, and bowls come from God's throne is by reporting what comes from the throne in 4:5—"lightnings, and rumblings and peals of thunder"—after each series of seven.

John next tells us in 4:5 that "before the throne were burning seven torches of fire, which are the seven spirits of God." John's epistolary greeting in 1:4 reads, "John to the seven churches that are in Asia: Grace to you and peace from him who is and who was and who is to come, and from the seven spirits who are before his throne, and from Jesus Christ." The Trinitarian nature of this greeting leads me to conclude that the reference to the "seven spirits" who are before the throne in 1:4 and 4:5 are references to the Holy Spirit (cf. 5:6). So John sees God on the throne, and the seven torches before the throne are the visible representation of the Holy Spirit.

John next tells us in verse 6, "and before the throne there was as it were a sea of glass, like crystal." This "sea of glass" seems to match what Ezekiel described when he saw God: "Over the heads of the living creatures there was the likeness of an expanse, shining like awe-inspiring crystal, spread out above their heads" (Ezekiel 1:22). This "expanse" or "sea of glass" seems to have been represented at the temple by a bronze sea (1 Kings 7:23–26). This thing that John sees, which looks like a sea of glass, before the throne seems to introduce the idea of distance and separation between God and everything else. He is transcendent, set apart, holy.

So John has been invited into the heavenly throne room (4:1), and there he seems to have started with the one on the throne (v. 2) and worked out from there in his description of what he saw. He tells us about the one on the throne and the rainbow around the throne (v. 3), then about the twenty-four elders on twenty-four thrones around the throne (v. 4), about the cosmic disturbances of lightning and thunder coming from the throne (v. 5), about the seven torches that are the seven spirits before the throne (v.5), and about the sea of glass before the throne (v. 6).

Let me encourage you to stop right now and ask the Lord to seal these images to your heart. God is on his throne being worshiped and praised as he rightly deserves. Pray that God would capture your imagination and lay hold on your desires, that he would make himself the supreme desire of your life. Pray that the next time you are confronted with some temptation, you would feel an overwhelming desire to conquer and gain your reward. Pray that God would make you feel that only a fool would choose the smutty, worthless, cheap imitation of pleasure Satan offers you over the reality and reward that God offers. Pray that you would not only feel contempt for the sin that tempts you, but that you would act accordingly. Resist. Turn. Flee. Conquer. Honor Christ.

Revelation 4:6b–11: The Worship of the One Seated on the Throne

Having worked outward from the throne from 4:2 to the first part of verse 6, it seems that John goes back to the throne in the second part of verse 6: "And around the throne, on each side of the throne, are four living creatures, full of eyes in front and behind." These four living creatures are similar to and may be the "seraphim" Isaiah saw (Isaiah 6:1–7) and the creatures Ezekiel saw (cf. Ezekiel 1:5–25).

John describes what they were like in 4:7: "the first living creature like a lion, the second living creature like an ox, the third living creature with the face of a man, and the fourth living creature like an eagle in flight." The three living creatures that are described like animals are not called a lion, an ox, and an eagle, but they are said to be "*like*" these animals. The third is said to have "the face of a man." The point of these descriptions seems to be the way these four living creatures reflect the glory of God. Something about God is captured by the likeness of these four living creatures. God is noble, royal, and fast like a lion. He has a massive, patient, slow, serving strength like an ox. God has the sensitivity and spirituality that we can see in the face of a human being, and he has a soaring transcendence like an eagle in flight.[5]

Behold your God! He will never bore you. He will never fail you. He cannot be overcome, outmuscled, outsmarted, or outdone, and his goodness will never fail.

The right response to this God is given for us in 4:8: "And the four living creatures, each of them with six wings," are full of eyes all around and within, and day and night they never cease to say, 'Holy, holy, holy, is the Lord God Almighty, who was and is and is to come!'" Like the seraphim Isaiah saw (Isaiah 6:2), the living creatures have "six wings." The fact that they are "full of eyes all around and within" seems to indicate that they see everything. Nothing escapes their notice. And it is precisely because they see everything, because they have all the facts laid out before them, because they behold God as he is and history as it happened, all the truth about the way things are now, and because they see God's character and how he will bring all things to resolution, because they "are full of eyes all around and within," they are continually compelled to confess the almighty, everlasting holiness of God.

They praise God because they have all the facts. What keeps us from praising God? We don't have all the facts. We don't see God the way these living creatures see him. We don't know all there is to know about the past, present, and future. And I suspect that it is our *ignorance* of God and reality that keeps us from praising him the way these living creatures praise him. Here's my question for you right now: will you accept their testimony, will you take them at their word?

Look at what they proclaim about God—they say the word "holy" three times. And they are constantly seeing new evidence of this, new reasons to cry three times over that he is holy; so they never stop.

You know the truth is that God's holiness is a scary thing. It's scary like that flash of lightning that you weren't expecting that suddenly brings to light what you're doing, like that big roll of thunder that catches you off guard and rattles your whole house and makes you wonder if God has just ripped the sky in half. God's holiness is absolute. He is personally offended at sin, and there is only one mediator between God and man. This will become more clear in chapter 5, but I have to tell you now: God will satisfy his holiness against your sin. He will do justice. His justice will either be done against your sin in Hell forever, or you will place yourself under the protection of Jesus, the one mediator between God and man. If you flee to Christ, if you trust in Jesus and place yourself under his cross, the penalty he paid for sin in his death on the cross will count for you. If you don't trust Jesus, you'll pay that penalty for yourself, and it will never end. Won't you trust him right now? Why would you refuse him? He has shown such love for you, and God is showing you such mercy in right now granting you this opportunity. "Everyone who calls on the name of the Lord will be saved" (Romans 10:13). Won't you call on him right now?

Having shown us how these four living creatures are praising God in 4:6–8, John shows us how those elders react in 4:9–11:

> And whenever the living creatures give glory and honor and thanks to him who is seated on the throne, who lives forever and ever, the twenty-four elders fall down before him who is seated on the throne and worship him who lives forever and ever. They cast their crowns before the throne, saying, "Worthy are you, our Lord and God, to receive glory and honor and power, for you created all things, and by your will they existed and were created."

The praise of the four living creatures acts as a catalyst for the praise of the twenty-four elders. Notice what these elders do with the rewards Jesus promised to those who overcome: they use the crowns to praise God, to whom credit for the crown is rightly due.

Don't you want to win crowns that you can use for the praise of God? This life is the one chance we have to stand against the world, the flesh, and the devil and to fight to be faithful to God. Here is the best possible motivation we could have for pursuing greater holiness, greater Christlikeness. Every triumph on the way will become one more laurel for us to cast at the feet of the one who sits on the throne. Pray right now that the next time you are tempted by sin, called to make a sacrifice, or confronted with a compromise, the Lord will remind you that what is before you is an opportunity to win a trophy you can place before him in his honor. On that day, when we see him as he is, when we are awed by the living creatures, but most of all by the one who sits on the throne, we will wish we had more to cast at his feet. We will wish we could have suffered more for him, sacrificed more for him, resisted greater temptations than the ones we gave in to. We will wish we had fought more for him, wish we had overcome more for him, and wish we had more with which to praise him.[6]

Conclusion

God is on his throne being worshiped and praised as he rightly deserves. John has shown us the scene in the heavenly court room. There is the throne, the Spirit before the throne in the form of the seven torches, the sea of glass, the four living creatures around the throne, and the twenty-four elders. And they are praising him.

I opened this study with a series of things that God says about himself. God announces his identity and glory, and all creation is made to be the echo of God's glory back to him. Revelation 4 shows us the world as it should be, praising the one who sits on the throne, and in doing so it summons us to live now so that we will echo God's glory to him now and forever. He is worthy. Trust him. Take the living creatures at their word. He is holy. Join them in worship.

14

The Lamb Standing
as Though Slain

REVELATION 5:1–14

WHAT WOULD IT BE LIKE IF there was no Jesus?

Jesus said, "I am the way, the truth, and the life" (John 14:6). Without Jesus, there would be no way, no truth, and no life. There would be no hope, no meaning, and no significance to what happens in this world. Without Jesus everything would be a hellish, howling wasteland.

The world would be a pagan wilderness full of meaningless suffering and pain where might really would make right. There would be no justice, no true righteousness, no vindication, and no mercy. The universe would be nothing but an awful, terrifying, trackless labyrinth in which we would all be lost.

Need

We need Jesus. Jesus lived the righteous life no one else was capable of living. Jesus obeyed God the way that God deserves and demands to be obeyed. And then Jesus laid down his life for us. He took the punishment we deserved, and he made available to us the righteousness that only he had. We need Jesus.

We need Jesus not only for our own personal salvation. We need Jesus so there is hope for the world. By his death and resurrection Jesus has taken control of history. Jesus has seized destiny—not just his destiny—all destiny. Jesus is the one who ensures that the universe will have meaning. Jesus is the one who will judge the wicked and vindicate those who have trusted in him. Jesus is the one who will right the wrongs and heal the hurts and wipe away the tears.

We need Jesus. Without Jesus there is no hope.

Main Point

Revelation 5:1–14 teaches us that Jesus is in control of the past, present, and future of world history. Revelation 5:1–14 teaches that Jesus has taken over.[1]

Preview

Revelation 5 breaks down into three parts:

Revelation 5:1–4   No One Can Open the Scroll
Revelation 5:5–7   The Conquering Lamb
Revelation 5:8–14   The Worship of the Lamb

Context

Jesus began to speak to John in chapter 1, dictated authoritative proclamations to seven churches in 2–3, and then in 4:1 invited John to "Come up here, and I will show you what must take place after this." The worship in Heaven that John recounts in chapter 4 is the setting for what John will be shown, and John sees the catalyst of the action in chapter 5. What Jesus intends to show to John, "what must take place after this," is then recounted in chapters 6—16 and in 17—22.

In 4:9–11 John relates how he saw God worshiped as the Creator. He tells us what he saw next in 5:1–14.

Revelation 5:1–4: No One Can Open the Scroll

John writes in 5:1, "Then I saw in the right hand of him who was seated on the throne a scroll written within and on the back, sealed with seven seals." So John saw the Father on the throne, and there in the Father's right hand is a scroll. The seven seals on this scroll will be opened by Jesus in chapters 6–8, and from what happens when Jesus does that, it appears that the writing on the scroll relates to the events that will bring history to its appointed conclusion.[2]

Next, John writes in 5:2, 3, "And I saw a strong angel proclaiming with a loud voice, 'Who is worthy to open the scroll and break its seals?' And no one in heaven or on earth or under the earth was able to open the scroll or to look into it." So as John was looking at the Father with that scroll in his hand, an imposing angel calls out this question in a mighty voice: "Who is worthy?" Answer: No one is worthy to approach the Father, take the scroll in hand, break its seals, and open the scroll. No one is worthy.

In 5:4 we see John's response to this situation: "and I began to weep loudly because no one was found worthy to open the scroll or to look into it." Why does John respond this way? Why is he weeping over the inaccessibility of the contents of this scroll? John desperately wants to know what is on that scroll, so much so that not knowing what is on it gives him such grief that he weeps loudly. What could be so important about this scroll?

We know from the rest of Revelation what happens once this scroll gets opened, so we can say what would not happen if the scroll were not opened. If the scroll were not opened,

- 5:9, Jesus would not be worshiped as worthy to open the scroll.
- 5:9, Jesus would not be worshiped as the world's Redeemer.
- 6:10, the martyrs of the faith would not be avenged.
- 8:4, 5, the prayers of the saints ("Your will be done; your kingdom come") would not be answered.
- 9:15, God's appointed plan would not come to pass.
- 11:15, the kingdom of the world would not become the kingdom of our Lord and of his Christ.
- 16–18, the wicked would not be judged.
- 19, 20, Jesus would not come back.
- 21, 22, God would not reign in glory in the new heavens and the new earth.

In short, if that scroll isn't opened, the Bible's promises don't come true. Hope is defeated.

Before we go on to 5:5, let's stop and think about what John is doing. He's weeping because he is so emotionally involved in what is happening, because he is concerned that things might not turn out the way that he had hoped they would.

Do you ever feel that way?

Isn't it encouraging to know that John, an apostle, a Bible author, also felt that way? Perhaps you feel the way John did when you think about the state of Christianity in the world. It seems that there is so much false teaching, so much hypocrisy, and so much failure. Maybe you feel the way John did when you think about the church. There is a lot to be discouraged about, isn't there? Just as John was discouraged by what he saw, sometimes we are discouraged by what we see.

The resolution to the pain that John feels is the same resolution that we need, and it comes in 5:5–7, where we see the conquering Lamb.

Revelation 5:5–7: The Conquering Lamb

John tells us in 5:5, "And one of the elders said to me, 'Weep no more; behold, the Lion of the tribe of Judah, the Root of David, has conquered, so that he can open the scroll and its seven seals.'" John's hopeless weeping is overcome by the reality that Jesus has conquered!

Jesus gives hope. Jesus wipes away tears. Jesus is mighty to save. Jesus lives! Hallelujah!

Jesus is identified here in 5:5 as "the Lion of the tribe of Judah," which reminds us of the way Jacob blessed Judah in Genesis 49:8–12: "Judah is a lion's cub . . . he crouched as a lion . . . " (49:9). Jesus is also identified here as "the Root of David," which recalls the promise in Isaiah 11:1, "There shall come forth a shoot from the stump of Jesse."

These are reminders of the Old Testament promises that were making John weep when he thought they might not be fulfilled because the scroll might not be opened. But this one, the Lion of Judah, the Root of David, has conquered! Because he has conquered, "he can open the scroll and its seven seals." So because he has conquered, he can make known the end of history. And since he has conquered, since he can make all God's promises come true, John should "weep no more."

Notice also who it is that makes this declaration to John in 5:5: "one of the elders said to me." In chapters 4, 5 we see a very clearly defined hierarchy. The Father is on the throne. In 5:6 we see Jesus there with the Father. The Spirit is there with the Father and Christ too (4:5). Then the members of the Trinity have this expanse between them and everything else (4:6), and they are surrounded by the four living creatures (4:6, 7). Outside the four living creatures are the twenty-four elders (4:4), and in 5:11 we will see the heavenly host. "A strong angel" calls out the question in 5:2, and "one of the elders" tells John not to weep in 5:5. Notice that this isn't a matter of one of the "many angels" in 5:11 piping up before the time is right. The people involved in this scene speak when it is right for them to speak. We need to learn to recognize when it is appropriate for us to speak and when it is appropriate for us to remain silent. This applies to all believers in all situations—children, students and professors, employers and employees. There is a time for us to speak and a time for us to keep quiet. There is a time for us to lead and a time for us to recognize that it is someone else's place to lead. We need discernment.

One of the elders encourages John, and note how he encourages him. He doesn't tell him that it's not as bad as he thinks. He doesn't tell him to take some medicine. No, he uses the language of the Bible to announce that Jesus has triumphed and has kept God's promises. We can take two things from this incident: first, let's look to Jesus when we're discouraged. There is a lot to be discouraged about in this world, but as long as there's Jesus there's hope, and "Jesus Christ is the same yesterday and today and forever" (Hebrews 13:8). He will never fail us, so he will always encourage us. Second, let's be sensitive to others and encourage others with the greatness and power of Jesus. Let's look to Jesus when we're discouraged, and let's encourage others with the truth that Jesus has conquered.

John describes what he saw next in 5:6, and here we see how Jesus conquered: "And between the throne and the four living creatures and among the elders I saw a Lamb standing, as though it had been slain, with seven horns and with seven eyes, which are the seven spirits of God sent out into all the earth." The throne room scene John described in chapter 4 is now complemented with the presence of the Lamb.

John told us in 5:5 that Jesus, the Lion of Judah, "conquered," and here in 5:6 he tells us how Jesus conquered: he was slain like a lamb. Jesus is a lion—royal, dignified, ruling, powerful—but is also a lamb—quiet, submissive, humble, slain. So there the Lamb stands. Jesus is depicted as a Lamb not because he is literally a wooly little beast but because of what he did. Do you know what lambs do? They get slaughtered, they get killed, and that's what Jesus did. Jesus conquered by getting killed. It is the greatest paradox in the world: the almighty King overcame all his enemies as his enemies seemingly overcame him. Satan surely thought he had won the decisive battle. He tricked God's chosen people into murdering their very own deliverer. Jesus was dead. But out of the ashes of the crucifixion rose salvation for the world.

Perhaps you've heard the story of Saint George and the dragon. The valiant knight slays the dragon and liberates the people of the beautiful Faerie Queene.[3] In the true story of the conquest of the Lamb, standing as though slain, it is as though the Lamb has conquered the dragon by being slaughtered by the dragon. How can this be?

Lambs not only get slaughtered, they get slaughtered as sacrificial animals. Jesus is not literally a lamb. But he was slaughtered, and he was slaughtered as a sacrifice. Lambs are common animals of sacrifice in the Old Testament. The most significant Old Testament sacrificial lamb is probably the Passover lamb. The death of Jesus is the final fulfillment of all those sacrifices.

What do you think about when you think of victory? God has redefined victory in Christ. If you don't think of a crucified Savior, dead, buried, raised on the third day, you don't know what victory is. Is this victory your victory? Or are you hoping to win some other kind of victory? Let me assure you, no one was found worthy to open the scroll in John's vision, and it wasn't because you weren't around yet. You are not worthy to stand before God. Your only hope is to be swept up in the defeat of Jesus' death on the cross so that his resurrection becomes your victory. In order for this to happen, you have to trust in Jesus. What keeps you from trusting in Jesus? If you don't, you will be defeated. If you do trust in Jesus, notice that 5:5 says he "conquered." This is exactly what Jesus called the churches to do in chapters 2, 3.

At the end of each of the seven letters, he makes promises to "the one who conquers." And the conquest he calls us to is an imitation of his conquest: he gave his life for the benefit of others. That's the conquest you're called to—the conquest of trusting Jesus and taking up your cross and following him for the spiritual benefit of other people.

Revelation 5:6 doesn't only have the paradox of a defeat that is really a conquest, it also has the paradox of a slain lamb "standing"—dead things don't stand, they don't live, but Jesus lives! And in addition this verse has the paradox of Jesus metaphorically described as a lamb, a sacrificial animal, who has "seven horns." The Bible regularly uses horns as a symbol of military might. So here is this paradoxical image of an animal of sacrifice, a meek little lamb, endowed with the fullness of military strength, which is what "seven horns" signifies. He came as a lamb. He will come again as a conquering king. If you do not identify with him in his death and triumph with him in the "defeat" of taking up your cross, he will triumph over you when he comes on a white horse. Jesus is also described here as having "seven eyes, which are the seven spirits of God sent out into all the earth" (5:6). This means that Jesus has the Spirit fully, and it means that he is fully apprised of all that is. Nothing escapes his notice.

Look at 5:7 and be astonished: "And he went and took the scroll from the right hand of him who was seated on the throne." This is breathtaking audacity. We saw in 5:3, "no one in heaven or on earth or under the earth was able to open the scroll or to look into it," and yet Jesus marches right up to the Father, seated on the throne, surrounded by the four living creatures crying "Holy, Holy, Holy!" and in full view of the twenty-four elders, takes that scroll!

Crucified, dead, buried, raised, now he assertively takes the reins of history. That's what this symbolizes. Jesus takes the scroll that describes the events of the end, whereby all the wrongs will be set right, all injustices accounted for, all crimes avenged. He takes it from the right hand of the Father, and the Father doesn't resist him, the four living creatures don't object, and the twenty-four elders do not stand in his way. This symbolic action shows that Jesus has taken control of history.

Jesus is the central figure in the history of humanity. He is without question the most important person who has ever lived. He is King. He is Lord. He is the way, the truth, and the life, and he has taken the scroll. Jesus controls your destiny. He controls the destiny of every individual on the planet.

And the response to this action that begins in 5:8 and continues through the rest of the chapter should be our response: the worship of Jesus. The four living creatures, the twenty-four elders, and "myriads of myriads and thousands of thousands" (v. 11) join with every creature to declare the rightful praise of the world's true King.

What makes this all the more remarkable is the Father's silent approval of all of this worship to Jesus. I refer to it as *silent approval* because we don't read that the Father has any objection to the heavenly host turning their eyes upon Jesus and voicing his praise. And this from the one who has said in Isaiah 42:8, "I am LORD; that is my name; my glory I give to no other." But he allows Jesus to receive glory with him.

This is nothing less than stupendous. Jesus walks right up to the Father and lays hands on the scroll, and all Heaven responds by praising Jesus. Is there any way that John could have more clearly communicated that Jesus is very God of very God, light from light, God from God, of the same essence as the Father? Even if John had simply stated, "Jesus is God," it would not have portrayed the deity of Christ as clearly as this episode.

Jesus has taken control of history. The rest of chapter 5 shows us the worship that takes place in Heaven in response to who Jesus is and what he has done.

Revelation 5:8–14: The Worship of the Lamb

Revelation 5:8 describes a remarkable scene: "And when he had taken the scroll, the four living creatures and the twenty-four elders fell down before the Lamb, each holding a harp, and golden bowls full of incense, which are the prayers of the saints." Reading chapter 4, you could legitimately ask the question, could anything make the worship in Heaven more fervent? Could anything add to the worship in Heaven? Could anything cause the hosts of Heaven to sing another song?

Jesus can! The appearance of the Lamb standing as though slain, with seven horns of military might and seven eyes of all-knowing wisdom, renews and refreshes the heavenly song.

There is an important thing for us to see here about worship: God will never cease to provide us with new reasons to praise him. We will see fresh visions of his worth forever. These things that appear to us to be new reasons to praise God are really eternal, but God brings them out as new.

Note what 5:8 tells us the four living creatures and the twenty-four elders are holding: "a harp, and golden bowls full of incense, which are the prayers of the saints." They have instruments with which they will praise Jesus, and they have "the prayers of the saints."

Prayer is implicit praise. Prayer assumes that God is able, that he is merciful, that he is good, that he is concerned, that he can and will overcome. When you pray, you praise God even in the very act of prayer. And just as Jesus instructed his disciples to pray in his name (John 14:13, 14; 16:24), now that Jesus has conquered by his death and resurrection and has taken control of history, these heavenly worshipers present to him the prayers of God's people.

In 5:9 we read the song they sang to Jesus: "And they sang a new song, saying, 'Worthy are you to take the scroll and to open its seals. . . .'"

Jesus is worthy of praise because he is able to do what no one else can (5:3).

The song continues in verse 9, "for you were slain, and by your blood you ransomed people for God from every tribe and language and people and nation."

What was implicit in 5:5, 6 is now made explicit: Jesus is worthy precisely because of what he accomplished by his death and resurrection. By his death he paid the ransom. He did not pay this ransom to Satan—God owes Satan nothing. Jesus paid the ransom in the sense that people were in bondage to sin and they deserved to be punished. In a way that is analogous to but greater than the ransom paid by the Passover lamb at the exodus from Egypt, Jesus ransomed his people.[4]

These people were ransomed "from every tribe and language and people and nation" (5:9). Often the number "four" in the Bible stands for the whole world—there are "four corners of the earth" (Isaiah 11:12; Revelation 20:8) and "four winds of the heavens" (Zechariah 2:6). So the fact that there are four terms here—"tribe . . . language . . . people . . . and nation"—means that Jesus has ransomed people from everywhere. The gospel levels all notions of racial superiority because it declares that all peoples stand in the same need of the Savior.

The song concludes in 5:10 with what Jesus did with those he ransomed: "and you have made them a kingdom and priests to our God, and they shall reign on the earth." When God put Adam and Eve in the garden, he enjoined them to rule over the earth and subdue it, which I take to mean that he wanted them to subdue all the land so that it was garden-like. The result would be that the glory of Yahweh would cover the dry lands as the waters covered the sea, as the place where Yahweh walked with his image-bearers expanded.

Adam and Eve failed, and they were thrown out of the garden. So they couldn't expand its borders. The same task was later given to the nation of Israel: they were to be a kingdom of priests, and as their borders expanded through military conquest, the place where God walked among his people would expand until his glory covered the dry lands as the waters cover the sea. Like Adam and Eve, Israel failed, and Israel was thrown out of the land just like Adam and Eve were exiled from the garden. But Jesus succeeded where they failed. Jesus made his people "a kingdom," and Jesus made them "priests." God's purpose of covering the dry land with his glory as the waters cover the sea will be realized because of what Jesus has done.

After John recounts the song, he tells us in 5:11, 12, "Then I looked, and I heard around the throne and the living creatures and the elders the voice of many angels, numbering myriads of myriads and thousands of thousands, saying with a loud voice, 'Worthy is the Lamb who was slain, to receive power and wealth and wisdom and might and honor and glory and blessing!'" To this point the cast of characters has included the one on the throne, the Lamb, the four living creatures, the twenty-four elders, and "a strong angel" who made the proclamation in 5:2. Suddenly John sees a vast host. The word *myriad* can mean ten thousand, or it can simply refer to an innumerable multitude. "Myriads of myriads" would be ten thousands of ten thousands, which would be a vast horde of angels. So imagine this roar of the multitude shouting these words. They are proclaiming the worth of the Lamb, and they are saying that he is worthy to receive anything that could be given to him in his honor. He will abuse no power. He will misuse no wealth. He will do good with might. He will respond rightly to and is worthy of honor and glory and blessing. The fact that there are seven items here in verse 12 points to the complete nature of the worth they ascribe to the Lamb.

The churches to whom John wrote probably felt outnumbered. They probably felt like a minority. They probably felt weak and insignificant. They probably felt that in the face of the vast and powerful Roman Empire, what was happening in their church was relatively small. John sees and describes reality. Those who worship Jesus are part of a vast multitude. We need to get the image of this multitude into our minds, because one way to deal with being sojourners—which is what we are—is to know where home is. Home, for us, means joining in that multitude praising Jesus.

But it doesn't stop with the multitude—it extends to "every creature," as we see in 5:13: "And I heard every creature in heaven and on earth and under the earth and in the sea, and all that is in them, saying, 'To him who sits on the throne and to the Lamb be blessing and honor and glory and might forever and ever!'" Do you know that creation exists for God's glory? Do you know that the animals exist for God's glory? The animals reflect the glory of God, and they exist to proclaim his great worth. All creation praises the skill and the worth of its maker. Imagine all the animals in the world—that's what John says here: "every creature in heaven and on earth and under the earth and in the sea"—all the birds, the fish, the cattle on a thousand hills, the bears, the lions, the whales, the dogs and cats, the mosquitoes, the eagles, the gnats, and all the animals whose names we don't know, all of them giving "blessing and honor and glory and might . . . to him who sits on the throne and to the Lamb . . . forever and ever."

And when all this has taken place, we see in 5:14, "And the four living creatures said, 'Amen!' and the elders fell down and worshiped." The story continues in chapter 6 as Jesus begins to open the scroll, but let's note here why this massive worship celebration by the heavenly host and the creatures of the world is taking place: Jesus has taken control of the world's destiny. Jesus takes the scroll, and everyone bursts into celebration.

Have you contemplated the fact that Jesus is in control of the way your life will turn out? Have you thought about the fact that Jesus is in control of the way your kids' lives will turn out? I am most easily brought to tears when I think about my children and when I pray for their salvation. Jesus is in control of their destiny, and I can join in this worship celebration because there is no better way for the world to be than under the control of Jesus.

Conclusion

The world would be terrible if there were no Jesus, but there is Jesus. He is trustworthy. He is good. And he has taken control of history.

In the spring of the year 2000, James Montgomery Boice, pastor of Tenth Presbyterian Church in Philadelphia, was diagnosed with cancer. He was sixty-two years old. Eight weeks later, on June 15, 2000, he died. On May 7, 2000, he addressed the congregation he served. In the midst of his remarks to the congregation that morning, he said to them, "If God does something in your life, would you change it? If you'd change it, you'd make it worse. It wouldn't be as good. So that's the way we want to accept it and move forward, and who knows what God will do?"[5]

The great comfort of our lives is the fact that Jesus is good, and he has taken hold of the scroll. He is in control.

15

God's Plan to Save and Judge

REVELATION 6—16

In A.D. 202–203, the persecution of Christians was so vicious that a Christian named Jude wrote an explanation of Daniel's seventy weeks that saw history terminating in his own time. The persecution was so fierce that he thought the rise of Antichrist had to be near.[1]

Eusebius's *History of the Church* has more accounts of martyrs than I have time to describe. And persecution is not only an ancient phenomenon. The Voice of the Martyrs website has accounts of a number of recent instances of the persecution of Christians. For instance, in China:

> On June 29, Pastor Dou Shaowen who is currently serving a one-year sentence for "engaging in illegal activities" was secretly transferred to Shifo Re-education Through Labor Center in Zhengzhou city, Henan province, according to China Aid Association.
>
> His family was not informed of his transfer. Pastor Dou, his wife Feng Lu and five other believers were arrested on June 14 when government officials raided and closed the Rock Church. The police confiscated computers and other church property from the church. Pastor Dou and his wife were sentenced to a year in prison and the other believers were sentenced to 15 days in detention and fined 500 Yuan (US $73). However, Feng Lu will serve her sentence at home so she can care for their 12 year-old daughter.
>
> China Aid reported that Pastor Dou has been treated inhumanely in the labor camp. According to China Aid, Pastor Dou was forced to squat when he wanted to talk to police officers, he was also forced to work 18 hours a day from 6 a.m. to 12 a.m. midnight. China Aid reports that some prisoners have contracted diseases while at the camp because of overcrowding, more than 70 people sleep in a room, the hot weather and poor sanitary conditions.[2]

Also in China, on July 3 of that same year, eight Christians were arrested when a house church was raided. Six of the eight are now detained in an undisclosed location. On July 5 a house church worship service was raided, and the Christians were accused of "disturbing social order." On July 13 thirty-two Christians were arrested at a youth camp. They were interrogated, threatened, and beaten.[3]

On June 26 sixteen homes belonging to Christians were burned to the ground in Pakistan, and sixty homes were damaged.[4]

I could go on and on with these accounts. What is it that holds Christians fast in the face of persecution? What is it that emboldens people to refuse to renounce Jesus? How do they hold up under intense persecution and the demand that they recant?

Need

Ultimately God sustains Christians by the power of the Holy Spirit. The Spirit uses the promises that God has made to sustain Christians through anything they face. Christians believe that it is worse to deny Christ and lose what has been promised than to have life ruined, or even ended, in this world.

So what has God promised to his people? We need to know, don't we? We need to be assured that our heavenly Father will come for us. We need to be assured of God's promises so that our faith in God will be as certain as that of a believer named Apollonia. Eusebius tells us that as her persecutors tried to compel her to deny Christ, they "broke out all her teeth with blows on her jaws," and when she held fast they burned her alive.[5]

God has not only made promises to us, he has disclosed his plan. The disclosure of God's plan is not the kind of blueprint that you could use to predict definitively what is going to happen, but it is the kind of disclosure that gives us what we need. We need to know that God is trustworthy, that he has a plan to deal with evil and pain, that he will be just, that he will be merciful, and that no matter what happens to us, he will come for us. We need this so that we can be like Dionysia, who was "the mother indeed of many children, who yet did not love them above the Lord" and was "put to death by the sword."[6]

Main Point

God's disclosure of his plan to judge evil and save his people frees us to trust him no matter what happens to us.

Revelation 6—16 liberates the people of God to trust him, regardless of the cost, because these chapters show that God is going to judge the wicked and save the righteous. These chapters enable bold, radical faithfulness to God because they show how things will turn out in the end.

God's disclosure of his plan to judge evil and save his people frees us to trust him no matter what happens to us.

If the earth shakes and buildings fall on us, if the laws change and we are persecuted for the word of God and the testimony of Jesus, if we face powerful temptations to give in to evil, these chapters show us that God will deliver his people from every calamity, he will avenge every injustice done to his faithful ones, and the temptations to do evil are Satan's attempts to make war on the saints.

Preview

This study is a little different because we are looking at a number of chapters. I want to do four things in this study:

First, we will look at the literary structure of this section of Revelation and summarize the contents of these chapters.

Second, we will look at the connections between chapter 6 and what Jesus said would happen before his coming.

Third, we will look at the similarities between the judgments of the trumpets and the judgments of the bowls.

Fourth, I am going to suggest that John has interpreted Daniel's seventieth week in the various references to three and a half years that we find in the book of Revelation.

My goal here is to set what John has written in chapters 6—16 within the wider story of the Bible in order to see how these events fit within what God has revealed of his plan. Whether my attempt to set out the details of the plan is correct or not, we can agree that there is a plan. The fact that there is a plan is reassuring.

The fact that God has revealed his plan to us in the context of the book of Revelation is meant to assure us so we can stand against temptation and persecution. As we look at the contents and literary structure of these chapters, at the connections between chapter 6 and the words of Jesus, and at the final trumpets and bowls of God's judgment, let's pray that what we read here would produce in us a childlike faith, a faith that clings to the promises our Father has made to us no matter what happens.

The Contents and Literary Structure of Revelation 6—16

The Contents of Revelation 6—16

After the letter-styled opening of the apocalyptic prophecy in 1:1–8, John recounts his vision of Jesus on the Lord's day in 1:9–20. Revelation 1:7

identified Jesus as Daniel's Son of Man from Daniel 7:13 and as the one pierced in Zechariah 12:10. Standing among the lampstands in 1:12–16, Jesus is also the typological fulfillment of Zechariah's two sons of oil, mentioned in Zechariah 4:14 (see ESV margin). John's account of his reaction to seeing Jesus, followed by Jesus addressing the seven churches in chapters 2, 3, is reminiscent in many ways of the vision Daniel recounts in Daniel 10—12. Then Jesus calls John up into the heavenly throne room in chapter 4, where John sees God and the Lamb worshiped in chapters 4, 5. In Revelation 5 a scene much like Daniel 7:9–14, where the Son of Man approached the Ancient of Days and received everlasting dominion, takes place as the Lamb approaches the Father seated on his throne and takes the scroll from his hand.

Flowing out of that throne room scene are the seals, the trumpets, the story, and the bowls that we see in chapters 6—16. In chapter 5 Jesus takes a scroll sealed with seven seals from the Father. Revelation 6 recounts how the opening of each of the seven seals on that scroll is accompanied by a judgment. Then in chapter 7 God seals his servants, and they worship him. The opening of the seventh seal comes at the beginning of chapter 8 and results in six trumpet blasts of God's wrath. These trumpet blasts and the judgments that follow them are described in chapters 8, 9. Before the seventh trumpet blast, the Lord sends John and the two witnesses to prophesy concerning the truth in chapters 10, 11. God seals his own in chapter 7, and in chapters 10, 11 he gives his word to his people.

The seventh trumpet sounds at the end of chapter 11, and the announcement is made that the kingdom of the world has become the kingdom of the Lord and of his Christ (v. 15). Then 12:1–13:10 shows satanic opposition to Jesus and the church. Revelation 13:11–18 depicts Satan trying to answer God's true prophets with his own false prophet. Then in chapter 14 the group that was sealed in chapter 7 stands with the Lamb, and the earth is harvested. In chapters 15, 16 the bowls of God's wrath are poured out.

The Literary Structure of Revelation

It has always puzzled me that the announcement that "the kingdom of the world has become the kingdom of our Lord and of his Christ" (11:15) comes in the middle of the book rather than at the end. Why is this so? I think the answer to that question is that the book of Revelation is structured chiastically.

The word *chiasm* comes from the Greek letter *chi*, which is in the shape of an X, but a chiasm only has one side of the X. You can think of a chiasm in terms of a picture frame: you have the actual wooden frame, then inside that you may have a mat, and sometimes there are multiple mats of complementary colors, and inside the frame and the mat you have the picture. The purpose of the frame and the mat is to highlight the picture. Similarly, the purpose of a chiasm is to highlight what is at the center of the chiasm. At the very center of the chiasm is the announcement that Christ is King.

Table 15.1: The Chiastic Structure of Revelation

1:1–8, Letter Opening: Revelation of Jesus and the Things That Must Soon Take Place

   1:9–3:22, Letters to the Seven Churches: The Church in the World

      4:1–6:17, Throne Room Vision, Christ Conquers and Opens the Scroll

         7:1–9:21, The Sealing of the Saints and the Trumpets Announcing Plagues

            10:1–11, The Angel and John (True Prophet)

               11:1–14, The Church: Two Witnesses Prophesy for 1,260 Days, Then Opposition from the Beast

                  11:15–19, Seventh Trumpet: "The kingdom of the world has become the kingdom of our Lord and of his Christ, and he shall reign forever and ever." Worship!

               12:1–13:10, The Church: The Woman Nourished for 1,260 Days, Then Opposition from the Dragon and the Second Beast

            13:11–18, The Deceiving Beast (False Prophet)

         14:1–19:10, The Redemption of the Saints and the Bowls of Wrath

      19:11–20:15, Return of Christ, He Conquers, Sets up His 1,000-Year Kingdom, and Opens the Scrolls

   21:1–22:7, New Heavens and New Earth: The Church in Glory

22:8–21, Letter Closing: Jesus Is Coming Soon

Another thing that chiasms accomplish is that they set mutually interpretive items across from one another. Thus, I would suggest that we should interpret 11:1–14, which describes the two witnesses, alongside 12:1–13:10, which describes the struggle between the woman who bears the male child (Jesus) and the great red dragon. Both sections deal with the church's struggle against satanic opposition.

So let's make some very basic observations on this chiasm, starting from the center and working out from there. We see in the center of this chiasm that the kingdom of the world will one day be the kingdom of the Lord and his Christ.

Moving out from there, we see that on either side of that we have sections on satanic opposition to God and his people in 11:1–14 and in 12:1–13:10.

Outside that we have matching sections on John the true prophet in chapter 10 and the devil's false prophet in 13:11–18.

Then there are broader sections: chapters 7—9 match chapters 14—18 and the first part of 19 (vv. 1–10). It falls out like this:

7, Sealing of the Saints   14, Sealed Saints and the Harvest of the Earth
8, 9, Trumpets   15—19, The Bowls and Babylon's Fall

Before we look more closely at the connections between the trumpets and the bowls, let's look at the connections between Revelation 6 and the Olivet Discourse.

Revelation 6 and the Olivet Discourse

Table 15.2 lists all the parallels I have noted between what Jesus said in Matthew 24, which is also recorded in Mark 13 and Luke 21, and Revelation 6. In both the Olivet Discourse and in Revelation 6, there are deceivers—people who look like Jesus in some ways, but they aren't Jesus.

In both the Olivet Discourse and in Revelation 6, wars are prophesied, and I would highlight the fact that Matthew 24:6 says, "the end is not yet," and 24:8 says these events are "the beginning of the birth pains." So neither false christs nor wars are an indication of the end.

In both the Olivet Discourse and in Revelation 6, famine, difficulty, and death follow the messianic pretenders and their wars.

In the Olivet Discourse, Jesus says the gospel has to be proclaimed to the whole world, "then the end will come" (Matthew 24:14). In Revelation 6:11 the martyrs are told that the full number of appointed martyrs has to be fulfilled before the end. I take this to mean that the gospel will go to the ends of the earth through the sacrifices of the martyrs, and the fact that there is an appointed number of martyrs in Revelation 6:11 means that their deaths are not accidental.

In both the Olivet Discourse and in Revelation 6, apocalyptic imagery accompanies the coming of Jesus (Matthew 24:29, 30; Revelation 6:12–17).

You and I may disagree on the specifics of exactly what these verses mean, but we will agree on the general picture: God has a definite plan to save his people and judge his enemies. The fact that God has a plan is revealed to us to enable us to trust him, to free us from sin, and to give us hope.

When God carries out his plan to save his people and judge his enemies, are you going to be saved or judged?

Table 15.2: Parallels between Daniel, the Olivet Discourse, and Revelation

Dan. 9:26: "And the people of the prince who is to come shall destroy the city and the sanctuary [cf. Rev. 11:2]. Its end shall come with a flood, and to the end there shall be war. Desolations are decreed."	Matt. 24:4, 5 (Mark 13:5, 6; Luke 21:8): warning not to be led astray by impostors who come in Jesus' name saying "I am the Christ."	Rev. 6:1, 2: at the opening of the first seal, a rider on a white horse goes out conquering and to conquer, similar to the way that Jesus comes in Revelation 19.
	Matt. 24:6 (Mark 13:7; Luke 21:9): wars and rumors of wars, "for this must take place, but the end is not yet" (cf. Rev, 4:1).	Rev. 6:3, 4: at the opening of the second seal, a rider on a red horse goes out to take peace from the earth, being given a great sword.
	Matt. 24:7 (Mark 13:8; Luke 21:11): famine, "the beginning of the birth pains"	Rev. 6:5, 6: at the opening of the third seal, a rider on a black horse goes out with scales, and the price of wheat and barley is greatly inflated.
	Matt. 24:7, 9–12: famine, tribulation, believers put to death, hated, falling away, betrayal, false prophets, lawlessness, lovelessness.	Rev. 6:7, 8: at the opening of the fourth seal, a rider named Death rides on a pale horse, and Hades follows, and they kill with sword, famine, pestilence, and wild beasts.
	Matt. 24:14: the gospel of the kingdom is proclaimed to whole world, "then the end will come."	Rev. 6:9–11: at the opening of the fifth seal, John sees martyrs under the altar, and they are told that the number of martyrs must be completed before the end comes.
Dan. 9:27: "And he shall make a strong covenant with many for one week, and for half of the week he shall put an end to sacrifice and offering. And on the wing of abominations shall come one who makes desolate, until the decreed end is poured out on the desolator."	Matt. 24:15 (Mark 13:14): "the abomination of desolation."	Rev. 11:2: the courts of the temple trampled for forty-two months; Rev. 13:14, 15: the image of the beast speaks and is worshiped.
	Matt. 24:29 (Mark 13:24, 25; Luke 21:25): "The sun will be darkened, and the moon will not give its light, and the stars will fall from heaven."	Rev. 6:12, 13: at the opening of the sixth seal, there is an earthquake (cf. Matt. 24:7), and "the sun became black as sackcloth, the full moon became like blood, and the stars of the sky fell to the earth" (cf. Rev. 8:12; 9:2).
	Matt. 24:32, 33 (Mark 13:28, 29; Luke 21:29–31): the parable of the fig tree: summer is near when its leaves appear, and these signs mean the end is near.	Rev. 6:13: "the fig tree sheds its winter fruit when shaken by a gale."
	Matt. 24:30 (Mark 13:26; Luke 21:27), "Then will appear in heaven the sign of the Son of Man, and then all the tribes of the earth will mourn, and they will see the Son of Man coming on the clouds of heaven with power and great glory."	Rev. 6:15–17: kings, great ones, generals, the rich, the powerful, everyone seeks to hide "from the face of him who is seated on the throne, and from the wrath of the Lamb, for the great day of their wrath has come, and who can stand?"
	Matt. 24:13, 14, 22, 24, 31: the elect will persevere until the end, the gospel will go to all the elect, the days will be cut short for the elect, the elect will not be led astray, and they will be gathered.	Rev. 7:1–17: the elect are sealed.
	Matt. 24:21: "great tribulation."	Rev. 7:14: "the great tribulation."
	Matt. 24:31: "he will send out his angels with a loud trumpet call."	Rev. 8:1–5: at the opening of the seventh seal, John sees seven angels with seven trumpets (does Matthew's single trumpet become seven trumpets the way that Jeremiah's seventy years became seventy sevens of years in Daniel?).
	Matt. 24:31: the angels "will gather the elect from the four winds, from one end of heaven to the other."	Rev. 14:14–16: the angels and the one like a son of man harvest the earth.

The Trumpets and the Bowls

Just as I have highlighted similarities between Revelation 6 and the Olivet Discourse, I want to highlight similarities between the trumpets in Revelation 8, 9 and the bowls of wrath in Revelation 15, 16.

Table 15.3: The Trumpets and the Bowls

Trumpets	Bowls
8:7: hail and fire, mixed with blood, thrown onto *the earth*, one third of trees burned up, and all green grass burned up.	16:2: bowl poured on *earth*, harmful and painful sores on those with the mark of the beast who worship its image.
8:8, 9: a great burning mountain thrown into *the sea*, one third of the sea becomes *blood, one third of living creatures die*, one third of ships destroyed.	16:3: bowl poured on the *sea*, became like *the blood of* a corpse, every living thing in the sea died.
8:10, 11: a star fell from Heaven on *one third of the rivers and springs of water*, many people died.	16:4–7: bowl poured on *rivers and springs of water*, became blood, the angel of the waters praises God.
8:12: one third of *the sun* struck, one third of the moon, one third of the stars, one third of their light darkened, and a third of the day kept from shining and likewise the night.	16:8, 9: bowl poured on *the sun*, allowed to scorch people, they cursed God, no repentance.
8:13: three "woes" announced by an eagle for the last three trumpets; cf. 9:12; 11:14.	
9:1–11: a star fallen from Heaven opens the bottom-less pit, scorpion-locusts like horses with wild hair and human faces, lion teeth, *five months of pain in their stings*.	16:10, 11: bowl poured on throne of the beast, kingdom darkened, *people gnawed their tongues* and cursed God, no repentance.
9:13–21: four angels released at the appointed time, two hundred million *mounted troops*, horses with lion-heads breathing fire, smoke, and sulfur kill one third of mankind, no repentance.	16:12–16: bowl poured on Euphrates, river dried up to prepare the way for the kings from the east, unclean frog-like spirits assemble the kings of the world for *Armageddon*.
10:1—11:14: An angel descends, gives John a scroll to eat and prophesy, two witnesses.	
11:15–19: The kingdom of the world becomes *the kingdom of our Lord and his Christ*, worship in heaven, temple opened, ark seen, *lightning, rumblings, thunder, earthquake, heavy hail.*	16:17–21: bowl poured into the air, loud voice from the throne, "*It is done.*" *lightning, rumblings, peals of thunder, earthquake* like no other, islands and mountains removed, *hailstones.*

Briefly, note:

- Both the first trumpet and the first bowl affect the earth.
- Both the second trumpet and the second bowl affect the sea, making it blood, and sea creatures die.
- Both the third trumpet and the third bowl affect the rivers and springs of water.
- Both the fourth trumpet and the fourth bowl affect the sun.

- Both the fifth trumpet and the fifth bowl result in humans experiencing terrible pain.
- Both the sixth trumpet and the sixth bowl depict armies massed for the final battle.
- Both the seventh trumpet and the seventh bowl result in the triumph of God in Christ.

So I think the trumpets and the bowls are presenting complementary descriptions of the final judgments. There are also similarities between the trumpets and the bowls and the plagues on Egypt; so I think John presents the trumpets and bowls in Revelation as the plagues that accompany the new exodus. God will save his people at the end the same way he saved them at the beginning: by judging his enemies.

These final plagues in Revelation, however, are not the only events in the New Testament that are presented as the new exodus. The death of Jesus on the cross is also spoken of as an "exodus" that Jesus accomplished at Jerusalem (Luke 9:31). God redeemed his people through the death of the new Passover Lamb, Jesus.

Have you placed the blood of the Passover Lamb over your lintel, or are you going to be destroyed by the angel of God's wrath? God *will* judge his enemies. The only way to be saved from God's wrath is to put yourself under the blood of Christ, just as those Israelites believed God's word and put themselves under the blood of the Passover lamb at the exodus.

Daniel's Seventieth Week

So we have looked at the contents of chapters 6—16, the literary structure of the book, the similarities between the trumpets and the bowls, and now we turn to the various references to a three-and-a-half-year period in the book of Revelation.

My wife and I are both graduates of Dallas Theological Seminary, which is a dispensational school. As such, we heard these things mentioned often. I heard the explanation of the dispensational system, and I think I understood the presentation. Still, I wanted to examine things for myself. So Jill and I had heard the Biblical phrase "time, times, and half a time" explained, but we still weren't sure what it meant. I think that over the years I've come to an understanding of this phrase, so I will try to set it out for you. We have to go back to Daniel's prophecy, but first let me remind you of a few things from Daniel's contemporary, Ezekiel.

In Ezekiel 4, Ezekiel is commanded by God to act out the siege of Jerusalem. God tells him to lie on his side for 390 days for the house of Israel and forty days for the house of Judah (vv. 1–8). This 430-day period symbolized the years of Israel's punishment. Now Israel was in Egypt for 430 years. So through the prophet Ezekiel the Lord seems to be saying that Israel's exile from the land would correspond to their sojourn in Egypt.

Then Daniel is given an encounter with the angel Gabriel, who gives him another interpretation of the time that Israel will be in exile, in Daniel 9. Gabriel tells Daniel that "seventy weeks are decreed" for Israel (v. 24). These "weeks" are universally understood to refer to weeks of years, seven-year periods. Seventy seven-year periods adds up to 490 years. Every seventh year Israel was to let the land have a Sabbath rest, and it was to lie fallow (Exodus 23:10, 11; Leviticus 25:1–7; cf. Deuteronomy 15:1–18). Every seven times seven years, in the forty-ninth year, Israel was to have a Jubilee (Leviticus 25:8–22). The land reverted to its original owners, all debts were canceled, and all the slaves went free. Leviticus 25:10 says that in the fiftieth year liberty is to be proclaimed in the land. The seventy weeks of years that Gabriel tells Daniel will go by before Israel experiences wholesale restoration add up to 490 years (490 is 49 times 10). Gabriel is telling Daniel that when Israel is restored to their land, it will be a tenfold Jubilee.

Gabriel also tells Daniel that after sixty-nine of those weeks of years, the Messiah will be "cut off" (Daniel 9:25, 26; the ESV mistranslates these verses;[7] see HCSB, NASB, NIV). If we start counting from the return of Nehemiah to rebuild the city of Jerusalem in 445 B.C., there are sixty-nine sabbatical year cycles down to A.D. 30/33.[8] Then Daniel 9:27 describes the last week of the seventy being split in half.[9]

One more point on the seventy weeks of years before we go back to Revelation: Leviticus 26:34, 35 promised in the curses of the covenant that if God exiled Israel from the land, the land would enjoy the Sabbaths that Israel refused to give it in obedience to God's instructions. Second Chronicles 36:20, 21 says that the seventy years of Israel's exile to Babylon, as promised by Jeremiah, were fulfilled so that the land could enjoy its Sabbaths. This might imply that Israel had refused to keep seventy sabbatical years.

If we back up 490 years from the time of the destruction of Jerusalem in 586 B.C., we land at 1076 B.C., which is about the time Israel's monarchy began with King Saul. So perhaps the Chronicler is suggesting that since Israel failed to keep the sabbatical years for 490 years, they were exiled for seventy years, and then once the decree is issued for the wall to be built in 445 B.C. (cf. Daniel 9:25) there would be sixty-nine sabbatical cycles to the cutting off of the Messiah, then one final week of years.

I think that final week of years is to be understood symbolically, not literally, and I think that John has interpreted Daniel's seventieth week in the book of Revelation. So I'm going to explain my view (see Table 15.4). You can examine the texts and draw your own conclusions.

Table 15.4: The Seventieth Week in Daniel and Revelation

	Time, Times, and Half a Time	Half of the Week	1,260 Days	Other Day Counts	42 Months
Daniel	7:25; 12:7	9:27		8:14 (2,300) 12:11 (1,290) 12:12 (1,335)	
Revelation	12:14		11:3; 12:6		11:2; 13:5

Even if you disagree with what I am about to say about John's interpretation of Daniel's seventieth week in Revelation, we can agree on this: God clearly has a plan, and we can trust him no matter what comes against us.

We just saw in Daniel 9:26, 27 that ". . . the prince who is to come . . . [will] make a strong covenant with many for one week, and for half of the week he shall put an end to sacrifice and offering." The thing I want to observe here is that Daniel's seventieth week is divided in half.

Earlier Daniel 7:25 referred to a three-and-a-half-year period, and that reference also seems to inform what John describes in Revelation. In Daniel 7:25 we read of the fourth beast, "He shall speak words against the Most High, and shall wear out the saints of the Most High, and shall think to change the times and the law; and they shall be given into his hand for a time, times, and half a time." The next verses speak of the way this beast will be destroyed and the kingdom will be given to the people of God (Daniel 7:26, 27).

A similar sequence of events can be seen in Daniel 12, where Daniel is told in verse 1 that the people of God will have "a time of trouble, such as never has been since there was a nation till that time"; but then those whose names are in the book of life will be delivered and raised from the dead (vv. 1b–3). When Daniel asks, "How long shall it be till the end of these wonders?" in verse 6, he is told in verse 7 that "it would be for a time, times, and half a time, and that when the shattering of the power of the holy people comes to an end all these things would be finished" (cf. also vv. 11, 12).

These two passages in Daniel seem to speak of a three-and-a-half-year period in which the people of God will face terrible persecution: they will be "worn out" and "given into [the] hand" of the beast (Daniel 7:25); it will be "a time of trouble, such as never has been . . . " (Daniel 12:1). But then both Daniel 7:25 and Daniel 12:1–13 indicate that after this three-and-one-half-year period of trouble, the power of the beast will be broken, and the people of God will be delivered.

In Revelation John gives us more insight into the nature of Daniel's seventieth week and the three-and-a-half-year period of intense persecution. Again, this is not the kind of insight that can be aligned with specific dates, months, and years. These things are symbolic. This is the kind of insight that assures the people of God that God has a plan, that no matter how bad the persecution gets he will break the power of the beast and raise his people from the dead.

In the book of Revelation John provides an interpretation of Daniel's seventieth week, and he accounts for both halves of it. From what we see in Daniel, it appears that the second half of the week will be a time of intense persecution after which the people of God will be raised from the dead. John seems to interpret the second half of Daniel's seventieth week the same way that Daniel presents it, while he adds that the church will be protected during the first half of Daniel's seventieth week. To be clear, I am suggesting that Revelation symbolically presents the church's being protected by God throughout its history during the first half of Daniel's seventieth week, while in the second half of the week there will be a period of intense persecution that immediately precedes the end of all things.

John indicates in Revelation that the church will be protected for a period of three and a half years, and then the beast will have three and a half years when he can "conquer"—"kill" (11:7)—the saints. Thus, in 11:1–3 John measures the temple, which seems to symbolize the people of God. Only the temple is measured, not the courts, which the nations will trample, along with the holy city, for forty-two months. This forty-two months is the first three-and-a-half-year period. During this time, we see in 11:3, the two witnesses will prophesy for 1,260 days, another reference to the first three-and-a-half-year period.

We read in 11:7 about the first three-and-a-half-year period coming to an end: "And when they have finished their testimony, the beast that rises from the bottomless pit will make war on them and conquer them and kill them." So it seems that the two witnesses, whom I take to symbolize the prophetic witness of the church, will prophesy for three and a half years, and then the beast will rise from the bottomless pit and kill them.

We next see this first half of Daniel's seventieth week in 12:6. John describes a "sign" that "appeared in heaven" (12:1). Using imagery from the Joseph story, John describes what appears to be Mary giving birth to Jesus (12:1–5). This male child is about "to rule all the nations with a rod of iron" (v. 5). The dragon stands ready to "devour" the child at his birth

(vv. 3, 4), but the child "was caught up to God and to his throne" (v. 5). This seems to symbolically represent the birth of Christ and his conquest of death followed by his ascension into Heaven. Then we read, "and the woman fled into the wilderness, where she has a place prepared by God, in which she is to be nourished for 1,260 days." I take this to mean that the woman will be nourished in the wilderness for the first half of Daniel's seventieth week.

Revelation 12:7–12 then seems to depict the heavenly implications of the triumph of God in the crucifixion and resurrection of Jesus. This passage tells of a war in Heaven and of Satan's defeat. He is cast down to the earth, and he knows that he has only a little time left (v. 12). The "short . . . time" that Satan has is Daniel's seventieth week, the final years of history. Satan (v. 9) first pursues the woman (v. 13), but in verse 14 she flees to the wilderness, "where she is to be nourished for a time, and times, and half a time." Satan's efforts against her are thwarted (vv. 15, 16), so he goes off to make war on the rest of her "seed" (v. 17).

In chapter 12 we see that the three-and-a-half-year period in which the church is to be protected symbolically represents all of church history until the time immediately before the end. It seems that during this time God protects his people—he has sealed them in chapter 7, and in 9:4, which describes locusts that rise from the bottomless pit, only those who have not been sealed can be harmed. This seems to indicate that at this point the demonic tormentors cannot harm the people of God.

Another indication that the church is protected during the first half of Daniel's seventieth week is that 11:3 says the two witnesses will prophesy for the duration of that period. When their prophecy is complete (which matches what Matthew 24:14 says about the gospel going to the whole world and what Romans 11:25 says about the full number of the Gentiles coming in), 11:7 says they will be killed by "the beast that rises from the bottomless pit."

Revelation 13 seems to describe this very beast, rising from the sea (v. 1). We read in 13:5 that this beast "was allowed to exercise authority for forty-two months." We then see in 13:7 that "it was allowed to make war on the saints and to conquer them." I would suggest that John is describing the same thing that Daniel described. The beast brings awful persecution on God's people for a three-and-a-half-year period, the second half of Daniel's seventieth week. At the end of that period, Jesus comes on a white horse, and we read in 19:20, "And the beast was captured, and with it the false prophet. . . . These two were thrown alive into the lake of fire that burns with sulfur."

Conclusion

So if it gets so bad that you think the Antichrist is going to arise at any moment, if they send you to a forced labor camp for "reeducation," if they break all your teeth with blows to your face, if they take you from your children and put you to death, God has a plan to save and judge. He will judge justly. He will save those who trust in Jesus. The gospel will go to the ends of the earth, and then the end will come.

16

The Seals on the Scroll

REVELATION 6:1-17

WHEN YOU THINK OF JESUS seizing control of history, what comes to mind? The way you answer that question will show what you think about God, and it will show whether God's concerns are your concerns, whether your concerns are derived from the Bible or from some other source.

When you think of Jesus taking over, do you think mainly about getting what you want? Do green grass and blue skies and happy smiles everywhere come first to mind?

Or are you concerned about what concerns God? When you are offended by people, is it because they are disregarding the first and greatest commandment? Do you think to yourself, *That person exists to love God with all his heart, mind, soul, and strength*? And when people offend you, do they offend you because in what they are saying or doing they are despising God? In other words, is your primary concern for God's glory? Are the uppermost thoughts in your mind thoughts of how people owe God honor and refuse to give it?

Here's why I ask these questions: If your concerns are derived from the Bible, Revelation 6 will not surprise you. If your concerns are not derived from the Bible, chapter 6 will be very surprising.

If you are primarily concerned with what concerns God, your primary concern will be for his glory. And if you are informed by the Bible, you will know that God is just, that God keeps his word. If God creates the world for his glory, and if he promises to punish those who do not glorify him as God or give thanks to him (cf. Romans 1:21), he will do it.

If you are not primarily concerned with God and his glory, and if your concerns are not derived from the Bible, then you will be surprised to read that

175

after Jesus has seized control of history in chapter 5, the wrath of God begins to be visited in chapter 6. These things will be surprising to you because you don't know God, you don't care about his glory, and you're not offended when his glory is trampled in the dust.

If you love God's glory, it offends you when people take the good gifts he has given and use them against him. If you love God's glory, it offends you when people refuse to honor God as God and give thanks to him. If you love God's glory, you want to see justice done.

If you love God's glory, it will not surprise you that when Jesus takes control by laying his hands on the scroll in chapter 5, the wrath of God begins to fall in chapter 6. It will not surprise you. It will satisfy you. God has been patiently storing up wrath for all these long ages. God has been allowing crimes and injustices and blasphemies and abominations for so long, and he has been tolerating such lies and calumnies to be spoken about him all these years. Revelation 6 promises that one day the wrath will begin to fall. The debt finally comes due. Justice will be done. The wicked will give account. The righteous will be avenged. God will be glorified in his justice.

Need

We need to have our minds and our affections shaped by the Bible. We need to love God with all our heart, mind, soul, and strength, and we need to love God's glory. We need what chapter 6 gives us, because it shows us how passionately committed to his own glory God is. We need to understand this so we can understand what the Bible shows us about God.

Main Point

God is just, and he will justly repay all the ways that his glory has been despised and his holiness defiled.

Preview

Revelation 6 presents the first six of seven seals. The opening of the first four seals results in actions that take place on earth. When the fifth and sixth seals are opened, John sees things in Heaven:

6:1–8   Four Seals and Four Horsemen
6:9–17   Martyrs and Signs in the Heavens

Context

The apocalyptic prophecy of the book of Revelation opens like a letter in its first eight verses. At that point John begins to describe a vision that he'd had of Jesus on the Lord's day. After John has described Jesus (1:9–20), he relates the authoritative proclamations that Jesus issued to seven churches (chapters 2, 3). Jesus then summons John into the heavenly throne room to show him "what must take place after this" (4:1). John beholds the worship of the Father in Heaven (chapter 4), and then the Lamb who is worthy, Jesus, takes the scroll from the Father's hand, prompting all of Heaven and earth to worship Jesus and the Father (chapter 5). Jesus begins to open the seven seals on the scroll in chapter 6.

Revelation 6:1–8: Four Seals and Four Horsemen

As we saw previously (see the study on Revelation 6—16), the sequence of events that John describes once Jesus takes the scroll and begins to open its seals closely parallels the sequence of events Jesus prophesied in Matthew 24. As we proceed through Revelation 6, I am going to interpret this chapter in light of Matthew 24 because I think that John would have known this chapter and expected his audience to know it. So I think that Revelation 6 and Matthew 24 are complementary presentations of world history between the first and second comings of Christ.

The judgments that are described in chapters 6—16 are linked back to the throne room vision of chapters 4, 5 in a variety of ways. One of the ways that the opening of the seals is linked back to the throne of God is by the activity of the four living creatures around the throne. At the opening of the first four seals, one of the four living creatures summons one of the four horsemen of the Apocalypse. The judgment that these horsemen bring is called for by these living creatures who worship God at his throne. It seems that a progression develops as we go from one horseman to the next, and we will note this development as we go forward.

We see the first of these in 6:1: "Now I watched when the Lamb opened one of the seven seals." Note here that the action is continuing from what we saw in chapter 5. The Lamb took the scroll, then a worship celebration broke out, and now the sequence of events continues with the Lamb opening the first seal. So John is about to see what he wept over not seeing in 5:4.

Once that first seal is open, John writes, "and I heard one of the four living creatures say with a voice like thunder, 'Come!'" (6:1). So one of these four living creatures who encircle God's throne speaks, and his voice sounds like the thunder that issues from the throne in 4:5. What he summoned to come is described in 6:2: "And I looked, and behold, a white horse! And its rider had a bow, and a crown was given to him, and he came out conquering, and to conquer." There is an obvious similarity between this rider on a white horse and the way that Jesus comes riding on a white horse in chapter 19. In view of the way that Matthew 24:4, 5 warns that many will come claiming to be Christ himself, it seems that this is a messianic pretender in Revelation 6. The phrase "a crown *was given* to him" (6:2) is a divine passive—in other words, God is the unnamed giver of this crown. God is in control of this horseman's activity. This rider on a white horse is not going to do anything other than what God gives him to do. He goes out "conquering, and to conquer," and when someone does that, you know there is going to be conflict with the ones he means to conquer. That conflict comes into view when the second seal is opened.

Let's think for a moment about messianic pretenders. This first horseman looks like Jesus, the rider on the white horse in chapter 19, but he isn't Jesus. Remember, those who do not worship the one true and living God who ever exists in three persons, the same in essence, equal in power and glory, will worship false gods. They may not call what they worship "god/s," but they will worship themselves or money or success or a sports team or a video game or learning or power or prestige or some utopian vision of the good life. Humans will worship. By the same token, those who do not know the divine Messiah, Jesus, will easily be led astray by false human messiahs. Some lyrical orator with passion and poise and style will come along promising hope and change, and all the sheep believe his promise to bring in the millennium. This is not new to the present political situation. These messianic pretenders have been followed around the world through the ages. God reveals this through Christ's opening the seal and having John record the vision so that God's people will not be duped by the fakes. Jesus is coming. He is our Messiah. He alone will bring in the kingdom, and his realm is our home. Followers of the Messiah Jesus do not worship the gods of this culture and do not follow the messiahs of this culture.

We read about what follows the messianic pretender in 6:3, 4: "When he opened the second seal, I heard the second living creature say, 'Come!' And out came another horse, bright red. Its rider was permitted to take peace from the earth, so that men should slay one another, and he was given a great sword." The conqueror on the white horse is followed by the rider on the red horse. Here again we have divine passives in the phrases in 6:4: "its rider *was permitted* to take peace" and "he *was given* a great sword." God gives the rider on a white horse a crown, and he comes out as a Christ-pretending conqueror. Then God gives this second rider the ability to take away peace, and God gives him the sword with which he will wage war. These are the very wars that Jesus predicted in Matthew 24:6 when he said, "you will hear of wars and rumors of wars. See that you are not alarmed, for this must take place, but the end is not yet." Jesus has taken hold of the scroll; he is opening it, and history is unfolding just as he said it would.

In the ancient world war had a devastating impact on the land. Invading armies made farming impossible. They camped in the fields. They stole crops for their own food. They destroyed crops they didn't steal with fire or simply by marching through the fields. Destroying the food would aid a siege. These realities inform what we read next in 6:5, 6: "When he opened the third seal, I heard the third living creature say, 'Come!' And I looked, and behold, a black horse! And its rider had a pair of scales in his hand. And I heard what seemed to be a voice in the midst of the four living creatures, saying, 'A quart of wheat for a denarius, and three quarts of barley for a denarius, and do not harm the oil and wine!'" This rider on the black horse has scales, and these scales are probably going to be used to measure out the wheat and the barley. The price stated here reflects severe inflation. This judgment comes from "a voice in the midst of the four living creatures," meaning that this voice comes from the throne. These judgments come from God. The oil and wine are not going to be harmed; these commodities were mainly enjoyed by the rich. The devastating conditions of war would immediately affect the poor, but the rich might not be affected at all.

Is your life affected by political upheavals and war? If it is not now, it might be in the near future. By revealing these things before they happen, God is preparing his people to trust him through the devastations that human governments create.

The consequences of war go beyond devastated land and resulting food shortages to the sickness and malnutrition and infection and disease that would accompany injuries, uncleanness, and inadequate supplies of food and water, and all this might be made worse in a walled city under siege. This seems to be what we read about in 6:7, 8: "When he opened the fourth seal, I heard the voice of the fourth living creature say, 'Come!' And I looked and behold, a pale horse! And its rider's name was Death, and Hades followed him. And they were given authority over a fourth of the earth, to kill with sword and with famine and with pestilence and by wild beasts of the earth." So here comes the pale horse, and his color seems to be the greenish color of ill-health that accompanies sickness, disease, and infection. Another divine passive can be seen in the statement in 6:8 that Death and Hades "were given authority over a fourth of the earth." They use this authority, and the way they use it summarizes these four horses: they kill with the sword, reflecting the wars started by the first two horses; they kill with the famine brought by the rider on the third horse who measures out the inflated cost of the wheat and the barley; and they kill with the pestilence reflected by the rider on the pale horse. So there is a sense in which the fourth horse summarizes the first four and ties them together.

The statement at the end of 6:8 about Death and Hades killing "by wild beasts of the earth" uses the same language that the Epistle to Diognetus would use, maybe seventy-five years after Revelation was written, to describe Christians being "thrown to wild beasts to make them deny the Lord, and yet they are not conquered."[1] Revelation 6:8 speaks of the kind of thing done by the Roman Empire when they put humans in the arena to fight against lions and other beasts.

Jesus talked about the things that unfold here in 6:1–8 in Matthew 24:4–9, when he spoke of false christs, wars, famines, lawlessness, lovelessness, and death. Jesus is in control of history. Now let me suggest that what we have just seen in 6:1–8 is relevant to us today because it tells us this: the history of humanity that we have witnessed is a history of these very things. Messianic pretenders, wars, famines, death—all these things mark the history of humanity. So I think this presentation of the four horsemen of the Apocalypse is a kind of schematic that represents the flow of history—inspiring rulers that leave wars and devastation in their wake.

Earlier I said that the opening of the seals results in judgments. How are these first four seals judgments? They are judgments against those who refuse to worship the real God and his King. Those who do not worship the real God and his King are handed over by God to false gods and false kings, and the consequences that result from these megalomaniacs and ruler cults are God's judgment against those who have rejected him.

Revelation 6 claims that Jesus is in absolute control of these things and that these events come as judgments from God. The four living creatures summon the four horsemen of the Apocalypse. God brings these things on humanity, but forces of wickedness are responsible for the evil they do. God gives the first rider the crown, permits the second to take peace and gives him a sword, sets the parameters for the third, and gives authority to Death and Hades.

Why would God allow these things? I think that God wants a clear contrast between what results from embracing his rule and what results from rejecting it. God wants people to see what happens when humans reject the true God and embrace false gods. God wants people to see what happens when humans reject the rightful King, the Lord's Messiah, Jesus, and replace him with some chump who looks good and speaks well. So God lets these fools have their day in the sun, and he lets all the mayhem and ruin that results from their pride and folly defile his world. God lets all this happen so that his wisdom, his power, his righteousness will be seen clearly. God wants people to know that only he can bring peace, justice, security, and happiness. God wants to be worshiped as God, and he wants people to embrace the rule of King Jesus, the Messiah.

All the pain and death and horror that makes up world history is a history of God's judgment being visited. God's judgment is visited because people do not honor God as God or give thanks to him (cf. Romans 1:21). They refuse to honor God, so God gives them over to their gods. But there is hope even in this. Jesus said that these things would happen, and he said in Matthew 24:6 that they "must take place, but the end is not yet."

In Matthew 24:8 Jesus said these judgments are "the beginning of the birth pains." Birth pains are awful. But just when they are at their worst, the baby comes. That these judgments are birth pains means that they are more than angry retribution. They are part of a necessary process that will bring forth new life.

Before Jesus can take his people to the new and better Eden, the new heavens and the new earth, he has to bring judgment for all the despising of God's glory and the defiling of his holiness. God is just, and Jesus has taken hold of the scroll. As he opens its seals, Jesus sets in motion the outworking of God's justice.

Revelation 6:9–17: Martyrs and Signs in the Heavens

The scene shifts when the fifth seal opens. The audience of Revelation is swept from the judgment of war on the earth to the altar in Heaven in 6:9: "When he opened the fifth seal, I saw under the altar the souls of those who had been slain for the word of God and for the witness they had borne." These are people who died for their faithfulness to the gospel. In 2:10 Jesus called the church in Smyrna to "Be faithful unto death." Those saints in Smyrna now hear of those who did just that. These souls under the altar have been faithful unto death.

We must come to the point where what matters most to us is faithfulness to God. Faithfulness to the word of God and the gospel must be more important to us than pleasure, more important to us than leisure, and more important than life itself. We must value faithfulness to God and his word more than we value the ability to go on living our peaceful, happy lives. That is what it means to be "faithful unto death." Knowing that others who have been faithful unto death before us are now in the presence of God can liberate us from any fear we may have about what comes after death. Death is not the end. This life is not the ultimate reason for your existence. You exist for the glory of God. Live in a way that testifies to that reality. Die in a way that testifies to that reality.

So John sees these souls under the altar in 6:9, and in 6:10 he tells us what they said: "They cried out with a loud voice, 'O Sovereign Lord, holy and true, how long before you will judge and avenge our blood on those who dwell on the earth?'" Let's stop and think about this so we can *feel* the injustice that has been done to these martyrs. People who are faithful to God, who are "slain for the word of God and for the witness they had borne" (6:9), are people who are rightly relating to God and to other human beings. They are doing no wrong. They are slain by people who are doing wrong. They are murdered for fulfilling the two greatest commandments—loving God and loving people.

The most loving thing you can do for another person is not leave them alone. The most loving thing you can do for another person is not affirm them in their sin. The most loving thing you can do for another person is bear witness to the word of God, share the gospel with them.

One of the great ironies of this life is the fact that humans find so many ways to treat evil as though it is good and good as though it is evil. Some people agitate for wickedness—they are activists for God-despising, humanity-destroying, depression-causing activities such as legalized abortion, legalized marijuana, legalized child pornography, and homosexual "marriage"—and these people are viewed by the media and the culture as champions of virtue.

Meanwhile, people who testify to God's truth—those who seek to win others to embrace the saving gospel of Jesus Christ and experience the liberating freedom of living according to Biblical morality—are viewed as unloving, negative hate-mongers who should be ashamed of themselves. We must resist the slow creep of the culture's conclusion that it is wrong to tell people the gospel, wrong to testify to God's truth.

The culture has not only called good evil and evil good, it has also succeeded in making this seem normal. The result is that if we are not careful, we will feel that the right thing to do is keep our mouths shut. We have to soak our minds in the Bible so that we know that the loving thing to do is speak the gospel and testify to the word of God. If we don't do that, we are basically saying to people, "I don't care if you go to Hell."

We must not say that to people! We have to tell them that we love them and that because we love them we want them to know Jesus. We have to tell them that even if it means they will repay our love by killing us. That's what happened to these souls John sees under the altar.

Because their love was repaid with hatred, they know that justice should be done. They want justice to be done so that God's goodness will be vindicated. So they call out for vengeance. Notice that they are not taking vengeance into their own hands. They are calling on God to avenge. Our culture has probably convinced most of us that vengeance is an evil thing altogether, but that's not what the Bible says. Romans 12:19 does not say vengeance is categorically wrong. Romans 12:19 says "Beloved, never avenge yourselves, but leave it to the wrath of God, for it is written, 'Vengeance is mine, I will repay, says the Lord.'" God's vengeance is a good thing, and these souls under the altar are calling for God to do his good work of vengeance in 6:10.

The time for the outpouring of God's vengeance has not yet come. We read in 6:11, "Then they were each given a white robe and told to rest a little longer, until the number of their fellow servants and their brothers should be complete, who were to be killed as they themselves had been." This verse states that there is a "*number*" of martyrs that has to be *completed*. This verse states that God will not avenge the blood of the martyrs until *all the martyrs that are to be killed have been killed*. Now, who do you think set that number? I guarantee it wasn't Satan. Why would God have an appointed number of martyrs who have to be killed before he avenges their blood? I suspect it has something to do with the way that believers' saying that God is better than life and sealing that confession with their life's blood testifies to the supreme value of knowing God.

Let me ask you another question: where are those martyrs going to come from? We've mentioned the people in Smyrna who were called to "be faithful unto death" in 2:10, but that call also goes out to every believer who seeks the blessing promised by this book to those who read it, hear it, and keep what is written in it. This scene is for me and you. This scene is to strengthen us to be faithful unto death, to tell us that some of us may be martyrs, so that we can be preparing ourselves for that now. Why is this passage here? To prepare us for martyrdom.

Do you know how to prepare for martyrdom? Soak yourself in the Bible. Cling to its promises. Live in the world the Bible describes, not in line with the world that rebellious humans reinvent for themselves.

Read the Bible like you might be martyred for it. Pray like you would if you knew they were going to kill you for it one day soon. Preach the gospel like you might be martyred for it. Cast your votes at church—for instance, when a congregation votes on whether or not to exclude the unrepentant from membership—like your life depends on it. Love your spouse like you would if you knew that they were coming for you. Hold your kids and teach them the faith like there is no tomorrow.

The truth is bloody. It is soaked in the blood of martyrs who have died in the past, who are suffering somewhere right now, and who will one day soon stand courageously and seal the confession with blood. Not long ago three Nigerian pastors were beheaded by Muslims.[2] One of those pastors was commanded to embrace Islam but instead preached Christ to his persecutors. A pastor preaching at one of the funerals told Christians to be ready to die for their Lord. Nigeria is not that far from the U.S.

Are you ready to die for the Lord Jesus Christ? Do you know how to get ready? Live like there is something worth dying for. That's how you prepare yourself for martyrdom. Put it in your mind: *God, Christ, the Bible, the truths of the faith—these things are worth more to me than life. Life without these things is not worth living. I would rather have my life taken from me than surrender the good confession. God will protect and provide for my widowed wife and my orphaned children. He is God, not my persecutors. I love my family and will serve them as long as there is breath in my chest, but all the while I will be teaching them Psalm 63:3—the steadfast love of the Lord is better than life.*

We must think about these things beyond this moment. When we're choosing whether to study the Bible and pray or to turn on the television, we need to ask, "What if five years from now they're going to demand that I renounce the faith or die?" When we go online or go to the mall looking for clothing, when we decide what we're going to do with our extra time or money, we need to factor into our considerations these questions: "Will this matter when they come for me?" "Will this help me make the good confession?" "Is this declaring that to live is Christ and to die is gain?"

Look what happens next in 6:12–17. The end has finally come: the sun goes black, the moon turns to blood, the stars fall, the sky is rolled up, the mountains and islands are removed, and people try to hide from the wrath of God and the Lamb. These images symbolize the end of all things everywhere in the Bible. It is going to come soon. Hang on. Hold fast. He's coming soon.

We read in 6:12, 13, "When he opened the sixth seal, I looked, and behold, there was a great earthquake, and the sun became black as sackcloth, the full moon became like blood, and the stars of the sky fell to the earth as the fig tree sheds its winter fruit when it is shaken by a gale." These cosmic signs that accompany the opening of the sixth scroll are very similar to the description in Matthew 24:29, and the next verse, Matthew 24:30, describes the coming of the Son of Man. With the opening of the sixth seal the moment when the Son of Man will come is drawing nigh.

The apocalyptic imagery continues in 6:14: "The sky vanished like a scroll that is being rolled up, and every mountain and island was removed from its place." These dramatic alterations in the order of things declare that the end is approaching. God no doubt stages this display of his might to provoke repentance. Repentance, however, does not result.

Rather than repent, people foolishly try to hide. We see in 6:15–17, "Then the kings of the earth and the great ones and the generals and the rich and the powerful"—these are people who are significant, dignified, and proud, but they stand no chance against God—"and everyone, slave and free, hid themselves in the caves and among the rocks of the mountains, calling to the mountains and rocks, 'Fall on us and hide us from the face of him who is seated on the throne, and from the wrath of the Lamb, for the great day of their wrath has come, and who can stand?'" Did you notice how the manifestation of the wrath of God functions as a leveler of humankind? Did you see how the reaction of the kings is the same as the reaction of the slaves? Did you see how the rich and the powerful are no better than the merely free? Status—"kings"—is nothing before the wrath of God. Human greatness—"the great ones"—is nothing before the wrath of God. An army—"generals"—is nothing before the wrath of God. Money—"the rich"—and influence—"the powerful"—are nothing before the wrath of God. All these people are looking for a place to hide, but there is no place to hide.

Everything people sell their souls to gain fails them when the great day comes. Politicians sacrifice their integrity to get elected, but their office won't help them when Jesus comes. The rich trade life for money, the powerful exchange loving relationships to gain influence, and people everywhere prefer enhancing their image to building character and learning truth. But when God knocks the mountains off their roots and yanks the earth's surface flat, when he rolls up the scroll of the sky, nothing that people forsook him to gain will protect them from his wrath.

How will you fare before the wrath of God? Do you think status or influence or wealth or greatness is going to help you on that day? There is only one shelter from the wrath of God on that day—the shelter of the cross of Jesus Christ. Only those who believe that Jesus died to pay the penalty for their sins, that he rose to conquer sin and death, only those who trust Jesus will be sheltered by Jesus from divine wrath on that day.

Interestingly, the gospel is a leveler of humanity in the same way that God's wrath is. The gospel declares that only Christ can save and that nothing you bring makes you closer to God. Money doesn't put you closer to God. Power doesn't, influence doesn't, greatness doesn't, freedom doesn't. The only thing that brings you to God is faith in Jesus Christ. Your pride will be demolished one way or the other. Do you want it demolished now by the cross and the gospel, or do you want it demolished on the last day by the wrath of the Lamb.

It might seem to you that "the wrath of *the Lamb*" shouldn't be that frightening. I think there might be a connection here between the martyrs and Jesus: both were overcome in that they were killed but overcame by being faithful. Perhaps John describes the wrath of Jesus here as "the wrath of *the Lamb*" because Jesus comes as the wrathful Lamb to avenge the wickedness of those who put him to death and of those who put his people to death.

You don't want to face that wrath. Even if the mountains and the rocks were to fall on these people, as they request in 6:16, they would not escape that wrath. There is only one way to avoid that wrath, and there is only "one mediator between God and men, the man Christ Jesus, who gave himself as a ransom for all" (1 Timothy 2:5, 6). What keeps you from trusting him? What evidence do you have that you will be able to survive without him? What gives you any hope that you will avoid the wrath of God without Jesus? Let me assure you: you have no other hope. He is worthy of your trust. You should trust him. Why don't you commit yourself to trusting him right now?

Conclusion

Do you love the glory of God? Are you offended when the glory of God is despised, when the holiness of God is profaned? Does it bother you that people have been put to death for the gospel? What do you expect to happen now that Jesus has taken hold of the scroll and has begun to open its seals?

It isn't altogether wrong to expect Jesus to bring in the golden age. But before the millennium dawns, Jesus will do justice. And we see that justice begin to fall in chapter 6. The first four seals show the wars that come in judgment of people's rejection of the one true and living God. The fifth seal shows the martyrs under the altar, crying out for justice. The sixth seal shows the wicked terrified before the one who sits on the throne and before the wrath of the Lamb.

There is still time for repentance. If you have not trusted Christ, won't you do so now? If you do trust in Christ, who do you need to talk to about the wrath to come? Perhaps there are some in your life you need to sit down with and ask them if you can read 6:12–17 to them. Then perhaps you could look them in the eye and invite them to the only shelter from the wrath of God, a shelter that mountains won't provide, the shelter of the cross of Christ.

17

The Sealing of the Servants of God

REVELATION 7:1–17

IN GREEK MYTHOLOGY, Achilles was the son of the nymph Thetis and the human king Peleus. When Achilles was born, his mother Thetis tried to make him immortal by dipping him in the river Styx. His only vulnerability was to be found at the place of his body where the water did not touch him, where his mother held him, which happened to be his heel. This is why a point of weakness is referred to as an Achilles heel.

I bring up this myth because it approaches something we all desire: invulnerability. We would all like to be as invulnerable as Achilles—except for his heel, which was his downfall. Paris shot an arrow that struck Achilles on the heel, and he died.

What if I told you that Christians have an invulnerability that is greater than that of Achilles?

Need

We need to understand the power of God and what it means for our lives. We need to understand that we are free to live, free to love, free to die for the gospel because the power of God is greater than death itself. The power of God is greater than all the power of Hell, and we need to know this and live on it.

We need earnestness to proclaim the gospel, willingness to suffer persecution, and ability to resist temptation as we are fueled by the power of God.

Main Point

God is able to seal his servants and protect them from all danger, winning praise from them.

Preview

Revelation 7 falls into two parts. In the first part the saints are sealed, and in the second part they praise God for their salvation.

7:1–8   The Sealing of the Saints
7:9–17   The Saints Worship God

Context

After the opening of the book of Revelation (1:1–8), John's vision begins with the glorified Christ (1:9–20) addressing the seven churches (chapters 2, 3). Then John is invited into the heavenly throne room, where he sees God and Jesus being worshiped (chapters 4, 5). In chapter 6 Jesus opens the first six seals on the scroll that he took from the hand of God, and in chapter 7 God seals the saints. This chapter is important because we will see later in 9:4 that those who are sealed will not be harmed, and we see in 14:1–5 that this group stands with Jesus, redeemed, on Mount Zion. The fact that God seals his servants also informs the number of the beast in 13:16–18, which seems to be a satanic imitation of God's sealing of his servants.

Revelation 7:1–8: The Sealing of the Saints

The focus of John's vision shifts from the judgment of God on the wicked at the end of chapter 6 to what will happen to the people of God at the beginning of chapter 7. John writes in 7:1, "After this I saw four angels standing at the four corners of the earth, holding back the four winds of the earth, that no wind might blow on earth or sea or against any tree." The phrase "After this" at the beginning of 7:1 seems to pertain only to what John saw next. It does not indicate that the events of chapter 7 come after the events in chapter 6 in terms of chronological sequence, for as we saw, the sixth seal deals with the events of the end.[1] So it seems that chapter 6 has given us the progress of history that fulfills what Jesus said in Matthew 24, and then chapter 7 gives us another perspective on that history, dealing mainly with how God's people are protected.

The reference in 7:1 to "the four corners of the earth" and "the four winds of the earth" points to the worldwide scope of the activity of these angels. The "four corners" and the "four winds" refer to the *whole* earth. John sees these four angels exercising worldwide restraint, and then we see what they are restrained from in 7:2, 3: "Then I saw another angel ascending from the rising of the sun, with the seal of the living God, and he called with a loud voice to the four angels who had been given power to harm earth and sea, saying, 'Do not harm the earth or the sea or the trees, until we have sealed the servants of our God on their foreheads.'" After the events of chapter 7, when the first trumpet is blown in 8:7, the earth and the trees are damaged, and then at the sounding of the second trumpet in 8:8 the sea is harmed. So this angel rises from the east, and whereas in chapter 6 the seals on the scroll have been opened, in chapter 7 God's people are about to be sealed. God will accomplish the sealing of his servants before the judgments fall.

In 7:2, 3 the four angels at the four corners holding back the four winds in 7:1 have "been given power to harm earth and sea." This is a divine passive. God gave these four angels this power. God also sends this angel with the seal in 7:2, saying in 7:3 that they are not to "harm the earth or the sea or the trees" until the servants of God have been sealed (cf. Ezekiel 9:1–11).

There are important lessons for us here: God is sovereign over the harmful forces in the world. The divine passive is a way to state that God has ultimate control over something while at the same time distancing God from it. This teaches us that the harmful things that happen do not surprise God. Satan has not tricked God. The world is not spinning out of God's control. God is in absolute control of everything that happens. Some things happen because he has given ability to an agent he has appointed to accomplish his purpose. God's purposes will be accomplished, even if humans and demons act wickedly (see 17:17).

In addition to the fact that God is sovereign over everything, even harmful things, we see in this passage that God actively protects his people. God keeps his own. Not one of them will be lost. The sealing in view here probably does not guarantee that the servants of God who are sealed will have no pain, but 9:4 indicates that those who are sealed are spared the pains of judgment. The sealing in view ensures the preservation of the servants of God in the faith. God seals them in the sense that he keeps convincing them that he is trustworthy. He keeps compelling them to trust him. He makes sure that they will always have compelling evidence to believe what he has said.

There is comfort here for us, isn't there? You can be confident that no matter how bad it gets, you will not suffer the smallest bit more than God allows you to suffer. God will not allow the suffering to go farther than you can bear. You can also be confident that if God is in control, the suffering is not meaningless. In addition, you can be confident that God will never let you go. If you trust in Jesus, God has sealed you. Unbelief will not swamp your ship.

This, my friends, is an invincibility that goes beyond the power of the

Greek gods, beyond what Thetis did for Achilles. This invincibility says that whatever happens to you, God will save you. You are sealed. God will keep you in the faith. Satan will not be able to make God's people deny the faith. So let me invite you to give praise and thanks to God in this moment. He will save you. He will bring you through whatever trial you're facing. Rest in his greatness. Cling to his word. The next time you're tempted, take up this word from God and use it to resist the devil. Say to him, *God has sealed me, Satan; so in the name of Jesus I will not yield to your temptation.*

In 7:4–8 we see John's account of those who are sealed. John explicitly identifies this group in verse 4: "And I heard the number of the sealed, 144,000, sealed from every tribe of the sons of Israel." Then he states in 7:5–8 that there were 12,000 from each tribe. This list raises interesting questions. The first is the question of who is and is not on the list. Jacob, who was renamed "Israel," had twelve sons. Joseph was replaced on later lists of the twelve tribes by his two sons, Ephraim and Manasseh. These two tribes are sometimes referred to as "half tribes," because if we drop Joseph and add his two sons, we have thirteen instead of twelve. This is in some part resolved by the fact that Levi was consecrated to the Lord (Numbers 3:11–13). For this reason, the tribe of Levi was not listed with the other tribes (Numbers 1:47–54; cf. the lists of the tribes in Numbers 1:20–43; 2:1–31). So by dropping Levi and Joseph and adding Joseph's two sons, the list in Numbers 1:20–43 has twelve tribes.

But in this list that John gives in Revelation 7:5–8, he leaves out Dan, lists Manasseh but not Ephraim, and lists both Joseph and Levi. So John has twelve tribes listed, but his list doesn't match the way that the Old Testament generally listed the twelve tribes. I doubt very much that John had forgotten those portions of the Old Testament. He no doubt knew these things more thoroughly than we do; so I suspect there is some explanation for the list being the way it is. The tribe of Dan was probably left out because that tribe fell into idolatry in Judges 18. Something similar is probably the case with Ephraim. Once Israel was split into a northern and a southern kingdom after Solomon, the Old Testament often referred to the Northern Kingdom as "Ephraim" (e.g., Isaiah 7). So the idolatry of the Northern Kingdom may lie behind the omission of Ephraim on John's list.[2] This is one way to explain the inclusion of Joseph and Levi in place of Dan and Ephraim.

We might not be exactly sure about why John includes the tribes he does on this list, but we can be sure of this: The twelve sets of 12,000 points to a full and complete number of the sealed. This very round, very perfect number is symbolic, and the point of the symbolic number is to say that God saves a vast multitude. God seals a huge, complete number of people, and by sealing them he ensures their perseverance. God provides a confidence that goes deeper than the kind of protection Achilles enjoyed. No arrow to the heel will ever kill the faith of someone God has sealed.

The way this list is presented in chapter 7 is similar to the militaristic arrangement of Israel's camp in Numbers 2.[3] The list in Numbers follows the exodus from Egypt as God's people are about to make their way toward the promised land to conquer it. So also here in Revelation God seals his servants, who are arranged in these legion-like battalions 144,000 strong. Then God brings the plague-like judgments of the trumpets and bowls to liberate his people before Christ conquers and brings the new heavens and the new earth. Perhaps you feel that your life is a little on the insignificant side. Let me say to you, if you're a Christian, John is revealing to you that the angel of the rising sun has suspended the judgment of God until you have been sealed. Your place, believer, is in the ranks of these 144,000. Are you living like one who belongs to this company? In the upper echelons of the United States Military, there are high-ranking officers who make coffee and basically serve as "gophers" for four-star generals. There are majors and lieutenant colonels who are errand boys for our highest-ranking officers. Do not conclude from the fact that you're changing diapers or teaching a five-year-old to spell that you are insignificant. Don't think that you don't matter because you're waiting tables or washing dishes or are stuck in what you think is a dead-end job. If you trust in Christ, your place is among the 144,000.

Perhaps you're not a believer. Let me ask you: What gives your life purpose? Your own ambition? Finding pleasure in a world that makes no sense and ultimately has no purpose? If you're an unbeliever, if Jesus is not your Lord, I don't want to encourage you—I want to discourage you. I want you to despair. Despair of any hope except the hope there is for you in Christ. If you don't join the ranks of the 144,000 by trusting in Jesus, the Warrior King who leads that army will crush you one day. Flee his wrath. Plead for mercy from him now. He is well-disposed to pardon your sin if you will repent of your sins and trust in him. You will be reconciled to God, and your life will have meaning. If you reject him, the only meaning your life will have will be the way you serve as an object of wrath, a demonstration of God's justice.

From what I have said thus far, I've tipped my hand as to who I think these 144,000 are. I think they symbolize all believers in Jesus, all Christians. Some think they are literal Israelites to be redeemed in a final seven-year period of tribulation. I find the other perspective more compelling, that the 144,000 is the same group as the one that will be described later in this chapter, the "great multitude that no one could number, from every nation, from all tribes and peoples and languages" in 7:9. There are two very clear differences between these groups: the first is both numbered and identified as Jewish, while the second is innumerable and from every nation, tribe, people, and language. On the other hand, we see in 7:14 that the innumerable multitude from every tribe are "the ones coming out of the great tribulation"; so it would seem that they are saved through the tribulation *because God sealed them*. This would strongly incline toward an identification of the 144,000 from the tribes of Israel with the innumerable multitude from every tribe. On this understanding, just as John *heard* that Jesus was a Lion in 5:5 and then "*saw*" Jesus as a Lamb in 5:6, so also John "*heard*" the number 144,000 in 7:4 and then *saw* an innumerable multitude in 7:9. This interpretation would hold that just as the Lion is the Lamb, Jesus, so the 144,000 is the innumerable multitude, all the people of God.[4] We will see more evidence that the 144,000 is the same group as the innumerable multitude as we proceed through the rest of this passage, particularly when we get to 7:14.

Whatever we conclude about the relationship between the 144,000 in 7:4 and the innumerable multitude in 7:9, what is clear is this: God seals his people and guarantees their salvation. God saves his people. They do not make themselves invincible—God seals them. And for this they praise him.

Revelation 7:9–17: The Saints Worship God

John writes in 7:9, "After this I looked, and behold, a great multitude that no one could number, from every nation, from all tribes and peoples and languages, standing before the throne and before the Lamb, clothed in white robes, with palm branches in their hands." No one can number the multitude. Does it seem to you now that there are only a few who are saved? It did not look that way to John. God's mercy is incalculable, and he has spread it widely.

The innumerable multitude is from "every nation" and "all tribes and peoples and languages" (7:9). The "four corners" and "four winds" in 7:1 pointed to the whole world, and the same dynamic is at work here where these four terms—"nation . . . tribes . . . peoples . . . languages"—point to people from all over the world. Look at where they are: they have joined the scene that was set for us in chapters 4, 5 and stand "before the throne and before the Lamb" (7:9). Fellow believers, we will stand there one day.

The mention of the white robes they wear reminds us of the promise of this reward to those who overcome in 3:5. In 19:14 "the armies of heaven" are "arrayed in fine linen, white and pure," and they are "following [Jesus] on white horses" into battle. This is in keeping with the marshaling of the twelve battalions of 12,000 each in the 144,000 seen earlier in chapter 7.

The "palm branches" they hold (7:9) call to mind the crowds at Jesus' triumphal entry into Jerusalem (e.g., John 12:13), and they are also reminiscent of the Feast of Booths, which celebrated God's provision for Israel in the wilderness on the way to the promised land (cf. Leviticus 23:40). These who have received their reward are celebrating the triumph of Jesus, and they are celebrating his provision on the way to the land of promise, the new heavens and the new earth.

They give credit where it is due in 7:10, "crying out with a loud voice, 'Salvation belongs to our God who sits on the throne, and to the Lamb!'" They do not credit themselves for overcoming. God sealed them. They state plainly that salvation belongs to God. This means that their salvation is not due to the right choices they made, the virtue of their character, the superiority of their wisdom, or the strength of their will. Salvation belongs to God. God saved them. So they praise God.

Then John gives us the rest of the heavenly scene in 7:11, 12: "And all the angels were standing around the throne and around the elders and the four living creatures, and they fell on their faces before the throne and worshiped God, saying, 'Amen! Blessing and glory and wisdom and thanksgiving and honor and power and might be to our God forever and ever! Amen.'" When we were examining 4:4 I suggested that the elders were likely angelic beings because elsewhere in Revelation they are grouped with the host of heaven rather than with redeemed humans, and we see that here in 7:11. The heavenly host praises God for his work in saving this innumerable multitude of human beings. They ascribe seven things to God: 1) "blessing," 2) "glory," 3) "wisdom," 4) "thanksgiving," 5) "honor," 6) "power," and 7) "might."

Look at the way the humans praise God in 7:10 and the way the heavenly host praises him in 7:12. The heavenly host says "Amen!" to the praise of the humans. So the humans God saves praise him (7:9, 10), and then those humans become reasons for the heavenly host to praise God also (7:11, 12). Who gets your instinctive praise? Are you someone who knows you deserve no credit for the redemption you have, or are you someone who expects to stand before God and be commended—by God and by others—commended for having made the right choice, commended for having been generous, commended for having been a good person? Do you feel that you should be commended, or do you feel, deep down in your soul, that if you got what you deserved you wouldn't be commended, you would be condemned? Salvation belongs to God. Everyone stands in need of salvation because everyone deserves to be condemned. No one is commendable to God. Remember what we saw at the end of chapter 6 in verse 17—"who can stand" before the wrath of the Lamb? Answer: no one. The redeemed proclaim that salvation belongs to God (7:10), and the heavenly host of angels, elders, and living creatures say "Amen!" (7:12).

If you're not a believer, you may be wondering how this innumerable multitude stands before God declaring that salvation belongs to him. I've just said that no one is worthy to stand before God, and here are these people standing before him. How? The answer is given to us in the exchange that follows.

We see an exchange between John and an angelic interpreter, one of the elders, beginning in 7:13: "Then one of the elders addressed me, saying, 'Who are these, clothed in white robes, and from where have they come?'" John tells us his response in 7:14: "I said to him, 'Sir, you know.' And he said to me, 'These are the ones coming out of the great tribulation. They have washed their robes and made them white in the blood of the Lamb.'"

These people clothed in white have "washed their robes . . . in the blood of the Lamb." The reference to "the blood of the Lamb" is a reference to Jesus' death on the cross. This is not a literal washing. They did not literally dip their garments in a pool of Jesus' blood. The point of this figurative expression is that the blood of Jesus cleansed them. How did the blood of Jesus cleanse them? When Jesus died he paid the penalty for sin, and when they trust in Jesus, his payment of the penalty is applied to them. Their sins are washed away when they trust in Christ.

This means that the innumerable multitude are believers in Jesus, people whose stain has been washed away by his blood. The angel also tells John, "These are the ones coming out of the great tribulation" (7:14). Dispensationalist interpreters understand "the great tribulation" to refer to Daniel's seventieth week (cf. Daniel 9:24–27), the final seven years of human history. I have indicated (in the chapter on Revelation 6—16) that I think Daniel's seventieth week is the whole period of time between the two comings of Christ. I think this because the New Testament indicates that with the resurrection of Jesus, the last days began. The eschaton has begun. Jesus says in John 5:25 that the time for the resurrection of the dead "is coming, and is now here." In Acts 2:16, 17 Peter says that the prophecy of Joel concerning the last days has come to pass. Paul says in 1 Corinthians 10:11 that Christians are those "on whom the end of the ages has come." So the age to come has been inaugurated. The final period of human history, Daniel's seventieth week, is the whole period between the ascension and the return of Jesus.

This also means that the whole period of time between the ascension and return of Jesus is a period of "tribulation." Jesus told his disciples in John 16:33, "In the world you will have tribulation." Paul told the churches in Acts 14:22, "through many tribulations we must enter the kingdom of God." In

Revelation 1:9 John told the churches that he was their "brother and partner in the tribulation." Jesus said to the church in Smyrna in 2:9, "I know your tribulation," then told them in 2:10 that they would have tribulation for ten days.

You might be thinking, okay, but this verse (7:14) talks about "the great tribulation." And I grant that this reference to "great tribulation" is also seen in Matthew 24:21, and both Matthew 24:21 and Revelation 7:14 are reflecting Daniel 12:1: "there shall be a time of tribulation, such as has not been from the time a nation came on the earth until that time" (my translation). But the phrase "great tribulation" does not *exclusively* refer to a final period of difficulty, for in 2:22 Jesus threatens to throw those in the church in Thyatira who commit adultery with Jezebel into "great tribulation."[5] This means that he threatened people alive in John's day with "great tribulation."

So it seems that the whole period of church history, the time between Jesus' ascension and return, is a period of tribulation. This period of tribulation is a time of birth pangs (cf. Romans 8:22). Right before the end, it does seem that there will be an intense period of persecution at the very end of history. But I think it is a mistake to expect a *literal* final seven years. I think if we do that, this innumerable multitude can only be the saints saved during that final seven years, and I think that is mistaken. So I am arguing that "the great tribulation" is the whole period between the ascension and return of Christ, that this is the period of "the messianic woes," and that the innumerable multitude and the 144,000 are all believers in Jesus. This innumerable multitude comes "out of the great tribulation" (7:14) because God put his seal on their forehead (7:3).

So rather than being a description of those saved in the final seven-year period, I think it more likely that John means this as a description of all believers in Jesus. Thus, what John sees and recounts in Revelation is meant to encourage the churches to whom he writes. They are facing tribulation, and John tells them that God seals his servants to preserve them through the tribulation. God makes it so that though they are killed, they will overcome because they will not stop trusting Jesus.

What are you trusting? Are you trusting in your ability to stand before God? Or are you trusting in the sacrifice of Jesus? Are you trusting in your ability to keep yourself from falling away? Or are you trusting in God who seals his servants? The angelic elder continues to describe the results of trusting in Jesus in 7:15–17:

> Therefore they are before the throne of God, and serve him day and night in his temple; and he who sits on the throne will shelter him with his presence. They shall hunger no more, neither thirst anymore; the sun shall not strike

them, nor any scorching heat. For the Lamb in the midst of the throne will be their shepherd, and he will guide them to springs of living water, and God will wipe away every tear from their eyes.

This glorious statement is a virtual catalog of Biblical promises. Those who trust in Christ will receive everything God has promised and more. It will go beyond anything we can ask or think.

Conclusion

So what threatens you? The loss of a job? Betrayal of a spouse? Children in danger? The economic downturn? Socialized medicine? Murderous unbelievers? The temptations of the world?

The main point of the book of Revelation is for Christians to see God in his glory, and that glory is on display as God shows justice and mercy. The awesome glory of God in mercy is what we see in chapter 7. He seals the saints, and the saints praise him.

Do you know what this means for you? It means you are invincible. It means your faith is unassailable—not because of the strength of *your* faith—salvation belongs to God! Your faith is unassailable because God has sealed his people. As Jesus said in John 10:29, "My Father . . . is greater than all, and no one is able to snatch them out of the Father's hand." So we say with the Apostle Paul in Romans 8:31–39:

What then shall we say to these things? If God is for us, who can be against us? He who did not spare his own Son but gave him up for us all, how will he not also with him graciously give us all things? Who shall bring any charge against God's elect? It is God who justifies. Who is to condemn? Christ Jesus is the one who died—more than that, who was raised—who is at the right hand of God, who indeed is interceding for us. Who shall separate us from the love of Christ? Shall tribulation, or distress, or persecution, or famine, or nakedness, or danger, or sword? As it is written, "For your sake we are being killed all the day long; we are regarded as sheep to be slaughtered." No, in all these things we are more than conquerors through him who loved us. For I am sure that neither death nor life, nor angels nor rulers, nor things present nor things to come, nor powers, nor height nor depth, nor anything else in all creation, will be able to separate us from the love of God in Christ Jesus our Lord.

18

Trumpeting the End of the World

REVELATION 8:1–13

HOW LONG? Psalm 4:2: how long will the wicked dishonor the Messiah and love what is worthless and seek lies? Psalm 6:1–3: how long until we're healed and no longer do things that provoke God's wrath? Psalm 13:1, 2: how long will it seem like God has forgotten us and is hiding his face while the enemy exalts over us? Psalm 35:17: how long will the Lord look on before he delivers? Psalm 62:3: how long will the righteous be attacked? Psalm 74:10: how long will the enemies of God scoff and revile his name? Psalm 79:5: how long will God's anger against his people who have sinned continue? Psalm 80:4: how long will God refuse to answer the prayers of his people? Psalm 90:13: how long before the Lord returns and has pity on his servants? Psalm 94:3: how long will God allow the wicked to exult and gloat? Psalm 119:84: how long must God's servants endure persecution? Revelation 6:9, 10: how long until God begins to avenge the blood of the martyrs?

We know what this feels like, don't we? How long must I suffer this painful disease? How long until God remakes the world so no more babies die of either Trisomy 18 or Trisomy 13? How long until no more babies are born with heart defects? How long until no more young wives die of tragic diseases? How long must we struggle with this temptation? How long until redemption comes? How long until the suffering ends? How long until God shows his glory and puts those who mock him to shame?

How long? That question has been ringing through the prayers of God's people for thousands of years now. What do you think it's going to look like when God decides it's time? In 6:11 the martyrs are told to "rest a little longer"; then in chapter 8 their prayers come before God, and he answers those prayers.

197

Need

Revelation 8 meets at least four needs that we have, but these are needs that we often overlook. First, we need encouragement to keep praying. We need to understand the relationship between our prayers and God's plan. Second, we often fail to make the connection between God's wrath against sin and the ravages of nature. The fact that the world is broken is evidence of God's righteous indignation against sin, and we need to understand this. Third, these judgments shout the glory of God. The severity of the judgments in chapter 8 are in direct proportion to the glory of the God avenged by these demonstrations of his righteousness and power. And fourth, we need to hear that our question, "how long?" is being answered by this book of Revelation with the answer, "a little longer," and we need to be encouraged to endure.

Main Point

So the main point of this study is this: the trumpet blasts in chapter 8 depict God hallowing his name in response to the prayers of his people as the holiness of God is visited upon the created order.

Or more simply, God answers the prayers of his people by hallowing his name and judging the world.

Now let me unpack it bit by bit before we go forward: the four trumpet blasts in chapter 8 are accompanied by judgments that fall upon the natural world—the land, the sea, the rivers, and the lights in the heavens (sun, moon, and stars). The two trumpet blasts in chapter 9 are accompanied by judgments that affect humanity. So in chapter 8 the created world is affected; in chapter 9 humanity is affected. That's what I mean when I say that this chapter shows the holiness of God being visited upon the natural elements of the created world.

These trumpet blasts and the events that accompany them in chapter 8 only happen because God is judging sin. Awful things happen in the world because of sin. Diseases, tsunamis, hurricanes, killer tornadoes, out-of-control fires, and every other kind of natural disaster all come as a result of God's judgment against sin. These things should make us fear God and hate sin.

The first part of chapter 8 shows us an angel presenting the prayers of all the saints to God, and then the trumpets are only blown after those prayers rise up before God. God is sovereign, and he will accomplish all his good purposes, but this chapter clearly shows God responding to the prayers of his people. God appoints the ends, and he appoints the means to those ends. One of the means to the ends that God has appointed is prayer.

The trumpet blasts in chapter 8 depict God hallowing his name in response to the prayers of his people as the holiness of God is visited upon the natural elements of the created world. God answers the prayers of his people by hallowing his name and judging the world.

Preview

Revelation 8 falls into three parts:

8:1–5   Our Prayers Will Be Answered
8:6–12   The First Four Trumpets: Wrath on the World
8:13   Woe to the Earth-Dwellers

Context

After the opening of the book of Revelation (1:1–8), Jesus appeared to John in glory and issued authoritative proclamations to the seven churches to whom John sent this book (1:9–3:22). Jesus then summoned John up into the heavenly throne room, where John saw God and Christ being worshiped (chapters 4, 5). What prompted the heavenly host to worship Jesus was his ability—because he conquered—to approach the Father, take the scroll from his hand, and open the seals on that scroll. Chapter 6 recounts what happened when the first six scrolls were opened, and those events seem to symbolize all of history from the time of Jesus until the end of the age. Then before the seventh seal is opened, chapter 7 shows all the people of God being sealed so they will be protected from God's wrath.

Once the people of God are sealed, the seventh seal is opened in chapter 8. The opening of this seal seems to initiate the events that will bring history to its appointed consummation. So what seems to have been written on that scroll that Jesus took from the Father in chapter 5, then opened in chapter 6 are the events that will take place at the end. Chapters 8, 9 show the first six trumpet blasts of God's wrath. Then just as there was a break in the action between the sixth and seventh seals, there is a break in the action between the sixth and seventh trumpets.

Revelation 8:1–5: Our Prayers Will Be Answered

After the interlude in chapter 7 when the saints are sealed, the seventh seal on the scroll is opened in 8:1: "When the Lamb opened the seventh seal, there was silence in heaven for about half an hour." This silence is appropriate in view of what is about to happen. This is the calm before the storm, in fulfillment of the call in the prophets to be silent before Yahweh.

• Habakkuk 2:20: "But the LORD is in his holy temple; let all the earth keep silence before him."

- Zephaniah 1:7: "Be silent before the Lord GOD! For the day of the LORD is near."
- Zechariah 2:13: "Be silent, all flesh, before the LORD, for he has roused himself from his holy dwelling."

John saw what was happening in Heaven in chapters 4, 5 before the seals were opened in chapter 6. He now has another glimpse into Heaven, and here he sees into the heavenly temple, before the trumpets are blown in the rest of chapters 8, 9. John will again see into the heavenly sanctuary in chapter 15 before the outpouring of the bowls of God's wrath in chapter 16.

Revelation 8:2 sets the scene for the blowing of the trumpets: "Then I saw the seven angels who stand before God, and seven trumpets were given to them." The four living creatures John saw around God's throne in 4:6–8 summoned the four horsemen in response to the opening of the first four seals in 6:1–8. The activity of those living creatures who are so near God's throne tied those judgments to the authority that issues from God's presence, and the giving of the seven trumpets to these seven angels "who stand before God" also serves to tie the judgments of the trumpets to the authority of God himself. These judgments issue from the very presence of God. This point is also established by the use of the divine passive in the phrase, "and seven trumpets *were given* to them." God gave these seven angels the seven trumpets. God is initiating the outworking of his plan to consummate history.

Before John tells us about those trumpet blasts, he shows us what is going on in the heavenly temple at the altar of incense in 8:3–5:

> And another angel came and stood at the altar with a golden censer, and he was given much incense to offer with the prayers of all the saints on the golden altar before the throne, and the smoke of the incense, with the prayers of the saints, rose before God from the hand of the angel. Then the angel took the censer and filled it with fire from the altar and threw it on the earth, and there were peals of thunder, rumblings, flashes of lightning, and an earthquake.

These verses return us to the scene at the opening of the fifth seal in 6:9–11, where John saw "under the altar"—probably the same altar that he now sees in 8:3—and under the altar in 6:9 were "the souls of those who had been slain for the word of God and for the witness they had borne." They were crying out, "how long before you will judge and avenge our blood on those who dwell on the earth?" (6:10). Then they were given white robes and told to rest a little longer until the number of martyrs would be complete (6:11). Those cries of "how long," those cries for God to "avenge" their blood, those cries for God to hallow his name by upholding justice and establishing righteousness are now the prayers that rise before God at this incense altar in 8:3–5. Notice the association of the incense with "the prayers of all the saints" in verse 3, then again in verse 4: "the smoke of the incense, with the prayers of the saints, rose before God."

Jesus taught his disciples to pray for God to hallow his name, for God's kingdom to come, and for God's will to be done (e.g., Matthew 6:9, 10). Now those prayers are about to be answered.

Will your prayers be among the prayers being answered when God takes action in these ways? If you trust in Christ alone for salvation, and *if you are praying*, they will be. Are you praying? Men, husbands and fathers, it is our responsibility to lead in this area. My wife is much better than me at making sure our family is praying and making sure that Jim and Jill are praying together. I need to repent of my laziness and prayerlessness, and I need to lead in this area. And I'm calling you, men, to join me in taking initiative on that point. It is our responsibility to lead our wives and children to be praying people. When our kids are grown and gone, we want them to look back and think of their parents as praying parents. More significantly, at the end of the age, when God begins to answer the prayers of all the saints, we want our prayers to be among the ones he is answering.

If you have been discouraged in prayer and wondered whether your prayers will ever be answered, John is testifying to you right now in 8:3–5 that God will answer your prayers one day.

If you have ever wondered whether you should pray the imprecatory prayers of the Psalms, let me encourage you to look again at the way the martyrs pray for God to "avenge" their blood in 6:9–11. You bet you should pray those imprecatory prayers. Pray that God would either save his enemies, those who oppose the gospel and the people of God, that he would bring them to repentance, or if he is not going to do that, that he would thwart all their efforts to keep people from worshiping God by faith in Christ. Pray that God would either save those who destroy families and hurt little children or thwart all their efforts and keep them from doing further harm. Those prayers will be heard. Pray that God would either redeem people who are right now identifying with the seed of the serpent, or if he is not going to redeem them, that he would crush them and all their evil designs. God will answer those prayers.

Don't miss the connection here between the prayers of God's people and the outworking of God's purposes to save and judge. These events go forward precisely in response to the prayers of God's people. Notice the divine passive again in 8:3, where the angel "*was given* much incense to offer with the prayers of all the saints." God gave that angel the incense that would accompany the prayers of his people, and God authorized that angel to do what we see in 8:5, where he fills that censer with fire and throws it on the earth. Then the peals of thunder, the rumblings, the flashes of lightning, and the earthquake we see at the end of 8:5 are the same things we saw issuing from the throne of God in 4:5. These judgments come from the very throne of God.

The trumpet blasts in chapter 8 depict God hallowing his name in response to the prayers of his people as the holiness of God is visited upon the natural elements of the created world. God answers the prayers of his people by hallowing his name and judging the world.

Revelation 8:6–12: The First Four Trumpets: Wrath on the World

As we begin to consider these trumpet blasts, we are going to see that the judgments that accompany these trumpet blasts correspond to the plagues on Egypt in significant ways. That is no coincidence. Remember that before God appeared to Moses to send him back to Egypt, we read in Exodus 2:23–25, ". . . the people of Israel groaned because of their slavery and cried out for help. Their cry for rescue from slavery came up to God. And God heard their groaning, and God remembered his covenant with Abraham, with Isaac, and with Jacob. God saw the people of Israel—and God knew." The mention of Abraham, Isaac, and Jacob calls to mind God's promise to deliver Israel in Genesis 15:13, 14, a promise that informs their cry for rescue. God's promises should inform our prayers.

God judged Egypt in order to deliver Israel, and in doing so God was responding to the prayers of his people. The book of Revelation is showing us the ultimate exodus, but this time it is not a mere nation that God is judging, but the wicked world system that is ranged against God and his people. As at the exodus from Egypt, God is going to judge the wicked world and deliver his people in response to their prayers.

So the fact that God brings on the world these judgments, which so closely correspond to the plagues on Egypt, points us to the significance of the deliverance that God is accomplishing through these judgments. As at the exodus, when Pharaoh and Egypt refused to repent, so here the earth-dwellers will refuse to repent (9:20, 21). But as with Pharaoh and Egypt, God is crushing the strong by worldly standards in order to deliver the weak by worldly standards.

John tells us what he saw next in 8:6, 7: "Now the seven angels who had the seven trumpets prepared to blow them. The first angel blew his trumpet, and there followed hail and fire, mixed with blood, and these were thrown upon the earth. And a third of the earth was burned up, and a third of the trees were burned up, and all green grass was burned up." Since the description here of the result of this plague focuses on what was burned up, with no mention of things being crushed by hailstones, it might be that these hailstones were fireballs of hail.[1] With the fire *and* ice in this description, the addition of blood to the mix would be absolutely horrifying and revolting. Imagine this devastation—one third of the earth burned, one third of the trees burned, and all the green grass burned. Picture in your mind the charred earth, the ash and smoke, and blood everywhere.

Revelation 8:7 says "all green grass was burned up," and 9:4 says that the locusts that come with the fifth trumpet "were told not to harm the grass of the earth." I doubt that we are intended to harmonize these passages by suggesting there was enough time between the trumpets for grass to grow back, and I also doubt that John would have viewed these two texts as contradictory if you had pointed out to him that he just said in 8:7 that all the grass was burned up, and now he's saying in 9:4 that there is grass the locusts aren't supposed to harm. I think this is probably an indication that we are not meant to read these scenes as being necessarily sequential, nor do we have in these descriptions a strictly linear, logical development. In these chapters John is not so much giving us a historical narrative of the future as he is giving us a collage of apocalyptic images.

The results of this first trumpet are very similar to the seventh plague that God brought against Egypt. We read in Exodus 9:23–25:

> Then Moses stretched out his staff toward heaven, and the LORD sent thunder and hail, and fire ran down to the earth. And the LORD rained hail upon the land of Egypt. There was hail and fire flashing continually in the midst of the hail, such as had never been in all the land of Egypt since it became a nation. The hail struck down everything that was in the field in all the land of Egypt, both man and beast. And the hail struck down every plant of the field and broke every tree of the field.

The first trumpet affects the dry land, and the second trumpet affects the sea, as we read in 8:8, 9: "The second angel blew his trumpet, and something like a great mountain, burning with fire, was thrown into the sea, and a third of the sea became blood. A third of the living creatures in the sea died, and a third of the ships were destroyed." This is like nothing anyone has ever seen. Picture in your mind a mountain; now in your mind's eye set that mountain on fire; then imagine some massive angelic being, so large that he can take the mountain in his hands and throw it into the ocean. There are tsunamis in every direction. Steam and smoke arise from the fire and water. A mountain thrown into the sea would result in a huge displacement of water. A burning mountain would definitely affect water temperature, and it is easy to imagine sea life dying and ships being destroyed. In addition, one third of the sea waters become blood. Stench. Filth. Disease. Nasty!

The results of this second trumpet blast are like the first plague on Egypt, where the Nile was turned to blood and all the fish died (Exodus 7:20, 21).

In these judgments God is making war on creation. This isn't a mere hailstorm or a little hurricane that affects a single coast. One third of *the world* is destroyed as a result of these judgments.

How serious do you think God is about his glory? Does God's glory matter this much to you? Do you think it is a serious crime that all the humans whom God made to know him and glorify him have used God's gifts to rebel against him? Do you find it heinous and deplorable that humanity has turned the world God made as a theater for his glory into a theater of idolatry and rebellion and sin? Do you think human sin warrants the kind of judgment that we see in this chapter?

If you think that God is overreacting, your view of God is too small. The scope of this devastation is meant to show us how great God is. The fury of this wrath is meant to declare how serious God is about his word.

The dry land was affected by the first trumpet, the sea by the second, and the rivers and springs will be affected by the third, as we read in 8:10, 11: "The third angel blew his trumpet, and a great star fell from heaven, blazing like a torch, and it fell on a third of the rivers and on the springs of water. The name of the star is Wormwood. A third of the waters became wormwood, and many people died from the water, because it had been made bitter." Like the second trumpet, the effects of the third trumpet correspond to that first plague on Egypt, which affected the Nile and its rivers and canals (Exodus 7:19).

Let me invite you to set what happens as a result of this third trumpet blast next to the current economic crisis. As bad as it may be, and as bad as it could get, we have not yet seen one third of the world's rivers turned to wormwood. Stop and think for a moment: every drink of clean water is mercy. We owe God thanks and praise and worship for every sip of clean water we enjoy. Are we as grateful as we should be? Are we as joyful as we should be in light of the mercy we have been and are being shown?

First trumpet—dry land; second—sea; third—rivers and springs; and fourth—sun, moon, and stars, as we see in 8:12: "The fourth angel blew his trumpet, and a third of the sun was struck, and a third of the moon, and a third of the stars, so that a third of their light might be darkened, and a third of the day might be kept from shining, and likewise a third of the night." Notice again the divine passives in this verse: one third of the sun "*was struck*," that one third of their light "*might be darkened*." God struck the sun, moon, and stars. God made them shine, and he can make them go dark.

The effects of this fourth trumpet match the ninth plague on Egypt, where the Egyptians suffered three days of darkness while the Israelites had light (Exodus 10:21–29).

If you're a non-Christian, you might be accustomed to taking for granted the ground beneath your feet, the water that comes from your faucet or fountain, and the light that shines morning by morning. What will you trust in case of nuclear war? What will you rely on if terrorists strike again? And even if you live out your years in peace and safety, what is going to happen when your body gives out on you or when your mind starts to go? In what are you trusting? If the world goes dark, will you have light?

We Christians want you to know the one who called himself "the light of the world" (John 8:12). We want you to understand that the reason God will judge the world the way chapter 8 says he will is because he made humans in his image. God then gave every good thing to humanity, and all we humans did was rebel against God and use the good gifts he gave us for evil. We hardly bother to think about God, much less thank him for all we have. So we deserve God's judgment. We have offended God at a deeply personal level, and he is righteous to condemn us. But God makes a way to show mercy to rebels by sending Jesus to redeem them. Jesus redeems us by living the righteous life we should have lived and then dying the death that we deserve to die. Jesus willingly went to the cross to pay the penalty for our sin. This means that everyone who trusts in Jesus can be justly forgiven by God. Let me invite you to trust in Jesus right now. If you do, you will have your biggest need met—your need to be reconciled to God. The only way to have that need met is to trust in Jesus. If you trust in Jesus, no matter how dark this world becomes, you will know the light of the world.

To this point in chapter 8, the first four trumpets have been blown, affecting land, sea, rivers and springs, and the lights of the heavens. It is interesting to observe that the blowing of the trumpets in chapters 8, 9 is matched by the outpouring of the bowls in chapter 16.

- The first trumpet affects the land, and the first bowl is poured out on the land.
- The second trumpet affects the sea, and the second bowl is poured out on the sea.
- The third trumpet affects the rivers and springs of water, and the third bowl is poured out on the rivers and springs of water.
- The fourth trumpet affects sun, moon, and stars, and the fourth bowl is poured out on the sun.

There are significant parallels between chapters 8, 9 and chapters 15, 16, and they are not limited to the actual trumpets and bowls. In chapter 7 the saints are sealed, and the number 144,000 seems to be a symbolic representation of the whole people of God. Then the trumpets follow in chapters 8, 9. This is paralleled by John's vision of the redemption of the 144,000 in chapter 14, followed by the outpouring of the bowls in chapters 15, 16. And as I noted earlier, the pause in the action at the beginning of chapter 8 (vv. 1–5), where John sees into the heavenly temple, is matched by the pause in the action in chapter 15, where John sees into the heavenly temple.

So chapters 7—9 seem to be paralleled by chapters 14—16, and then there are also parallels between the depiction of John as the true prophet in chapter 10 and the third beast as the false prophet in 13:11–18. Within that there are parallels between the opposition to the people of God in 11:1–14 and the opposition to the people of God in 12:1—13:10. In the middle of all these parallels is the blast of the seventh trumpet, when it is announced that the kingdom of the world has become the kingdom of our Lord and of his Christ in 11:15–19. So all this material forms a chiasm:[2]

Table 18.1: The Chiastic Structure of Revelation 7—14

7:1–9:21, The Sealing of the Saints and the Seven Trumpets

    10:1–11, The Angel and John (a True Prophet)

        11:1–14, The Church: Two Witnesses Prophesy for 1,260 Days, Then Opposition from the Beast

            11:15–19, the Seventh Trumpet: "The kingdom of the world has become the kingdom of our Lord and of his Christ, and he shall reign forever and ever." Worship!

        12:1–13:10, The Church: The Woman Nourished for 1,260 Days, Then Opposition from the Dragon and the Second Beast

    13:11–18, The Deceiving Beast (False Prophet)

14:1–19:10, The Redemption of the Saints and the Bowls of Wrath

The trumpet blasts in chapter 8 depict God hallowing his name in response to the prayers of his people as the holiness of God is visited upon the natural elements of the created world. God answers the prayers of his people by hallowing his name and judging the world.

Revelation 8:13: Woe to the Earth-Dwellers

The opening of the first four seals in chapter 6 resulted in things that took place on earth, and then at the opening of the last three seals John saw things taking place in Heaven. Similarly with the trumpets, after the first four trumpet blasts John sees the earth and the elements of the natural world affected. In 8:13 we get a pronouncement of woe before the last three trumpet blasts, at which time John will see spiritual realities that result in the judgment and salvation of people. So there is a pattern in the seven seals and trumpets—the first four affect the earth, then the last three depict heavenly and spiritual scenes.

We read in 8:13, "Then I looked, and I heard an eagle crying with a loud voice as it flew directly overhead, 'Woe, woe, woe to those who dwell on the earth, at the blasts of the other trumpets that the three angels are about to blow!'" We saw a living creature like an eagle at the throne of God in 4:7; so this eagle is probably meant to be another connection between these judgments and God's own personal indignation against sin. These judgments are not the outworking of impersonal forces. They come from God himself. The angel pronounces one woe for each of the three trumpets, and notice that the woes are directed at "those who dwell on the earth," the earth-dwellers. These are people who live for this world. These are people who are not concerned with God and his purposes. God will judge them for their refusal to honor him as God and give thanks to him.

If you're a non-Christian, these woes are directed at you. But don't think that's unkind of God, and don't think that I'm not being nice to you to tell you this. This is actually an expression of God's mercy to you, because God is giving you a chance to repent of your sins, trust in Christ, and be saved from the woes that are coming upon you. If you refuse to repent, woes await you. This is certain, on the basis of the very word of God. Let me plead with you, for your own good, repent of your sin and trust in Christ!

If you're a Christian, let me invite you to consider a scenario: the prophet Ezekiel was told that he had been appointed as a watchman to the house of Israel, and it was explained to him that if he warned the wicked to repent and they refused to repent, the wicked would die for their own iniquity. But Ezekiel was also told that if he did not warn the wicked, they would pay for their own sin, but "his blood I will require at your hand" (Ezekiel 3:16–21). Christian, is there going to be blood on your hands? Are you warning the wicked? We shouldn't only warn them because we don't want to be responsible for them, but the Lord did give that reason to Ezekiel in order to motivate him to warn the wicked. It's never pleasant to tell people that they need to repent, that the wrath of God is hovering over them, but if we don't tell them, God will hold us responsible.

Let's pray that God would cause us to love people enough to tell them the truth. Let's pray that God would make us faithful to proclaim the gospel as Jesus charged us to do.

The trumpet blasts in chapter 8 depict God hallowing his name in response to the prayers of his people as the holiness of God is visited upon the natural elements of the created world. God answers the prayers of his people by hallowing his name and judging the world.

Conclusion

God answers prayer. He really does. D. A. Carson writes of his father:

> Dad's practice in private prayer was to kneel before the big chair that he used and pray loudly enough to vocalize, so as to keep his mind from wandering. Outside the door we could hear him praying, even if we could not hear what he was saying. I can remember countless days when he prayed for forty-five minutes or more; strange to tell, at this juncture I cannot recall days when he didn't. Jim [D. A. Carson's brother] recalls barging in on Dad's study unannounced, finding him on his knees praying, and quietly backing out. [Jim wrote] "But the image has always remained with me, especially during my later, rebellious teen years. While walking away from God, I could not get away from the image of my father on his knees, praying for me. It is one of the things that eventually brought me back."[3]

God will answer the prayers of his people. Let's be sure that we pray as Jesus taught us to pray, so that our prayers will be among those that God answers.

The awesome displays of God's wrath in chapter 8 show how seriously God takes the glory that is due him. Let's pray that this chapter will make us hate sin, which is judged by these devastations, and let's pray that God would use us to call people to repentance. Then let's get to work doing that.

If you're not a believer, repent, believe, and be saved. "Everyone who calls on the name of the Lord will be saved" (Romans 10:13), and Revelation 8 is a glimpse of the wrath from which those who call on the name of the Lord will be saved.

The trumpet blasts in chapter 8 depict God hallowing his name in response to the prayers of his people as the holiness of God is visited upon the natural elements of the created world. God answers the prayers of his people by hallowing his name and judging the world.

God does not reject the prayer in 6:10, "how long?" He answers it in 6:11, "a little longer." Let's trust him until the time comes.

19

The Unimagined Horrors
of God's Judgment

REVELATION 9:1–21

PERHAPS THE MOST TERRIFYING ENEMIES IN J. R. R. Tolkien's The Lord of
the Rings are "the Fell Riders out of Minas Morgul," "the Black Riders," the
Nazgûl—former kings who were once noble, but are now like living dead,
riding huge dragon-like beasts. Consider this description of these frightful
enemies in *The Return of the King*:

> The Nazgûl came again, and as their Dark Lord now grew and put forth his
> strength, so their voices, which uttered only his will and his malice, were
> filled with evil and horror. Ever they circled the City, like vultures that
> expect their fill of doomed men's flesh. Out of sight and shot they flew, and
> yet were ever present, and their deadly voices rent the air. More unbearable
> they became, not less, at each new cry. At length even the stout-hearted
> would fling themselves to the ground as the hidden menace passed over
> them, or they would stand, letting their weapons fall from nerveless hands
> while into their minds a blackness came, and they thought no more of war,
> but only of hiding and of crawling, and of death.[1]

We will see creatures much like Tolkien's Nazgûl in chapter 9. Why is
this chapter in the Bible?

Need

We have a great need to see evil for what it is. The sins that tempt us are not
pleasant things that we could enjoy if it weren't for those pesky, unnecessary,
burdensome commands that God has given to us. The sins that tempt us are

traps set by a Dark Lord far more evil than Sauron, and his lieutenants are far more frightful than the Nazgûl. We need to feel the evil of sin, so that we will be convinced that God's commands are *good*. God's commands keep us from the traps and snares of the ancient dragon. We need to feel this, and we also need to be convinced that God will indeed judge sin. We need to be convinced that God alone can save. And we need to be convinced that idolatry and sin will not profit us. God gives us chapter 9 to meet these needs.

Main Point

God's judgment is painful and terrifying, and only those whom God seals will be protected from his judgment.

Preview

9:1–12	The Fifth Trumpet: The First Woe
9:13–19	The Sixth Trumpet: The Second Woe
9:20, 21	Unrepentant Sinners

Context

Jesus appears to John in glory in Revelation 1, then dictates the letters to the seven churches in chapters 2, 3. Next Jesus summons John into the heavenly throne room, and John describes the worship of God and Christ that he saw there in chapters 4, 5. Jesus told John he was going to show him "what must soon take place" (4:1), and that begins in chapter 6. Jesus had taken the scroll from the Father in chapter 5, and in chapter 6 he begins to open its seals. Before the seventh seal is opened, chapter 7 shows the people of God being sealed so they won't be harmed by God's judgments. Chapter 8 begins with the opening of the seventh seal; then the angel offers up the prayers of God's people, in response to which the angels begin to blow their trumpets. The first six trumpets are blown in chapters 8, 9—the first four in chapter 8, then the fifth and sixth in chapter 9.

We saw in chapter 8 that the first four trumpet blasts are accompanied by judgments that affect the created world. The two trumpet blasts depicted in chapter 9 will result in damage and death to human beings. The seventh trumpet blast comes in 11:15–19. This pattern with the trumpets—four affect the elements of creation, two affect humanity, then the last one comes after an interlude—matches the pattern seen in the seals, where the opening of the first four seals results in consequences on earth, then the next two result in heavenly consequences, with the last one coming after an interlude.

We also saw in chapter 8 that the judgments that follow the first four trumpet blasts match the plagues on Egypt, and the same will be true of the judgments that accompany the two trumpets blown in chapter 9. Just as at the exodus God heard the cries of his people (Exodus 2:23–25) and delivered them by judging their enemies, so here in Revelation God has heard the prayers of his people (8:3, 4), and he is delivering them through the judgment of their enemies. Just as at the exodus God led his people out by a pillar of cloud and fire, so also after the trumpets, which bring judgments like the plagues, in 10:1 John sees an angel come down who is "wrapped in a cloud" with "legs like pillars of fire." Just as at the exodus, when the people journeyed through the wilderness to the promised land, so in Revelation the people of God are journeying toward the new heavens and the new earth.

Table 19.1: Revelation's Trumpets and the Exodus Plagues

Trumpet in Revelation	Plague in Exodus
1. 8:7: hail, fire	7th: 9:23–25: hail, fire
2. 8:8, 9: sea turns to blood, one third of living creatures die	1st: 7:20, 21: Nile turns to blood, fish die
3. 8:10, 11: rivers and springs made bitter	1st: 7:19: rivers, canals filled with blood
4. 8:12: one third of sun, moon, and stars darkened	9th: 10:21–29: three days of darkness
5. 9:1–11: darkness, locusts like scorpions	9th and 8th: 10:21–29: darkness; 10:12–20: locusts
6. 9:12–19: angels released, mounted troops, fire, smoke, and sulfur kill one third of humanity	10th?: 11:1–10; 12:29–32: death angel?
10:1: angel wrapped in a cloud with legs like pillars of fire	Israel led out of Egypt by the pillar of cloud by day and fire by night

Table 19.2: Revelation's Bowls and the Exodus Plagues

Bowl in Revelation	Plague in Exodus
1. 16:2: sores	6th: 9:10: boils/sores
2. 16:3: sea to blood, all living things die	1st: 7:17–21: Nile turns to blood, fish die
3. 16:4–7: rivers and springs turn to blood	1st: 7:17–21: rivers and springs turn to blood
4. 16:8, 9: sun burns people	
5. 16:10, 11: darkness	9th: 10:21–29: darkness
6. 16:12–15: Euphrates dries up, and the demons prepare for battle	10th?: 11:1–10; 12:29–32: death angel?; 14: Red sea parted
7. 16:17–21: earthquake, hail	7th: 9:13–35: hail

Revelation 8:13 ended with the announcement of three woes to come. We see the first of those three woes in 9:1–12, where John describes what happens when the fifth trumpet is blown.

Revelation 9:1–12: The Fifth Trumpet: The First Woe

In 9:1 John writes, "And the fifth angel blew his trumpet, and I saw a star fallen from heaven to earth, and he was given the key to the shaft of the bottomless pit." Look back at 8:10, where after the third angel blew his trumpet "a great star fell from heaven." That star in 8:10, 11 fell on the rivers and springs and made the waters bitter. This star in 9:1 "was given"—note the divine passive—"the key to the shaft of the bottomless pit." This is very similar to what we see in 20:1 where an angel comes down from heaven "holding in his hand the key to the bottomless pit." Satan will be locked up in the pit in 20:1–3, which contrasts with what we see in 9:2: "He opened the shaft of the bottomless pit, and from the shaft rose smoke like the smoke of a great furnace, and the sun and the air were darkened with the smoke from the shaft." We'll see more about this smoke in verse 3, but here we can observe that the darkness caused by this smoke again matches the ninth plague on Egypt—darkness (Exodus 10:21–29). We should remember what Jesus said of himself back in 1:18: "I have the keys of Death and Hades." Jesus is in control, even of the opening of "the shaft of the bottomless pit" (9:1; cf. 3:7).

John tells us in 9:3, "Then from the smoke came locusts on the earth, and they were given power like the power of scorpions of the earth." So locusts come from the smoke, like the eighth plague on Egypt (Exodus 10:12–20). Notice again the divine passive: the locusts "were given power," and then that power isn't said to be the power of scorpions but is likened to the power of scorpions. So these are biting, poisonous locusts.

Revelation 9:4 ("They were told not to harm the grass of the earth or any green plant or any tree, but only those people who do not have the seal of God on their foreheads") is reminiscent of 7:3: "Do not harm the earth or the sea or the trees, until we have sealed the servants of God on their foreheads." Both texts mention not harming the earth and trees, and both texts mention the seal of God on the forehead. Revelation 7:3 introduces the sealing of the saints, and 9:4 states that those who don't have that seal will be harmed by these scorpion-like locusts, which are so numerous that the clouds of them darken the sun (9:2).

Note that these locusts "were told" what they could and could not harm. That's another divine passive, and it tells us that God is in absolute control of what or who gets judged and how severe the judgment will be. The agents of God's judgment will not go farther than God allows and intends for them to go. Furthermore, the only people protected from these scorpion-like locusts are those with the seal of God on their foreheads, which itself tells us that people cannot by their own power avoid these locusts—only God can shield you from this pain.

Back in 7:3 it was the servants of God who were sealed, and we see in the letters to the seven churches in chapters 2, 3 the kinds of things the servants of God suffer. But no matter how bad it gets, when the scorpion-like locusts show up, you want to be among the servants of God! You want to have the seal of God on your forehead. Satan will try to counterfeit this seal with the number of the beast, and he'll try to make life miserable for those who don't have the mark of the beast (13:16–18). Revelation shows us that we definitely want the seal of God on our forehead, not the mark of the beast. God makes the servants of Satan miserable in chapter 9, and Satan makes the servants of God miserable in chapters 2, 3. God will comfort and sustain his servants, but Satan will only abuse and abhor his. You don't want to serve Satan.

Do you have the seal of God on your forehead? Of course, it's not a literal seal, but what is it? God's servants are the ones sealed in 7:3, and in 1:5, 6 God's servants are those who have been freed from their sins by the blood of Jesus and made into a kingdom and priests. Have you been freed from your sins by the blood of Jesus? Do you believe that since he shed his blood on the cross, you are free from the penalty due your sin? Do you believe that since he shed his blood on the cross, you are free from the dominion of sin? Have you been transferred from the domain of darkness into the kingdom of Jesus? Is Jesus your King? And are you serving him as a priest? A priest worships God and mediates the knowledge of God to others—is that what your life looks like?

When the judgments of God begin to fall, you want to have the seal of God on your forehead. If you fear that you don't have that seal, confess all your sins to God right now, turn from them, and believe in Jesus. Pray for God to show you mercy. Ask him to give you his Holy Spirit. Jesus promised in Luke 11:13 that the Father would give the Holy Spirit to those who ask him.

If you refuse to do so, terrors like the ones we see in 9:5, 6 await you: "They were allowed to torment them for five months, but not to kill them, and their torment was like the torment of a scorpion when it stings someone. And in those days people will seek death and will not find it. They will long to die, but death will flee from them." God's sovereignty over this judgment is stressed (1) in the divine passive, "they were allowed," (2) in the specified duration of the torment, "for five months," (3) in the limit as to the extent of the torment—they were not allowed to kill their victims, and (4) in the fact that the victims want to die and cannot. Imagine a pain so bad you want to die, and imagine the futility and frustration of not being able to find death. This text clearly says that human beings are not in control of their lives—God is in control. How are you responding to God's control over your life?

The horrors of 9:1–6 are elaborated upon in 9:7–12, and this section functions in two ways. First, in 9:7–12 we see the way Satan is imitating and perverting what God does, and second, we have the awful pains described in verses 1–6 made worse by the psychological terrors brought about by the physical description of these locusts in verses 7–12. As if the physical pain wasn't bad enough, emotional duress is added by the frightful description of these scorpion-like locusts. The Nazgûl have nothing on these terrors of chapter 9.

Revelation 9:7, 8 says, "In appearance the locusts were like horses prepared for battle: on their heads were what looked like crowns of gold; their faces were like human faces, their hair like women's hair, and their teeth like lions' teeth." Horses prepared for battle are not average, tame horses. Battle steeds were bred large. Their teeth and hooves were sharpened, and they were trained to kick and bite. These are fearsome horses, and the crowns on their heads point to their authority. These awful scorpion-like locusts who look like battle stallions seem to be perverse imitations of the living creatures around God's throne—one like a lion, one like an ox, one like a man, and one like an eagle (4:6, 7). Rather than reflecting the majesty and glory of God, however, these locusts are a grotesque blend. These are terrifying, revolting beasts.

Whereas the living creatures at God's throne reflect the character of God, these scorpion-like locusts reflect the character of Satan. The best that Satan can do is twist something that God created good. That's the way that Satan tempts us, too. Everything that tempts us is a twisted, perverse, satanic corruption of something that God meant for us to enjoy. We must fight the lure of temptation by trusting that God means for us to enjoy the real thing in his way and at his time.

It gets worse in 9:9–11: "they had breastplates like breastplates of iron, and the noise of their wings was like the noise of many chariots with horses rushing into battle. They have tails and stings like scorpions, and their power to hurt people for five months is in their tails. They have as king over them the angel of the bottomless pit. His name in Hebrew is Abaddon, and in Greek he is called Apollyon." The iron breastplates mean that these locusts are themselves well protected. The noise of their wings being like chariots increases the dread horror of those who know these beasts are coming and know they can't overcome or escape them. Then there is the unpleasant reminder of their five-month sting. These are frightful legions (perhaps they are demons), and their king is called Abaddon and Apollyon—both names have to do with destruction. This king appears to be either Satan or one of his chief lieutenants.[2]

Verse 12 informs us, "The first woe has passed; behold, two woes are still to come."

This passage teaches us that God's judgment is painful and terrifying and that only those whom God seals will be protected from his judgment. You cannot keep the judgment of God from falling. You cannot protect yourself from it. You are not stronger than the scorpion sting of those locusts, and they are more scary to you than you are to them.

Your only hope is to repent of your sin and trust in Christ.

Revelation 9:13–19: The Sixth Trumpet: The Second Woe

The second woe begins in 9:13:"Then the sixth angel blew his trumpet, and I heard a voice from the four horns of the golden altar before God." That this voice comes from the "altar before God" again ties these judgments to God himself. This continues in 9:14, where the voice is "saying to the sixth angel who had the trumpet, 'Release the four angels who are bound at the great river Euphrates.'" Revelation 9:15 exposits this for us: "So the four angels, who had been prepared for the hour, the day, the month, and the year, were released to kill a third of mankind." These angels being prepared for precisely this moment—stressed by the four references to time ("hour," "day," "month," and "year")—points to God's meticulous sovereignty. God has left nothing to chance. These events are depicted as taking place exactly when God has appointed them to take place.

Brothers and sisters in Christ, let me encourage you to rest in the comforting truth of God's sovereign plan at this time of financial uncertainty. God's plan extends to what the stock market does to your retirement plans and to what it might do to your employment status. Let's respond to these things in ways that reflect our knowledge that God is sovereign. Let's live like we believe that God has a plan that will be accomplished. Let's be confident: his seal is on our foreheads; so we are protected from his wrath. He is our shepherd, and he will care for us better than money ever could.

The release of the appointed angels in 9:13–15 opens the way for the massive cavalry we see in 9:16–19. There is a movement in Deuteronomy 28 from a locust plague (v. 38) to a human army (vv. 49–68). The same thing seems to happen in Joel, where the locusts come in Joel 1, and then Joel 2 describes an army. Those judgments are typological of what happens here in Revelation 9, where we saw the locusts in 9:3–11, and now we seem to see an army in 9:13–19. The host is numbered in 9:16: "The number of the mounted troops was twice ten thousand times ten thousand; I heard their number." This is twenty thousand ten thousands, which adds up to 200,000,000. The horses and riders are described in 9:17: "And this is how I saw the horses in my vision and those who rode them: they wore breastplates the color of fire and of sapphire and of sulfur, and the heads of the horses were like lions' heads, and fire and smoke and sulfur came out of their mouths." The riders have breastplates that have the orange of fire, the deep blue of a sapphire, and the pale yellow of sulfur. We again see the perverse combination of animal features in these horses. Having lion heads and with fire and smoke and sulfur coming from their mouths, we know these are no ordinary horses. Verse 18 tells us, "By these three plagues a third of mankind was killed, by the fire and smoke and sulfur coming out of their mouths." One third of humanity is killed. One in every three is dead. Those probably aren't all adults, which would mean there are an awful lot of corpses for the remaining adults to bury. This is a death toll like nothing ever seen in human history.

But these horses don't just kill, they also wound, as we see in 9:19: "For the power of the horses is in their mouths and in their tails, for their tails are like serpents with heads, and by means of them they wound." That is one horrifying horse—with a lion head and a serpent with a biting head for a tail. You don't want to face the judgment of God.

God's judgment is painful and terrifying, and only those whom God seals will be protected from that judgment.

Revelation 9:20, 21: Unrepentant Sinners

At various points in Revelation John will tell us about how people respond to God's judgment (cf. 11:13; 16:9, 11, 21). Here in 9:20, 21 he tells us that humanity continues in unrepentant sin in response to these six trumpet blasts: "The rest of mankind, who were not killed by these plagues, did not repent of the works of their hands nor give up worshiping demons and idols of gold and silver and bronze and stone and wood, which cannot see or hear or walk, nor did they repent of their murders or their sorceries or their sexual immorality or their thefts." These people do not repent, even though they are breaking the two great commandments; their sins match the two divisions of the Ten Commandments. Rather than worship God, they worship idols. Rather than love their neighbors, they murder, manipulate through magic, commit adultery, and steal.

Their gods have not delivered them from the judgments of the one true and living God, and their deeds have brought God's awful wrath down upon their heads. Yet they cling to their addictions and their superstitions. They refuse to turn from the very things that ruin their lives.

What keeps people from Heaven? The worship of gods that cannot save, gods that cannot protect, gods that cannot satisfy, gods that cannot even see, hear, or walk.

What keeps people from Heaven? Their love of meanness to other people—murder, magical manipulation, immorality, theft.

God's commands do not deny us good things. God's commands protect us from evil.

God is not holding something good from us by telling us not to murder; he wants us to love other people, not kill them.

God is not keeping power from us by forbidding sorcery; he wants us to trust him as God.

God is not withholding pleasure from us by telling us not to commit adultery, not to be sexually immoral; he wants us to enjoy pure, undefiled sexual fulfillment within the context of the covenant union of one man and one woman joined as one flesh.

God is not relegating us to poverty by telling us not to steal; he wants us to have clear consciences, to be content with what he has given to us, and to know that he can and will meet all our needs.

God is not withholding good from us; he is calling us to trust him.

There is no greater fulfillment than that of knowing God. There is no greater joy than the joy of obeying God.

People who refuse to worship God and obey him choose death rather than life, darkness rather than light, bondage rather than freedom, guilt rather than peace, shame rather than honor, and Hell rather than Heaven.

As Christians, let's not envy the wretched choices that unbelievers make. Let's not desire their sins. Let's not gaze on their idols. We can see from movies and television that our culture loves murder and immorality. Modern culture does not cultivate the honor of God as God or the giving of thanks to him. Secular culture advocates idols of every kind and promotes murder, superstition, adultery, and theft. Those things are worthless and self-destructive and unsatisfying and corrupting and defiling.

Let's love God, and let's love our neighbors.

Our problem is that we are born dead in trespasses and sins (Ephesians 2:1–3). We need God's kindness to lead us to repentance (Romans 2:4). We need him to "give repentance" to us (Acts 5:31). We need him to grant us "repentance that leads to life" (Acts 11:18). The surest sign that you are a Christian is repentance from sin. If you find yourself unrepentant, the only hope you have is to cry out to God to grant you repentance, to show you his kindness by leading you to repent. Won't you repent of your sins and turn to Jesus?

God's judgment is painful and terrifying, and only those whom God seals will be protected from his judgment.

Conclusion

Let me ask you, Christian, what will you do with this chapter of the Bible? Let me urge you to use it in your fight against sin. Let me call on you to connect the vicious beasts of Hell that we see in this chapter to the seemingly pleasing things that tempt you away from obedience to God and his word.

God's judgment is painful and terrifying, and only those whom God seals will be protected from his judgment. We who are sealed can benefit from the horrors of this chapter—the terrifying scorpion-like locusts and the awful battle steeds with lion heads and serpent tails—because they show us evil for what it is.

Temptation to engage in idolatry, murder, sorcery, immorality, and theft does not really offer us a secret path into the garden of Eden. Rather, temptation lays a trap for us; it sets us up to be attacked by the locusts that sting like scorpions and the horses who kill with fire, smoke, and sulfur from their mouths.

By the grace of God, let's use the true picture of the world given to us in chapter 9 in our fight against sin. Perhaps you feel that your fight against sin is futile. Let me encourage you to trust God and his word, and let me encourage you with the valor of a woman and the courage of a hobbit. Tolkien describes the way these unlikely warriors defeated the Lord of the Nazgûl in *The Return of the King*.

King Théoden has been crushed beneath his fallen horse, and the Nazgûl descends to defile the dead. Only one warrior has remained to defend the fallen king. This warrior was named Dernhelm, but it was really the maiden Éowyn in disguise. The presence of the Nazgûl startled the horse that Éowyn and the hobbit Merry rode, and they were thrown from their crazed mount.

> Merry crawled on all fours like a dazed beast, and such a horror was on him that he was blind and sick.
> "King's man! King's man" his heart cried within him. "You must stay by him. . . ." But his will made no answer, and his body shook. He dared not open his eyes or look up.

Éowyn disguised as Dernhelm then commanded the Nazgûl, "Leave the dead in peace!"

> A cold voice answered: "Come not between the Nazgûl and his prey! Or he will not slay thee in thy turn. He will bear thee away to the houses of lamentation, beyond all darkness, where thy flesh shall be devoured, and thy shriveled mind be left naked to the Lidless Eye."
> A sword rang as it was drawn. "Do what you will; but I will hinder it, if I may."

"Hinder me? Thou fool. No living man may hinder me!"

Then Merry heard of all sounds in that hour the strangest. It seemed that Dernhelm laughed, and the clear voice was like the ring of steel. "But no living man am I! You look upon a woman. Éowyn I am, Éomund's daughter. You stand between me and my lord and kin. Begone, if you be not deathless! For living or dark undead, I will smite you, if you touch him."

The Black Rider rises to kill Éowyn.

But suddenly he too stumbled forward with a cry of bitter pain, and his stroke went wide, driving into the ground. Merry's sword had stabbed him from behind. . . .

"Éowyn! Éowyn!" cried Merry. Then tottering, struggling up, with her last strength she drove her sword between the crown and mantle, as the great shoulders bowed before her. The sword broke sparkling into many shards. The crown rolled away with a clang. . . . and a cry went up into the shuddering air, and faded to a shrill wailing, passing with the wind, a voice bodiless and thin that died, and was swallowed up, and was never heard again in that age of this world.

Stand, brothers and sisters, against the onslaught of evil. Stand and fight against temptation. The book of Revelation is pulling back the mask of beauty that evil wears, and underneath that mask is exposed the perverse and destructive reality of what tempts us. Stand and fight for your life.

20

Eat This Scroll (and Prophesy the History of the Future)

REVELATION 10:1–11

MY PARENTS HAD COME TO VISIT MY SISTER AND ME. We were working at Kanakuk, a Christian sports camp in Missouri. But that night the softball game I was playing in wasn't over when my parents and sister were ready to go. I told them to go on, and they did. These were the days before cell phones. I knew my parents would be staying at a resort called Holiday Island, but that was all I knew. After the game, on the drive to Holiday Island, I began to wonder how in the world I would find my family. I got to Holiday Island and pulled into what looked like an office. Thankfully, someone came to the door, but when I asked if they could help me find which time-share my parents were in, I was told there were thousands of time-shares at Holiday Island. To make matters worse, there was no central system that logged all the units. He couldn't help me.

Suddenly I realized that I was alone in the world, with no idea where to go, no clue as to where to start, and no way to contact my family. So I despondently got in my car and started driving farther into Holiday Island. Then I saw a familiar sight: there was my sister's car! And under a windshield wiper was a note—I have it with me to this day. It reads as follows:

Jimbo,
    We are at 15 Ironwood Dr. on the Island. Go to the Island—turn right on Apaloosa Dr.—2nd street is Ironwood Dr. Go to the end of the street. 15 Ironwood Drive.
    Love, Dad
PS: It is 7:20 pm—we will be back here at 8:20.

It was 8:15 when I found that note. As I began to follow the directions, I soon crossed paths with my dad coming to get me, just as he said he would.

Need

Apart from divine revelation, can we really know anything in this world? Apart from the Bible, do we have any hope of understanding who we are, how we got here, what has gone wrong, what God has done to address the problem, and what will become of the world?

We need the Bible like I needed that note from my father that night. If God does not communicate with us, we are lost, adrift, uncertain, hopeless, and without purpose, significance, or any sense of meaning.

Main Point

Almighty God sent his angel to his servant John to show his servants the things that must soon take place (1:1).

Preview

10:1–3   The Angel of Salvation through Judgment
10:4–7   No More Delay at the Seventh Trumpet
10:8–11   John Eats the Scroll

Context

Jesus appeared to John in chapter 1, dictated the letters to the seven churches in chapters 2, 3, invited John into Heaven to see the worship of God in chapter 4, took the scroll from the Father in chapter 5, and opened its seals in chapters 6—8. In chapters 8, 9 God gave seven trumpets to seven angels, and the first six angels blew their trumpets. Just as there was a break between the sixth and seventh seal in chapter 7, so now there is a break between the sixth and seventh trumpet here in Revelation 10:1–11:14. Before the seventh trumpet is blown at the end of chapter 11, here in chapter 10 a strong angel is going to bring the scroll Jesus opened to John, and John is going to eat that scroll.

Revelation 10:1–3: The Angel of Salvation through Judgment

As we have moved through chapters 8, 9, we have observed the parallels between these chapters and what took place at the exodus from Egypt. Just as the Lord responded to the prayers of the children of Israel (Exodus 2:23–25), raised up Moses, and judged Egypt through the plagues, by which Israel was delivered (through all this Pharaoh refused to repent), so in Revelation 8,

9 we have seen the Lord respond to the prayers of his people (8:3–5) with the judgments of the six trumpets of his wrath. The wicked who survive the trumpet judgments are like Pharaoh in that they refuse to repent (9:20, 21). Meanwhile God's people are being delivered through these judgments on the world. Just as Israel was led out of Egypt through the wilderness to the promised land by the pillar of cloud by day and fire by night, so now in Revelation an angel who is wrapped in a cloud and has legs like pillars of fire is going to lead God's people. Just as Israel was led to Mount Sinai, where God revealed himself to Israel and gave them his word, so this angel in chapter 10 is going to give God's word to John.

What shapes your identity? Do you get your concept of who you are from your performance at work, from the respect—or lack of respect—with which other people treat you? Are you someone who is really fussy about your image? Are you afflicted with an excessive concern for your style, for your reputation, and for what other people think of you? One of the reasons this exodus pattern is repeated in chapters 8—10 is so that the people of God will have their identities shaped by the fact that God has redeemed them. If you're a believer, do you think of yourself as someone who was a slave until God redeemed you from slavery? If you're a believer in Jesus, that's your identity, and that identity matters more than your image, your style, and your reputation. The defining truth about who you are, about your identity is that you are someone whom God has gone to extravagant lengths to redeem. Think of yourself in the terms and categories the Bible gives to you.

The angel bringing these revelations is described in 10:1: "Then I saw another mighty angel coming down from heaven, wrapped in a cloud, with a rainbow over his head, and his face was like the sun, and his legs like pillars of fire." This angel is "wrapped in a cloud" with "legs like pillars of fire" just like the pillar of cloud and fire that led Israel through the wilderness. So John is telling us that this angel is going to lead the people of God to the new and better promised land, the new heavens and new earth. A similar idea is also communicated by the mention of the "rainbow over his head." We know about rainbows from Genesis 9, where we read that God saved Noah through the judgment of the world, and when Noah got off the ark in land newly brought forth out of the waters, God gave him the rainbow as a sign of his covenant. Those themes of God saving through judgment and giving the redeemed a new heavens and new earth are recalled by this rainbow over the angel's head. What God did for Noah and the children of Israel by saving them through the judging of their enemies, then bringing them into a new land, he is going to do again when he saves us through the judgment of this world and brings us into the new heavens and new earth.

Because of what we see in 10:2, 3, some suggest that this angel might be Christ himself. But this figure is called "another mighty angel" in the first part of 10:1, and the word "another" is there because we saw a "mighty angel" back in 5:2 (the ESV renders it "strong angel" in 5:2, but the Greek phrase is the same in 5:2 and 10:1), and we'll see a third "mighty angel" in 18:21. So I don't think this angel is Jesus because there are other "mighty angels" in Revelation. Another reason not to identify this angel with Jesus is that 1:1 tells us that God made the revelation of Jesus Christ known "by sending his angel to his servant John."

This angel does, however, reflect the glory of Jesus. So just as John says of Jesus in 1:16, "his face was like the sun shining in full strength," so this angel's face in 10:1 "was like the sun." There are other ways in which this angel reflects the glory of Jesus. In 10:2 we see that he is bringing the scroll that Jesus opened to John—the scroll is probably described as "little" because of how big this angel evidently is. We see there in 10:2, "And he set his right foot on the sea, and his left foot on the land." That's a big angel! In the imagery employed in the Bible, when you put your foot on something it means you have authority over what is under your foot. So Psalm 8:6 declares, "You have given him dominion over the works of your hands; you have put all things under his feet"; then verses 7, 8 go on to talk about the animals that inhabit the land and the sea. So this angel puts one foot on the land and one foot on the sea, and that means he represents the one who is Lord of the land and the sea—Jesus.

The angel's representation of Jesus continues in 10:3: he "called out with a loud voice, like a lion roaring." Just as the living creatures around God's throne in chapter 4 embody aspects of God's character, so this angel embodies aspects of the character of Jesus, "the Lion of the tribe of Judah" (5:5). This angel's being "like a lion roaring" also reminds us of several statements in the prophets that indicate that when God arises to save and judge, he roars like a lion.

> Joel 3:16: "The LORD roars from Zion, and utters his voice from Jerusalem, and the heavens and the earth quake."
>
> Amos 1:2: "And he said: 'The LORD roars from Zion and utters his voice from Jerusalem.'"

So it is natural for the "loud voice" of this angel who represents King

Jesus to be "like a lion roaring," and it also follows in 10:3 that "When he called out, the seven thunders sounded."

> Psalm 29:3: "The voice of the LORD is over the waters; the God of glory thunders, the LORD, over many waters."

> Isaiah 29:5, 6: "And in an instant, suddenly, you will be visited by the LORD of hosts with thunder and with earthquake and great noise, with whirlwind and tempest, and the flame of a devouring fire."

So this angel in 10:1–3 is described in terms that explicitly recall God's acts of salvation through judgment, and these verses are also expositing the statement in 1:1 about God sending his angel to his servant John to show his servants what must soon take place. The things that must soon take place are the things written on that scroll that Jesus took from the Father in chapter 5 and opened in chapters 6—8. Now the angel comes down from Heaven as the representative of the Lord Christ to give the scroll to John.

Take heart, believer, for your Lord is King over land and sea. Your Lord will save you through judgments like the flood and the plagues of Egypt, and he will send his angel to lead you through the wilderness in a pillar of cloud and flame. Your Lord has opened the scroll and has given it to an angel who roars like a lion, and thunders roll in response.

If this is how impressive one who reflects God's glory is, how much more impressive must the Lord himself be? Do you want to be encouraged? Look at this angel and multiply his greatness, size, power, and authority by infinity! Behold your God! Behold your Savior!

God has revealed himself. Almighty God has sent his angel to his servant John "to show his servants the things that must soon take place" (1:1).

Revelation 10:4–7: No More Delay at the Seventh Trumpet

Revelation 10:1–3 exposits the phrase in 1:1 about God sending his angel to his servant John to show his servants what would "soon take place," and 10:4–7 exposits the little word "soon." Are you ready for these events that will soon take place?

Johnny Cash's album *American V: A Hundred Highways* was released after his death. The song "I'm Free from the Chain Gang Now" seems to use the idea of being released from prison as a metaphor for dying. The dead man sings:

> I got rid of the shackles that bound me
> And the guards that were always around me
> There were tears on the mail mother wrote me in jail

But I'm free from the chain gang now.

All the years I was known by a number
How I kept my mind is a wonder
But like a bird in a tree I got my liberty
And I'm free from the chain gang now[1]

How do you view your approaching death? Do you view it as a moment of release? If you're a believer in Jesus, you will be freed from bondage to corruption. You will be in the presence of the Lord. You will never again abuse yourself with sin. Believers in Jesus, let us not fear death!

Perhaps you're not a believer in Jesus, though, and if that's the case, let me tell you with all the concern for your soul that I am able to feel, you have everything to fear. Once the events of the end begin, they will take place quickly, and your worst nightmares will not do justice to the wrath of Almighty God. Let me plead with you: save your soul! Repent of your sin and trust in Christ. You are not guaranteed tomorrow. If you don't repent and believe in Jesus, you won't ever be free from the chain gang. You will never be like a bird in a tree who got his liberty. The shackles will only get worse, and the guards will be meaner and more abusive than I dare say. It will be just, and it will be awful, but it will never end. And you will deserve every minute of it for refusing to honor God as God and to give thanks to him, for refusing to repent and trust in Christ. But now, in this moment, God is offering you mercy. Trusting Christ *now* means liberty, freedom, salvation, redemption, adoption, justification, forgiveness, glorification, and the joy of worshiping God forever! If you don't trust Christ, you will regret this missed opportunity every moment of your long eternity in Hell.

We saw the seven thunders respond to the lion-like voice of the angel in 10:3, and we see in 10:4, "And when the seven thunders had sounded, I was about to write, but I heard a voice from heaven saying, 'Seal up what the seven thunders have said, and do not write it down.'" This seems to indicate that just as the opening of the seventh seal gave way to the seven trumpets, the blast of the seventh trumpet might have given way to the roaring of seven thunders of God's judgments.[2] Rather than go forward with the thunder-judgments, however, God seals them up because, as we see in 10:5–7, the seventh trumpet will bring things to completion:

And the angel whom I saw standing on the sea and on the land raised his right hand to heaven and swore by him who lives forever and ever, who created heaven and what is in it, the earth and what is in it, and the sea and what is in it, that there would be no more delay, but that in the days of the trumpet call to be sounded by the seventh angel, the mystery of

God would be fulfilled [finished], just as he announced to his servants
the prophets.

I want to observe four things about these three verses: (1) what the angel
is doing, (2) how God is described, (3) what is going to be completed, and (4)
when it will be completed.

First, we see in 10:5 what the angel is doing. He has one foot on the sea,
one on land, and he raises his hand to Heaven. Note how these three spheres
of the created world are mentioned in verse 6 as encompassing everything that
God made. By standing where he stands and doing what he does, this angel
shows the universal significance of what he gives to John. There is no place
in the world where God's word does not apply.

Second, look at how God is described as the one by whom the angel
swore in 10:6: God is the one "who lives forever and ever." He is eternal.
The other descriptions state that God made everything in Heaven, on earth,
and in the sea, in a way that recalls the second of the Ten Commandments
in Exodus 20:4: "You shall not make for yourself a carved image, or any
likeness of anything that is in heaven above, or that is in the earth beneath,
or that is in the water under the earth." God made everything that is in all
the parts of the world that he made. The angel swears by the only living and
true God, the only self-existing being in the universe, the one who made
everything that is.

Third, look at what is going to be completed in 10:7, ". . . the mystery
of God would be fulfilled, just as he announced to his servants the prophets."
The reference to the prophets here probably encompasses both Old and New
Testament prophets. God's plan for all creation, announced by everyone
from Moses to Malachi, Matthew to John in Revelation is in view here. Paul
describes this in Ephesians 1:9, 10: God "made known to us the mystery of
his will, according to his purpose, which he set forth in Christ as a plan for
the fullness of time, to unite all things in him, things in heaven and things on
earth." The history of the world, recounted and prophesied in the Old and New
Testaments, is what will be completed.

Fourth, look at when the history of the world will be completed in 10:6,
7 as the angel swears by the everlasting and all-creating God: ". . . that
there would be no more delay, but that in the days of the trumpet call to be
sounded by the seventh angel, the mystery of God would be fulfilled, just
as he announced to his servants the prophets." I don't take this to mean that
right now there will be "no more delay," but rather "in the days of the trumpet
call to be sounded by the seventh angel," *then* there will be "no more delay."
As noted above, this seems to be in response to the thunders. Rather than

delay things with seven thunder-judgments, the seventh trumpet will bring all things to completion.

This is our hope: God who created this world will bring to pass in it everything that he has planned to accomplish. The angel has sworn *by God* that everything will be completed "just as he announced to his servants the prophets" (10:7). God has revealed to us what he will do. He will judge, and through that judgment he will save. This is the true story of the world. Your life finds its meaning and significance in the context of this story.

Almighty God has sent his angel to his servant John "to show to his servants the things that must soon take place" (1:1).

Revelation 10:8–11: John Eats the Scroll

Revelation 1:1 announces that God gave this "revelation of Jesus Christ" by "sending his angel to his servant John" so that he could "show to his servants the things that must soon take place." To this point in the book of Revelation, John has recounted the way that Jesus appeared to him in chapter 1, spoke the letters to the seven churches in chapters 2, 3, then invited him into the heavenly throne room to see God being worshiped in chapter 4. Then in chapter 5 Jesus took a scroll from the Father, and in chapters 6—8 he opens the seven seals on that scroll.

We have just seen in 10:1, 2 that an angel descends from Heaven with that scroll. The scroll that Jesus took from the Father, opened, and apparently gave to the angel is now going to be given to John in 10:8: "Then the voice that I had heard from heaven spoke to me again, saying, 'Go, take the scroll that is open in the hand of the angel who is standing on the sea and on the land.'"

The reference to "the voice" John heard "from heaven" speaking "again" has 10:4 in view, where we read that John "heard a voice from heaven saying, 'Seal up what the seven thunders have said.'" Let me point out that John is not presenting these things as things that he made up out of his own mind. He is claiming to have "heard a voice from heaven" (10:4). We can also say that since what the thunders "said" was sealed up and not written down (10:4), we have not been given an *exhaustive* revelation. But the fact that we don't know *everything* doesn't mean we don't know *anything*. God has given us revelation.

The burden of 10:8–11 is to show that John is a true prophet. John's status as a true prophet is established as he has an experience that is very similar to the call of Ezekiel in Ezekiel 2:9–3:4, as can be seen from a comparison of those verses with this passage.

Table 20.1: Ezekiel and John Eat the Scroll

Ezekiel 2:9–3:4	Revelation 10:2; 5:1;10:9, 10
2:9: "And when I looked, behold, a hand was stretched out to me, and behold, a scroll of a book was in it."	10:2: "He had a little scroll open in his hand."
2:10: "And he spread it before me. And it had writing on the front and on the back, and there were written on it words of lamentation and mourning and woe."	5:1: "Then I saw in the right hand of him who was seated on the throne a scroll written within and on the back, sealed with seven seals."
3:1: "And he said to me, 'Son of man, eat whatever you find here. Eat this scroll, and go, speak to the house of Israel.'"	10:9: "So I went to the angel and told him to give me the little scroll. And he said to me, 'Take and eat it; it will make your stomach bitter, but in your mouth it will be sweet as honey.'"
3:2: "So I opened my mouth, and he gave me this scroll to eat."	10:10a: "And I took the little scroll from the hand of the angel and ate it."
3:3: "And he said to me, 'Son of man, feed your belly with this scroll that I give you and fill your stomach with it.' Then I ate it, and it was in my mouth as sweet as honey."	10:10b: "It was sweet as honey in my mouth, but when I had eaten it my stomach was made bitter."
3:4: "And he said to me, 'Son of man, go to the house of Israel and speak with my words to them.'"	10:11: "And I was told, 'You must again prophesy about many peoples and nations and languages and kings.'"

The structure of the whole book of Ezekiel is roughly paralleled by the book of Revelation. In Ezekiel 1, Ezekiel has a vision of God's indescribable glory. Then in Ezekiel 2, 3 Ezekiel is commissioned to go and prophesy to the children of Israel. This is matched in Revelation as John has a vision of the indescribable glory of God and Christ in Revelation 1—5, then the scroll is unsealed in Revelation 6—8, the trumpets sound in Revelation 8, 9, and now John is commissioned to prophesy in Revelation 10. Ezekiel prophesied of God's judgment (Ezekiel 4—32), and then he prophesied of God's future salvation (Ezekiel 33—48). Similarly, John will prophesy of God's judgment (Revelation 11—18), and then he will prophesy of the salvation God will bring in Christ (Revelation 19—22).

The idea behind the eating of the scroll is that the prophet John is taking in the message, ingesting and digesting it, then delivering it to the people of God.[3] This sequence presents John as a true prophet. Whereas Ezekiel was commissioned to speak to Israel, John was commissioned to prophesy about the consummation of world history.

Conclusion

God gave this revelation. Jesus took the scroll from the Father and opened its seals. The angel then took the scroll to John. John obeyed. He ate the scroll. He prophesied. Now the message comes to you. What will you do with it? Let me suggest some ways we should apply the teaching of chapter 10 to our lives.

First, be confident that God is Lord of all and will accomplish his purposes. The angel stands on the sea and the dry land, reminding us that all things are under Jesus' feet. No terrorists, no rogue governments, no dictators, no usurpers of democracy, no kings, no tax collectors, no corrupt government officials, no hypocritical senators are going to stand in the way of God's accomplishing his purposes. If Russia puts a military base on Cuba, if terrorists strike the USA again, if democracy comes to an end in this country, God's purposes will still come to pass. God is Lord of history, and his will is going to be done.

Second, we can know truth because God has revealed himself. We will never have exhaustive knowledge because only God is omniscient, but we can have reliable knowledge because God gave the scroll to Jesus, who opened it, and then the angel gave it to John, who ate it. John ate the scroll and prophesied, and we can trust what God has shown us about "the things that must soon take place" (1:1).

My dad left me a note telling me exactly where my family was and when he was coming to get me. Jesus said to his disciples in John 14:1–3, "Let not your hearts be troubled. Believe in God; believe also in me. In my Father's house are many rooms. If it were not so, would I have told you that I go to prepare a place for you? And if I go and prepare a place for you, I will come again and will take you to myself, that where I am you may be also."

Almighty God has sent his angel to his servant John "to show to his servants the things that must soon take place" (1:1).

21

Bearing Witness 'til Kingdom Come

REVELATION 11:1–19

IN HIS AUTOBIOGRAPHY John Paton writes of the opposition he encountered when he volunteered to go as a missionary to the islands of the New Hebrides:

> Even Dr. Symington, one of my professors in divinity, and the beloved Minister in connection with whose congregation I had wrought so long as a City Missionary . . . repeatedly urged me to remain at home. He argued that ". . . I was leaving certainty for uncertainty—work in which God had made me greatly useful, for work in which I might fail to be useful, and only throw away my life amongst Cannibals."
>
> I replied, that "my mind was finally resolved; that, though I loved my work and my people, yet I felt that I could leave them to the care of Jesus, who would soon provide them a better pastor than I; and that, with regard to my life amongst the Cannibals, as I had only once to die, I was content to leave the time and place and means in the hands of God, who had already marvelously preserved me when visiting cholera patients and the fever-stricken poor; on that score I had positively no further concern, having left it all absolutely to the Lord, whom I sought to serve and honor, whether in life or by death."
>
> . . . Amongst many who sought to deter me, was one dear old Christian gentleman, whose crowning argument always was, "The Cannibals! You will be eaten by Cannibals!"
>
> At last I replied, "Mr. Dickson, you are advanced in years now, and your own prospect is soon to be laid in the grave, there to be eaten by worms; I confess to you, that if I can but live and die serving and honoring the Lord Jesus, it will make no difference to me whether I am eaten by Cannibals or by worms; and in the Great Day my resurrection body will arise as fair as yours in the likeness of our risen Redeemer."[1]

Need

We need to know that God knows us. We need to know that God will empower us. We need to know that God will protect us. We need to know that God has given us a liberating message to proclaim. We need to know that even if we are killed in his service, God is more powerful than even death and will vindicate us. We need to know that the kingdom will come, that God and Christ will reign, that the righteous will be rewarded, and that the wicked will be judged.

Main Point

The main point of chapter 11 is simple, even if you disagree with me about what the temple is that gets measured in 11:1, 2 and who the two witnesses are in 11:3–14. In other words, we can disagree on the meaning of the first two sections of this chapter, but I think we will agree on what the main point of this chapter is. We'll agree on the main point of this chapter because it is simple.

Here it is: God will protect his people against all satanic opposition, and they will proclaim the gospel until the kingdom comes. If everything else in this study is utterly mystifying to you, and if you disagree with what I suggest the symbols in this chapter mean, don't miss this main point: God will protect his people against all satanic opposition, and they will proclaim the gospel until the kingdom comes.

Preview

11:1, 2   Measuring the Temple
11:3–14   The Two Witnesses
    11:3–6   The Three-and-a-Half-Year Ministry of the Two Witnesses
    11:7–14   The Three-and-a-Half-Day Defeat of the Two Witnesses
11:15–19   The Seventh Trumpet: The Kingdom Belongs to God and Christ

Context

John ate the scroll in chapter 10, and it would seem that now he begins to prophesy in response to the contents of that scroll. I think that the literary structure of these chapters is very significant for their interpretation, so this literary structure needs to be developed in some detail.

We begin by asking why the announcement that "the kingdom of the world has become the kingdom of our Lord and of his Christ" comes in 11:15 rather than at the end of the book. Why would John put it right in the middle? The reason it comes in the middle, I think, is that John wants it to be centrally located, with the things on either side of this announcement matching one another. So I think the whole book of Revelation is structured as a chiasm, with the celebration of the kingdom of Christ in 11:15–19 right in the middle of the whole thing.

Right before and right after 11:15–19 we have sections that describe the persecution of the people of God in terms drawn from the Old Testament. Revelation 11:1–14 describes the measuring of the temple and the ministry and martyrdom of the two witnesses. I would suggest that 12:1–13:10 basically retells the same story in different terms.

Before the depiction of the church's being persecuted and preserved in chapter 11, we have the depiction of John, a true prophet, in chapter 10. After the picture of the church's being persecuted and preserved in chapters 12, 13, at the end of chapter 13 we have the depiction of the false prophet in 13:11–18.

We will look more fully at this chiastic structure as we continue through the book, but what we want to think about now is its significance for our interpretation of chapter 11. Revelation 11 is matched by chapter 12, which symbolically depicts the birth of Christ and Satan's opposition to the church. This means, I think, that chapter 11 is also about the church and the way Satan opposes the church.

Revelation 11:1, 2: Measuring the Temple

John writes in 11:1, 2, "Then I was given a measuring rod like a staff, and I was told, 'Rise and measure the temple of God and the altar and those who worship there, but do not measure the court outside the temple; leave that out, for it is given over to the nations, and they will trample the holy city for forty-two months.'" The end of chapter 10 depicted John eating a scroll just as Ezekiel had eaten a scroll (Ezekiel 2:8–3:4), and now the beginning of chapter 11 depicts John measuring the temple just as Ezekiel had watched the temple being measured in Ezekiel 40–48 (cf. also Zechariah 2:1–5). Notice that in 11:1 John says he "was given" a measuring rod, and the one who begins to speak to John in 11:1 is still speaking in 11:3 when he refers to "my two witnesses." These "two witnesses" belong to Jesus; so it seems that Jesus is the one who gave the rod to John and told him to measure the temple.

Many believers think that the temple measured here is a future temple—a literal building—that will be rebuilt in Jerusalem. I am more persuaded by those who argue that this temple is a figurative way to describe the people of God. Notice in 11:1 that "those who worship there" are to be measured. The Bible's theology of the temple is not about a building so much as it is about God being with his people.

The early chapters of Genesis present the Garden of Eden as a temple in which God communes with man.[2] After the expulsion from Eden, the tabernacle and temple are built so that God can dwell among his people, and the tabernacle and temple are thereby meant to recapture the Edenic experience. When Jesus comes, he fulfills and replaces the temple, and as God he once again walks with man. Then Jesus fulfills the sacrificial system through his death on the cross, and he pours out the Spirit on the church. The indwelling of the Spirit makes the church the new temple. The goal of this whole trajectory is not a rebuilt temple in Jerusalem, but a day when the whole of creation will be like the Holy of Holies in the new heavens and the new earth. So I don't think Revelation predicts there will be a rebuilt temple in Jerusalem. Rather, the temple becomes a symbol for the church, which is God's temple because the church is indwelt by the Holy Spirit (1 Corinthians 3:16; 6:19).

Many believers also think that the reference to forty-two months here is to a literal period of time, but just as I think the temple is a symbol of God's people, I find the view that this is a symbolic period of time more persuasive. Forty-two months is thirty-six months (three years of twelve months each) plus six months; so this is a period of three and a half years.

This three-and-a-half-year period interprets what many refer to as "Daniel's seventieth week." In Daniel 9:24–27, the angel Gabriel tells Daniel, "seventy weeks are decreed about your people" (v. 24). These "weeks" are seven-year periods. Gabriel then explains to Daniel that there will be sixty-nine weeks from "the going out of the word to restore and build Jerusalem to the coming of an anointed one, a prince" (v. 25). I think this sixty-nine week period refers to the time between Nehemiah, who returned to rebuild the walls of Jerusalem in 445 B.C., and Jesus, who was crucified around A.D. 30. A sixty-nine week period adds up to 483 years, and if we simply add 30 to 445, we get a total of 475 years. Harold Hoehner has argued that if you adjust for leap years and other calendrical variations, there are exactly 483 years from Nehemiah to the triumphal entry.[3] And Daniel 9:26 states that at the end of that sixty-nine-week period, "an anointed one shall be cut off and shall have nothing," which I think prophesies the crucifixion of Jesus. So Gabriel says that "seventy weeks are decreed" in Daniel 9:24, then discusses the first sixty-nine of those seventy weeks in Daniel 9:25, 26.

The last week, the "seventieth week," is described in Daniel 9:27: "And he ["the prince who is to come" who destroys the sanctuary in verse 26] shall make a strong covenant with many for one week, and for half of the week he shall put an end to sacrifice and offering. And on the wing of abominations shall come one who makes desolate, until the decreed end is poured out on the desolator." Notice how this seventieth week is divided in half when Daniel 9:27 says, "for half of the week he shall put an end to sacrifice." The first part of the verse speaks of "a strong covenant"; then we see sacrifice ended, followed by the abomination of desolation, and then "the decreed end is poured out on the desolator." So it looks to me like the first half of this seventieth week will consist of "a strong covenant," and then sacrifice will be ended during the second half of the week, which will also see the rise of "one who makes desolate." And the end of the week seems to be marked by the destruction of the desolator.

It is important to see these things in Daniel because it seems that when John refers to three-and- a-half-year periods in Revelation, he is interpreting the two halves of Daniel's seventieth week. We see here in Revelation 11:2 that John refers to "forty-two months," which adds up to three and a half years. In 11:3 we have a reference to "1,260 days," and that number assumes thirty days in a month, multiplied by forty-two months; so it also refers to three and a half years. In 12:14 we see a reference to "a time, and times, and half a time," and this also refers to three and a half years.[4]

I think that John interprets both halves of Daniel's seventieth week. More will be said on that shortly, but at this point let me say that I don't think it's a literal seven-year period, which means that I don't think this reference to "forty-two months" in Revelation 11:2 refers to a literal three-and-a-half-year period. Rather, I think this "forty-two months" refers to the whole time from Jesus' death and resurrection until just before he comes. As we go forward I'll seek to defend that understanding from the other things we see about this three-and-a-half-year period.

The measuring of God's people that we see in 11:1 is a symbolic depiction of God's knowing exactly where all his people are. He is taking stock of them, so he can protect them all. None of God's people are overlooked. None of God's people will be forgotten. Do you believe that? Ask the Lord right now to assure you that he knows you by name, that he will protect you. He has stretched the measuring line over you. You belong to him.

This means that "the court outside the temple" and "the holy city" that is trampled for "forty-two months" is a reference to the way wicked people will rule over the world (on "the holy city," cf. 11:8). I am suggesting that "the temple" in 11:1 is a reference to the church, and the reference to "the court" and the "city" in 11:2 signifies the rest of the world. The world is God's. He made it. He owns it. He deserves glory from it. But for this forty-two-month period, he protects only the church. The rest of the world, though it belongs to God, will be trampled by "the nations." Thus, I think what John describes here in Revelation 11:2 interprets and fulfills Daniel 7:23: "there shall be a fourth kingdom on earth, which shall be different from all the kingdoms, and it shall devour the whole earth, and trample it down, and break it to pieces." I take Daniel's "fourth kingdom" to have been typified by the Roman

Empire, which was the reigning world power when John wrote Revelation. The fulfillment of these words is not limited to the Roman Empire, though, because John attributes the trampling of the whole world to "the nations" in Revelation 11:2.

Even if you think that this temple that gets measured in 11:1 is a literal building in Jerusalem, we can agree that its being measured signifies God's protection of it. Even if you think that the reference to "forty-two months" in 11:2 is a literal period of time, we can agree that throughout that time the temple will be protected while the court and the city are trampled. So we can agree that the main point of 11:1, 2 is that God will protect his people.

Revelation 11:3–14: The Two Witnesses

There are two parts of this section on the two witnesses in 11:3–14. In the first part, the two witnesses "prophesy for 1,260 days" (11:3). Then in 11:7, "when they have finished their testimony, the beast that rises from the bottomless pit will make war on them and conquer them and kill them." There is a parallel to this in 13:1 where John sees "a beast rising out of the sea"; then in 13:5 the beast "was allowed to exercise authority for forty-two months," and with that authority we see in 13:7 that "it was allowed to make war on the saints and to conquer them." In 11:7 the beast from the pit "make[s] war" and "conquer[s]" the two witnesses, and in 13:7 the beast from the sea "make[s] war" and "conquer[s]" the saints.

Here is one way to put together this information: the people of God are protected and the two witnesses prophesy for a three-and-a-half-year period, the first half of Daniel's seventieth week. Then the beast rises from the pit, kills the two witnesses, and makes war on the saints. His authority will last for three and a half years, the second half of Daniel's seventieth week. So I would suggest that John is depicting the church's being protected for the first half of the week, then severely persecuted for the second half of the week. This is not the only way to interpret these references to three and a half years, but I think it makes best sense of the information in Daniel and Revelation. Daniel clearly divides the seventieth week in half (Daniel 9:27), and in Daniel 7:25–27; 12:1–13 the people of God receive the kingdom after a three-and-a-half-year period of intense persecution.

Again, even if you disagree with me on what John *refers to* when he describes the temple, the three-and-a-half-year period, and the two witnesses, we can agree on their *significance*: we are being shown that God preserves his people to proclaim the gospel in spite of all satanic opposition. Let's look more closely at the ministry of the two witnesses in 11:3–6.

Revelation 11:3–6: The Three-and-a-Half-Year
Ministry of the Two Witnesses

Before we read these verses, let me tell you up front what I think they symbolize: these two witnesses are symbols of the church proclaiming the gospel. Again, some think there will literally be two witnesses who will arise in the future, but I find the view that the church is symbolically portrayed in 11:1–14 more convincing.

In 11:3–6, John uses images from Old Testament passages that depict God's preserving the prophetic witness in Israel to describe the way God will preserve the prophetic witness of the church. There are four primary images, and they work backward from the end of Israel's history in the Old Testament to the beginning of Israel's history in the Old Testament. The four images are: first, the two olive trees from Zechariah 4, where the community that returned from exile was empowered to rebuild the temple by the two anointed figures, Joshua the high priest and Zerubbabel the governor; second, the fire that fell from Heaven and killed those whom Israel's wicked king sent to summon Elijah the prophet (2 Kings 1:9–12); third, Elijah's prayer that it would not rain (1 Kings 17:1; James 5:17); and fourth, the plagues that Moses visited upon Egypt (Exodus 7—12).

Table 21.1: Old Testament Imagery in Revelation 11:4–6

OT Image	OT Reference	OT Personage	Revelation
two olive trees	Zechariah 4	Joshua the high priest Zerubbabel the governor	11:4
fire consumes enemies	2 Kings 1:9–12	Elijah, wicked king Ahaziah and his men	11:5
no rain	1 Kings 17:1	Elijah, Ahab	11:6a
waters to blood, plagues	Exodus 7 — 12	Moses, Pharaoh	11:6b

The one speaking to John in 11:1, 2 continues to speak to him in 11:3: "And I will grant authority to my two witnesses, and they will prophesy for 1,260 days, clothed in sackcloth." We know that Jesus is speaking to John here because these are his witnesses: he calls them "my two witnesses" in 11:3, and there is a reference to "their Lord" being "crucified" in 11:8. There are two witnesses because in the Bible everything must be confirmed on the authority of two witnesses (Deuteronomy 17:6; 19:15; Matthew 18:16; 26:60; 2 Corinthians 13:1; 1 Timothy 5:19; Hebrews 10:28). Putting 11:3 together with 11:1, 2, I take it that the church, symbolized by the temple, will be protected to proclaim the gospel, symbolized by these two witnesses, throughout history until the time when the beast is given authority, and this whole period of the church's history is symbolized by the two references to the first half of Daniel's seventieth week—the three-and-a-half-year period called "forty-two months" in 11:2 and "1,260 days" in 11:3.

Having stated that the church will proclaim the gospel in 11:3, Jesus introduces the first of the four images from the Old Testament in 11:4, where the two witnesses are explained: "These are the two olive trees and the two lampstands that stand before the Lord of the earth." In Zechariah 4, the two olive trees stand beside one lampstand (Zechariah 4:2, 3), feeding it oil. The olive trees are identified as "two sons of oil" (Zechariah 4:14, literal translation), meaning that they are anointed with the Spirit to empower the people to rebuild the temple (Zechariah 4:6). The Spirit-empowered leadership of Joshua and Zerubbabel inspired the people of Israel to rebuild the temple "not by might, nor by power, but by my Spirit, says the LORD of hosts" (Zechariah 4:6). The lampstand was a symbol of the presence of God among the people in the temple. So this is another connection between "the temple" and "those who worship there" (11:1), another indication that the temple is a symbol of God's people. In 11:4 "the two olive trees" are identified with "the *two* lampstands." Revelation 1:20 states that the lampstands John saw symbolized churches, and that's what I take them to symbolize here in 11:4. Therefore, I understand the identification of the two witnesses as two olive trees and two lampstands to mean that the church, which is what the lampstands symbolize, has a prophetic witness that meets the Old Testament requirement that everything be confirmed by two witnesses, and the church's prophetic witness is empowered by the Spirit, which is what the olive trees symbolize.

Revelation 11:5 states, "And if anyone would harm them, fire pours from their mouth and consumes their foes. If anyone would harm them, this is how he is doomed to be killed." Recalling the way God shielded Elijah from those who summoned him to Israel's wicked king, this amounts to a declaration of divine protection for the church's prophetic witness.

Revelation 11:6 adds another Elijah-like element to the church's witness: "They have the power to shut the sky, that no rain may fall during the days of their prophesying." Elijah called for a drought during the days of the wicked King Ahab. Interestingly, James 5:17 says, "for three years and six months it did not rain" (cf. Luke 4:25; 1 Kings 17:1; 18:1), the same amount of time these two witnesses prophesy in Revelation 11. The drought in Elijah's day was a demonstration of Yahweh's superiority over the false gods that Ahab trusted. I would suggest that the invocation of this aspect of Elijah's ministry points to the many ways the church demonstrates that Yahweh is superior to any other spiritual power, greater than any other so-called god.

The second part of 11:6 brings in the ministry of Moses: ". . . and they have power over the waters to turn them into blood and to strike the earth with every kind of plague, as often as they desire." The turning of the waters to blood and the visitation of the plagues on Egypt demonstrated Yahweh's greatness and brought Egypt to its knees. Through the judgments of the plagues, Yahweh brought Israel out of the land of Egypt, out of the house of slavery. Stating that the church has the ability to do this means that the church has the power necessary to liberate people from bondage, to enable people to experience the new exodus. This power comes through the preaching of the gospel, when the Spirit gives life to someone dead in trespasses and sins. The church's power is in the proclamation of the gospel.

Let's put the meaning of these four images from the Old Testament together. The olive trees symbolize the Spirit's empowering the church, because olive oil is associated with anointing, and anointing is associated with the coming of the Spirit. The fire that consumes enemies symbolizes divine protection for the church. The power to shut the sky points to demonstrations that Yahweh is the only living and true God, and the ability to bring the plagues highlights the church's ability to liberate people from bondage through the proclamation of the gospel. The church, then, is empowered by the Spirit, protected by the Father, and able to liberate people through the gospel of Jesus Christ.

Do you know this power? Is this your experience of what it means to be the church? This is what makes the church potent—not money, not political influence, not marketing gimmicks, not anything that involves worldly strategy. The church's power is in Spirit-empowered, Father-protected proclamation of Jesus Christ and him crucified.

Being a Christian is about being liberated from bondage to sin by faith in the death and resurrection of Jesus Christ. Being a Christian is about being confident that the Father is greater than all, that nothing can overcome Almighty God. Being a Christian is about relying on the power of the Spirit, not the power of our own abilities. If you don't know Christ, what keeps you from being set free from your sin by Jesus, protected by the Father's care, and experiencing the Spirit's power? Won't you trust Jesus now?

If you do know Christ, this is who you are. You are measured by the Father, indwelt and empowered by the Spirit, protected to proclaim the good news so that slaves might be freed.

Revelation 11:7–14: The Three-and-a-Half-Day
Defeat of the Two Witnesses

Look at the first phrase of 11:7, "And when they have finished their testimony
. . ." Now look back at 11:3: "they will prophesy for 1,260 days. . . ." It seems
that the church will finish its testimony at the end of a three-and-a-half-year
period. Again, I think that the three-and-a-half-year period symbolizes all
of church history, and this period of time is the first half of Daniel's seventieth week. In 13:5 we read that the beast "was allowed to exercise authority
for forty-two months," which I take to be a reference to the second half of
Daniel's seventieth week. So the beast's time of authority seems to come after
the 1,260 days that the two witnesses prophesy according to 11:3, when, as
11:7 puts it, the two witnesses "have finished their testimony."

So at the midpoint of Daniel's seventieth week, we see in 11:7, 8 that "the
beast that rises from the bottomless pit will make war on them and conquer
them and kill them, and their dead bodies will lie in the street of the great city
that symbolically is called Sodom and Egypt, where their Lord was crucified."
Jerusalem is clearly in view in 11:8, because that's where Jesus was crucified.
These two witnesses are also identified as belonging to Jesus, because it was
"their Lord" who was crucified. Identifying Jerusalem with Sodom associates Jerusalem with an adulterous city that came under God's judgment, and
identifying Jerusalem with Egypt associates it with the country that enslaved
the people of God, from which God delivered his people. This is a symbolic
or spiritual identification. Jerusalem is not literally Sodom and Egypt, but
Jerusalem has come to play a role in God's purposes that is similar to the role
played by Sodom and Egypt—places judged by God, places from which the
people of God (Lot and the nation of Israel) were delivered through judgment.
So I think this is another indication that a literal temple and the literal holy
city are not in view back in 11:1, 2.

In Revelation 11:9–13 we read:

> For three and a half days some from the peoples and tribes and languages
> and nations will gaze at their dead bodies and refuse to let them be placed
> in a tomb, and those who dwell on the earth will rejoice over them and
> make merry and exchange presents, because these two prophets had been
> a torment to those who dwell on the earth. But after the three and a half
> days a breath of life from God entered them, and they stood up on their
> feet, and great fear fell on those who saw them. Then they heard a loud
> voice from heaven saying to them, 'Come up here!' And they went up to
> heaven in a cloud, and their enemies watched them. And at that hour there
> was a great earthquake, and a tenth of the city fell. Seven thousand people
> were killed in the earthquake, and the rest were terrified and gave glory
> to the God of heaven.

So the dead bodies of the two witnesses are left unburied for three and a half days, while the wicked world rejoices over them. At the end of the three and a half days, they are resurrected and summoned up to Heaven. Then an earthquake destroys a tenth of the city and kills seven thousand people. It may be that this three-and-a-half-day period of time is to be taken literally, but let me suggest an alternative explanation. I am not certain that this alternative explanation is correct, but I think it might be. I pose it as a question: what if the three-and-a-half-year period of the beast's authority is symbolically depicted here as a three-and-a-half-day period? Revelation 17:10, 12 might support this notion: 17:10 speaks of a king to come remaining "only a little while," and 17:12 says the time of the beast's power will be "one hour." So these texts seem to indicate that the time of the final, vicious persecution of the church has undergone prophetic foreshortening.[5] If this is correct, the resurrection of the two witnesses and their being summoned into Heaven symbolizes the vindication of the church. They are raised from the dead and invited into God's presence. Meanwhile, the three-and-a-half-year period of the beast's authority is presented as a short period of time—three and a half days.

Table 21.2: Interpretations of Daniel's Seventieth Week

	Symbolic Understanding of Daniel's Seventieth Week (not seven literal years)	
The View Presented Here	First half: church history from the cross until the beast	Second half: the time of the beast's authority
Roger Beckwith's View [6]	First half: from the cross to the destruction of Jerusalem in A.D. 70	Second half: From the destruction of Jerusalem in A.D. 70 to the end of history
	Literal and Symbolic Understanding of Daniel's Seventieth Week (three and a half literal years at the beginning of the seventieth week, then three and a half symbolic years to the end of history; for the preterists, three and a half symbolic years leading up to A.D. 66, then three and a half literal years until Jerusalem is destroyed in A.D. 70)	
Meredith Kline's View [7]	First half: terminates at the cross of Christ	Second half: church history until the second coming
Preterists	A.D. 66–70	destruction of Jerusalem
	Literal Understanding of Daniel's Seventieth Week (the final seven years before the millennium)	
Gleason Archer's View [8]	Church history	Seven-year tribulation

So I am suggesting that this three-and-a-half-day period is a symbolic representation of the beast's time when the wicked world will rejoice over the people of God. The beast and his followers will prevail, but not for long.

That's true whether what I am proposing about this three and a half days is right or not. The time when Satan and the opponents of God appear to be victorious will be short.

Three woes were promised in 8:13. The first ended after the fifth trumpet, and now in 11:14 we read, "The second woe has passed; behold, the third woe is soon to come." This seems to indicate that everything from the blowing of the sixth trumpet in 9:13 through chapter 10 and to this point in chapter 11 is included in the second woe.

Whether the two witnesses are two literal prophets or, as I am suggesting, symbolize the church, the point of the text is that evil forces may even kill those who belong to God, but God overcomes death and vindicates his people. Whether the three-and-a-half-year period when the two witnesses prophesy is a literal forty-two-month period or, as I am suggesting, symbolizes the whole church age, the point of the text is that those who belong to God will be empowered by the Spirit and protected by God to proclaim the gospel.

God will protect his people against all satanic opposition, and they will proclaim the gospel until the kingdom comes.

Revelation 11:15–19: The Seventh Trumpet: The Kingdom Belongs to God and Christ

The fact that at the seventh trumpet blast the kingdom comes in 11:15–19 supports the idea that the three and a half days in which the two witnesses are unburied is a prophetically foreshortened version of the beast's three-and-a-half-year period of authority. There is a consistent pattern in Daniel 7:25–27, 9:27, and 12:7–12: the people of God are shattered, and then the ravaging beast is destroyed, and the people of God receive the kingdom. That is the pattern that we see here in Revelation 11, as the two witnesses are slain, mocked, and rejoiced over, and then God's enemies are defeated and his witnesses vindicated, and the kingdom comes in 11:15–19.

We read in 11:15, "Then the seventh angel blew his trumpet, and there were loud voices in heaven, saying, 'The kingdom of the world has become the kingdom of our Lord and of his Christ, and he shall reign forever and ever.'" I think that this seventh trumpet blast falls here at the middle of the whole book of Revelation because the book is structured chiastically, so that everything is centered on this moment. This is the moment when the trumpet is blown, the voices are raised, and the rebellion against the world's rightful Lord comes to an end. The true King is enthroned, and his reign will never end. As I meditated on this section of Revelation, I wrote the following poem:

Through flame and flood, with plague and blood,
The gospel is proclaimed
The Spirit flows, the church it grows
The beast he is enraged

Measuring rod and line outstretched
The Father knows his own
As martyrs die the saints will sigh
And they cry out, How long?

And then at last, the trumpet blast
And Christ will reign as King
Creation sings, the praises ring
For this the world was made.

James M. Hamilton Jr.
March 10, 2009

The response to the enthronement of the Lord Christ as King comes in 11:16–19:

> And the twenty-four elders who sit on their thrones before God fell on their faces and worshiped God, saying, "We give thanks to you, Lord God Almighty, who is and who was, for you have taken your great power and begun to reign. The nations raged, but your wrath came, and the time for the dead to be judged, and for rewarding your servants the prophets and saints, and those who fear your name, both small and great, and for destroying the destroyers of the earth." Then God's temple in heaven was opened, and the ark of his covenant was seen within his temple. There were flashes of lightning, rumblings, peals of thunder, an earthquake, and heavy hail.

Revelation 11:15 states that "The kingdom of the world has become the kingdom of *our Lord* and of *his Christ*," and once the trumpet is blown John takes us back to the heavenly throne. There the twenty-four elders surrounding the throne of God fall down and worship God who has brought all things to completion. As they praise God, they thank him in verse 17 because he has begun to reign. Then in verse 18 they acknowledge the long opposition to God's rule, his just wrath, and the arrival of the moment of judgment. The judgment will result in the rewarding of God's servants—whether God's servants were "small" or "great," both "the prophets and saints" and "those who fear your name." God's servants will be rewarded!

Conversely, judgment will come on the enemies of God. "The destroyers of the earth" (v. 18) will be destroyed. Interestingly, it might surprise many modern-day environmentalists that opposition to God and his rule is regarded here at the end of verse 18 as destroying the earth.

As we were given a vision into the heavenly temple after the seventh seal was opened in 8:1–5, and as we saw there lightning, thunder, and an earthquake, so also here in 11:19 after the seventh trumpet the temple of God is opened. The ark of the covenant becomes visible. The heavens went dark, the veil was split, the earth shook, and the dead were raised also when Jesus died on the cross (Matthew 27:50–53). This is what happens at the day of the Lord. The lightnings, thunder, earthquake, and hail seen emanating from God's throne in 4:5 also punctuate the events of the seventh trumpet and remind us that these judgments are God's judgments.

God will protect his people against all satanic opposition, and they will proclaim the gospel until the kingdom comes.

Conclusion

God knows his people and protects them. This is symbolically presented by the measuring of the temple in 11:1, 2. God's people are protected by him to proclaim the gospel by the power of the Spirit. This is symbolically presented by the two witnesses who are empowered by the Spirit, protected by the Father, and given power to stop the rain and bring the plagues in 11:3–6.

God's people may be killed for the gospel, as the two witnesses are in 11:7, and there may be a period of time in which they are mocked and scorned. The two witnesses are not immediately vindicated in 11:8–10, but the time of their dishonor will be short.

God's people will be vindicated, raised from the dead, and invited to join God and Christ in Heaven, as we see in 11:11–14. And then the kingdom will come, as depicted in 11:15–19.

God will protect his people against all satanic opposition, and they will proclaim the gospel until the kingdom comes.

John Paton was enabled by these truths to look death in the face and herald the gospel. May the Lord so work in our hearts and lives.

22

The Seed of the Woman Conquers the Serpent

REVELATION 12:1–17

CAN YOU IMAGINE anything more vulnerable than a woman laboring to give birth? Women in labor are completely occupied with giving birth. They are not thinking about defending themselves. They cannot strategize about how to escape from danger. They are focused on one thing: giving birth. The process of giving birth is a colossal struggle for life. The whole of a woman's mental energy, emotional strength, and bodily power are focused on what seems impossible and is nothing short of miraculous. A human being is about to come into the world out of her body, and the baby seems bigger than the birth canal. It looks impossible. It is a miracle of frantic human determination and astonishing divine design.

Can you imagine anything more frightening or threatening than a huge dragon? Let me suggest a way to make a dragon even more dreadful: give it seven heads. Now put a horn on each head, and three of the heads have two horns; so there are seven heads and ten horns.

Put the two images together and you have a powerful drama. A pregnant woman is in the process of giving birth, and she is threatened by a massive dragon who wants to eat her baby the moment he is born. She cannot run. She cannot hide. What hope does she have?

Do you want to heighten the desperation and urgency of the situation? The child about to be born, sure to be eaten by the dragon, is the world's last hope. This is an epic pageant of intense, unprotected goodness confronted with a shocking evil that looks powerful, inevitable, devastating.

Need

We need to know the danger we face. We need to know that it always looks like the odds are that Satan will win, but he always loses. And we need to know that victory has been secured, that no satanic accusation will stand against those who trust in Christ, and that God can and does protect his people.

Main Point

Satan wants to accuse us before God, but Jesus has defanged him.

Preview

Revelation 12 falls into three parts:

12:1–6	Enmity between the Serpent and the Seed of the Woman
12:7–12	The Cross Defeats the Accuser
12:13–17	On the Wings of an Eagle

Context

In 11:1–14 we saw a symbolic depiction of the church being protected by God as the temple in which he dwells (11:1, 2), and we saw a symbolic depiction of the church's prophetic witness throughout church history (11:3–14). Then in 11:15–19 the seventh trumpet was blown at the midpoint of the book of Revelation. I think that here in 12:1–17 we have another symbolic depiction of the church being protected by God and testifying to the gospel throughout church history.

The center of the whole book is the announcement that Christ is King in 11:15–19. The section before that announcement is matched by the section after that announcement, and they say the same thing in different ways: God will protect his people against all satanic opposition, and God's people will proclaim the gospel until the kingdom comes. Satan wants to accuse God's people before God, but Jesus has defanged him.

Revelation 12:1–6: Enmity between the Serpent and the Seed of the Woman

John writes in 12:1, 2, "And a great sign appeared in heaven: a woman clothed with the sun, with the moon under her feet, and on her head a crown of twelve stars. She was pregnant and was crying out in birth pains and the agony of giving birth." The first thing we should note is that this woman is a "sign." She is a portent of symbolic significance. So the symbol is a pregnant woman about to give birth, and she is "clothed with the sun."

Imagine a woman wearing the sun as a garment. She has "the moon under her feet," and she has a crown on her head. The crown is made of twelve stars. These heavenly bodies are reminiscent of Joseph's second dream in Genesis 37:9, where Joseph says, "Behold, the sun, the moon, and eleven stars were bowing down to me." Joseph's father Jacob, aka Israel, interprets the dream in 37:10 saying, "Shall I and your mother and your brothers indeed come to bow ourselves to the ground before you?" So in Joseph's dream, Jacob/Israel is the sun, Joseph's mother Rachel is the moon, and Joseph's eleven brothers are the eleven stars, with Joseph evidently the twelfth.

When God created the heavens and the earth, he made the two great lights on the fourth day—the greater light to rule the day, the lesser light to rule the night with the stars (Genesis 1:16), and they were "for signs and for seasons, and for days and years" (Genesis 1:14). Portraying the family of Israel as these ruling signs seems to communicate that Israel will rule the world, and the patriarchal luminaries of Israel will bow to Joseph. Revelation 12:1 seems to evoke Genesis 37:9, 10 to portray Jesus as a new and greater Joseph.

As for the woman being pregnant, Micah 4:10 presents the "daughter of Zion" as being "in labor," and it seems that Israel will remain in exile until the child is born in Bethlehem (Micah 5:2). Micah 5:3, 4 says, "Therefore he shall give them up until the time when she who was in labor has given birth; then the rest of his brothers shall return to the people of Israel. And he shall stand and shepherd his flock in the strength of the LORD, in the majesty of the name of the LORD his God. And they shall dwell secure, for now he shall be great to the ends of the earth." Psalm 72:8 and Zechariah 9:10 also speak of the Messiah reigning "to the ends of the earth." So this woman seems to symbolize the nation of Israel in general and in particular Mary, the maiden of Israel, daughter of Zion, who gave birth to Jesus. The birth of Jesus is interpreted here as the fulfillment of Old Testament prophecies that point to the birth of the child who brings redemption for God's people and rules over all the nations of the earth. This child is the hope of the world.

There is a second sign in 12:3, 4: "And another sign appeared in heaven: behold, a great red dragon, with seven heads and ten horns, and on his heads seven diadems. His tail swept down a third of the stars of heaven and cast them to the earth. And the dragon stood before the woman who was about to give birth, so that when she bore her child he might devour it." Imagine seeing this huge red dragon, but it isn't an ordinary dragon with one head—it has seven heads! On those seven heads are ten horns. If the horns are evenly distributed among the heads, three of the heads would have two horns. It seems that in 12:17–13:1 the dragon summons a beast from the sea that also has seven heads and ten horns. We can see from 16:13 that there is a false trinity in Revelation: the dragon, the beast, and the false prophet. In chapter

13 we will see the beast that rises from the sea, which seems to correspond to the fourth beast in Daniel 7:7, which I would take to symbolize Rome in both Daniel and Revelation. This dragon in Revelation 12, however, is identified in verse 9 as "Satan," the ruling principality behind the wicked kings of the earth. In 17:9, 10 the seven heads of the beast from chapter 13 are interpreted as seven mountains (consider the seven hills of Rome) and as seven kings, and in 17:12 the ten horns are ten kings. The dragon exercises his power through the beast. The dragon is Satan. The beast is a symbol of the wicked human rulers of the world; the heads and horns of the beast symbolize the authoritative powers that are under the sway of the devil (cf. 1 John 5:19; Ephesians 6:12).

The portrayal of the dragon's tail sweeping down a third of the stars of Heaven and casting them to the earth depicts a dragon massive in proportion to have a tail so large. This event seems to portray something that took place before the war in Heaven that will be described in 12:7–12. Revelation 12:4 tells us that Satan swept a third of the stars out of Heaven, and this is very similar to the description of the "little horn" in Daniel 8:10, where he makes war on the host of Heaven, throws the stars to the ground, and tramples them. This seems to match the way the Old Testament describes other kings in satanic terms, such as the king of Babylon in Isaiah 14 and the king of Tyre in Ezekiel 28. Perhaps the dragon sweeping these stars out of Heaven and casting them to earth refers to Satan's convincing one third of the heavenly host to join him in rebellion against God.[1]

The dragon being ready to devour the child about to be born to the woman reminds us that God cursed the serpent in Genesis 3:15, putting enmity between the seed of the serpent and the seed of the woman and promising that the seed of the woman would crush the head of the serpent. These symbols depict the cosmic, epic battle between God and Satan. Satan looks like he has all the advantages—he's a dragon with seven heads and ten horns against a pregnant woman! Who would you bet on in that conflict?

In 12:5 we see the identity of the child about to be born to the woman: "She gave birth to a male child, one who is to rule all the nations with a rod of iron, but her child was caught up to God and to his throne." This clear allusion to Psalm 2:7–9 identifies the child as the Lord's Anointed, his Messiah, Jesus. Out of the mouths of babes God has established strength. Satan goes to war as a dragon, and God overcomes him by a pregnant woman giving birth to a baby boy.

Does it sometimes seem to you that Satan has the upper hand in the struggle of the ages? Does it look like he is the one who knows how to fight to win, and God always seems to pick the losing strategy? Turn the other cheek. Bless those who persecute you. Love your enemies. Preach Christ and him crucified and not with what the world thinks is eloquent wisdom. Choose the weak things of the world. It's almost as though God shows up on the playground to pick his team, and instead of picking the guys who look like they can play, he picks the obviously inferior team. And how does it always turn out? God triumphs every time.

Do you ever look around your life and feel like God has dealt you a losing hand? If you're a student of the Bible, when you see what looks like a losing hand, you know that God is about to triumph in a way that will give him all the credit for the victory. Isn't that the kind of victory you want? So when everything in your life looks unimpressive, sure to lose, insignificant, trust Christ and watch for the glory of God to be demonstrated.

When you feel like a loser, when you feel like a failure, when you feel like you're incompetent, praise God! You're exactly the kind of person God uses. God uses people like us to defeat the great dragon.

This is precisely what happens when the child is caught up to God and to his throne in 12:5. In verse 4 the dragon is poised to devour the child. God looks like he has the short end of the stick. Satan is a dragon, and God has left this poor pregnant woman and her newborn baby to face the dragon alone. Suddenly victory is snatched from the dragon's jaws as the child is caught up to God and his throne.

This being caught up to Heaven seems to collapse the whole life of Jesus, from ministry to cross and resurrection, so that we go straight from the birth to the ascension.[2] When Jesus died on the cross, it looked like Satan had conquered. But God turned certain and total defeat—his own people rejecting and crucifying the Messiah—into the victory that saves the world. When it looked like the last defense against evil had fallen, Christ rose from the dead, decisively breaking the back of evil.

Do you know this victory? Do you believe that God turns loss into gain? Do you believe that God has irrevocably defeated Satan through the death of Jesus on the cross? Faith comes by hearing, and hearing by the word of Christ (Romans 10:17). Believe it.

Before we move on to 12:6, let's summarize what we have seen so far: the woman seems to symbolize the people of God as a whole (cf. Micah 4:10), and 12:5 summarizes the Messiah's career from birth to ascension. What happens after the ascension? The church begins to spread, beginning from Jerusalem. Revelation 12:6 is a symbolic depiction of God's protecting the church after the ascension of Jesus. Note the imagery in that verse: "and the woman fled into the wilderness, where she has a place prepared by God, in which she is to be nourished for 1,260 days." Look where she goes: to the wilderness. Just as Israel went into the wilderness after the exodus from Egypt, so the people of God go into this symbolic wilderness after the new and greater exodus is accomplished by Christ on the cross. Just as Israel was provided for by God throughout their time in the wilderness, with manna from Heaven and water from the rock, so the church will be nourished for 1,260 days.

Where is your home? Do you think you're home now? Or do you think of yourself as a pilgrim passing through, sojourning on the way to the land of promise? Have you been redeemed, bought out of slavery and delivered in an exodus greater than that of Israel from Egypt? Do you want to know how to participate in that, how to make that true for you? It's simple: begin to trust Jesus right now and never stop. You will either trust him, or you will go to war against him with Satan and so face certain defeat. However much it may look like the dragon has all the advantages, he loses every time.

What about this period of time, 1,260 days? I think this is the same 1,260 days during which the two witnesses prophesy as described in 11:3. We read of forty-two months in 11:2, and forty-two months of thirty days each adds up to 1,260 days; so I think this is the same forty-two months in which the nations will trample the court outside the temple in 11:2. Again, my view is that the temple in 11:1 is a symbol of the church. The two witnesses in 11:3 also symbolize the church, focusing on its prophetic witness to the gospel, and now the woman nourished in the wilderness in 12:6 is another symbolic statement that God will protect and provide for his people for the whole of their appointed time. This is a three-and-a-half-year period, described in three different ways: 1,260 days, forty-two months, and "a time, and times, and half a time" (12:14). This three-and-a-half-year period in Revelation is John's interpretation of the splitting of Daniel's seventieth week in half, as described in Daniel 9:27. To what does Daniel's seventieth week refer? Here are the possibilities:

- Dispensationalists take it literally, and they take Daniel's seventieth week to refer to the final seven years of history: the great tribulation.
- Preterists see this as a literal three-and-a-half-year period between A.D. 66 and A.D. 70 when Jerusalem was destroyed.
- Some amillennialists take the first half of Daniel's seventieth week literally as the three years of the public ministry of Jesus, and they then see the second half of Daniel's seventieth week symbolically as the whole period of time between the first and second comings of Jesus.
- There are other variations, such as Roger Beckwith's proposal that the first half of Daniel's seventieth week goes up to A.D. 70, and the second half covers the rest of church history.[3]
- As I said in the previous study on chapter 11, my view is that the first half of Daniel's seventieth week is church history until the time right before the end, and then at the end of history the beast kills the two witnesses

and has authority for forty-two months (11:7; 13:5, 7). The beast then engages in a final vicious persecution of the people of God, but Revelation presents his forty-two months as being prophetically foreshortened to "three and a half days" (11:9) and "one hour" (17:12).[4]

Revelation 12:7–12: The Cross Defeats the Accuser

The ramifications of Christ's death, resurrection, and ascension in 12:5 are depicted in 12:7–12. I take this section to be a dramatic depiction of all of Satan's accusations being rejected in the heavenly court—note how in 12:10 he is described as "the accuser" who "accuses." The reason Satan's accusations are rejected and his standing in court removed is the blood of Christ (12:11).

Jesus said in John 12:31, "Now is the judgment of this world; now will the ruler of this world be cast out." He also said in Luke 10:18 that he saw Satan fall from Heaven like lightning, and both statements appear to reflect Jesus' understanding that his death would remove Satan's standing in Heaven. Christ accomplished the victory, and apparently God sent Michael to enforce it, as we read in 12:7: "Now war arose in heaven, Michael and his angels fighting against the dragon. And the dragon and his angels fought back." Note that Michael and his angels are presented as joining battle with Satan and the devil's forces fighting back as though on the defensive. They are unsuccessful, as we see in 12:8: "but he was defeated, and there was no longer any place for them in heaven." Satan's power is in accusation. By his death and resurrection, Jesus broke that power. Satan is defeated and expelled from Heaven. Jesus defanged him.

Table 22.1: Differences in Detail between Revelation 12:7–12 and 20:1–3

Action	12:9, cast to earth	20:2, 3, seized, bound, thrown into a pit
Place of Confinement	12:9, earth	20:1–3, bottomless pit
Henchmen	12:9, his angels with him	20:1–3, Satan alone; cf. 19:20, beast and false prophet in lake of fire, where Satan joins them in 20:10
Result	12:12–13:18, Satan makes war on the saints (12:13–17) and deceives the nations (13:3–8, 14), over whom he has authority (13:2) for 42 months (13:5)	20:1–3, no war on the saints; no deception of the nations; no authority for Satan and his beast
Time	12:12, Satan has a little time to make war and deceive	20:3, Satan cannot deceive the nations for a thousand years; after that he will be released for a short period

So what happens to him? We see in 20:1–3 that Satan is bound and thrown into the abyss, and the abyss is shut and sealed over him so that he cannot deceive the nations for a thousand years. Compare that with what happens here in 12:9: "And the great dragon was thrown down, that ancient serpent, who is called the devil and Satan, the deceiver of the whole world—he was thrown down to the earth, and his angels were thrown down with him." Amillennialists think that the binding of Satan in 20:1–3 is the same event being described here in 12:7–9, but let's observe the differences between the two passages.

From these differences, I think it is clear that John does not mean for us to view the thousand-year period described in 20:1–10 as *the same period of time* as the forty-two months that follow Satan's being cast out of Heaven as a result of Christ's death, resurrection, and ascension.

Satan is called by four names in 12:9, and then his activity is described. He is (1) "the great dragon," which identifies him as the dragon trying to devour the male child in 12:1–6, (2) "that ancient serpent," which identifies him as the snake of Genesis 3, (3) the one who is called "the devil," which identifies him with the antagonist described in the Gospels, and (4) "Satan," marking him as a figure known from the Old Testament (cf. 1 Chronicles 21:1). If there was any uncertainty about whether the serpent and the devil and Satan and the dragon are the same character, John removes it in 12:9. John also tells us what Satan *does* in 12:9—he is "the deceiver of the whole world." Satan does not have legitimate claims, and he does not offer real paths to happiness. He deceives.

Christ defeated Satan on the cross (12:5). On the basis of that victory, Michael and his angels defeated Satan in pitched battle and drove him from the heavenly field (12:7–9). The announcement of victory comes in 12:10: "And I heard a loud voice in heaven, saying, 'Now the salvation and the power and the kingdom of our God and the authority of his Christ have come, for the accuser of our brothers has been thrown down, who accuses them day and night before our God.'" If we read this statement in isolation, if we pull it out of its context in this chapter and out of the context of the whole of Revelation, we might conclude that everything is consummated because of the way the first half of verse 10 states that "salvation and the power and the kingdom of our God and the authority of his Christ have come." But after this announcement is made in verse 10, we see at the end of verse 12 that the devil has come down to the earth "in great wrath, because he knows that his time is short." This means that the first half of 12:10 does not mean that the end of all things has come. In fact, I think the sense in which "the salvation and the power and the kingdom of our God and the authority of his Christ have come" in 12:10a is explained in the rest of verse 10: "for the accuser of our brothers has been thrown down, who accuses them day and night before our God." *Salvation* has come in the sense that all grounds of satanic accusation have been removed by Christ's death on the cross, demonstrating God's *power*, the righteousness of his *kingdom*, and the *authority* of Christ.

Revelation 12:11 tells us that salvation comes to those who believe it is better to trust in Jesus than to go on living: "And they have conquered him by the blood of the Lamb and by the word of their testimony, for they loved not their lives even unto death." Who are "they" at the beginning of 12:11? Those whom Satan was accusing in 12:10. Note the connection between the blood of Jesus and the triumph over satanic accusation in 12:10, 11.

When you feel guilty, how do you respond to that guilt? Let me urge you to respond to that guilt by trusting in Christ's death on the cross to pay for it, to remove any power Satan has to accuse you because of it, and to secure your justification before God. There is no condemnation for those in Christ Jesus (Romans 8:1), and none of the charges that Satan brings against them will stand up in court. This message of Christ crucified to pay for sin, raised to secure justification, nullifying all of Satan's allegations against those who trust in Jesus is what verse 11 means when it refers to "the word of their testimony." That's the testimony of believers. If that's not your testimony, I call on you to trust Jesus right now and experience reconciliation with God and freedom from all of Satan's accusations.

If that's already your testimony, wrap your arms and heart around the final phrase of 12:11, "for they loved not their lives even unto death." If you know that God is holy and will keep his word to punish sin, you know that it is better to die trusting Christ and clinging to the gospel than to go on living by denying that gospel. Better to die with the gospel than to live without it, because if you live without the gospel, you still face the alarming prospect of standing before God. Without the gospel, when you stand before God, all Satan's accusations will ring true, and you will be damned with Satan, your master who will turn on you, accuse you, then take his pleasure in your pain. But you can be delivered from Satan. You need only turn from your sin and trust in Christ.

Consider 12:12: "Therefore, rejoice, O heavens and you who dwell in them! But woe to you, O earth and sea, for the devil has come down to you in great wrath, because he knows that his time is short!" Those in the heavens rejoice because the death, resurrection, and ascension of Jesus have secured Michael's ability to go on the offensive against Satan and drive him out of Heaven. Those on the earth have the woe pronounced over them because when Satan was driven out of Heaven because of the cross, he was cast down to the earth. He has a little time in which to pursue his malice on earth.

When you think of the world, do you think of it in these terms? You should. When we open our eyes, we should remind ourselves that there is an unseen dragon who—look at that phrase in 12:12—"has come down to you in great wrath." He is massive. He is deceptive. He is frightening. And he's mad. He knows his time is short. He knows his cause is lost. So he comes against you with the desperation and recklessness of one who has no hope of redemption, no reason to show mercy, and no desire to make terms. Imagine the ferocity of one who knows that death and damnation are certain. He hates God, he hates goodness, and he hates us. Our only hope is to heed the words of this book and trust in Christ to deliver us.

Revelation 12:13–17: On the Wings of an Eagle

The death, resurrection, and ascension of Jesus (12:5) authorized Michael to forcefully expel Satan from Heaven because he has been defanged and his accusations are now toothless. They have lost all their bite (12:7–12). We see his response to defeat in 12:13–17. He is relentless in his destructive intentions.

Robbed of the child he sought to devour in 12:5, he turns on the mother in 12:13, 14: "And when the dragon saw that he had been thrown down to the earth, he pursued the woman who had given birth to the male child. But the woman was given the two wings of the great eagle so that she might fly from the serpent into the wilderness, to the place where she is to be nourished for a time, and times, and half a time." Satan sees that he has been thrown out of Heaven, that he has been defeated, but he does not give up. He is like a rabid wounded animal that knows he is going to die but wants to kill as much as he can while he has life; so he pursues the woman. The word used to describe his pursuit of the woman ($\dot{\epsilon}\delta\dot{\iota}\omega\xi\epsilon\nu$) is used elsewhere in the New Testament (cf. Acts 7:52; 9:4; 22:4) to describe the persecution of the church, and that is probably what this pursuit symbolizes.

Revelation 12:14 has a rich Old Testament background: after the exodus from Egypt, when Israel arrived at Mount Sinai, God said to them in Exodus 19:4, "You yourselves have seen what I did to the Egyptians, and how I bore you on eagles' wings and brought you to myself." In addition Isaiah prophesied about the return from exile that would happen after the new exodus: "they who wait for the LORD shall renew their strength; they shall mount up with wings like eagles; they shall run and not be weary; they shall walk and not faint" (Isaiah 40:31). John has just recorded the loud voice in Heaven speaking of Christ's death and resurrection in terms of his being the new Passover lamb in 12:10, 11: "they have conquered him *by the blood of the Lamb.*" So like Israel at the first exodus being carried on eagles' wings to God at Mount Sinai in Exodus 19:4, in fulfillment of Isaiah 40:31 promising that those who wait on the Lord will mount up with wings like eagles, John now shows the woman, who symbolizes the people of God, the church, flying from Satan into the wilderness on "the two wings of the great eagle" (12:14). In the wilderness, like Israel, the woman will "be nourished for a time, and times, and half a time" (12:14). The parallel with 12:6, where the woman is nourished in the wilderness for 1,260 days, shows that the 1,260 days refers to the same amount of time as "a time, and times, and half a time" in 12:14.

We noted that Satan's sweeping a third of the stars from Heaven in 12:4 is similar to what seems to be a prophecy about Antiochus Epiphanes in Daniel 8:10, and we see Satan described in terms reminiscent of another wicked human king, Pharaoh, in Revelation 12:15: "The serpent poured water like a river out of his mouth after the woman, to sweep her away with a flood." This is reminiscent of Exodus 1, where after Pharaoh fails to compel the midwives to kill the male children of the Hebrew women, he commands his people to throw the male children of the Hebrews into the Nile (v. 22). In this connection, Ezekiel 29:3 is very interesting: "speak, and say, Thus says the Lord GOD: 'Behold, I am against you, Pharaoh king of Egypt, the great dragon that lies in the midst of his streams, that says, "My Nile is my own; I made it for myself."'" John seems to be interpreting the satanic impetus behind Pharaoh's persecution of Israel in the Old Testament, and he also seems to be saying that the way Satan has opposed the people of God in the past is similar to the way he opposes them now that Christ has come.

Russell Moore is right: Satan hates babies.[5] Abortion is his work. The struggle against it is not battle with flesh and blood but with the devil himself.

Look how encouraging 12:16 is. Just as God delivered Israel from Pharaoh, preserving Moses alive even though Pharaoh wanted him dead in the Nile, and just as the earth swallowed whole those who opposed Moses (cf. Numbers 16:30–34; Deuteronomy 11:6), so we read in 12:16, "But the earth came to the help of the woman, and the earth opened its mouth and swallowed the river that the dragon had poured from his mouth." God has accomplished the new exodus in Christ, and God will protect his people through the return from exile that is happening right now as we sojourn toward the promised land. Satan wants to accuse us before God, but Jesus has defanged him.

Satan is defanged, but he is foolishly persistent. Look at 12:17: "Then the dragon became furious with the woman and went off to make war on the rest of her offspring, on those who keep the commandments of God and hold to the testimony of Jesus. And he stood on the sand of the sea." In this statement John shows that in his view there is a singular seed of the woman (Jesus) and a collective seed of the woman (those who believe in Jesus). Look at the contrast, too, between the seed of the woman and the dragon, in light of what

Jesus said about those who hear and do his words in Matthew 7:24–27. Jesus compared them to those who build their house on the rock, while those who reject his teaching build their house on sand. The seed of the woman in 12:17 are "those who keep the commandments of God and hold to the testimony of Jesus," and the dragon "stood on the sand of the sea."

Are you building your house on the rock by listening to Jesus and doing what he says? Are you part of the seed of the woman? Is Satan making war on you? If so, let me remind you that though he looks powerful, God always defeats him. Jesus has defanged him. None of his accusations against you are going to stick.

Perhaps you recognize that you don't keep the commands of Jesus, you don't trust him, and you really prefer money or sex or drugs or pride to him. Do you know what Jesus says about you? He says you're like a foolish man building his house on sand, and the rains will fall, the floods will rise, the winds will blow, and there will be a great crash when your house falls. You don't want to stand on the sand with Satan. Turn from your sins and trust in Jesus.

Conclusion

Satan is at enmity with the woman and her seed. He wants to accuse us before God, but Jesus has defanged the dragon, and all his accusations are now toothless against those of us who trust in Christ. The new exodus has happened, and God is carrying us, those who trust him, on eagles' wings, sustaining us in the wilderness as we sojourn toward the promised land. Satan is making war on us, but the outcome will be as it has been throughout history. Strong as Satan may look, the seed of the woman will crush his head.

23

The Beast

REVELATION 13:1–10

ASTROLOGERS HAD PROPHESIED THAT Nero would be vindicated somehow from the East.[1] Even after Nero committed suicide in A.D. 68, rumors began to circulate that he was not dead. Legends sprang up that Nero had actually fled to Parthia and that he would lead the Parthian horde against Rome to reclaim his lost power. The legends were so plausible that at least three impostors appeared claiming to be Nero and trying to take power, in A.D. 69, 80, and 88 or 89.

This is relevant to us as we approach Revelation 13 because Nero was so vicious—he even killed his own mother—that he was referred to as a beast.[2] So in the Nero legend, with which John's churches were probably familiar, a beast who seemed to have died would return and rule the whole known world. We should also note that in the eastern parts of the Roman Empire, to which Nero was rumored to have fled, Nero was worshiped as a living god in the imperial cult.[3]

Need

Second Thessalonians 2:8 states that a "lawless one will be revealed," and Jesus himself said that "false christs and false prophets will arise and perform signs and wonders, to lead astray, if possible, the elect" (Mark 13:22). We need to be equipped to heed what Jesus said in Mark 13:23: "Be on guard; I have told you all things beforehand." Satan is a powerful deceiver, and we need to be able to tell the difference between the real Jesus and the fake Jesus that Satan will use to deceive the world.

Do you feel this need? Are you certain that your idea of who Jesus is matches who he is in reality? How do you know that Satan has not deceived you into following some imitation of Jesus?

Main Point

Revelation 13:1–10 shows us how Satan deceives and how he responds to those who are not persuaded by his deception. This chapter enables us to believe the truth and endure until the end. This passage can keep us from being deceived by Satan into following his fake christ. This passage will prepare us to stand strong against the satanic persecution of those who do not worship his fake messiah. This passage enables us to be saved.

Preview

Satan's strategy is really pretty simple: he acts like he is God, and he tries to kill anyone who isn't fooled by his impersonation. So in 13:1–4 Satan's beast will try to convince the world that he is Jesus. Then in 13:5–8 Satan will go to war against everyone who isn't convinced. Revelation 13:9, 10 calls the people of God to endure until God vindicates them.

Revelation 13:1–4	Satan's Fake Christ
Revelation 13:5–8	The Murderous Blasphemer
Revelation 13:9, 10	The Call to Persevere

Context

This section of Revelation begins in 12:1 and continues through 13:10, and it matches what we saw in 11:1–14. By his death, resurrection, and ascension Christ defanged the dragon with seven heads and ten horns (12:5). Satan no longer has any standing in Heaven to accuse believers (12:7–12). He knows his time is short (12:12), and he is making war on the woman and her seed (12:13–17). Revelation 11:3 says that the two witnesses "will prophesy for 1,260 days." I take that to be simultaneous with, in 12:6, the woman being "nourished for 1,260 days" in "the wilderness, where she has a place prepared by God" (see also 12:14).

When the two witnesses have finished their testimony, and when the gospel has been proclaimed to all nations (Mark 13:10), 11:7 says that the beast from the bottomless pit is going to kill the two witnesses. I take the two witnesses to symbolize the prophetic witness of the church; so the killing of the witnesses symbolizes a persecution so vicious that the church is almost completely stamped out. This would match what we read in Mark 13:19, 20: "For in those days there will be such tribulation as has not been from the beginning of the creation that God created until now, and never will be. And if the Lord had not cut short the days, no human being would be saved. But for the sake of the elect, whom he chose, he shortened the days." In Mark 13:21, 22 Jesus goes on to warn about "false christs and false prophets" who will do "signs and wonders, to lead astray, if possible, the elect." The signs and wonders of these false christs and false prophets are exactly what we see in Revelation 13.

Revelation 13:1–4: Satan's Fake Christ

John writes in 13:1, "And I saw a beast rising out of the sea," and this calls to mind Daniel 7:3: "And four great beasts came up out of the sea, different from one another."[4] The sea is a dark, unknown place, and it was often associated with evil, which seems to be the reason that the sea will be no more in the new heaven and new earth (21:1).

The beast that John sees in 13:1 has "ten horns and seven heads, with ten diadems on its horns and blasphemous names on its heads." The dragon in 12:3 also had "seven heads and ten horns, and on his heads seven diadems," and in 12:17 (Greek 12:18) the dragon was standing "on the sand of the sea." The dragon seems to be summoning forth from the great deep this beast in his own image. We might say that the beast is the image of the invisible dragon. I put it this way because from what the beast and the dragon are going to do, and from the way John describes them, it seems that they are intent on putting themselves in the place of God and Christ. It may even be that the description of "blasphemous names on its heads" refers to claims that the beast is making to be the real Messiah, and the obvious implication of the beast's claim to be the Messiah would be that Jesus is not the Messiah. This would mean that the beast's blasphemy is in who he claims to be.

John then describes the beast again in terms that are reminiscent of Daniel 7. We read in 13:2, "And the beast that I saw was like a leopard; its feet were like a bear's, and its mouth was like a lion's mouth." Daniel's first beast was like a lion, his second like a bear, and his third like a leopard (Daniel 7:4–6). Then Daniel saw a fourth beast with ten horns (Daniel 7:7), and the angel explained to Daniel, "These four great beasts are four kings who shall arise out of the earth" (Daniel 7:17). The ten horns of Daniel's fourth beast are identified with ten kings (Daniel 7:24), and a king will arise into whose hand the saints will be given "for a time, times, and half a time" (Daniel 7:25). This king will be judged and destroyed, however, and God's kingdom will come (Daniel 7:26, 27).

In Revelation 17 the beast's seven heads and ten horns will be interpreted as seven kings and ten kings (vv. 10, 12). John's beast in 13:2 combines elements of Daniel's first three beasts, and at the same time John's beast seems to be Daniel's fourth beast. In both Daniel and in Revelation, the beasts symbolize kings. So Revelation 13 seems to be depicting Satan pursuing his war against the woman and her seed by bringing onto the stage of history this beast who combines in himself all the wickedness of the evil empires of human history.

There is also a connection in the Bible between evil empires and demonic powers. In Daniel 10:13 an angelic being tells Daniel that he was opposed by "the prince of the kingdom of Persia," and we also see the relationship between Satan and the kings that the beast symbolizes in Revelation 13:2: "And to it the dragon gave his power and his throne and great authority." This beast seems to symbolize an end-time government that will initiate vicious persecution, and it has Satan's own authority.

There were four living creatures around God's throne in Revelation 4, and those living creatures reflect the beauty, power, majesty, and character of God. The best Satan can come up with are perverse and twisted parodies of God, and Satan's beast reflects his character just as the four living creatures reflect God's character. Satan's beast is a grotesque and unnatural blend of brutal and bloodthirsty animals of prey, and that's what Satan is like.

There is no neutrality between God and Satan. The kingdoms of the world are not the kingdom of God. "The whole world lies in the power of the evil one" (1 John 5:19). Satan is "the prince of the power of the air" (Ephesians 2:2; cf. 6:11, 12). The world powers opposed to the gospel get their authority from Satan, and they do the works of their father the devil, whose business is to "steal and kill and destroy" (John 10:10). They will not all be as bad as possible, but to the degree that they are not subjected to Scripture and submitted to the Lordship of Christ, they are against him. Satan's beast is depicted in 13:1, 2 as the culmination of all the wickedness at work in the evil empires of history.

The point of application for us here is very simple: let's disabuse ourselves of any false hope that some merely human government is going to bring in the kingdom of God. God's King, Jesus, is going to bring in the kingdom of God. And until he does, we're not to be fooled by any cheap imitations.

We see in 13:3 the cheap imitation of a satanically empowered king setting himself up as a messianic pretender: "One of its heads seemed to have a mortal wound, but its mortal wound was healed, and the whole earth marveled as they followed the beast." The healing of the seemingly mortal wound is Satan's knock-off of the cross and resurrection of Jesus.[5] Perhaps John's audience would have made a connection between this and the legend of Nero's return. The world should, of course, follow Christ who died and rose again.

Instead it worships Satan's beast who only imitates what Jesus did and who only "seemed to have a mortal wound." Nor does this wounding and healing accomplish anything for anyone. The death and resurrection of Jesus accomplished salvation. Satan's cheap trick is just a smoke-and-mirrors magic show that people find impressive.

We see the blasphemous world response in 13:4: "And they worshiped the dragon, for he had given his authority to the beast, and they worshiped the beast, saying, 'Who is like the beast, and who can fight against it?'" Rather than worship God, the whole earth worships Satan. Rather than worship Jesus, they worship Satan's fake christ. And the language of their praise is clearly taken from the praise of God in Exodus 15:11 where God is praised for his deliverance of Israel at the exodus: "Who is like you, O LORD, among the gods?" Satan has no new ideas. He has no creations of his own. He has no originality. All he can do is twist and pervert the good things God has made. He is worthy of neither your allegiance nor your worship; so don't give to Satan what belongs to God alone.

Are you worshiping Jesus as he really is? Or is there a possibility that you are worshiping what you think is Jesus but is really only a satanic imitation? Can you tell the difference? The Bible is the only sure guide for telling the real Jesus from the counterfeits. Do you know your Bible well enough to be sure that you're worshiping Jesus and not some false christ?

Revelation 13:5–8: The Murderous Blasphemer

Let's remember where we are in the wider narrative that began in chapter 12. The dragon hoped to devour the male child of the woman, the Messiah, but failed (12:1–5). Then he chased the woman, and she was given the wings of an eagle and fled into the wilderness to her place where God will nourish her for three and a half years (12:13–16). Again the dragon failed. He was furious with the woman and went off to make war on the rest of her seed (12:17). Now look at how he prepares for this war on the seed of the woman: he summons up this beast from the sea that symbolizes some brutal, dictatorial emperor, and he fakes the crucifixion and resurrection of Jesus. In response the whole world worships Satan and thinks the beast is invincible (13:1–4). All this is preparatory for the war that Satan is plotting against the seed of the woman in 12:17. Having impersonated God and Christ in 13:1–4, Satan will blaspheme God and kill Christians in 13:5–8.

We read in 13:5, "And the beast was given a mouth uttering haughty and blasphemous words, and it was allowed to exercise authority for forty-two months." Notice how even here God's sovereignty over the beast is stressed as the beast "was given" the ability to blaspheme and "was allowed" to exercise his authority, and notice how this reiterates the point that only God is the Creator. Satan and his beast cannot create anything. They can only corrupt what God creates. The "haughty and blasphemous words" that the beast is allowed by God to utter are probably verbal claims to be God. The beast is probably making verbal assertions that lay claim to what only God can legitimately claim. Notice, too, that the beast will have "authority for forty-two months." I think this is the second half of Daniel's seventieth week. This means that the beast's time of authority is determined—and it isn't the beast who has determined it. God has allotted to this beast a certain, short period of time. That's all he has, forty-two months, and he uses it to blaspheme.

The beast's attack in the war on God and his people begins verbally and then becomes physical. We see the beast's verbal attack in 13:6: "It opened its mouth to utter blasphemies against God, blaspheming his name and his dwelling, that is, those who dwell in heaven." Make no mistake about it—to claim privileges that belong to God alone is to blaspheme God and attack him. The beast wants the dragon in God's place; so he has to go to war against God.

Look at how the dwelling of God is equated with the people of God in 13:6—"his dwelling, that is, those who dwell in heaven." The beast is not only attacking God directly—he is attacking the people of God. The refusal to agree with God about who his people are and what they are to believe is an attack on those who believe what God would have them believe. The beast is blaspheming God and God's people by speaking against them in 13:6.

Do you wonder what it means to be a Christian? To be a Christian means that you are reconciled to God through faith in the salvation that God accomplished through the death and resurrection of his Son, Jesus Christ. To be a Christian is to believe that faith in Jesus is the only way to be reconciled to God. There are no other ways to be made right with God. If something else could reconcile you to God, Jesus did not need to die (cf. Galatians 2:21). Christians believe that the death of Jesus was necessary to pay for sin, and Christians believe that the only way to have the death of Jesus count for anyone is to believe in Jesus. To claim that people can be reconciled to God apart from Jesus is to attack Christianity because it asserts that what Christians believe is wrong. So both universalism and inclusivism are attacks on Christianity.

Universalism holds that all people everywhere will be saved, and inclusivism holds that some people will go to Hell but that those who are faithful to whatever religion they adhere to will be saved, even if they do not believe in Jesus. These are attacks on Christianity because they are repudiations of Christianity. They reject the idea that the only way to be saved is by faith in the good news that Jesus died to pay for sin and rose to accomplish justifica-tion. To assert that people can be reconciled apart from faith in Jesus Christ is to blaspheme and belittle what Jesus did.

Now it is one thing to recognize that the different religions are making different competing claims and then allow the different religions to com-pete with one another in an open marketplace of ideas—to let the religions convince who they will. It is another thing to define a religion such that you have denied the very things that religion claims. Or perhaps what we have today is more like an equation of all religions as the same thing, which denies them all, so that only those who truly believe the claims of their religion find themselves out of favor with the opinion-shapers of the world. In such a setting I would suggest that Christianity will be particularly open to attack because its claims are so different from the claims of the other world religions. Christianity is the only religion that does not believe in a works-based salva-tion. Only Christianity holds that salvation is only by grace through faith in what God has done in Jesus Christ.

Do you believe that people who do not believe in Jesus are going to Hell? If we believe that, the way we spend our time and money should prove it. We have a responsibility to take the gospel across the street and around the world.

The beast's attack moves from words to wounds in 13:7: "Also it was allowed to make war on the saints and to conquer them." The beast's war against and conquest of the saints in 13:7 matches his war against and con-quest of the two witnesses in 11:7: "the beast . . . will make war on them and conquer them and kill them." Those two witnesses symbolize the church. The beast conquers and kills them "when they have finished their testimony" (11:7). That seems to point to the day when the gospel has gone to all nations (cf. Mark 13:10). Once that has happened, the beast is granted this ability (note again the divine passive in 13:7: "it was allowed to make war on the saints and to conquer them"). I take these two statements, in 11:7 about the two witnesses and in 13:7 about the saints in general, to be referring to the same thing. This vicious persecution will be such that the church is almost completely wiped off the face of the earth.

The beast will enjoy worldwide, universal reign, as we see in the rest of 13:7: "And authority was given it over every tribe and people and language and nation." Clearly this period of time when the beast has universal authority over the nations is to be contrasted with the millennium, when the beast and false prophet are in the lake of fire and Satan is shut up in a pit so he can no longer deceive the nations (cf. 19:20; 20:1–3).

Note again the divine passive: this authority "was given" to the beast. Satan has been allowed to put himself in the place of God and to put the beast in the place of Christ. Together Satan and his beast fake the crucifixion and resurrection, and they make war on anyone who sees through their tricks. So they blaspheme God and God's people, and then they kill Christians.

Satan's Antichrist is ruling over all the nations, and 13:8 is a sad statement: "and all who dwell on earth will worship it." All earth-dwellers will worship the beast. This shows that they want to worship it. This shows that they are impressed by things like the crucifixion and resurrection. But they prefer Satan's version to God's. Unfortunately, Satan's version does nothing for them but ensure that they will suffer Satan's fate. Almost everyone worships the beast; in fact we see in the rest of verse 8 that "everyone whose name has not been written before the foundation of the world in the book of life of the Lamb who was slain" worships the beast. Those whose names were written in the Lamb's book of life before the foundation of the world don't worship the beast. God's elect don't worship the beast. Those whose names God recorded before time began will not worship the beast.

As I've said, I think that the beast's forty-two months are prophetically foreshortened to three and a half days, the amount of time the two witnesses lie in the street before they are resurrected in 11:8–12. The beast's forty-two months are also prophetically foreshortened to "one hour" in 17:12. I take Mark 13:20 to mean that Jesus also indicated that the beast's time would be shortened: "And if the Lord had not cut short the days, no human being would be saved. But for the sake of the elect, whom he chose, he shortened the days."

In Mark 13:21–23 Jesus warns about false christs and false prophets who do signs and wonders that are so compelling that they would "lead astray, if possible, the elect" (v. 22). If it were possible for the elect to be led astray, these signs and wonders would be convincing enough to do it. But it isn't possible for the elect to be led astray because God wrote their names in the Lamb's book of life before the foundation of the world.

Christian, do you take the comfort you should from the doctrine of election? Do you feel in your soul the fact that if God has chosen you, it is not possible for you to be lost? How do you know whether God has chosen you? The clearest indication is how you feel when you sin. If you feel awful when you sin—not because you got caught but because you have offended God—that's good evidence that God has done the work in your soul that only he can do.

Perhaps you have no idea whether or not God has chosen you. Let me encourage you to trust in Jesus. God created you to worship him. You have the capacity to know God. Sadly, instead of using our God-given capacity to know God and enjoy him, we have all defiled ourselves with lesser things than God himself. We have also actively rebelled against God, incurring his almighty wrath. We need Jesus to die for us because only Jesus can satisfy

God's infinite wrath against sin. If you're not sure whether or not you have been chosen, think about the fact that God loved you by sending Jesus to die to pay the penalty for your sin. Trust in Jesus. Repent of your sin. Recognize that the reason Jesus died was to atone for your sin. Repudiate that sin, and hope fully in Christ. He is mighty to save, and he is worthy of your trust.

Revelation 13:9, 10: The Call to Persevere

Revelation 13:9, 10 gives us the brutal facts so we can prepare ourselves to deal with what is coming upon us: "If anyone has an ear, let him hear: If anyone is to be taken captive, to captivity he goes; if anyone is to be slain with the sword, with the sword must he be slain. Here is a call for the endurance and faith of the saints." The logic of these statements is simple: there is no avoiding what God has predestined to happen to you. If God has predestined you to be taken captive so that you will have the opportunity to show that God means more to you than freedom, you will be taken captive. If God has predestined for you to be slain with the sword so that you will have the opportunity to show that God means more to you than life, you will be slain with the sword. That is why this is "a call for the endurance and faith of the saints."

Revelation 13:9, 10 crowns the description of Satan's war on the woman and her seed (12:13–17). Satan is going to imitate God (13:1–4), and he is going to try to kill anyone who isn't convinced (13:5–8). The revelation of this before it happens is a call for believers to endure and keep believing once it begins to unfold. This statement is here to keep believers from deciding they will renounce Christ so they can avoid imprisonment or execution. This statement is here to preserve God's people in faithfulness through the war Satan prosecutes against them.

Conclusion

Do you know Jesus? Or is the Jesus you know a satanic imitation? The real Jesus is described in the four Gospels, and the significance of the real Jesus is explained in the rest of the New Testament. The real Jesus died on the cross to ransom those who believe from the consequences of their sin. The real Jesus is going to come and visit destruction on all his enemies. The real Jesus demands exclusive loyalty and worship. Does he have yours?

24

The False Prophet

REVELATION 13:11–18

YOUR LIFE DEPENDS ON your knowledge of the gospel. Not just your life now, though that is certainly true, but your eternal life depends on your knowledge of the gospel. Are you ready? Do you know the gospel so well that you will stake your life on it?

If someone claimed to be a representative of Christianity but taught that you should do exactly what the Bible says not to do, would you be prepared to dispute his claim to speak for God? I'm not envisioning Muslim extremists speaking for God—I'm talking about people who claim to be Christians. If they not only called you to do what the Bible says not to do, but made demands and threatened to kill you if you didn't do them, would you be ready to put your life on the line? Would you be ready to die because you were certain that the gospel such a person was preaching was not in fact the gospel the Bible teaches? Do you know your Bible well enough to know when someone is telling you to do exactly what the Bible says not to do? And if you do, has the Bible so shaped your convictions that you don't just disregard the Bible but are prepared to be faithful to God even unto death?

Need

We need to be able to tell the difference between God's work and Satan's. Paul wrote in 2 Corinthians 11:14, 15, "Satan disguises himself as an angel of light. So it is no surprise if his servants, also, disguise themselves as servants of righteousness." Can you tell the difference between a genuine servant of righteousness and a servant of Satan who has disguised himself as a servant of righteousness? We need to know that this is the way Satan operates, and we need to know how good at it he is. Knowing that, we need to be able to tell the difference between God's work and Satan's.

Let me be clear: there are people writing books sold by "Christian" publishers that help Satan's cause against the gospel. There are people preaching sermons on "Christian" radio and television, claiming to speak for God, claiming to represent Christianity, but they are not preaching the gospel, they are not helping people love God and love others. In fact they are in many cases telling people to do exactly what the Bible says not to do.

And too many Christians don't even notice the discrepancy!

Main Point

Revelation 13:18 states that the situation set out in 13:11–17 "calls for wisdom," and the wisdom in view is the ability to distinguish between God's truth and Satan's counterfeits. God's truth is found in the Bible; it exalts Jesus and the good news of his death and resurrection; it calls us to trust in Jesus and live out the gospel by laying down our lives in service to others. Satan's counterfeits claim to be God's truth, but they contradict the Bible; they blaspheme Jesus by teaching that the cross isn't necessary; and Satan's counterfeits promote self-centeredness at the expense of other people.

Preview

Revelation 13:11–18 falls into three parts:

13:11, 12	The False Prophet and His Work
13:13–15	Signs That Deceive and Produce Idolatry
13:16–18	The Mark of the Beast

Each of these sections is concerned with distinguishing between God's truth and Satan's counterfeit. God's true prophet John was commissioned in 10:1–11, and now Satan's false prophet rises in 13:11, 12. God's true gospel power was displayed by the church and the two witnesses in chapter 11, and now Satan's false prophet will do convincing signs that woo people into idolatry. God's true seal was put on his saints in 7:1–3, and now Satan's false prophet will counterfeit God's seal with the mark of the beast in 13:16–18.

Context

At the middle of the whole book of Revelation is the announcement that Christ is King in 11:15–19. On either side of this announcement there are depictions of the persecution of the church, in 11:1–14 and 12:1–13:10. The book of Revelation is depicting reality for us: Jesus really is King, and Satan really is opposing the church. Our Lord reigns, but it does not seem that way today. Right now it seems that the church is afflicted, but we are being protected until the gospel has been proclaimed to all nations. Once the gospel has gone to the whole world, the Antichrist will arise, and it will seem as though Satan has gotten the upper hand. It will seem as though Christianity is almost entirely stamped out. This seems to be what these two sections on the church, 11:1–14 and 12:1–13:10, mean.

So in the middle is the announcement that Christ is King. Before and after that is a picture of the church, protected, then persecuted. Before and after these sections on the church are sections on a true prophet and a false prophet. In 10:1–11 we have the section on the true prophet, John. In 13:11–18 we have the section on the false prophet.[1]

The false prophet in 13:11–18 matches the section on John the true prophet in 10:1–11. Revelation 13:11–18 also serves as a kind of exposition of the beast's war on the saints in 13:7, 8. Revelation 13:7, 8 tells us that the beast conquers and kills the saints and makes all the non-elect worship him for his faked crucifixion and resurrection. Revelation 13:11–18 gives us further insight into how the beast accomplishes the killing of the saints and the persuasion of unbelievers.

Revelation 13:11, 12: The False Prophet and His Work

Revelation 13:11 describes "another beast," and then 13:12 summarizes this beast's activity. That activity will be exposited in verses 13–18. Let's look at this beast who is identified in 16:13 as "the false prophet."

When John writes in 13:11, "Then I saw another beast rising out of the earth," we are referred back to 13:1, "And I saw a beast rising out of the sea."[2] John seems to be describing the fulfillment of Daniel 7. Daniel sees four beasts ascending from the sea in Daniel 7:3, and then the angel explains that these are four kings who will arise out of the earth in Daniel 7:17. Daniel's four kings were rulers of Babylon, Medo-Persia, Greece, and Rome, all of which controlled the Holy Land in the time between Daniel and Jesus. It seems that by alluding to Daniel in this way, John understands the four empires prophesied by Daniel to be typological precursors of the final world powers that will arise in the future.

It is also worth observing that the first beast comes from the sea in 13:1, and then the second beast comes from the earth in 13:11. These points of origin, sea and earth, are in contrast with the true servants of God, the angels who are in Heaven and the one who comes down from Heaven in 10:1.

We see in the rest of verse 11 that the false prophet looks like Jesus but talks like Satan: "It had two horns like a lamb and it spoke like a dragon." The appearance of the false prophet is reminiscent of John's description of Jesus in 5:6: "I saw a Lamb standing, as though it had been slain, with seven horns." So this false prophet is christlike, which may indicate that he will arise from within the church. Jesus said in Matthew 7:15, "Beware of false prophets, who come to you in sheep's clothing but inwardly are ravenous wolves." He also said in Matthew 12:34, "out of the abundance of the heart the mouth speaks," and this second beast in Revelation 13:11 "spoke like a dragon."

Are you familiar with the Bible's depiction of the way the dragon speaks? In Genesis 3:1 we're told that the serpent is "crafty," and he asks Eve, "Did God actually say . . . ?" In John 8:44 Jesus said of the devil, "He was a murderer from the beginning, and has nothing to do with the truth, because there is no truth in him. When he lies, he speaks out of his own character, for he is a liar and the father of lies." So we can identify at least three characteristics of the dragon's way of speaking: he craftily raises questions about God's word; he lies; and he lies to kill. Who does he want to kill? Jesus and those who follow him.

If someone claims to speak for God and claims to be Christian but craftily causes others to doubt the word of God, they're speaking like the dragon. If someone claims to be a Christian minister but craftily tells lies that result in opposition to Jesus and those who follow Jesus, they're speaking like the dragon. This passage is telling us there will be a supreme manifestation of these characteristics of a false prophet.

Revelation 13:12 points back to what we saw in 13:1–10 and forward to what we will see in 13:13–15. Using the first beast's authority, the false prophet is going to induce people to worship the first beast. In this way the false prophet, this other beast, is a satanic parody of the Holy Spirit. In the real Trinity, Jesus points people to the Father, and the Holy Spirit points people to Jesus. In the satanic false trinity, the first beast points people to the dragon, and the second beast, this false prophet, points people to the first beast, the one who faked the crucifixion and resurrection.

This passage is giving us fair warning: just because someone claims to be a Christian does not mean he or she is. Just because someone uses the language of Christianity does not mean he or she is promoting Christianity. Just because someone looks like Jesus does not mean he or she genuinely represents him. We must know what Christianity really is from the Bible so that we can see past the surface level of Christianity to discern whether what we see is the real thing or a satanic deception.

So how can we tell the difference? This beast speaks like Satan, and Satan speaks against God's word, blasphemes Jesus, and tells lies meant to result in the death of Jesus and his people. Christians do not reject or speak against the Bible. Christians do not blaspheme Jesus. Christians do not tell lies to get other people killed. The tricky thing is that the beast looks like a lamb. So we have to be discerning. If someone holds up the Bible and says, "This is my Bible. I am what it says I am. I have what it says I have. I can do what it says I can do," we must ask, does this person ever open the Bible and say what it actually says in context? Does this person ever do anything other than pull things out of the Bible that he likes to use for his own purposes? Does this person say that we are what the Bible says we are—sinners under the wrath of God? Does he say that our greatest possession is having Christ by faith through the power of the Holy Spirit? When this person talks about what we can do, does he talk about proclaiming the good news of the gospel?

If he says that people are basically good, that it doesn't help people to tell them they are sinners, that the important thing to have is a lot of money and worldly treasure, and that you can be a good person apart from faith in Christ and the power of the Holy Spirit, he is talking like the dragon. He is blaspheming Jesus by denigrating the power and significance of the cross and saying that we really don't need Jesus, Jesus really isn't the great treasure, and Jesus didn't need to go to the cross at all. Watch out for lambs who talk like dragons. They come in the clothing of sheep, but they are wolves inside.

Revelation 13:13–15: Signs That Deceive and Produce Idolatry

There is a progression here as the false prophet's activity is described in three steps: first, the false prophet does signs that look like the work of God; second, he uses the signs to deceive people into idolatry; and third, he enforces the idolatry with the death penalty. The activity of the false prophet in leading people to worship the first beast was summarized in 13:12; now it will be explained more fully in 13:13–15. Similarly, it seems that the false prophet's activity of enforcing the worship of the beast is summarized in 13:15 and then explained more fully in 13:16–18.

Jesus said in Mark 13:22, "For false christs and false prophets will arise and perform signs and wonders, to lead astray, if possible, the elect." We saw the beast fake the crucifixion and resurrection in 13:1–4, and now in 13:13 the false prophet will do things that look very much like the work of God: "It performs great signs, even making fire come down from heaven to earth in front of people." This looks like the work of the two witnesses in 11:5, but there the fire consumed the enemies of the two witnesses. It did something—it defended the people of God. Here when the false prophet does it, it doesn't defend anyone—it's just a neat trick. The trick, though, looks like the work of God through Elijah (1 Kings 18:38), and it looks like what the disciples expected would be done to the enemies of Jesus (Luke 9:54). When something looks Christian, looks like the work of God, how do you know whether it really is of God?

One way to know is to look at its purpose. That is, what is this thing that looks Christian being used to accomplish? There are four Christian purposes: (1) to exalt Jesus, (2) to impress on people their great need to believe in him and be saved by his death and resurrection because they are sinful and God is holy, (3) to encourage people to read the Bible and heed its message, and (4) to encourage people to love others and serve them so they can know the love of God in Christ by the power of the Spirit. If these purposes are not being accomplished, however Christian something may seem, it isn't Christian at all.

You can be sure, too, that if something is being used to do exactly what the Bible forbids, it isn't Christian. That's what we see in 13:14: "and by the signs that it is allowed to work in the presence of the beast it deceives those who dwell on earth, telling them to make an image for the beast that was wounded by the sword and yet lived." This is idolatry. The Lord commanded in the Ten Commandments that no carved images were to be made of him (Exodus 20:4), and the New Testament reaffirms the command against idolatry (1 John 5:21). So no matter what the sign looks like or how impressive it seems, if it is used to persuade people to do exactly what the Bible forbids, it isn't Christian—it's demonic, satanic. Notice how this satanic idolatry wants to look Christian—they are making "an image for the beast that was wounded by the sword and yet lived" (13:14). If you didn't know better, you might think these people were actually worshiping Jesus. But if people are doing exactly what the Bible says not to do, they are not worshiping Jesus.

Jesus sets people free by bringing them into the light, into the truth (John 8:36). That's not Satan's agenda. Satan's false prophet does not want the truth. He deceives, as we see in 13:14: "it deceives those who dwell on earth." There will come a day when for a thousand years Satan will be bound and prevented from deceiving the nations (20:1–3). Before that day comes, Satan works powerful deception through false teachers throughout history (e.g., 2 Corinthians 11:4, 5, 13, 20) and through this false prophet who will arise at the end of history. But God is sovereign over what the evil forces at work in the world will do. Notice in verse 14 that the false prophet was "allowed" to do these things.

This passage is telling us that at the end of history, when the gospel has gone to all nations (11:7), the way that Satan will prosecute his war against the woman and her seed (12:13–17) will be by counterfeiting the work of God in Christ (13:1–4). The false prophet here in 13:11–14 arises with a powerful deception to compel people to commit idolatry by worshiping the beast.

He first does signs in 13:13; then in 13:14 he uses the signs to validate idolatry, and he enforces his program in 13:15: "And it was allowed to give breath to the image of the beast, so that the image of the beast might even speak and might cause those who would not worship the image of the beast to be slain." This is almost like Frankenstein. The false prophet does what looks like a miracle by giving breath to the image of the beast. Notice that God is sovereign over this activity—the false prophet "was allowed" to do this. And once he has done it, the image speaks! This has to be the work of God, right? Wrong. No matter how miraculous it seems, if it is not leading people to believe the gospel of Jesus Christ, it isn't Christian. Satan can produce counterfeits that look like the real thing, but his counterfeits smell like the dragon from which they come. His counterfeits will blaspheme Jesus and suppress the truth and seek to deceive. His counterfeits will be murderous. The image of the beast to which the false prophet gives breath speaks, and what he says is that anyone who doesn't worship the image deserves to die. While he was saying this he was probably also claiming that it was liberal and tolerant, and most university professors probably agreed with him.

Notice the progression of the false prophet's work in verses 13–15: powerful signs in verse 13 are used to promote idolatry in verse 14, and the idolatry is enforced with the death penalty in verse 15. The people of God have been through this before—remember Daniel 3 where we read that Shadrach, Meshach, and Abednego are told to bow to the image or be burned alive? The people of God have been through this before, and we will go through it again.

In order to be faithful to God at that moment, we have to be absolutely certain about the difference between the work of God and the work of Satan. Christianity exalts Jesus by stressing the necessity of his death on the cross for salvation because of the Father's holiness and human sinfulness. Jesus died and rose from the dead to satisfy the Father's justice against sin and to establish the justification of those who trust in him. If someone is doing what looks like the work of God, but they're not promoting that message, not proclaiming the gospel, they're not doing the work of Christianity, even if they call themselves a Christian ministry. If your life is at stake, you need to be absolutely certain that you're right. Do you believe this message? I invite you to start believing it right now. We must think hard about the gospel. We must get a clear understanding of the gospel. And then we must believe the gospel and be ready to die for the gospel.

Calling down fire from Heaven and giving breath to an idol so that it speaks isn't really that impressive. Do you know what's impressive? Do you know what is genuinely miraculous? People repenting of sin. People confessing their sin and asking forgiveness. People staying true to the gospel no matter what it costs them, even if they get killed for it. People inconveniencing themselves to serve others. That's impressive. What the gospel produces is impressive, and such results only come from the gospel. Satan can't counterfeit the gospel and what it produces.

Revelation 13:16–18: The Mark of the Beast

The work of the false prophet in making worldlings worship the beast is introduced in 13:12, then explained in 13:13–15. Similarly, the work of the false prophet enforcing idolatry is introduced in 13:15, then explained in 13:16–18.

The beast requires the mark of the beast in 13:16, 17, and then John hints at its meaning in 13:18. We read in 13:16, "Also it causes all, both small and great, both rich and poor, both free and slave, to be marked on the right hand or the forehead." This is standard satanic procedure: counterfeit the work of God. In 7:3 the servants of God were sealed on their foreheads. Now Satan wants his servants sealed. Farther back than chapter 7 and the sealing of the saints, Moses said to Israel in Deuteronomy 6:8 that God's word was to be bound as a sign on their hand and as frontlets between their eyes—they were to have God's word on their hands and on their foreheads. Satan wants his seal where only God's word should be. If you have been sealed by God through the Holy Spirit, the way God intends to keep you is by the Spirit applying the Word of God, the Bible, to your thinking. If you are a believer, the Bible is the grid through which you are to see the world. If you don't see things God's way through the grid of the Bible, you will see things Satan's way.

Look at the way the false prophet uses the mark in 13:17: "so that no one can buy or sell unless he has the mark, that is, the name of the beast or the number of its name." So the false prophet is seeking to impose tremendous psychological pressure on anyone who disbelieves his signs and does not worship the image of the beast and take the mark of the beast. This is not put into effect all at once. Rather, this will involve the imposition of the standard and then an ongoing, day-by-day resistance to the demand as those who refuse to take the mark grow more and more hungry, more and more concerned for the welfare of their families, and more and more uncertain about how they will procure what they need to live. We know from 13:7 that the beast wants to kill Christians, but now we are informed that the execution will be a long time in coming rather than happening swiftly. The waiting makes it worse.

John interprets the mark of the beast and the number of his name in 13:18: "This calls for wisdom: let the one who has understanding calculate the number of the beast, for it is the number of a man, and his number is 666." The statement "This calls for wisdom" parallels the statement at the end of 13:10, "Here is a call for the endurance and faith of the saints" (cf. also 14:12; 17:9). So the depiction of the persecution in 13:1–8 leads to a focused call for endurance and faith in 13:9, 10, and the depiction of the persecution from the false prophet in 13:11–17 leads to a focused call for wisdom in 13:18.

What kind of wisdom? The rest of 13:18 describes the one who has "understanding" calculating "the number of the beast, for it is the number of a man, and his number is 666." This reference to calculating numbers in 13:18 seems to point to what is known as *gematria*, which is a symbolic interpretation of the numerical value of Hebrew letters. The Hebrew language does not have separate symbols for numbers but assigns numerical value to the letters of the alphabet. This means that the consonants of a word can be added together to achieve a number that can then be used as a numeric symbol for that word or name. If you put the name Nero Caesar into Hebrew consonants, their numerical value is 666.[3] Similarly, if you transliterate the Greek word for *beast* into Hebrew consonants, the numerical value is also 666.[4] This appears to be what John means when he mentions in 13:18 "the number of the beast, for it is the number of a man, and his number is 666."

If this is a reference to the Emperor Nero, what does it mean? We saw the legend of Nero's return from the dead when we considered the beast whose mortal wound was healed in 13:1–4. I think that John is using the pattern of Nero as a type of the final ruler of an evil world empire through whom Satan will persecute the church. So Nero was a wicked tyrant who persecuted Christians and was worshiped as a god and had expectations that he would return from the dead the way only Jesus has really done. I think that John is now seeing in his vision the typological fulfillment of the historical Nero in this final Antichrist who is a seven-headed, ten-horned beast and who has a false prophet who enforces the worship of the beast with the threat of death.

What does this mean for us today? John wrote in 1 John 2:18, 19, "Children, it is the last hour, and as you have heard that antichrist is coming, so now many antichrists have come. Therefore we know that it is the last hour. They went out from us, but they were not of us." These "antichrists" have gone out from the true church. They are false teachers who have gone away from the gospel. John can evidently say that "many antichrists have come" because there were several instances of this. We could look around today and identify people who claim to be doing Christian ministry, but their aim is not to cause people to see God's holiness, realize their own sinfulness, and trust in Christ by the power of the Spirit so they can be saved according to the Bible's teaching. If that is not their aim, they can call themselves Christian ministers and teachers, but the reality is that they are antichrists. They fit the pattern, and one day the pattern will be fulfilled in the ultimate Antichrist.

In 13:18 John says, "This calls for wisdom." I think John wants to give us the wisdom necessary to discern between true and false prophecy. He wants us to be able to tell the difference between the true gospel and false gospels. John wants us to be able to tell the difference between those who exalt God and teach the truth about his holiness and those whose teaching leads to the conclusion that God is not holy—not because they say that God is unholy but because their teaching leads to the conclusion that God is not going to punish sin. John wants us to tell the difference between those who teach the truth about the sinfulness of human beings and our inability to save ourselves and those who teach that we're basically good people who can make ourselves better apart from the new birth and the power of the Spirit working through faith. John wants us to be able to tell the difference between those who exalt Jesus by celebrating his death and resurrection and his unique ability to accomplish salvation and those who blaspheme Jesus because their teaching leads people to think they don't really need Jesus or his death and resurrection. John wants to give us the wisdom that leads to salvation. John wants us to be able to tell the difference between the work of God and Satan's counterfeits. John wants us to know the Bible so that we will know whether someone is teaching the Bible or claiming to teach it while actually inducing people to do exactly what the Bible says not to do.

Conclusion

John's original audience in the churches he addressed in Asia Minor may have understood the mark of the beast to refer to participation in the Roman Imperial Cult. Failure to participate in the idolatrous activity of that cult, with the Caesar at its head—beastly Nero and those who followed him—could result in financial and economic consequences like those described here. So how would John's original audience have been enabled to persevere in such circumstances, and how can we be enabled to persevere as we face similar things? To take it one step further, if the events of the end come upon us and the Antichrist arises, how will we stand against him? Does John give us any help here? It is likely that the whole book of Revelation would have been read aloud all at once in early Christian worship services; so John's original audience would have seen what happens in the very next chapter. In 14:1–5 the redeemed, those sealed with the Father's name on their foreheads, stand with God's Lamb, Jesus, on Mount Zion. Then in 14:9–11 those who have the mark of the beast drink the full cup of God's wrath. So John's original audience would have been encouraged to remain faithful by the promise that they would be redeemed and their enemies would be judged. We take our encouragement from these truths, too. If Satan and his minions starve us and kill us, judgment day is coming, and we will be raised in glorified bodies while those who take the mark of the beast will experience God's wrath. "This calls for wisdom" (13:18). Let us distinguish between God's truth and Satan's counterfeits, and let us hold fast the gospel that glorifies Jesus and reconciles us to the Father as taught by the Holy Spirit in the Bible.

25

The Song of the Redeemed

REVELATION 14:1–13

IN HIS BOOK *A Portrait of the Artist as a Young Man*, James Joyce describes a saint's visionary experience of Hell:

> [H]e stood in the midst of a great hall, dark and silent save for the ticking of a great clock. The ticking went on unceasingly; and it seemed to this saint that the sound of the ticking was the ceaseless repetition of the words: ever, never; ever, never. Ever to be in hell, never to be in heaven; ever to be shut off from the presence of God, never to enjoy the beatific vision; ever to be eaten with flames, gnawed by vermin, goaded with burning spikes, never to be free from those pains; ever to have the conscience upbraid one, the memory enrage, the mind filled with darkness and despair, never to escape; ever to curse and revile the foul demons who gloat fiendishly over the misery of their dupes, never to behold the shining raiment of the blessed spirits; ever to cry out of the abyss of fire to God for an instant, a single instant, of respite from such awful agony, never to receive, even for an instant, God's pardon; ever to suffer, never to enjoy; ever to be damned, never to be saved; ever, never; ever, never. O, what a dreadful punishment! An eternity of endless agony, of endless bodily and spiritual torment, without one ray of hope, without one moment of cessation, of agony limitless in intensity, of torment infinitely varied, of torture that sustains eternally that which it eternally devours, of anguish that everlastingly preys upon the spirit while it racks the flesh, an eternity, every instant of which is itself an eternity of woe. Such is the terrible punishment decreed for those who die in mortal sin by an almighty and a just God.[1]

Hell will be awful, worse than even these words tell. Those who believe in Jesus will be saved from God's awful wrath. Those who endure, who persevere in faith to the end, will be saved.

279

Need

In chapter 13 John has shown Satan's war against the church using powerful deception, and he doesn't want anyone who believes in Jesus to decide that it would be easier to give in than to resist. He doesn't want anyone to conclude that it would be better to join the world and Satan than to be faithful to Jesus. Satan's persecution of the church will be awful. People might not be able to buy or sell food. Fathers might not be able to provide for their families. Christians will be put to death, and it might even look like Christianity has been stamped out altogether. Still, John gives us this passage so that we will never give up. John gives us this passage so that we will never stop resisting Satan. John gives us this passage so that we will never join the world in its idolatry and immorality. John gives us this passage to enable us to persevere to the end and be saved.

Main Point

Revelation 14:1–13 enables endurance to the end by showing the salvation of the redeemed and the judgment of the wicked.

Preview

Revelation 14:1–5	The Song of the Redeemed (assurance)
Revelation 14:6–11	Three Angelic Pronouncements (warning)
Revelation 14:12, 13	A Call to Persevere and a Blessing on the Faithful (encouragement)

Context

Think of a picture frame on a mantelpiece. The picture in the middle of the frame is the declaration that Christ is King in 11:15–19. The mat on either side of the picture is the depiction of the church persecuted throughout the church age in 11:1–14 and 12:1–13:10. The frame around this matted picture has the true prophet John on one side in 10:1–11 and the false prophet on the other side in 13:11–18.

The framed picture is not the only thing on the mantelpiece. There are matching sets of decorative candles on each side. The first candles match each other, and the second candles match each other. The first candle on each side represents the depiction of the sealed 144,000 redeemed saints of God in chapter 7 on one side and the same sealed 144,000 in chapter 14 on the other side. The second candles on each side match each other as well: on one side the second candle represents the six trumpets of God's wrath in chapters 8, 9 (with the seventh trumpet in 11:15–19), and on the other side the candle represents the seven bowls of God's wrath in chapters 15, 16. So the framed picture on the mantelpiece looks like this:

Table 25.1: The Framed Picture of Revelation 11—16

Christ is King
11:15–19

Persecuted Church	Persecuted Church
11:1–14	12:1–13:10
True Prophet John	Satan's False Prophet
10:1–11	13:11–18
144,000 Sealed — Six Trumpet Plagues	144,000 Sealed — Seven Bowls of Wrath
Revelation 7, 8 — 9	Revelation 14, 15 — 16

Revelation 14:1–5: The Song of the Redeemed

Let's remember that John is writing to churches that are struggling, as we saw in the letters to the seven churches, and John has just told these churches in chapter 13 that Satan is going to make war on them by using deceptive signs to initiate persecution. Now John tells the embattled Christians in his audience that Satan will not have the last word. John will give assurance to the redeemed in 14:1–5, warn the wicked in 14:6–11, and then encourage the righteous in 14:12, 13.

John tells us what he saw in 14:1, what he heard in 14:2, what the 144,000 were doing in 14:3, and the characteristics of the 144,000 in 14:4, 5. Everything in this depiction is meant to motivate endurance. Those who are embattled behold those who have overcome. They see those who have received the promises. They see the conqueror on Mount Zion with his army ready to wage the messianic war. They hear the song being sung before the Father in Heaven. All of this inspires us to seek to be faithful, to endure to the end, to overcome.

In 12:17, the beast "stood on the sand of the sea." Now in 14:1 John writes, "Then I looked, and behold, on Mount Zion stood the Lamb." Satan does not have firm footing on the sand of the sea, for Jesus stands on Mount Zion. We read in chapter 7 of the sealing of the 144,000, and now we see that group again in the rest of verse 1: "and with him 144,000 who had his name and his Father's name written on their foreheads." Jesus promised the Philadelphians in 3:12, "The one who conquers . . . I will write on him the name of my God . . . and my own new name." These 144,000 were sealed in chapter 7, they conquered, and now they have received the promise that Jesus made to those who overcome.

The redeemed will stand with Jesus on Mount Zion. They will bear the name of the Father and the Son, showing forth his glory. We want to be numbered among them. God will keep his promises. There is more to this life than our years here; death is not the end.

The voice of Jesus was "like the roar of many waters" in 1:15. Now in

14:2 John hears "a voice from heaven like the roar of many waters and like the sound of loud thunder." This describes a loud, overpowering voice. The redeemed no longer seem outnumbered and weak. Now they roar. They sound like Jesus because they have followed in his steps. John will again hear the redeemed speak with a voice like many waters and loud thunders in 19:6. Here in chapter 14 John goes on to describe what he heard at the end of verse 2 and on into verse 3: "The voice I heard was like the sound of harpists playing on their harps, and they were singing a new song before the throne and before the living creatures and before the elders. No one could learn that song except the 144,000 who had been redeemed from the earth."

There are several observations to be made here. First, in verse 1 the Lamb and the 144,000 are on Mount Zion, but in verse 2 John hears "a voice from heaven," and the song in verse 3 is being sung "before the throne and before the four living creatures and before the elders." Hebrews 12:22 describes the "Mount Zion" that is part of "the heavenly Jerusalem." So that seems to be the Mount Zion that John has described in verse 1. Second, on this Mount Zion the 144,000 are like harpists making music before the Father on his throne in the presence of the heavenly court. The redeemed are singing "a new song," just as we saw the heavenly court sing a new song in 5:9 when Jesus took the scroll. New acts of conquest call for new songs of praise. Finally, note that this is an exclusive song: none but those sealed by the Father, redeemed by Jesus, can learn this song. There will not be Hindus, Buddhists, or Muslims singing that song, nor will there be decent people who were consistent with their own atheism. Only those who put explicit faith in Jesus will sing this song.

John tells us four things about these singers in 14:4, 5: they are pure; they follow Jesus; they were redeemed; and they tell the truth. The first three of these are seen in 14:4 and the fourth in 14:5.

The first thing John says about them is in 14:4: "It is these who have not defiled themselves with women, for they are virgins." The point here is not that these people never married, nor is it that these are all men. I think this figurative description of the 144,000 as virgins means they were pure. They did not defile themselves with the sexual immorality that accompanies idolatry. Look at the reference to "the wine of the passion of [Babylon's] sexual immorality" in 14:8, and notice how Babylon "made all nations drink" it. The redeemed refused to drink the wine of the sexual immorality of Babylon's worldliness. We're not talking about the literal kingdom of Babylon. Babylon is a symbol of the world powers that refuse to submit to God. So this first description of the 144,000 means they were pure in their devotion to God and abstained from worldliness. They did not commit spiritual adultery against him.

How are you doing on this front? Are you pure in your devotion to God?

While the description of these people as "virgins" is figurative, we can say that no one who is sexually immoral is pure in his or her devotion to God. Do you need to repent? Let me exhort you to renew your commitment to sexual and spiritual purity right now. If the Spirit has sealed you, you will do so. Do it with all your might.

John's second description of the 144,000 in 14:4 states, "It is these who follow the Lamb wherever he goes." The Lamb is Jesus. Jesus leads through his Word, and he has given clear commands to his people in the Bible. Following Jesus is the opposite of idolatry. Do you know how to keep from being deceived by the beast who looks like the Lamb but talks like the dragon? Follow Jesus wherever he goes. These first two descriptions of the 144,000 show that they did not commit idolatry and the sexual immorality that accompanies it.

Are you following Jesus wherever he goes by obeying the commands of Jesus in the Bible? Are you remaining in his Word? Are you doing everything you can to make disciples of Jesus from all nations?

The third description of the 144,000 in 14:4 tells us how they became who they are: "These have been redeemed from mankind as firstfruits for God and the Lamb." They did not redeem themselves. They did not secure their own salvation. God saved them through Jesus. Note the passive: "These *have been* redeemed." If you think you are going to stand before God and be accepted because you are a good person, you are wrong. If you think you are going to redeem yourself from slavery to sin, you are wrong. It will never happen. The 144,000 are redeemed as "firstfruits," and the full harvest of the righteous is depicted in 14:14–16. The 144,000 are redeemed "for God and the Lamb."

If you are redeemed, you are redeemed for God and the Lamb. Let me encourage you to be what you are. Do you believe the gospel? If you have been redeemed, you have been redeemed for God. Live like you are an offering consecrated to God—as Paul puts it, like "a living sacrifice" (Romans 12:1, 2). Is that the way you think of yourself?

The fourth thing that John says about the redeemed is in 14:5: "and in their mouth no lie was found, for they are blameless." They tell the truth. They tell the truth, but the dragon lies about who made the world and what it is for. They tell the truth, but the dragon lies about the useless death and resurrection of the beast. They tell the truth, but the dragon uses the false prophet to deceive. Do you see what this means? It means the redeemed tell the truth about God, about who the Messiah is, about how to be reconciled to God through faith in Jesus, about why people need to be reconciled—we're all sinners! They tell the truth about where true revelation can be found—in the Bible. While the dragon, the beast, and the false prophet are constructing their alternative explanation of the world, of what deserves worship, and of how truth can be known, the redeemed are telling the truth. They are proclaiming the truth of the Scriptures and the good news of the gospel.

Note the connection in 14:5 between blamelessness and truth-telling. The Bible never presents blamelessness as something that results from perfect obedience or absolute sinlessness. Blamelessness results from the gospel. Those who believe in Jesus, repent of their sins, and trust in his death on the cross to pay the penalty for their sins are blameless.

Are you blameless? Are you telling the truth? Or are you deceived by Satan's lies? Do lies come from your mouth? If you know that to be so, let me exhort you to repent of those lies right now and come to the truth.

Revelation 14:6–11: Three Angelic Pronouncements

John now describes the proclamations of three angels in 14:6–11. The first, in 14:6, 7, proclaims the gospel, which is the truth that exposes the lies told by Satan and believed by the world. The second, in 14:8, announces that the world's party is over because Babylon has fallen. The third, in 14:9–11, describes the everlasting torment with no rest that God will bring on those who worship the beast and align themselves with the world against God and the gospel.

First the gospel in 14:6, 7:

> Then I saw another angel flying directly overhead, with an eternal gospel to proclaim to those who dwell on earth, to every nation and tribe and language and people. And he said with a loud voice, "Fear God and give him glory, because the hour of his judgment has come, and worship him who made heaven and earth, the sea and the springs of water."

This message is described as "an eternal gospel." This message is always true, from everlasting to everlasting, and it is good news. Be astonished by this claim of a message that is forever and good! Have you contemplated the majesty of the truth of the gospel? This is not just some old story—it is the eternal gospel. Let me encourage you to let your mind contemplate this until the grandeur of it rests on you with a weight that will change your life. If you know the gospel, you know truth that is true from eternity past and that will still be true in eternity future. If you know the gospel, you know the good news—everlasting good news.

This message is not just "true for you" either. This message is not only for Jews, or only for Americans, or only for people in the Bible Belt. This message is for *everyone*—the angel is going to proclaim it "to those who dwell on earth, to every nation and tribe and language and people." This is the everlasting good news for everyone everywhere. Do you recognize what this statement does? It excludes the possibility of "local truths" that apply only to those people over there. This means that the gospel is the everlasting good news for the Muslims in the Arab world, for the Buddhists in Southeast Asia, for the Hindus in India, and for the atheists in Europe. The gospel applies to them—they don't have some other way to God. The only way they will know God is by faith in Jesus Christ. There is not some other religious message that was true before the Bible, and there is not some other religious message that will be valid when the gospel no longer applies—the angel's message is the "*eternal* gospel." And the angel's message is the only message that is *gospel*.

If you know the gospel, you know everlasting good news. And if you know the gospel, you should feel an enormous weight of responsibility. This is the only saving message, and so many people have never heard it. My prayer for the church is that our lives would be given to the proclamation of the gospel and that our highest commitment will be to make disciples of all nations.

Look at the message of the eternal gospel in 14:7: "Fear God and give him glory, because the hour of his judgment has come, and worship him who made heaven and earth, the sea and the springs of water." This is a simple message. God is the Creator. God made all that is. Because of this, God alone is to be feared, God alone is to be worshiped, and God alone will judge. These truths are as basic as gravity, and yet many people foolishly deny them. No one can make gravity not apply to them; no one can levitate, no one can fly. And no one can escape the implications of this eternal gospel.

O God, give us lives that demonstrate our embrace of this eternal gospel.

The second angel's message is in 14:8: "Another angel, a second, followed, saying, 'Fallen, fallen is Babylon the great, she who made all the nations drink the wine of the passion of her sexual immorality.'" In 14:4 we saw the sexual purity and unmixed devotion to Jesus of the 144,000 redeemed. Now we will see the sexual immorality and idolatry of the world addressed by these second and third angels. Here we see the world's sexual immorality with the harlot Babylon. The kingdom of Babylon is a symbol of the wicked world system that rejects God and does as it pleases. In 17:5 the kingdom of Babylon will be symbolically depicted as a "prostitute." The idea is that the powers at work in the world are enticing people to commit spiritual adultery against the one to whom they owe their faithfulness and devotion. Have you noticed that the world wants to lead you away from God?

Let's think about this proclamation in 14:8. John here describes a visionary experience of an angel who proclaims Babylon's fall before it happens. It hadn't happened in the vision when the angel proclaimed it—that will come in chapters 17, 18. So before Babylon is depicted as falling, the angel announces that Babylon has "fallen." This means that Babylon's fall is certain. What Babylon symbolizes—the world's temptations that would lead us away from God—still hasn't fallen, has it? But the fall of Babylon is certain, so certain that the angel can speak as though it has already happened.

Are you living as if Babylon has fallen? Are you living as if Babylon's fall is certain? To the extent that we are guilty of worldliness, we are not living like we believe Babylon will fall. And if we believe Babylon will fall and are still living in worldly ways, then we are guilty of trying to please ourselves with pleasures that God has condemned and will destroy.

This second angel's proclamation is a warning and a call to repentance. It warns us to flee from Babylon lest we share her doom, and it commands us to repent of our attempts to combine the pleasures of God with the pleasures of the world. The two do not mix. Let us repent of our worldliness. Let us pursue faithful, undiluted purity and devotion to God alone. Let us live in the assurance that Babylon has fallen.

The Bible gives us ammunition for the fight against Babylon the prostitute, weapons with which we can fight for sexual purity. Proverbs 5:3, 4 says, "For the lips of a forbidden woman drip honey, and her speech is smoother than oil, but in the end she is bitter as wormwood, sharp as a two-edged sword." Proverbs 6:25 adds, "Do not desire her beauty in your heart, and do not let her capture you with her eyelashes."

The third angel proclaims the punishment that God will bring on those who commit sexual immorality with Babylon and idolize the beast. After the end of 14:8 refers to sexual immorality, notice how 14:9, 10 addresses idolatry:

> And another angel, a third, followed them, saying with a loud voice, "If anyone worships the beast and its image and receives a mark on his forehead or on his hand, he also will drink the wine of God's wrath, poured full strength into the cup of his anger, and he will be tormented with fire and sulfur in the presence of the holy angels and in the presence of the Lamb."

Worshiping the beast will keep Satan from persecuting you. Taking the mark of the beast will enable you to buy and sell. For a while, a short while, idolatry and identification with Satan may make your life better. But there is a terrible price to pay. This message is meant to preserve believers and to call unbelievers to repent. Believers are told here that giving in to the pressure and persecution described in chapter 13 places one squarely under the wrath of God. Unbelievers are warned of the wrath that is over them. Those who "drink the wine" of Babylon's "immorality" (14:8) will drink "the wine of God's wrath" (14:10). That wine is "poured full strength into the cup of his anger" (14:10), which means that this wine is undiluted. God's fury is neither softened nor slowed. God will torment his enemies with fire and sulfur, heat and stench, and the shame and pain and disgrace will not be hidden. God will visit his justice "in the presence of the holy angels and in the presence of the Lamb" (14:10). God will not hide the display of the glory of his justice, and the presence and observation of the holy ones will only make the torment of the wicked that much worse.

Revelation 14:11 tells us that this punishment will never end: "And the smoke of their torment goes up forever and ever, and they have no rest, day or night, these worshipers of the beast and its image, and whoever receives the mark of its name." The smoke goes up forever because the fire never goes out. They have no rest day or night because the wrath of God against them will never be exhausted, because the punishment fits the crime. The crime of refusing to "fear God and give him glory" (14:7) is infinite in heinousness and effrontery. Therefore the punishment such an infinite crime deserves is infinite in scope and duration. Hell lasts forever because God is infinitely important. Hell is about the worth and majesty of God. If you understand what it means for God to be God, you will understand why Hell lasts forever. If Hell is offensive to you, it is because you have not yet realized how significant God is.

No one has sufficiently felt the weight of God and eternity, and to get at it I want to quote James Joyce again:

Last and crowning torture of all the tortures of that awful place is the eternity of hell. Eternity! O, dread and dire word. Eternity! What mind of man can understand it? And remember, it is an eternity of pain. Even though the pains of hell were not so terrible as they are, yet they would become infinite, as they are destined to last for ever. But while they are everlasting they are at the same time, as you know, intolerably intense, unbearably extensive. To bear even the sting of an insect for all eternity would be a dreadful torment. What must it be, then, to bear the manifold tortures of hell for ever? For ever! For all eternity! Not for a year or for an age but for ever. Try to imagine the awful meaning of this. You have often seen the sand on the seashore. How fine are its tiny grains! And how many of those tiny little grains go to make up the small handful which a child grasps in its play. Now imagine a mountain of that sand, a million miles high, reaching from the earth to the farthest heavens, and a million miles broad, extending to remotest space, and a million miles in thickness; and imagine such an enormous mass of countless particles of sand multiplied as often as there are leaves in the forest, drops of water in the mighty ocean, feathers on birds, scales on fish, hairs on animals, atoms in the vast expanse of the air: and imagine that at the end of every million years a little bird came to that mountain and carried away in its beak a tiny grain of that sand. How many millions upon millions of centuries would pass before that bird had carried away even a square foot of that mountain, how many eons upon eons of ages before it had carried away all? Yet at the end of that immense stretch of time not even one instant of eternity could be said to have ended. At the end of all those billions and trillions of years eternity would have scarcely begun. And if that mountain rose again after it had been all carried away, and if the bird came again and carried it all away again grain by grain, and if it so rose and sank as many times as there are stars in the sky, atoms in the air, drops of water in the sea, leaves on the trees, feathers upon birds, scales upon fish, hairs upon animals, at the end of all those innumerable risings and sinkings of that immeasurably vast mountain not one single instant of eternity could be said to have ended; even then, at the end of such a period, after that eon of time the mere thought of which makes our very brain reel dizzily, eternity would scarcely have begun.[2]

Are you ready to face eternity? The only thing that will deliver you from the eternal wrath of God is the eternal gospel of God. God's eternal and undiluted wrath was poured out on Christ at the cross. He drank the whole cup of the full fury of God's justice against sin. If you trust in Jesus, he drank that cup for you. You will either trust in Christ, or you will drink that cup for yourself. I invite you to place your confidence and hope in Jesus, to trust in him now.

Revelation 14:12, 13: A Call to Persevere and a Blessing on the Faithful

Satan's deceptions may be powerful, his beast may be convincing, and his false prophet may persuade every unbeliever in the world to worship the beast and kill Christians. It will not be fun to have the ancient dragon wage war against us. Revelation 13:10 indicates that some of us may be taken captive and others slain with the sword. Revelation 13:17 says that those who refuse the mark of the beast will not be able to buy or sell. We may suffer, and because of our faithfulness to Jesus, our families may suffer as well.

But chapter 14 tells us that as bad as it may get for believers before Jesus comes, when he comes he will reward those who have been faithful to him and will punish his enemies. It will be worse for unbelievers when he comes than it was for believers while Satan attacked them. So we see the recipients of the promises in 14:1–5, and we see the punishment of the idolatrous and sexually immoral in 14:6–11. Now (14:12) John tells us why he has shown us these things: "Here is a call for the endurance of the saints, those who keep the commandments of God and their faith in Jesus."

Do you need motivation to keep the commandments of God and to keep believing in Jesus? Brand your brain with the images of the redemption of the faithful and the punishment of the wicked in 14:1–11. Do you need help fighting the temptations of the world? Ask God to bring to mind the fall of Babylon and the wine of God's wrath that those who worship the beast will drink. When Babylon tempts you, think of how she will fare on the Day of Judgment.

When the beast calls for your worship, think of the torment his worshipers will experience in the presence of the Lamb. Think of the fact that they will never rest, day or night. Think of the fact that the smoke will rise forever. Endure in keeping the commands of God and believing in Jesus by seeing the outcome of the things that would tempt you to disobedience and unbelief.

Trusting in Jesus and obeying God's commands may get you killed by Satan. But the temporary suffering before death and death itself will be overcome by God's resurrection power. Consider what John says in 14:13: "And I heard a voice from heaven saying, 'Write this: blessed are the dead who die in the Lord from now on.' 'Blessed indeed,' says the Spirit, 'that they may rest from their labors, for their deeds follow them!'" The voice from Heaven blesses those who are killed because they obey God and believe in Jesus. They are blessed because they will not suffer God's wrath. Then the Spirit chimes in and says that unlike those who worship the beast, those who are killed for obedience to God and faith in Jesus will "rest." And the Spirit also says that "their deeds follow them," which means that everything we do in obedience to God's commands and out of faith in Jesus will be remembered before God on the Day of Judgment.

Conclusion

After the incident of the golden calf, the Lord commanded Israel not to commit idolatry and sexual immorality with the inhabitants of Canaan in Exodus 34:14–16. Solomon became sexually immoral and fell into idolatry in 1 Kings 11:1–8. After the people returned from exile, Ezra and Nehemiah were both opposed to intermarriage with the peoples of the land because they feared the sexual immorality and idolatry that would result (Ezra 9:11, 12, 14; Nehemiah 13:23–31).

The church is now the bride of Christ (Ephesians 5:22–33). The 144,000 are described as "virgins" who "follow the Lamb wherever he goes" in 14:4 because they are those who will partake in the "marriage supper of the Lamb" (19:9); they are "the Bride, the wife of the Lamb" (21:9). We pursue sexual and spiritual purity for the sake of the one who is to come.

26

The Harvest of the Earth

REVELATION 14:14–20

WHAT WILL YOU DO between now and judgment day?

When Antonio James was a teenager, he got mixed up with a gang in New Orleans. They would rob tourists in the French Quarter at gunpoint. "Most of the time, the victims did not resist. Except one. Antonio shot him, and he died." His gang members ran, then testified against him to save themselves. Antonio James was sentenced to death. He was on death row for fourteen years.

Before he died, he became a Christian. He used his time on death row to teach others on death row to read so that they, too, could read the Bible. He taught Bible studies and cared about other men facing death.

In the death chamber he asked forgiveness from the victim's family and told them he was sorry for what he had done. The warden of Angola prison, Burl Cain, also a believer in Jesus, took the hand of Antonio James and said, "Antonio, the chariot is here; get ready for the ride. Here we go; you are about to see Jesus."

When Burl Cain announced that the execution had taken place, he said, "we have sent Antonio James to his final judgment."[1]

What will you do between now and judgment day?

Need

We must face the fact that the earth will be reaped. The actions that we have sown, whether to the flesh or to the Spirit, will bear fruit, and that fruit will be reaped. What kind of fruit are you sowing and bearing? The judgment is certain. Will you spend your time between now and then living for Jesus, trusting in him, so that you have nothing to fear from death? Or will you spend your time between now and then living for yourself, avoiding the thought of what will inevitably come?

We must face the fact that the earth will be reaped. We need to look this reality squarely in the face and live our lives as though we have seen what is coming.

Main Point

God will keep his word to the righteous and to the wicked.

God will keep his word—he will save those who trust in Jesus and will judge those who do not worship him as God or give thanks to him. God will keep his word and will reward righteousness and punish wickedness. The earth will be reaped. Judgment will happen, and justice will be done.

God will keep his word to the righteous and the wicked, but he will show mercy to those who trust in Jesus.

Preview

We see two harvests in 14:14–20:

| Revelation 14:14–16 | The Grain Harvest of the Earth |
| Revelation 14:17–20 | The Grape Harvest of the Earth |

Context

It seems to me that one of the most important questions we can ask about 14:14–20 is this: Why did John put these two harvests at this place in his book? We saw in 14:9, 10 that the wicked will "drink the wine of God's wrath." That wine comes from the grapes that are harvested in 14:19, then trod in the winepress in 14:20. The wine ferments as the events of chapter 15 unfold, and it seems that the bowls that are poured out in chapter 16 are full of the wine of God's wrath. Note 16:19: "God remembered Babylon the great, to make her drain the cup of the wine of the fury of his wrath." So the wine of God's wrath that Babylon will drink in 16:19 comes from the grapes harvested in 14:19. That's bad news. The wicked, according to 14:9, "will drink the wine of God's wrath, poured full strength into the cup of his anger."

But I have good news, too. Do you remember what Jesus prayed in the Garden of Gethsemane? "Father, if you are willing, remove the cup from me. Nevertheless, not my will, but yours, be done" (Luke 22:42). Jesus drank the whole cup. He took all God's wrath. No one who trusts in Jesus has to drink the wine of God's wrath because Jesus drank that cup for us.

Revelation 15, 16 depicts the outpouring of God's wrath in the seven final bowls of his judgment, and then chapters 17, 18 show the fall of Babylon. John is giving us a carefully selected collage of images. These images of the harvest of the earth in 14:14–20, of the outpouring of the final bowls of wrath in chapters 15, 16, and the fall of Babylon in chapters 17, 18 all depict the same thing. They all depict the events of the end of history.

This harvest pertains to people and to *what people have done*. There is a strong tradition in the Bible of people *sowing* deeds and the fruit of those deeds being *reaped*. Hosea 8:7 speaks of those who "sow the wind, and . . . reap the whirlwind." Jesus spoke of the man who planted a fig tree that bore no fruit, so he gave orders to cut it down. The vine dresser said he would fertilize it, and if it still bore no fruit it could be cut down (Luke 13:6–9). Paul told the Galatians, "Do not be deceived: God is not mocked, for whatever one sows, that he will also reap" (Galatians 6:7). People's deeds are reaped in this passage in Revelation. The deeds of the wicked are the grapes that are trodden to produce the wine of God's wrath that will be poured out of the seven bowls in chapter 16.

We can also say that John employs the different imagery—a harvest, the outpouring of the bowls of wrath, the desolation of a harlot city mourned by its merchants—for at least two reasons. First, these different images communicate the implications of the events of the end. Second, these different images gather together the various prophetic depictions of the end of history from earlier passages of the Bible, bring them together, and show them all being fulfilled.

So by showing the harvest of the earth, this passage shows one aspect of how God's promises of judgment are going to be kept. Daniel 7:13 says one like the Son of Man will come "with the clouds of heaven," and in Revelation 14:14 he does just that. Joel 3:13 describes the earth being harvested, and Revelation 14:14–20 declares that Joel 3:13 will be fulfilled. Isaiah 63:2, Jeremiah 25:30 (LXX 32:20), and Lamentations 1:15 speak of God's judgment in terms of the treading of the winepress of God's wrath, and Revelation 14:20 shows those promises being fulfilled. When we look more closely at the bowls of God's wrath (chapters 15, 16) and at the downfall of the harlot city (chapter 17) and the mourning of her merchants (chapter 18), we will see that these images also depict God's keeping the promises he made through the prophets.

What about the placement of 14:14–20 in the context of chapter 14? I have suggested that the first part of chapter 7, with its sealing of the 144,000, matches the first part of chapter 14, where the 144,000 stand with the Lamb on Mount Zion. What follows chapter 7, the trumpet judgments in chapters 8, 9, also matches what follows chapter 14, the bowl judgments in chapters 15, 16.

You'll remember that the first part of chapter 7 deals with the sealing of the 144,000 (vv. 1–8), and then the second half of the chapter shows an innumerable multitude with palm branches in their hands worshiping God (vv. 9–17). The palm branches remind us of the Feast of Tabernacles, which celebrated God's provision for his people in the wilderness after the exodus from Egypt.

The structure of chapter 14 is similar to that of chapter 7. We see the 144,000 with the Lamb on Mount Zion (vv. 1–5), hear three angelic pronouncements and a benediction (vv. 6–13), and then see two harvests of the earth (vv. 14–20). After the harvest of the earth in chapter 14, John sees the overcomers singing the song of Moses in 15:2–4, celebrating the fulfillment of the exodus, just as the innumerable multitude in 7:9–17 had palm branches to celebrate the fulfillment of God's provision in the wilderness.

John is describing the vision he had of final redemption, and in the vision *everything* is fulfilled. This is the fulfillment of the exodus, the fulfillment of God's provision for his people, the fulfillment of everything Jesus and the prophets had to say about the harvest of the earth. John describes his vision of what happens when the end has come. In 14:14–20 we will see two harvests, grain and grapes.

Revelation 14:14–16: The Grain Harvest of the Earth

So with the benediction of 14:13 ringing in our ears, John writes in 14:14, "Then I looked, and behold, a white cloud, and seated on the cloud one like a son of man, with a golden crown on his head, and a sharp sickle in his hand." Daniel 7:13 described "one like a son of man" coming "with the clouds of heaven." In Matthew 24:30 Jesus said the tribes of the earth would "see the Son of Man coming on the clouds of heaven." When the high priest asked Jesus if he was the Messiah, Jesus told him he would "see the Son of Man seated at the right hand of Power and coming on the clouds of heaven" (Matthew 26:63, 64). When Jesus was received into the clouds of Heaven at his ascension, the angels told the disciples that Jesus would come just as he went, on the clouds of Heaven (Acts 1:9–11). John himself announced in Revelation 1:7 that Jesus is coming on the clouds of Heaven and that every eye would see him, "even those who pierced him." John sees this come true in his vision. He sees Jesus coming on the clouds of Heaven in 14:14.

The fact that Jesus is coming in the clouds identifies him with the one "like a son of man" who will receive the kingdom from "the Ancient of Days" in Daniel 7:13. The fact that Jesus is "seated" identifies him with the one seated at the Lord's right hand in Psalm 110. Jesus himself is described in terms that put Daniel 7:13 and Psalm 110:1 together in Matthew 26:64:

"from now on you will see the Son of Man seated at the right hand of Power and coming on the clouds of heaven." John seems to allude to this connection in his description of Jesus in Revelation 14. This indicates that John (and Matthew) learned to interpret the Old Testament from Jesus. Jesus is wearing "a golden crown." He has conquered and received what he promised to those who overcome in 2:10 and 3:11. Jesus has "a sharp sickle in his hand." He comes to harvest the earth.

I wonder how often you think of the day when he will come on the clouds of Heaven, wearing the crown of gold, for the harvest of the earth? We don't think of this as often or as deeply as we should. John is telling us about it to force the issue. Our actions have consequences. What fruit is your life producing? How is the soil around the tree of your life? What kind of rain falls? Is anyone fertilizing the ground around you? Are you being cultivated? If we want to bear fruit for God's glory, we need to think about soil and fertilizer and clean water. Ultimately we must be branches connected to the true vine, Jesus, by faith. Apart from that, the other influences in our lives are meaningless. So we must believe the gospel, trust in Jesus, and then think of our lives as though we are trees. A tree needs the light of the world (Jesus), the living water of the Word (the Spirit working through the Bible), and the Gardener (the Father) cultivating the soil. In short, we need to trust in Christ, hear his Word proclaimed, and fellowship with the family of God in the church.

You will bear rotten, stinking, worthless fruit if you fertilize your tree with television shows, water it with worldliness, and hide your sin from the light of Christ. If you don't trust in Christ, you are cut off from the true vine, and if you don't repent of your sins and trust in Jesus, you will be gathered up and thrown in the fire.

Our lives are to be lived longing for the day when he will come on the clouds. Our lives are to be lived in light of the fact that the prophecy will be fulfilled and he will come on the clouds of Heaven.

How soon the day will be upon us, when what John describes in 14:15 will take place: "And another angel came out of the temple, calling with a loud voice to him who sat on the cloud, 'Put in your sickle, and reap, for the hour to reap has come, for the harvest of the earth is fully ripe.'" So in this scene Jesus is coming on the clouds, and an angelic emissary comes from the heavenly temple to announce that the time to reap has come. "The hour to reap" comes when "the harvest of the earth is fully ripe." What is it that makes the earth ripe?

The answer to that question turns on what kind of harvest this is. Some interpreters think that both sections of this passage are harvests that result in judgment.[2] If 14:14–16 is depicting a harvest that leads to judgment, the ripening of the earth would be the filling up of transgressions (cf. Genesis 15:16; Matthew 23:32; 1 Thessalonians 2:16). This may be correct, but I'm inclined to agree with those interpreters who see a harvest of the righteous in 14:14–16, followed by a harvest of the wicked in 14:17–20. The wicked are definitely harvested in 14:17–20, for the grapes are cast into the winepress of God's wrath (v. 19). I think the harvest in 14:14–16 contrasts with that judgment for at least three reasons: first, the 144,000 are described as the "firstfruits" in 14:4, which points to a full harvest in 14:14–16; second, the harvesters are different—Jesus harvests the righteous, then another angel harvests the wicked; third, this matches the judgment of the righteous whose names are in the Book of Life in 20:12, followed by the judgment of the unrighteous whose names are not in the Book of Life in 20:13–15.[3] So if 14:14–16 is a harvest of the righteous, the ripening of the earth might refer to the gospel going to all nations (Matthew 24:14), the full number of the Gentiles being brought in (Romans 11:25), people from every tribe being saved (Revelation 5:9), and the two witnesses finishing their testimony (11:7).

Jesus Christ will come on the clouds when the harvest is ripe. Are you hastening the day of redemption (2 Peter 3:12)? Do you know what that looks like? It means holiness and godliness (2 Peter 3:11), and it means proclaiming the gospel so that every single one of God's elect will be saved (2 Timothy 2:10). Live for this! Don't waste your life on promotions, on reputation, on padding your stats and making a name for yourself. Live for the day when he appears.

This is the only opportunity we will have to live for that day. Today is the day of salvation (2 Corinthians 6:2). We have a window of opportunity. It is as though the ark is being built while the thunderclouds form. All God's elect will be saved. The question is not whether they will hear the gospel and believe. The question is whether we will have the joy of proclaiming the gospel to them, the joy of teaching them everything Jesus commanded and making disciples (Matthew 28:18–20). Will you be a part of this great work? Will you sacrifice your time, your money, your very life so that the elect may obtain salvation (2 Timothy 2:10)? We have a short time before what John writes in 14:16 takes place: "So he who sat on the cloud swung his sickle across the earth, and the earth was reaped."

All God's elect will be saved. The Father chose them. The Son died for them. The Spirit sealed them. Who does God send to tell them the good news? Us! This is our life. This is our mission. The fields are white for harvest. Others have labored, and we enter into the joy of their work (John 4:35–38). God will save, and he is pleased to allow us the privilege of being his hands and feet. Can there be a higher calling? Could there be a more significant task?

God will save, and God will judge. We see the harvest of the righteous in 14:14–16 and the harvest of the wicked in 14:17–20. God will keep his word to those who trust in Christ for salvation, and he will save them all, every one.

Revelation 14:17–20: The Grape Harvest of the Earth

Salvation is not the only possible fate for human beings. Make no mistake about it, the wicked will be judged. God will keep his word to them, and he will visit terrible judgment upon them. John writes in 14:17, "Then another angel came out of the temple in heaven, and he too had a sharp sickle." The angel in 14:15 came out of the temple with the word that the harvest of the earth was fully ripe and it was time for the one "like a son of man" to gather in the righteous. That angel in 14:15 is called "another angel" because of the three angels who made their pronouncements in 14:6–13. Now yet another angel appears in 14:17, and like the one "like a son of man" in 14:14, he has "a sharp sickle."

This angel is the reality behind the legendary "grim reaper." Evil is frightening, and sinful humanity has cultivated perversions that are indeed terrifying. Let me suggest to you that there are realities far more frightening than anything wicked humans could begin to imagine. Look the holiness of God full in the face. He is absolutely pure . . . altogether righteous . . . unfailing in his goodness . . . absolutely truthful . . . overwhelming in the power and force of his rightness. Now let's look the reality of our sin full in the face. This holy God has given us every good gift and called us to love him and enjoy him with all our might. But we have fled from his presence . . . used his gifts against him . . . tried to make ourselves into gods of our own . . . transgressed his every command. And he overlooks none of it.

The only refuge is Jesus. Jesus died on the cross so God can justly show mercy to sinners. Those who trust in Jesus will be forgiven for all their sins.

If you are not trusting in Jesus, or if you are trusting him and care for someone who isn't, consider the implications of the appearance of this true grim reaper. He comes to bring the wrath of God. He comes to call the wicked to account. He comes to harvest the fruit of their deeds. What the unrighteous have sown shall be reaped. They will not escape. They will not be overlooked. They have rejected their only chance for mercy. There is no place to hide. All the weight of their sin will come crushing down upon them. God's time of patiently bearing with the "vessels of wrath prepared for destruction" (Romans 9:22) has run its course. He will now show his wrath and make known his power. Satan is not scarier than God.

God will arise in almighty holiness to do justice, and there is nothing between the wicked and the full outpouring of his wrath. No Christ stands between them and God. The outpouring of his justice on the wicked is meant to augment and highlight the beauty of the salvation accomplished by Christ on the cross. Think how great this display of justice will be. The greater it is, the better Jesus looks. There will be no limit to the magnitude of the powerful display of God's righteousness—tremendous majesty unleashed in absolute justice. Behold the glory of God's holiness!

"Christ Jesus came into the world to save sinners" (1 Timothy 1:15). Could there be better news? "Everyone who calls on the name of the Lord will be saved" (Romans 10:13). You will not find a better gospel. Won't you believe this one?

If you refuse to believe this gospel, look with me at what awaits you (14:18–20):

> And another angel came out from the altar, the angel who has authority over the fire, and he called with a loud voice to the one who had the sharp sickle, "Put in your sickle and gather the clusters from the vine of the earth, for its grapes are ripe." So the angel swung his sickle across the earth and gathered the grape harvest of the earth and threw it into the great winepress of the wrath of God. And the winepress was trodden outside the city, and blood flowed from the winepress, as high as a horse's bridle, for 1,600 stadia.

This angel in 14:18 comes from the altar and "has authority over the fire," most likely the fire of the altar. So this appears to be the same angel that we saw in 8:3–5. There he offered up incense with the prayers of the saints—the martyred saints who were under the altar crying out for vengeance in 6:9–11. The incense and prayers rose before God (8:3, 4); then the angel cast fire from the altar onto the earth (8:5). Now in 14:18 that same angel comes from the altar and gives the word for the holy angel who is the grim reaper to do his work.

This means that those who will be judged are those who have oppressed and murdered Christians. Those who will be judged are those who reject the gospel and oppose God's right to rule the world. Those who will be judged will suffer God's vengeance. This judgment will be so awful that we should pray for those who persecute us. We don't want anyone to face God's wrath.

The harvest is comprehensive because just as 14:15 spoke of "the harvest of the earth," so now 14:18 shows the ingathering of "the clusters from the vine of the earth." The "grapes are ripe" (14:18). Iniquity is completed. The wicked have filled up the full measure of their sin. They have cultivated and cultured the full measure of transgression for the awesome display of God's justice.

By your deeds, thoughts, statements, and affections, your life is ripening right now for one of these two harvests. Which is it? If you are not trusting in Jesus, you are grapes ripening for the winepress of God's wrath. If you are trusting in Jesus, you are grain growing for the glory of God. Everything you do prepares for the harvest.

Revelation 14:19 describes the moment when the bubble is burst. All the deceptive power of the sins that look romantic and appealing, all the false promises and untrue enticements, and all the whispering wishes will be exposed for what they are by the outcomes they produce. The weeds and barren trees will be reaped. There will be no fruit on them for God's glory, no nourishing and refreshing yield, but only grapes for the winepress of wrath. Will you be part of that harvest, or will you repent of your sin and trust in Jesus?

The winepress will be trodden, and the blood will flow. The blood flows as high as a horse is tall, and the 1,600 stadia are equal to almost 200 miles, which is approximately the length of the land of Israel. It will be a full display of wrath.

Conclusion

When Eugene Tanniehill was about twenty years old, in the early 1960s, he and his young wife were out drinking at a local tavern. Something was said, or thought to have been said, that irritated the wife, whom Tanniehill quickly took outside. Then he killed a man. The man was a Pentecostal preacher. Serving a life sentence in Angola, Tanniehill was enslaved to the moonshine alcohol made by the prisoners, when one night he cried to God for redemption. That was 1963, and over the years he has come to be known as the Bishop of Angola. Faithfully trusting Christ through persecution from other prisoners, blessing those who persecute him, he now counsels other prisoners and preaches on Sundays and throughout the week. The consequences of this man's actions cost him freedom, cost him his marriage, and cost him his relationship with his child. But in prison he has proclaimed the gospel and has pointed countless men to the saving knowledge of Jesus Christ.[4]

God will keep his word to the righteous and to the wicked.

What will you do between now and judgment day?

27

Seven Angels with Seven Plagues

REVELATION 15:1–8

DID YOU SEE THE MOVIE *The Family Man*? Nicolas Cage is a rich and successful single man, and he is shown the beautiful life he could have had if he had chosen love instead of his career. The life he would have had was with a wife who truly loved him, children who respected him and delighted in playing with him, and friends who were genuinely involved in his life. The beauty of that life exposes his loneliness and emptiness.

There is a sense in which what we see in chapter 15 shows us what we might have been. But instead of taking us back in time to show us what could have been, this passage takes us forward in time to show us what can be. This passage is going to show us the buildup to the final outpouring of God's wrath, and it will show us the redeemed who will worship God for his justice. Here is what the future can be for you: you can be someone who, instead of being terrified by the justice of God, is thrilled by it.

We all have an unremitting sense of answerability to our Maker, as one person put it. We know his justice is over us. But there is a comfort that is as strong and deep as the very justice of God.

Need

Let me invite you to imagine something better than winning the Heisman Trophy, better than being the MVP of the team that wins the World Series. Imagine being the doctor who discovers the cure for cancer, and now try to conceive of something better than that.

The highest military decoration awarded by the United States government is the Medal of Honor, which is "bestowed by the President in the name of Congress on members of the United States Armed Forces who distinguish themselves through 'conspicuous gallantry and intrepidity at the risk of his or her life above and beyond the call of duty while engaged in an action against an enemy of the United States.'"[1] Imagine something better than being honored to receive the Medal of Honor.

What could be better than the Heisman Trophy, better than being the World Series MVP, better than finding a cure for cancer, and better than winning a Medal of Honor? I'll tell you what's better. One day the dead will be raised, and the multitudes will stand before Almighty God. On that day King Jesus will say to those who trusted him and lived for him, "Well done, good and faithful servant," and on that day no Heisman Trophy, no World Series MVP, no medical or military achievement will be worth more than those words.

What will motivate us to live for that commendation?

Main Point

The display of God's justice in saving his people and winning him praise is meant to make us want to be among the redeemed, not the condemned.

Preview

This passage seems to be structured by the three times John uses the phrase "I saw" or "I looked" in Revelation 15:1, 2, 5.

15:1	Another Sign in Heaven
15:2–4	The Song of Moses
15:5–8	The Seven Angels and Seven Bowls

Context

In this section of Revelation, chapters 4—16, we are being shown the judgments that issue from God's throne. We have seen the throne room (chapters 4, 5), the opening of the seven seals and the sealing of the saints (chapters 6, 7), the seven trumpets and the true prophet John whose message is proclaimed by the church, symbolized by the two witnesses (chapters 8—11), the child born to slay the dragon, who though driven from Heaven makes war on the woman and her seed (chapters 12, 13), and the harvest of the earth (chapter 14). Chapter 15 depicts for us the buildup to the outpouring of God's wrath in chapter 16. The mounting tension in chapter 15 increases the magnitude of the display of God's wrath in chapter 16.

Revelation 15:1: Another Sign in Heaven

John writes in 15:1, "Then I saw another sign in heaven." This reference to "another sign" seems to point us back to the two signs he described in 12:1–3. The first sign in 12:1 was the pregnant woman, "clothed with the sun, with the moon under her feet, and on her head a crown of twelve stars." The second sign in 12:3 was "a great red dragon, with seven heads and ten horns, and on his heads seven diadems." These two signs seem to symbolize the cosmic conflict between the righteous and the wicked, the woman and the serpent. This third sign in 15:1 points to the outcome of the conflict. John tells us that he "saw another sign in heaven, great and amazing, seven angels with seven plagues, which are the last, for with them the wrath of God is finished." Like the plagues on Egypt, these plagues will visit God's justice on his enemies. Unlike the plagues on Egypt, these plagues will *finish* the wrath of God.

Why is God wrathful? Recently I was watching my sons play together, and it struck me that Adam and Eve watched Cain and Abel play together. Can you imagine living in the Garden of Eden, where there was no sin, and being expelled from the garden because of your transgression, then living in a world where your son murders his brother? Imagine the horror and sorrow that Adam felt. His son murdered his brother because he, Adam, got everyone thrown out of Eden.

Now let me invite you to consider these things from God's perspective: God makes this pristine world where everything is good. He gives humans everything they need for life and happiness. And he gives only one command. They break it, and then they start devising ways to be offensive and abominable. They start stealing and boasting and murdering and fornicating, and their thoughts are only evil all the time.

God is a just God. He is holy, righteous, and good, and he is personally offended by sin. Imagine how much sin there is in this world to offend God.

We are to love God with all our heart, soul, mind, and strength. Look over the last seven days of your life and consider how many seconds you were doing that and how many you were not. When you were not walking by faith and loving God, you were sinning. Now multiply all your own personal sin by 6,000,000,000 people alive today, then multiply that heap of transgression by about 6,000 years.

Can you imagine what it will take to finish the wrath of God? Go ahead and try.

No wind can be colder than what we deserve.

No snow too deep.

No terror too haunting.

No night too dark.

No crash too startling.

No cut too deep.

And that's just the physical. Imagine the emotional anguish of knowing that you had everything you needed to please God—the Bible, the gospel, the church, people for whom you could lay down your life, people you could have served—and instead of pleasing God by loving him and others, you loved only yourself. Our selfishness and sin has made us nothing but miserable all our lives, and if we do not repent and trust in Christ and love God and others by faith, sin and selfishness will make us miserable forever.

What do you want—life or death? Joy or pain? Satisfaction or anguish? Holiness or defilement? "Well done" or "depart from me"?

The wrath of God will be finished one day. He will be satisfied. Sinners will not escape. Will you face that wrath for yourself, or will you flee to Christ, who faced that wrath for all who would trust him when the Father forsook him at Calvary?

These are the last plagues. When they are poured out, the conflict will be over. The serpent's head will be crushed. The seed of the woman will be triumphant. God's justice will be fulfilled, and through that display of justice his people will be delivered to praise him, which is what we see in verses 2–4. The display of God's justice saving his people and winning him praise is meant to make us want to be among the redeemed, not the condemned.

Revelation 15:2–4: The Song of Moses

In 15:2–4 John sees two things—first, "a sea of glass," and second, the overcomers. Having told us what he saw, John tells us about the song the overcomers sing. He told us the wrath of God will be finished, and now he shows us those who will not suffer the wrath of God.

We only see this "sea of glass" one other place in Revelation, in 4:6, where "before the throne there was as it were a sea of glass, like crystal." So when John sees "what appeared to be a sea of glass" here in 15:2, we can assume that this is the "sea of glass . . . before the throne" in 4:6. Here in 15:2 it is "mingled with fire," and that fire swirling in the sea of glass appears to be a depiction of the cosmic disturbance resulting from the wrath of God. The fire is about to fall. Judgment is about to be visited on all the rebels who refused to give God the honor and gratitude rightly due him.

Look at the identity of these people in Revelation 15:2: "those who had conquered the beast and its image and the number of its name." Do you know how to conquer the beast? Look back at 12:11: "And they have conquered him by the blood of the Lamb." You conquer the beast by the blood of Christ, but 12:11 continues, "and by the word of their testimony." These people have testified. This means that they trusted in Christ and his death and resurrection. They then testified that Christ is the only way of salvation. His death was for them. As Lecrae puts it in his rap, "Don't Waste Your Life":

> Your money your singleness marriage talent and time
> They were loaned to you to show the world that Christ is Divine
> That's why it's Christ in my rhymes
> That's why it's Christ all the time
> See my whole world is built around him
> He's the life in my lines
> I refuse to waste my life
> He's too true to chase that ice
> Here's my gifts and time
> Cause I'm constantly trying
> To be used to praise the Christ[2]

Then look at the last phrase in 12:11, "for they loved not their lives even unto death." And they "conquered the beast" (15:2)! Trust Jesus. Testify to Jesus. Live and die for Jesus. Conquer the beast (cf. 13:1–10).

If you understand the severity of the completion of God's wrath, the gospel will be more precious to you than life. If you understand the severity of God's wrath, you will look 13:10 in the face: "If anyone is to be taken captive, to captivity he goes; if anyone is to be slain with the sword, with the sword must he be slain. Here is a call for the endurance and faith of the saints." You will stare captivity and the sword in the face and say, better that than the wrath of God! Better to be put in prison for the gospel than face God's wrath. Better to be slain with the sword for the gospel than to face God's wrath.

There is nothing you can imagine that is worse than God's wrath will be. There is nothing in existence that is worse than God's wrath will be.

Look back at 15:2, where they also conquered the beast's "image." You'll remember the deceptive power of the image of the beast that was granted the power of speech in order to deceive the world in 13:11–15. What enables people to see through such powerful deception? The knowledge that God's wrath is going to fall. That's what causes people to examine an argument until they see its flaws. That's what gives people eyes to see through the fakes.

The next phrase in 15:2 says that the redeemed conquered "the number of its name." We read about that in 13:16–18, where no one can buy or sell unless they have the "mark" of the beast or "the number of its name." How do you overcome that? By knowing that God's wrath is worse than starving because you can't buy food.

The rest of 15:2 says the redeemed were "standing beside [literally "on," see NASB] the sea of glass with harps of God in their hands." The redeemed have harps, just as the 144,000 had harps in 14:2. They are about to praise God for the awesome display of his justice.

Revelation 15:3 states, "And they sing the song of Moses, the servant of God," which recalls the song that Israel sang after God brought them through the waters of the Red Sea only to close the sea on the Egyptians. God saved Israel by judging Egypt. So also God's people here are going to be finally delivered when God visits wrath on the world. They are singing "the Song of Moses . . . and the song of the Lamb" (15:3). This points to the redemption accomplished by Christ, the true Passover Lamb, through whose death God's people are redeemed. As with the first Passover, those whom the Lamb's blood covers are not destroyed by the destroyer. Through the destruction accomplished by the destroyer, those covered by the blood are brought out of their bondage to corruption in this world.

In 15:3, 4 we see the song they sang. The first four lines are in the second half of verse 3, then there are five lines in verse 4. The first four lines at the end of verse 3 are made up of two couplets, or two two-line sets. Each consists of a statement about God in the first line, followed by an address to God using significant titles for him in the second. The first couplet in 15:3 is:

"Great and amazing are your deeds,
O Lord God the Almighty!"

So in the first line you have a statement about God—that his deeds are "great and amazing." Then in the second line the redeemed address God as "Lord God the Almighty." The second couplet at the end of verse 3 is similar:

"Just and true are your ways,
O King of the nations!"

These are not bland truths. God is "great and amazing," but this statement isn't smoke and mirrors. It isn't special effects. It isn't a big charade. It isn't corrupt. It isn't bribed or partial or crooked. It is "just and true." He is the only one who can be called "Lord God the Almighty," and he is the only "King of the nations." Those titles belong to God alone.

There are five lines in 15:4. The first two lines are parallel, and the next three lines give three reasons for the statements in the first two. The first two lines are:

Who will not fear, O Lord,
and glorify your name?

These lines are parallel—*fearing the Lord* is synonymous with *glorifying his name*. When we see the "great and amazing . . . deeds" of the Lord and the "just and true ways" of the "King of the nations," we should fear him and honor him. Everyone should. Look at the three reasons stated for fearing the Lord and glorifying his name in the rest of 15:4:

> For you alone are holy.
> All nations will come and worship you,
> for your righteous acts have been revealed.

The first reason given is that God alone is "holy." No one else is holy like the Lord. He is absolute.

The second reason given is that "all nations" will "worship" him. Imagine that for a moment. Picture in your mind's eye the gathered multitudes before the great throne. It will be a crowd like no crowd that has ever gathered. Every human who has ever lived has been raised to stand before the Maker. Who could gather such a crowd? Where will there be space for the hordes of humanity? Who could command such an audience?

Only the one who is worthy of fear and worship. This God is worthy of your worship. No one else can do what he does. He will call every soul to account. No one else can do what he can do, and no one else is worthy of his glory.

The greatness of this God may not seem so apparent now, but the third reason stated here tells us why all will fear him and glorify his name on that day: "for your righteous acts have been revealed." Imagine someone who has always done everything right; from this moment all the way back through the entirety of eternity past he has been true, solid, on target. Every decision was correct, every action appropriate. No failings. No infelicities. No weak points. No wrong thoughts or actions. When this God is revealed, everyone will fear. Everyone will worship.

By showing us those who sing the song of Moses in 15:2–4, John means to motivate his audience to overcome "the beast and its image and the number of its name" (v. 2). He shows the overcomers here to make us want to overcome. He is forcing this question: how will you relate to God's "great and amazing . . . deeds" (v. 3)? Will his just and true ways mean deliverance for you or will they mean judgment? Will you rejoice on that day or will you wail?

Revelation 15:5–8: The Seven Angels and Seven Bowls

As we move into 15:5–8, the question for us is this: does the drama that is about to unfold give you hope or does it terrify you? In 8:3, before the opening of the seventh seal, John sees "the golden altar before the throne." That altar appears to be in the temple in Heaven. In 11:19, after the seventh trumpet, the temple in Heaven was opened and the ark seen. Now in 15:5, before the seven bowls are poured out, John writes, "After this I looked, and the sanctuary of the tent of witness in heaven was opened." The temple is going to be opened. God is going to be revealed. And the wicked are going to get their due.

Revelation 15:6 tells us, "and out of the sanctuary came the seven angels with the seven plagues, clothed in pure, bright linen, with golden sashes around their chests." Look at the beauty and formality and author- ity communicated by the way these angels come from the presence of God clothed like the royal Son. These angels are described the way John described Jesus in 1:13. They look like him because they represent him. Their task is holy. Their errand is righteous. So they wear pure, bright linen, and sashes adorn their chests. They seem to come rushing out of the temple with the zeal of furious devotion to their task—the glad visitation of God's long-awaited justice.

These seven angels are commissioned by God, who commissioned the four living creatures to summon the events of history in chapter 6 (see vv. 1, 3, 5, 7). Now we read in 15:7, "And one of the four living creatures gave to the seven angels seven golden bowls full of the wrath of God who lives forever and ever." It seems that in the flow of events in Revelation, these bowls of wrath are full of "the wine of God's wrath" (14:10), which was made from the grapes of wrath trodden in "the great winepress of the wrath of God" after the "harvest of the earth" (14:19, 20). These seven angels are given seven bowls, and the use of the number seven points to completion. This will be a full outpouring of wrath.

John is seeing into the heavenly temple (15:5), and this is the heavenly counterpart of Israel's tabernacle and temple. When the tabernacle and later the temple were built, God filled both with the cloud of his glory (Exodus 40:34–38; 1 Kings 8:10, 11). Revelation 15:8 tells us, "and the sanctuary was filled with smoke from the glory of God and from his power, and no one could enter the sanctuary until the seven plagues of the seven angels were finished." No one can enter the sanctuary until the plagues are finished, and the plagues are going to finish the wrath of God. This seems to indicate that this final, purging judgment will purify the world. God will then take up residence in his cosmic temple, and the earth will be filled with the glory of the Lord as the waters fill the seas. The manifestation of God's justice saves his people and wins him praise.

Conclusion

So will God's justice mean deliverance or judgment for you? What hope do any of us have? How could anyone be delivered from God's justice?

The gospel of Jesus Christ is good news. The world's true King has come as a noble prince born to die. The one who was rich became poor, so that we by his poverty might become rich (2 Corinthians 8:9). The one offended sympathized with those who were offensive. He took our transgressions on himself, and he endured the wrath of God to the very end. God's wrath has been propitiated by his gift of love. Behold the paradoxical display of almighty wrath quenched by everlasting love as Christ bore our sins in his body on the tree. Everyone who trusts him will be saved.

See how precarious the great plan of redemption was—God risked everything on the baby born to the peasant couple in Bethlehem. And the Son did not fail! He crushed the serpent's head, propitiated the Father's wrath, drove Satan from the heavenly field, and secured redemption for everyone who calls on his name.

Won't you call on him? Won't you look to him to be saved? The justice of God will save you and win praise from you if you will trust in Jesus. Otherwise the one who lives forever and ever will hunt you down and satisfy his justice against you. The baby in the manger is our only hope.

28

The Seven Bowls of Wrath

REVELATION 16:1–21

CONSIDER CHRISTMAS FROM GOD'S PERSPECTIVE. Having created this astonishing universe, he made this earth that is perfectly fitted for human life in every detail. Then he created human beings in his image and likeness, and everything was very good. Think of the gifts he has given us. Life. Five senses. Friendship. Family. Love. And yet if we had the opportunity to murder God and seat ourselves on his throne, we would do it. Every sin we willfully commit is an implicit declaration that we are usurping God's throne and doing as we please.

How has God responded to those who treat him this way? Instead of crushing the rebellion, he initiated a plan to forgive the rebels. If we were to try to anticipate what God might do to redeem rebellious humanity, none of us would expect him to do it the way he has. God chose to send his Son in the most vulnerable way possible—as an innocent, helpless baby.

If we were to look at God's timing from a worldly perspective, we might accuse him of parental negligence. He did not arrange for his Son to be born into the world at a time when universal health care was available. He did not plan for it to happen when modern medicine was a possibility. He did not even secure a room in an inn, to say nothing of a hospital.

The Son of God came in the most vulnerable way possible, perhaps in the worst conditions possible, but God pulled it off. The baby lived, even though born without hospitals, doctors, or even a room in the inn.

My wife and I are often struck by the sweet innocence and purity of our young sons. At their young age and in their sheltered lives they are unbesmirched by so much of the world's filth. But they're sinners nevertheless. It is difficult to imagine the innocence, purity, honesty, nobility, and wholesomeness of a man who never sinned, ever. I suspect that in our pride most of us would probably find him objectionable, until he loved us in some disarming way.

So God creates this pleasure dome of a world that we live in and gives us more than we could dream of or imagine experiencing. To show our thanks to him, we rebel against him and try to usurp his kingdom. In response God sends a love gift, his Son. Perfect. Innocent. Pure. A little baby who grows to be the most noble, most upright, most loving, most understanding, best human being who has ever lived. To show our gratitude, we crucify him. And then we go on about our business as if nothing significant has happened. We are all like the adulteress described in Proverbs 30:20: "she eats and wipes her mouth and says, 'I have done no wrong.'"

None of us is just like God. None of us is holy like God. But we all know how we would feel and how we would respond if someone treated us the way the world has treated God. We would feel a righteous indignation. Transpose the righteous indignation you would feel into perfect holiness, multiply it by all the sins of all the people who have ever lived or ever will, and we can begin to understand why Revelation 16 is in the Bible.

Need

We really do need to read chapter 16 from God's perspective. If we read this chapter from the perspective of a sinner, we will think that maybe this is awfully harsh of God. We will think that maybe the people who suffer in these seven plagues from the seven bowls of wrath have not been treated fairly. So we need to take God's perspective on the matter, because our sinful, limited perspective is grossly inaccurate. Our sin-tainted view on the matter is unfair to God. So as we examine this chapter, we must remember that God created the world and humanity good. We must remember the thanks humanity showed God for that—rebellion. And we must remember the innocent baby in the manger who grew up to be the most righteous man who ever lived. We must remember the way humans responded to him—crucifixion.

Main Point

The main point of this text is that God is glorified in justice as he brings awesome wrath that fits the crimes human beings have done.

Context

In 14:19 the grape harvest is reaped and thrown into the winepress of God's wrath so that, as 14:9, 10 state, those who take the mark of the beast will "drink the wine of God's wrath." In 14:20 the winepress is trodden; then the wrath ferments as the scene shifts to the redeemed worshiping God in 15:1–4. After that the temple in Heaven opens, the seven angels come out with their seven plagues (15:5, 6), and in 15:7 one of the four living creatures gives them seven bowls full of God's wrath. These bowls seem to be full of the wine of God's wrath that results from the trodding of the grapes from the harvest of the earth. Then in 15:8 the temple is filled with smoke, and no one will be able to enter until the seven plagues of the seven angels are finished. Here in chapter 16 we will see the seven angels pour out their bowls of wrath.

Preview

Revelation 16 can be broken into two parts. The first part deals with the first three bowls, where plagues are poured on earth, sea, and rivers and springs in verses 1–7. After the first three bowls are poured out in verses 1–4, there is a celebration of God's justice in verses 5–7.

Then the last four bowls, the fourth through seventh, are poured out in verses 8–21. In contrast to the first three bowls, after which the righteous worshiped God for his justice, after the last four bowls we see that the wicked refuse to repent, instead cursing God.

What is shocking about this chapter is the way unrepentant humanity reacts to the wrath of God. Rather than recognizing that the rebellion is doomed and surrendering to the Almighty, they are enraged by the claims the Almighty makes upon them and gather for what they must know is a futile war against him.

God is glorified in awesome wrath that shows the bankruptcy of the false gods people worship, and the punishments God brings on his enemies fit their crimes. This calls the wicked to repentance, and it serves to encourage the righteous as they persevere.

16:1–7   The First Three Bowls and the Response of the Righteous
16:8–21   The Last Four Bowls and the Response of the Wicked

Revelation 16:1–7: The First Three Bowls and the Response of the Righteous

So the temple in Heaven has just been opened in 15:5, then the seven angels came out in 15:6, one of the four living creatures gave them the seven bowls in 15:7, and now the word comes from the temple for the bowls to be poured out in 16:1: "Then I heard a loud voice from the temple telling the seven angels, 'Go and pour out on the earth the seven bowls of the wrath of God.'" The speaker is not identified, but the voice comes from the temple where God's throne is. So whether this is God speaking or one of the four living creatures or some other authority near God, the commission comes from the temple to the seven angels who have just come out of the temple. The seven bowls will be poured out on the earth, the sea, the rivers and springs, the sun, the beast's throne, the Euphrates River, and into the air, but all seven are summarized here in 16:1 with the umbrella statement, "pour out on the earth the seven bowls of the wrath of God."

Because of the way John will note in 16:9–11 that in response to these bowls of wrath the people curse God and refuse to repent, it appears that these bowls are intended as a final warning, a final call to repentance. God sent his witnesses, the church proclaimed the gospel, and people have been given every evidence that God is Lord, that God is creator, that God has provided redemption through Jesus, and that God will judge. And the world refuses to repent.

Wicked humans have persisted in calling on and worshiping gods that are not worthy. They have continued to serve themselves. And so in mercy God is going to demonstrate to them one final time that they cannot protect themselves against him and that the gods they worship cannot save them. It seems that God means to force upon them the truth that he alone is worthy of their trust. He alone can save them from his wrath. He alone can give them the mercy they need. He alone can provide atonement for the sins they have committed. He alone can reconcile them to himself. He alone can give them the satisfaction they seek from things that were not created to satisfy them.

So God is mercifully judging the world. God is lovingly showing how futile and vain and broken are the false religions and the selfish pursuits and the proud imaginings. It seems that God is going to show the rebels an awesome display of his unconquerable might to offer them a final opportunity to surrender. God is proving to humanity that there are two possibilities: repent of sin and worship God, or persist in rebellion and face unavoidable judgment. These bowls of wrath will prove that false gods cannot deliver from the true God.

In 16:2 we read, "So the first angel went and poured out his bowl on the earth, and harmful and painful sores came upon the people who bore the mark of the beast and worshiped its image." People took the mark of the beast in 13:16–18 so they could buy and sell, so they could meet basic needs and provide for themselves and their families, so they could get for themselves what God provides for those who trust him. And they worshiped the image of the beast in 13:11–15 because the beast and its image did things that counterfeited the work of the Lamb of God and the Holy Spirit. A warning was announced against those who do these things in 14:9–11, and that warning promised God's wrath against those who took the mark of the beast. So now God is demonstrating to these people that the image of the beast and the mark of the beast cannot protect them. God is proving to them that there is something worse than not being able to buy or sell—the displeasure of almighty God.

Revelation 16:2 states that those who trust something other than God will suffer God's wrath in the form of "painful sores." If you have ever experienced something like a painful sore, you know that there is a great longing for the pain to be over. There is an eager desire for the time when the sore will be healed, when things will be better. But it isn't going to get better for those who suffer the wrath of God. If they refuse to repent, it will only get worse.

We read in 16:3, "The second angel poured out his bowl into the sea, and it became blood like that of a corpse,[1] and every living thing died that was in the sea" (author's translation). There has never yet been an act of God like this in the world's history. The blood of a corpse is partially coagulated, thick, dead, and disgusting. Imagine the smell and the horror of the waters of the oceans of the world being made into something like the blood that remains in a dead body, and in the filthy liquid are the dead creatures of the deep. So in addition to the "painful sores" there is this worldwide stench, no doubt accompanied by heretofore unknown bacteria and infections and unexpected consequences.

It isn't hard to imagine how those who refuse to acknowledge God would explain this away. They would probably blame it on climate change or on some poor politician who has no control over the forces of nature. They would probably argue that if they propitiated the gods they worship with climate change initiatives or new entitlement programs, such problems could be solved. What they need to do is bend the knee to the God who has created the world and is visiting wrath on mankind in order to warn of coming judgment, so they will repent of their sins, trust in Christ, and be reconciled to God. But they hate God, so they will not do that.

Douglas Wilson has said that the two statements atheists make are: first, there is no God; second, I hate him.

People suffer "painful sores" from the first bowl, the sea is inconceivably ruined from the second bowl, but at least they still have clean water to drink—until the third bowl. We read in 16:4, "The third angel poured out his bowl into the rivers and the springs of water, and they became blood." So now the clean water is gone.

God sustains the world in such a way that water is clean. God deserves praise and thanks for every drink of water we take. God deserves praise and thanks for every breath of fresh air. God deserves praise and thanks for every moment we live without painful sores. God sustains our lives, and we should all repent of refusing him the praise and thanks that is due him. We should all repent of ignoring the Giver when we enjoy his gifts. We should all repent of wrong thinking that attributes to false gods what is due to the true God alone.

In 7:1 four angels were "holding back the four winds of the earth." In 14:18 an angel had "authority over the fire." And now in 16:5 we read of the "angel in charge of the waters." Some commentators understand this to be the angel who poured the third bowl onto the rivers and springs.[2] How does this angel, who apparently has authority delegated from God over the waters, respond to the waters being turned to blood? He responds by celebrating God's righteousness. He says in 16:5, 6:

> "Just are you, O Holy One, who is and who was,
> for you brought these judgments.
> For they have shed the blood of saints and prophets,
> and you have given them blood to drink.
> It is what they deserve!"

Note how the angel confesses God's *holiness*, calling him in verse 5 the "Holy One." And he identifies God as the one "who is and who was." Unlike the beast, who rises to power and seems to prosper for a time, a time that is appointed by God, God is and has always been the same. This angel of the waters is not upset at what has happened to the element under his control, water; he confesses that God is in the right: "Just are you" (16:5). Nor is this angel confused about what caused the waters to turn to blood. He states plainly to God, "for you brought these judgments" (16:5). This is not some accident of history. It does not result from human technology but from God's judgment against human sin.

In 16:6 the angel explains that the waters have been turned to blood because the wicked "have shed the blood of saints and prophets." The wicked poured out the blood of the righteous; so God pours blood out for the wicked to drink. The punishment fits the crime, as the angel states at the end of verse 6: "It is what they deserve!"

Back in 6:9–11 the souls of the martyrs were under the altar crying out, "O Sovereign Lord, holy and true, how long before you will judge and avenge our blood on those who dwell on the earth?" The answer that came to them was that they were to rest "until the number of their fellow servants and their brothers should be complete, who were to be killed as they themselves had been." Then in 8:3, 4 the angel offered up the prayers of the saints with incense on the altar, in response to which God commissioned the seven angels to blow the seven trumpets. When we read in 16:7, "And I heard the altar saying, 'Yes, Lord God the Almighty, true and just are your judgments!'" we are to understand that the souls under the altar are being avenged—note the connection between the martyrs and the altar in 16:6, 7 and 6:9–11. The martyrs are being avenged, and as God visits just judgments against the wicked, the desire the martyrs have for justice is satisfied.

So we see the first three bowls poured out in 16:1–4. Then we see the response of the angels and the martyrs in 16:5–7. As we see the next four bowls poured out, John will tell us how the wicked respond to God's justice. God is glorified in justice as he visits awesome wrath that fits the crimes human beings have done.

Revelation 16:8–21: The Last Four Bowls and the Response of the Wicked

In Greek and Roman mythology, the god Apollo was worshiped both as the god of healing and as the god of the sun. Then there was Neptune (or for the Greeks, Poseidon) who was god of the sea, and there were a whole series of river gods. The worshipers of these gods are being shown by these bowls of wrath that their gods cannot heal if Yahweh wounds, their gods cannot protect the waters that Yahweh made, waters that Yahweh sustains, and their gods have no control over the sun that Yahweh keeps in the sky. Yahweh is Lord. He alone deserves worship, and he does not appreciate people giving the worship he deserves to demons.

We have our own version of the Greco-Roman pantheon and cult today. In place of those who worshiped Poseidon and Neptune we have the environmentalists who worship the earth and its plants and animals. In place of those who worshiped Apollo the god of healing we have the worshipers of modern medicine who believe that health care is what they need and are panicked at the thought of losing access to it or at the thought of someone not having access to it, as though that were the worst thing that could possibly happen. The devotees of these modern cults need to know the one true and living God, Yahweh. Yahweh will crush the things they worship. They will either see Yahweh's justice and worship him for it, as we just saw in 16:5–7, or they will respond the way the idolaters do in 16:8–21.

Apollo does not control the sun, nor do modern-day champions of environmentalism. We read in 16:8, "The fourth angel poured out his bowl on the sun, and it was allowed to scorch people with fire." Note the words, "it was allowed." God is the one doing the allowing. Verse 9 tells us how the wicked respond: "They were scorched by the fierce heat, and they cursed the name of God who had power over these plagues. They did not repent and give him glory." The plagues are demonstrating the futility of the false gods. The plagues are showing that nothing can deliver from Yahweh's hand. The plagues are irrefutable evidence that the only way to be delivered is to repent of sin, surrender to Yahweh, and seek his mercy. But rather than repent and seek mercy, the wicked curse Yahweh's name. So Yahweh continues to make war on the wicked, seeking to break them down and bring them to himself.

Revelation 16:10 states, "The fifth angel poured out his bowl on the throne of the beast, and its kingdom was plunged into darkness." So here we have seen the sun go wrong in both directions—first it flashes out at people and burns them, and now its light fails. The rest of verse 10 through verse 11 tells us how the wicked responded: "People gnawed their tongues in anguish and cursed the God of heaven for their pain and sores. They did not repent of their deeds." Rather than do the only thing that will bring them relief—repent—these people cause themselves further pain by gnawing their tongues, and they do more wickedness by cursing God, for which they will face more judgment.

People who refuse to give God the praise and thanks that is due him have rejected him. They refuse his right to reign over them as their creator and sovereign Lord. They rebel against his authority. If they could kill him and seize his throne they would do so. The impulse to take God's place is implicit in every willful sin. What we see in 16:12–16 is the wicked going to war against God. What is ironic about this is that God himself is the one who sets up the opportunity, which the wicked will seize, for the armies to gather. This is ironic because even the setup of their opportunity to gather for battle comes from God. He is in absolute control of all that takes place. Their attempt to unseat him is worse than futile, more vain than hopelessness itself. This battle is going nowhere, and still they choose to fight it.

Revelation 16:12 states, "The sixth angel poured out his bowl on the great river Euphrates, and its water was dried up, to prepare the way for the kings from the east." So the angel pours out the bowl of God's wrath, and the result is that God's enemies can all gather themselves in one place to launch their grand assault against the Almighty. This may look wise and noble and valiant, but John shows us what it truly is—a stupid and rebellious and shameful waste that is really little more than a suicide mission.

In addition to the futile waste, it is a deceitful sham initiated by hateful demons, as we see in 16:13, 14:

> And I saw, coming out of the mouth of the dragon and out of the mouth of the beast and out of the mouth of the false prophet, three unclean spirits like frogs. For they are demonic spirits, performing signs, who go abroad to the kings of the whole world, to assemble them for battle on the great day of God the Almighty.

So here Satan and the beast and the false prophet are a false trinity, a twisted parody of the Father and the Son and the Holy Spirit. And these "unclean spirits like frogs" that come from their mouths (16:13), "demonic spirits, performing signs" (16:14), are the powers that produce the world's network of assumptions and conclusions. These are the demonic powers that teach the world the common set of "given facts" that convince "the kings of the whole world, to assemble them for battle on the great day of God the Almighty."

John here gives us a powerful explanation for why the wicked respond to God the way they do. There is a plausibility structure at work in the world that makes certain realities believable and other realities unbelievable. Those who repent of sin and trust in Christ are amazed that the world would be so foolish as to believe that the right course of action would be to go to war against one who can never be defeated, one who controls all that is. Those who refuse to repent, John explains, see through a grid of meaning that has been built by demonic powers. They are deceived.

The demons are hard at work constructing the plausibility structure that will convince people to go to war against God. They do their teaching through false teachers in the church, through worldly forms of media and entertainment, and through those who have rebelled against God and seek to convince others to join them in a grand wasted life of rebellion. Many of these rebels teach at prestigious universities.

John is equipping believers to understand what is happening. The demons are preparing people to make war against God. And John is also seeking to convince people of the futility of the campaign against God. He wants to convince people to repent of sin and trust in Christ.

It seems that in 16:15 Jesus himself speaks: "Behold, I am coming like a thief! Blessed is the one who stays awake, keeping his garments on, that he may not go about naked and be seen exposed!" Jesus' saying he is "coming like a thief" reinforces what he said in Matthew 24:42–44:

> "Therefore, stay awake, for you do not know on what day your Lord is coming. But know this, that if the master of the house had known in what part of the night the thief was coming, he would have stayed awake and would not have let his house be broken into. Therefore you also must be ready, for the Son of Man is coming at an hour you do not expect."

Paul too said the day of the Lord would come "like a thief in the night" (1 Thessalonians 5:2).

The blessing on those who stay awake and ready in 16:15 is the third of seven benedictions in Revelation (1:3; 14:13; 16:15; 19:9; 20:6; 22:7; 22:14). John is calling the faithful to be ready, to watch, to stay clothed so they won't be shamed. How do we do that? How do we guard ourselves against the demonic spirits of 16:13, 14? How do we see through their lies and keep ourselves clothed and ready?

There's no magical formula here, just simple truths that always apply. Here's what you must do: repent of your sin, trust in Christ, join a church where the gospel is preached and the Bible is explained, read your Bible, and pray. Walk with God. Know your Bible. Read the world through the interpretive grid built for you by the Bible. Reject the interpretive grid pushed by the world. Be a student of Scripture, and reflect on life informed by the Scriptures.

So the righteous are urged to stay ready in 16:15, but the wicked are duped by the demons in 16:16: "And they assembled them at the place that in Hebrew is called Armageddon." The great battle is about to be fought. Before it happens in 19:11–21, the fall of Babylon will be lamented and celebrated in 17:1–19:10.

War on God is a futile cause. He cannot be defeated. How does this message strike you? Are you angered by the fact that God would lay claim to what is rightfully his? Or do you rejoice that one day the rebels will be crushed and the world will be liberated from their wicked ways? Every corrupt scoundrel will receive justice; so every one of us should repent.

If you are an unbeliever, let me assure you that if you do not repent and trust in Christ, you are a fool who is vainly trying to continue in a lost cause. If you do not repent and believe, Jesus is going to slay you with the sword of his mouth and feed your flesh to the birds of Heaven; then you will suffer eternal conscious torment, and you will deserve every minute of it. You should repent. You should trust Christ. Do so today.

If you are a believer, are you a good soldier of Christ Jesus or are you a traitor? Are you double-minded? Are you convinced that Jesus is Lord, that God is Almighty, or are you still harboring fantasies or affections that entail making yourself Lord of the Universe instead of God? Are you aiding and abetting the enemy's causes in that way? Is Christ reigning in your heart through his Word? That's how he exercises his rule in the lives of his people—through the Bible.

So the final warnings have been issued. The power of God has been displayed one final time. He has absolute authority over land, sea, rivers, and sun; he can afflict the throne of the beast, and his enemies can only gather against him because he gives them the opportunity by drying up the Euphrates. Rather than repenting, they have gathered for war. So now the seventh bowl will be poured out, and its results show that the time has come.

John writes in 16:17, "The seventh angel poured out his bowl into the air, and a loud voice came out of the temple, from the throne, saying, 'It is done!'" This loud voice comes from God's throne and announces that with the outpouring of the seventh bowl, his wrath has been poured out. These are, as 15:1 states, the last plagues that finish the wrath of God.

We saw lightning and thunder and rumblings issuing from God's throne in 4:5, after the seventh seal in 8:5, and after the seventh trumpet in 11:19. Now we see the same after the seventh bowl in 16:18: "And there were flashes of lightning, rumblings, peals of thunder, and a great earthquake such as there had never been since man was on the earth, so great was that earthquake." This is like a punctuation mark after judgment that reminds us that judgment issues from God's throne.

The earthquake is the strongest in world history. It is God's judgment. And we read of the effects of that earthquake in 16:19, 20:

> The great city was split into three parts, and the cities of the nations fell, and God remembered Babylon the great, to make her drain the cup of the wine of the fury of his wrath. And every island fled away, and no mountains were to be found.

So the earthquake splits the great city into three, brings down all the other cities of the nations, flattens the mountains, and covers the islands with water. It is as though God seized the surface of the earth and yanked it flat like you would a bedsheet. This is what it means for God to remember "Babylon the great." The identification of "Babylon the great" with "the cities of the nations" points to this being the destruction of the wicked world system that opposes God and the gospel. This judgment does not fall on one city but on all human political arrangements that fail to acknowledge God as creator and Christ as Savior and Lord. They are all brought low. The cup of God's wrath, promised in 14:9, 10, prepared by the harvest of the earth and the treading of the winepress in 14:17–20, filling the bowls that were prepared for in chapter 15 and poured out in chapter 16, is drained in full. God visits unmitigated justice on his enemies.

Besides the earthquake, we read in 16:21, "And great hailstones, about one hundred pounds each, fell from heaven on people; and they cursed God for the plague of the hail, because the plague was so severe." Imagine hundred-pound blocks of ice raining out of the sky like cannonballs. Still they refuse to repent but instead curse God. The wicked are resolute in their vain rebellion.

Conclusion

God is good, and he made the world good. Humanity responded to God's goodness by rebelling against him and exalting themselves as gods. Rather than obliterate the rebels, God sent his Son as a love gift to reconcile the world to himself by offering Jesus as a sacrifice of propitiation. Jesus willingly obeyed, giving his own life to pay the penalty for the sins of humanity. Humanity responded to God's generous gift of Jesus the same way that we responded to his generosity in giving us life and this world in which to live: we crucified Jesus. Apart from the new birth and the regenerating work of the Holy Spirit, if we had the opportunity we would crucify the Father along with the Son and place ourselves on the throne. And one after another we would assassinate each other seeking to make ourselves God.

But there is only one who is truly God. He mercifully shows that everything humans worship instead of him is bankrupt, and he does so to display his wealth, which he offers to all who will repent and trust in Jesus. But rather than surrender their rebellion, wicked humans respond to the terms he offers by cursing him and gathering to make war upon him.

Are you letting the rebels tell you how the world works? Are you reading their books and letting them shape your expectations? Are you letting these scallywags and bandits and God-hating blasphemers tell you what it means to be significant?

God has given you the sword of the Spirit, the Word of God, with which to fight their message. He has given you the shield of faith to quench their darts, the helmet of salvation to protect your head, the gospel of peace to protect your feet, the belt of truth with which to gird your loins, and the breastplate of righteousness with which to go into battle. You will either make war on the world and conquer it by believing the gospel, repenting of sin, and living to lay down your life for others, or you will join the world in its war on God.

29

The Harlot and the Beast

REVELATION 17:1–18

ARE YOU WORRIED about where the world is going? Does the health care debate concern you? I know one lady in bad health whose finances are a mess, and she thinks the government can't take over quickly enough because she believes she won't have to pay for the care she needs. Others are concerned about what they will have to pay in taxes or about the outcome of the next few elections. Maybe you're concerned about Al Qaeda or about what the world your kids will grow up in will be like.

Perhaps your concerns are less global and more personal. Maybe what is most on your mind today has to do with resolutions you made last New Year's Day, with your work performance, or maybe even with persecution you might face.

Need

Two ways of life are ever before us:

- One way serves the Lamb, the other the beast.
- One way fellowships with the church, the Lamb's pure bride; the other sells its soul to the world, the beast's foul whore.
- One way lives for what will last forever, the other for what will look good for a short while before being destroyed.
- One way pleases God through obedience; the other carries out his purpose by filling up the measure of transgression on which he will display his wrath.
- One way leads to the new Jerusalem, the other to Hell.

We need to be convinced that it is better to live for the Lamb than for the beast, with the pure bride than with the nasty whore, for eternal things rather than the temporary, to please God and not enrage him, to enter his city rather than being thrown into the lake of fire.

Main Point

Live for the Lamb and his pure bride, not for the beast and his whore.

Preview

In chapter 17 God has revealed the future to us. He has given us symbols, not specifics, but these symbols enable us to live for Jesus and the church, not for the world and Satan. This chapter falls into two parts:

17:1–6   John Sees the Harlot and the Beast
17:7–18   The Angel Explains the Mystery

Revelation 17:1–3 introduces 17:1–19:10. In the context of chapter 17, 17:3–6 describes the beast and the woman. Then in 17:7–14 an angel interprets the beast (17:8, 11), the seven heads (17:9, 10), and the ten horns (17:12–14). In 17:15 the angel interprets the waters; then 17:16, 17 tells what the beast and horns will do to the harlot and why. Finally, in 17:18 the angel interprets the harlot.

Context

We have seen Jesus and the letters in chapters 1—3, the throne and the judgments in chapters 4—16, and now we move to the section on the harlot, the King, and the bride in chapters 17—22. Look at the language of 17:1–3, and then look at 21:9, 10 (see Table 1.1). Several phrases occur in both places, and in both places one of the seven angels who had one of the seven bowls of wrath invites John to come look at a symbolic female, first Babylon, then the new Jerusalem, and then the angel carries John away in the Spirit. The use of the same language at the beginning of the sections on the foul harlot and the pure bride indicates that the two are to be contrasted with each other. The world is a whore. The church is the bride of Christ. For which do you want to live?

Revelation 17:1–6: John Sees the Harlot and the Beast

The seven bowls of God's wrath in chapter 16 took us to the end of history, with the capital city of the rebellious nations, Babylon, being split into three parts from an earthquake that causes the nations to fall (16:19). Now Babylon is going to be personified so that we, John's audience, will be able to feel what we should about who the world is and how it has acted.

We read in 17:1, "Then one of the seven angels who had the seven bowls came and said to me, 'Come, I will show you the judgment of the great prostitute who is seated on many waters.'" The angel tells John (beginning in 17:7) in 17:15, "The waters that you saw, where the prostitute is seated, are peoples and multitudes and nations and languages." Then he tells him in 17:18, "the woman that you saw is the great city that has dominion over the kings of the earth." So John sees the ruling city of the world personified as a human female who is a prostitute, and the world under her control is personified as waters on which she sits.

Is this the way you think of the world? The harlotry in view is spiritual adultery. The whole world owes allegiance, fidelity, to God. The whole world should relate to God as a wife does to a husband, in pure devotion. But the world has forgotten God, betrayed him, and sold herself to anyone who will pay. The world is a whore. Every human government that does not honor Christ is prostituting itself to agendas and worldviews and national interests that are nothing but pimps and customers. This description of the world as a prostitute is a statement about how the world should relate to God but does not. This description of the world as a prostitute reveals the discrepancy between what the world was made to do and what it has done instead.

We should be as emotionally dismayed by the way the world is as we would be to behold a woman who had been so degraded as to prostitute herself.

The angel tells John two things about the prostitute in 17:2: "with whom the kings of the earth have committed sexual immorality, and with the wine of whose sexual immorality the dwellers on earth have become drunk." There is one statement here about the world's rulers and another about its inhabitants. Rather than be faithful to God and render to him what is due to him alone, the world's rulers have gone to the great prostitute by pursuing their own glory, their own name, their own purposes, all the while ignoring God's law, God's glory, and God's purposes. And all the unbelieving inhabitants of the earth have become intoxicated with the world rather than loving and serving God. The wine of the world's disregard of God has made all unbelieving humans drunk. They live in a godless stupor, blind to God's claims on them, staggering about in stupid self-importance, like drunks who think themselves funny and smart but are only witless and uninhibited because they are inebriated.

This is what the angel says to John, and then John writes in 17:3, "And he carried me away in the Spirit into a wilderness, and I saw a woman sitting on a scarlet beast that was full of blasphemous names, and it had seven heads and ten horns." The beast with blasphemous names recalls the blasphemous words the beast was speaking in 13:5, and it also ties this beast in Revelation to the little horn "speaking great things" in Daniel 7:8. The beasts described in Daniel

7:3–7 have a total of seven heads, and this beast here in Revelation 17:3 also has seven heads. The fourth beast in Daniel 7:7 had ten horns, and this beast in Revelation 17:3 also has ten horns, just as he was described in 13:1.

We will see more about the beast in 17:7–14, but at this point John describes the woman in 17:4: "The woman was arrayed in purple and scarlet, and adorned with gold and jewels and pearls, holding in her hand a golden cup full of abominations and the impurities of her sexual immorality." These clothes and jewels may look nice for a season, but look what happens to the whore in 17:16: "They will make her desolate and naked, and devour her flesh and burn her up with fire." If you disregard God and live for the world, you may look nice for a little while, but it will not last. Only God is trustworthy. Only God can provide lasting satisfaction, lasting significance, lasting beauty, and lasting pleasure. That "golden cup full of abominations and the impurities of her sexual immorality" will ruin your life. Do not drink it.

John identifies the woman in 17:5: "And on her forehead was written a name of mystery: 'Babylon the great, mother of prostitutes and of earth's abominations.'" In the Bible, Babylon is the capital city of Satan's realm. It is the hometown of the seed of the serpent. This symbol of the oppressive kingdoms of the world that disregard God and do not recognize Christ as King is here personified as a human female who sells herself and gives birth to abominations.

She produces things that God hates. She teaches others to disregard God the way she does, to be unfaithful to their rightful Lord the way she is, and to sell themselves the way she does. She gives birth to people who let others use them for pleasure in exchange for a little cash, as though people made in the image and likeness of God are commodities to be used if the price is right.

John tells us the spiritual status of the whore in 17:6: "And I saw the woman, drunk with the blood of the saints, the blood of the martyrs of Jesus. When I saw her, I marveled greatly." She is "drunk with the blood of the saints" because there has been an excess of blood, just as an excess of alcohol makes people drunk. This image also communicates that this whore is complicit in the murder of Christians because they hold fast to the gospel—they are martyrs of Jesus. So those who are faithful to God, those who believe the gospel, those who seek to love others by telling them the good news of Jesus, have been murdered by foul unfaithful, degraded sluts who sell themselves to the world and its agenda.

This image should shock us. The offense we take at the personifications involved here is the kind of offense we should feel when people disregard God and kill his messengers. John tells us that the image had a striking effect upon him: "I marveled greatly" (17:6).

Before we go on to the angel's explanation of what John saw, note the way prostitution defiles and degrades people. That is what disregarding God does to us. That is what selling ourselves for the world's "stuff" instead of trusting God and keeping ourselves chaste for him does to us. Believers in Jesus are the bride of Christ. Let us not whore ourselves out for the world's passing pleasures, adornments, and commendations. Live for the Lamb and his pure bride, not for the beast and his whore. Live for the church and for Jesus, not for the world and its God-dishonoring rulers.

Revelation 17:7–18: The Angel Explains the Mystery

In response to John's amazement at what he has seen, the angel says to him in 17:7, "Why do you marvel? I will tell you the mystery of the woman, and of the beast with seven heads and ten horns that carries her." Most of the book of Revelation consists of John relating what he saw and heard. There are only a few places where heavenly beings interpret what he sees for him. Jesus tells John the meaning of the mystery of the stars and the lampstand in 1:20, one of the elders tells him who the 144,000 are in 7:13–17, and now one of the seven angels who had the seven bowls explains the mystery of the prostitute, the beast, and the beast's heads and horns here in 17:7–18.

The angel's explanation is going to focus on the beast, its heads, and its horns. Commentators are at a loss as to who exactly these symbols signify, but everyone agrees on how these symbols function. These symbols represent the kingdom of the world that will be defeated and will become the kingdom of our Lord and of his Christ. I am going to offer my take on *who* these symbols signify, but before I do that let's be clear on *how* they function. These are the enemies of God who are troubling God's people—governments that put Christians to death or imprison them, social networks and dynamics among groups of people that build a plausibility structure in which the truth of the Bible is regarded as backward and shallow and for the weak, and so on—and these are powers at work in the world to make Christianity seem negative or weak or foolish or not respectable.

The angel explains the beast to John in 17:8: "The beast that you saw was, and is not, and is about to rise from the bottomless pit and go to destruction. And the dwellers on earth whose names have not been written in the book of life from the foundation of the world will marvel to see the beast, because it was and is not and is to come." Just as the beast faked the crucifixion and resurrection of Jesus back in 13:3 when one of its heads had a mortal wound and was healed, so now it seems that the beast will imitate Jesus in another way. Jesus came on earth, and he has gone away, and he will come again. The beast appears to try to fake this too. We see here at the end of 17:8 that like the healing of the mortal wound back in 13:3, this wins worship for the beast. Look how bankrupt Satan and his forces are—the only way they can amaze people is by imitating God and Jesus. They don't write their own songs—they just do twisted covers of songs sung by the Triune God. We will return to this idea of the beast who "was, and is not" when we see it again in 17:11.

The next several phrases about the beast in 17:8 pick up earlier statements from Revelation and bring them together. In 11:7 the beast rises from the bottomless pit to kill the two witnesses when they have finished prophesying for 1,260 days. Then in 13:1 the beast rose from the sea (not from the bottomless pit as in 11:7), but here in 17:8 the beast "is about to rise from the bottomless pit."

The beast rising from the sea back in 13:1 identifies the beast John sees with the beasts Daniel saw rise from the sea in his vision in Daniel 7:3. John then shows us that the beast in 11:7 is one and the same with the beast in chapters 13 and 17 by repeating a phrase from 13:8 almost verbatim in the description in 17:8: "the dwellers on earth whose names have not been written in the book of life from the foundation of the world will marvel to see the beast." By describing the beast here in chapter 17 in phrases used both in chapters 11 and 13, John indicates that these three different descriptions of the beast are different perspectives on the same thing: the church (symbolized by the two witnesses in chapter 11) has a symbolic three-and-a-half-year period of time in which it will proclaim the gospel, and then the beast will rise, kill the two witnesses, and "go to destruction" (17:8). This is exactly what happens to the little horn in Daniel 7:11 (cf. also Daniel 8:11, 25; 11:45), and we will see the beast thrown into the lake of fire in Revelation 19:20.

The angel then gives John two interpretations of the beast's seven heads. The first is in 17:9: "This calls for a mind with wisdom:[1] the seven heads are seven mountains on which the woman is seated." Here the angel gives John one interpretation of the beast's seven heads: they are seven mountains. This identifies the beast with the seven hills on which Rome was built. The second interpretation of the seven heads is in 17:10: "they are also seven kings, five of whom have fallen, one is, the other has not yet come, and when he does come he must remain only a little while." These are not different interpretations, for the seven kings and the seven hills both convey, in a slightly veiled way, the idea that the beast represents the evil empire that rules the world. It may be that these seven kings in 17:10 are to be identified with the Caesars of Rome, but commentators are uncertain, and I would like to suggest a different interpretation. It may or may not be correct. Daniel prophesied of four kingdoms—Babylon, Medo-Persia, Greece, and Rome (see Daniel 2, 7). In Daniel 8, Daniel focused on the second and third kingdoms, Medo-Persia and Greece, and he prophesied of an antichrist figure in Daniel 8:9–14, 23–26. Similarly, we read of an antichrist figure that came from the fourth kingdom in Daniel 7:8 and Daniel 11. I am inclined to think that when John writes of the five kings who have fallen, one who is, and the other who has not yet come (17:10), he reports on what the angel told him as an interpretation of the book of Daniel. The number seven points to the complete number of rulers, and perhaps John has in view a particular set of the rulers Daniel prophesied. This possibility calls for further study.

The angel then tells John in 17:11, "As for the beast that was and is not, it is an eighth but it belongs to the seven, and it goes to destruction." Commentators connect this to the myth of Nero's return, but again I am inclined to think this interprets Daniel. For instance, in Daniel 7:7 the fourth beast (Rome) has ten horns, and then in Daniel 7:8 a little horn plucks up three of the ten. That would leave seven horns, and the little horn would be an eighth that belonged to the seven, just as we see in Revelation 17:11.

We saw at the beginning of 17:8 that the beast "was, and is not." The same phrase occurs again at the end of 17:8, and now we see in 17:11 that the beast "was and is not." Here again some point to the myth of Nero's return, but once again I think the book of Daniel is being interpreted. I noted above that in Daniel 8 an antichrist figure arises from the third kingdom, Greece, and conservatives identify this figure with Antiochus Epiphanes. In Daniel 7 an antichrist figure arises from the fourth kingdom. Perhaps the beast that was and is not is the Antichrist, typified by Antiochus Epiphanies but also still expected in the future in the final kingdom. The beast might be imitating the two comings of Jesus by means of the two comings of these antichrists, first Antiochus and then the end-time manifestation in the final kingdom.

In 17:12 the angel tells John, "And the ten horns that you saw are ten kings who have not yet received royal power, but they are to receive authority as kings for one hour, together with the beast." So the beast is a symbol of the wicked world of governments that refuse to honor Christ as King, and when the time comes for him to exercise his forty-two months of authority (13:5) for the second half of Daniel's seventieth week, there will be this tenfold alliance of world powers. I think this is symbolic of all the world, not necessarily ten specific kings. Revelation 17:10 told us that the seventh king would "remain only a little while," and now in 17:12 we see that these kings will have authority with the beast for "one hour."

The angel explains in 17:13, "These are of one mind, and they hand over their power and authority to the beast." The angel is speaking here of what we saw depicted in chapter 13, as the whole world seemed to join together to kill Christians.

Then the angel says in 17:14, "They will make war on the Lamb, and the Lamb will conquer them, for he is Lord of lords and King of kings, and those with him are called and chosen and faithful." This war on the Lamb is the great battle for which the nations prepared after the sixth bowl when they gathered to "the place that in Hebrew is called Armageddon" (16:12–16; particularly v. 16). We read about the Lamb's conquest in that battle here in 17:14, and John describes the conquest in 19:11–21.

The details of this passage may be confusing, and the interpretations and identifications may be at many points disputed, but I think we can be sure of this: the end is coming. It will be very bad for Christians for a little while. But then Jesus will conquer his enemies and deliver his people, "for he is Lord of lords and King of kings" (17:14).

Note that last phrase in 17:14: "and those with him are called and chosen and faithful." Those who will ride with Jesus to victory on white horses are "called"—they heard the summons of the gospel. God is holy. You have sinned, but Jesus died to pay the penalty for your sin. I call you to trust in Christ right now! I summon you to join the army of the Lamb. Trust Christ and be saved. Those who are called are also "chosen." God has chosen who will believe. Those whom God chooses he also calls, and he makes them "faithful."

By contrast, look at the situation in the unbelieving world in 17:15–18. If 17:18 identifies the prostitute as Babylon, and the seven hills in 17:9 identify the beast as Rome, then the harlot sitting on the beast in 17:3 points to an alliance between Rome and Babylon. I don't think this points to a literal alliance. Rather, Rome and Babylon are symbols of the powers of the world that have always opposed God and his people.

If you are not faithful to God, no one is going to be faithful to you. If you are not faithful to God, anyone who enters into an alliance with you is not being faithful to God either. You cannot trust anyone who is not faithful to God. The kings of the world turn on the very things that they use for their pleasure. The harlot is destroyed by her customers in 17:16. The world self-destructs because evil is self-defeating. But this isn't blind fate. This is God's justice, as the angel explains in 17:17: "for God has put it into their hearts to carry out his purpose by being of one mind and handing over their royal power to the beast, until the words of God are fulfilled."

Revelation 17:17 is an astonishing verse. I want to highlight two things in it. First, notice how God works his will in the hearts of these wicked kings who are opposed to his purposes. God is absolutely sovereign, even over what his enemies plan to do. You cannot overcome such a God! They are his enemies, and he puts it into their hearts to carry out his purposes by doing their wicked deeds. God is holy, righteous, and good. He is not evil. He is not tempted by evil, nor does he tempt anyone to it. He never does evil. But no evil is outside God's control.

The second thing I want to note about 17:17 is in the last phrase that refers to "the words of God" being "fulfilled." We get our understanding of the Bible from verses like this. God will keep all his words. He will fulfill every promise he has made. I have mentioned at several points that I think chapter 17 presents an interpretation of several prophecies in Daniel. If that's correct, then Daniel's words are called "the words of God." Even more staggering than that, "the words of God" in view in 17:17 are the things that John has written in this chapter and in this book. I think John is claiming that Revelation is God's Word and that it will all be fulfilled.

Conclusion

Will you live for the beast and the whore or for the Lamb and his pure bride? Will you do God's will by obeying him and living by his word, or will you do his will as his enemy who unwittingly carries out his purposes?

Think with me about this image of the world as a prostitute. Men go to prostitutes to pay to have a "husband and wife" kind of experience, but no amount of money buys the true joys of marriage. Think of how foolish and twisted and hopeless is the attempt to buy the joys of marriage. Could you pay someone to give you the joys of any other relationship? Could you pay someone to give you a father's wisdom when you need it? Could you pay someone to tell you they love you the way only a mother can? Could you pay a little child to run to your arms like a laughing toddler? You only get these joys by being in real relationships with people. Those who go to prostitutes may purchase a physical pleasure, but it is stripped of all the relational and emotional richness that is only to be found in marriage.

Now think about how John uses the image. Unbelievers are trying to purchase from the world system what God offers them for free, if they will commit to a relationship to him. Unbelievers are looking for security, health care, faithful provision for the future, but no whore can give what only God is able to give. You cannot purchase the joy of knowing God any more than you can purchase the experience of marital joy.

Live for the Lamb and his pure bride, not for the beast and his cheap whore.

Here are some specific ways to do that:

- *Read the Bible* every day. It does not have to be a long passage, but do not let a day go by without reading from the Scriptures.
- *Memorize the Bible.* Make a list of verses and put it where you eat. While you eat your food, read the verses out loud over and over. Everyone at the table with you will learn them too.
- *Meditate on the Bible* that you have read and memorized. If you catch yourself waiting on someone or sitting in traffic, think about the Scripture you have been reading and saying at mealtimes.
- *Pray the Bible* that you read and memorize for yourself and others. Pray through the church directory. Pray through your relatives. Ask. Seek. Knock.

Go to God to have your needs met, not the world's spiritual red-light district.

30

Lamenting or Rejoicing over Babylon's Fall?

REVELATION 18:1–24

WHERE ARE YOU GETTING YOUR NEEDS MET? The world is a spiritual red-light district. Are you going to a spiritual prostitute for your safety, security, health, purpose, provision for the future, and self-esteem?

You might ask, what would that look like? The following questions seek to get at what it means to go to the spiritual red-light district of the world instead of to God:

Do you feel good about yourself because the world respects you? Or do you feel good about yourself because you trust in Jesus and are united to him by faith, and that makes you righteous and right with God?

Do you feel good about yourself because you think you can make a lot of money and ensure your future? Or do you feel good about yourself because you trust your heavenly Father to meet all your needs because he is good and you can trust him?

Do you feel good about yourself because you know your agenda, know your goals, and are chasing your dreams? Or do you feel good about yourself because you are seeking your joy in the joy of those you love and it feels so good to make sacrifices for them that benefit them?

Do you feel good about yourself because you have a sound mind and a strong body and you have great health insurance? Or do you feel good about yourself because the purpose of your life is to make much of Jesus and death will be gain to you because you will be in his presence and you are confident that he will raise your body to be like his glorious body on the last day?

Do you feel good about yourself because you have a great security system in your home and you pack a weapon that you know how to use? Or do you feel good about yourself because you trust God's providential plan for you and are ready to preach the gospel every chance you get while you live?

Need

We need to be freed from the attractions of the world's spiritual red-light district. We need to see God's power to provide freely everything the world would sell us. We need to see that those who trade God in for the world's misuse of God's gifts will have all of God's gifts taken away from them. We need to see that the world does not love us. Worldly people love only themselves. We need to see Babylon fall, and we need to hear the call to come out of her that we might sojourn toward the Land of Promise. Revelation 18 gives us just what we need.

Main Point

Revelation 18 promises that godless worldliness will be judged, calling the worldly to repent and calling believers to separate themselves from the world's idolatry.

Preview

This chapter falls into three parts, and all three are comprised mainly of what is spoken by heavenly beings.

18:1–3   Announcement One: Judgment
18:4–20   Announcement Two: What Results from Judgment
18:21–24   The Angel and the Millstone

Context

After the outpouring of the seven bowls in chapter 16, with the seventh bowl resulting in the city of Babylon being split into three parts (16:19), John saw the prostitute and the beast, which were interpreted for him by the angel in chapter 17. The angel finished his interpretation of the woman and the beast at the end of chapter 17, and chapter 18 returns to John's describing what he saw and heard.

Chapter 17 drew out the implications of Babylon's behavior in the graphic description of her as a prostitute. Rather than go to the Lord, who offers every form of satisfaction freely to those who enter into covenant with him, the world has gone to a prostitute it must pay for tawdry imitations of God's good gifts. That prostitute is the world's leading city, and the whole world is drunk on her immorality. But the world turns on her and destroys her, and chapter 18 draws out the implications of Babylon's fall. This chapter deals with the way Babylon will be punished and with the way her cohorts and purveyors will respond. God is glorified in salvation through judgment: through the judgment of Babylon God calls his people home from exile.

John describes two proclamations from two voices in 18:1–20. The first announces the fall of Babylon, and the second announces both the salvation for God's people that comes through her fall and the way that she will be paid back for her sin. The chapter closes with a symbolic action involving a millstone that recalls Jeremiah's prophecy and the words of Jesus (18:21–24).

Revelation 18:1–3: Announcement One: Judgment

John writes in 18:1, "After this I saw another angel coming down from heaven, having great authority, and the earth was made bright with his glory." John also saw an angel "coming down from heaven" back in 10:1, and he will see another do the same in 20:1. In 14:18 we read of an angel who "has authority over the fire," and now we read of one with "great authority." The light that radiates from this angel is so powerful that his approach makes the earth bright.

This powerful, resplendent angel comes down to earth, and his glory enlightens the lands, and he will make the first pronouncement in 18:2, 3. He will say what *will be* found in Babylon after her fall, and later in the chapter another angel will declare what *will not be* found in Babylon after her fall (vv. 21–23). After declaring what will inhabit Babylon in 18:2, the angel will say why in 18:3. John writes in 18:2, "And he called out with a mighty voice, 'Fallen, fallen is Babylon the great! She has become a dwelling place for demons, a haunt for every unclean spirit, a haunt for every unclean bird, a haunt for every unclean and detestable beast.'"

The fall of Babylon is a dramatic reversal that paradoxically unveils reality. It seems that Babylon is an important place inhabited by glorious people, but the fall of Babylon is like the removal of the veneer. The demons, unclean spirits, birds, and hated beasts befit Babylon's rejection of God. This fulfills what Jeremiah prophesied in Jeremiah 51:37: "Babylon shall become a heap of ruins, the haunt of jackals, a horror and a hissing, without inhabitant." Rejecting God is rejecting what is pleasant, and the rejection of what is pleasant results in fellowship with what is unpleasant. Are you living in a way that matches the clean and holy presence of God? Or are you living in ways that fit you for fellowship with demons and unclean beasts?

In 18:3 the angel explains why Babylon is punished this way: "For all nations have drunk the wine of the passion of her sexual immorality, and the kings of the earth have committed immorality with her, and the merchants of the earth have grown rich from the power of her luxurious living." This verse reiterates what we saw in 17:1, 2, 15. The nations have intoxicated themselves with Babylon's for-pay services, which they substitute for what God offers freely to those who love him. The kings have gone to bed with Babylon, and their merchants have profited by serving as the purveyors of her smut. The rest of chapter 18 will show the demise of Babylon and the merchants and kings lamenting her.

Revelation 18:4–20: Announcement Two: What Results from Judgment

The second announcement is made in 18:4–20. The first and last things that this voice from Heaven says are addressed to the righteous. The first thing the voice says in verses 4, 5 calls the people of God to come out of Babylon. The last thing the voice says in verse 20 commands the righteous to rejoice over Babylon. Between these two statements are a command to pay Babylon back (18:6–8) and a description of how the wicked react to the fall of Babylon (18:9–19).

The voice that John hears in 18:4 speaks of the people of God as "my people," at the same time referring to "God" and "the Lord God" in verses 5, 8. Perhaps this means that Jesus is the one who speaks in 18:4–20.

Come Out of Her (18:4, 5)

In 18:4, 5 we see a call to the people of God to return from exile in verse 4 and a statement that explains why God is judging Babylon in verse 5. John writes in 18:4, "Then I heard another voice from heaven saying, 'Come out of her, my people, lest you take part in her sins, lest you share in her plagues.'" The first part of this statement is reminiscent of several statements in the Old Testament:

- Isaiah 48:20: "Go out from Babylon, flee from Chaldea."
- Isaiah 52:11: "Depart, depart, go out from there; touch no unclean thing; go out from the midst of her; purify yourselves, you who bear the vessels of the LORD."
- Jeremiah 50:8: "Flee from the midst of Babylon, and go out of the land of the Chaldeans."
- Jeremiah 51:6: "Flee from the midst of Babylon."
- Jeremiah 51:45: "Go out of the midst of her, my people! Let everyone save his life from the fierce anger of the LORD!"

In the Old Testament these statements anticipate the return from exile. Babylon carried Judah into exile after destroying Jerusalem and the temple in

586 B.C. The prophets pointed to a glorious eschatological future for Israel, when God would gather them from exile in a new act of salvation that would eclipse the exodus from Egypt. He would then restore them to their land. The New Testament authors interpret what God did in Christ in the categories of these Old Testament prophecies. The death of Jesus is the new salvific event like the exodus from Egypt, and Jesus fulfills the role played by the Passover lamb. That new exodus was to be accompanied by a return from exile. So by picking up on the prophecies of the return from exile, this statement in 18:4 is a call to God's people to return from exile, to come home from Babylon.

God's people are not now literally in exile in Babylon as they once were, so what does this mean? First, it is a call to trust in Jesus and the liberation he has accomplished (cf. 1:5). Second, it is a call to separate from the world and live for God as sojourners on the way to the land of promise. If you are not believing in Jesus right now, the words, "Come out of her, my people" are a call for you to abandon the sinking ship of the world and step onto the ark of salvation: trust in Christ. If you do not heed this call, you will do what the rest of verse 4 describes—you will partake of the sins and plagues of Babylon. By trusting Christ and coming out of Babylon, you will avoid Babylon's sins and plagues. You will no longer live like a Babylonian, like someone who does not know God. And you will not be punished with Babylon.

Revelation 18:5 tells us why God is going to punish Babylon: "for her sins are heaped high as heaven, and God has remembered her iniquities." Her sins are piled up, and God has not forgotten any of them. He will pay her back for all of them, as we see in verses 6–8.

Pay Her Back (18:6–8)

Revelation 18:6 gives a command to pay Babylon back, and then verses 7, 8 explain why. There is a threefold statement of retribution in 18:6: "Pay her back as she herself has paid back others, and repay her double for her deeds; mix a double portion for her in the cup she mixed." The consequences of sin are inescapable. Ecclesiastes 8:11 says, "Because the sentence against an evil deed is not executed speedily, the heart of the children of man is fully set to do evil." It may look as though sinners are going to get away with their crimes, but make no mistake about it, God will be just. The only way to avoid that justice is to trust in Christ and obey Proverbs 28:13, which promises mercy to those who confess and forsake their sin.

We see how punishments fit crimes in 18:7, 8. Babylon's proud disregard for God is stated in 18:7: "As she glorified herself and lived in luxury, so give her a like measure of torment and mourning, since in her heart she says, 'I sit as a queen, I am no widow, and mourning I shall never see.'" Rather than glorify God who controls where people are born, what they have, and who they are, Babylon glorifies herself. She will be punished according to the measure of her self-glorification and sensual living. Look at the "as . . . so" construction in verse 7. This means that to the degree that she has disregarded God and glorified herself, she will be punished. To the degree that she has engaged in pleasure without thanking God for those pleasures or staying within the boundaries God sets for pleasure, she will be punished.

God does not continue to provide his gifts to those who do not thank him and praise him for them. God gives Babylon gifts that Babylon glorifies herself for and uses without regard for the way God intended the gifts to be used. So God will teach Babylon that the gifts are his and that those who do not use his gifts the way he wants them to be used will be punished. God removes the gifts and "give[s] her a like measure of torment and mourning" (18:7).

Are you thanking God for the gifts he has given you or are you thanking yourself? Are you enjoying the gifts God has given within the boundaries he has set for them or are you trying to indulge in God's gifts any way you want whenever you want?

The voice from Heaven gives specifics about which gifts are in view. We see these gifts of stature, of companionship, and of safety in the final statements of 18:7. Babylon presumes on her stature as queen: "I sit as a queen." God made her queen, and she thanked him by killing his servants (18:24). Babylon presumes on her companionship: "I am no widow." God gave her companionship, and she lived in sensuality and became a prostitute. Babylon presumes on her future security: "and mourning I shall never see." God gave her joy, and she celebrated only herself.

All the good gifts will be removed and replaced with things fit for those who disregard God and kill his servants: "For this reason her plagues will come in a single day, death and mourning and famine, and she will be burned up with fire; for mighty is the Lord God who has judged her" (18:8). The "plagues" will come. Why plagues? Because the return from exile heralded in 18:4 is going to follow the consummation of the new exodus. The plagues will come "in a single day." It will be a sudden, shocking reversal. As Babylon is lamented by her accomplices, the kings say she was judged in an "hour" in 18:10, the merchants say she was destroyed in an "hour" in 18:17, and the men of the sea say she was destroyed in an "hour" in 18:19. These statements that the destruction will come in an "hour" show that the reference to "a single day" is not to a literal day. The point is that Babylon's destruction will be swift and sudden.

Notice how the "plagues" in 18:8 match Babylon's boasts in 18:7. She said she was "no widow" and would not mourn, but "death and mourning" come upon her. She said she was "queen," which implies luxury and excess, but she will meet "famine." She will be "burned up with fire," just as 17:16 described. This is guaranteed because the Lord God is "mighty," and he has "judged her." God's enemies will not overcome him, and they will not escape him. Do not test him.

The Wicked Weep for Her (18:9–19)

Rather than learn from what happened to Babylon, her consorts and those who purveyed her filth lament her fall. This affects all levels of society, from kings to merchants to men of the sea.

Kings (18:9, 10)

The voice from Heaven continues to speak in 18:9, 10:

> And the kings of the earth, who committed sexual immorality and lived in luxury with her, will weep and wail over her when they see the smoke of her burning. They will stand far off, in fear of her torment, and say, "Alas! Alas! You great city, you mighty city, Babylon! For in a single hour your judgment has come."

The kings pleased themselves with Babylon, but when she falls they want no part of her punishment. Notice how their grief does not result from the injustice Babylon did. Their grief does not spring from the lives they ruined in alliance with Babylon. They do not grieve about the way they dishonored God and led others to do the same. They wail for Babylon, but their concern is not for Babylon—notice how they do not seek to help her. Rather, they "stand far off, in fear of her torment" (18:10). They are not about to risk themselves in order to help Babylon. This shows that they do not love Babylon. They love themselves. They are only mourning because Babylon will give them no more sensual and immoral favors.

Are you sad when you see sin punished? Why? Because you got caught? Because you won't get away with that way of sinning anymore? Or because you defamed God's glory and goodness, told lies about his character, and wasted opportunities to enjoy him? Are you concerned for those your sins hurt? Or are you only concerned for yourself?

These kings are fools. Notice how they call Babylon a "great city" and a "mighty city." Fools! The truth is in verse 8, where God is called "mighty." They should regard his might, not Babylon's. Babylon's might was *nothing* when the hour of judgment came.

Merchants (18:11–17a)

The kings enjoyed Babylon's sensuality and luxury, and the merchants carried it to the ends of the earth, enriching themselves along the way. The voice from Heaven describes them in 18:11: "And the merchants of the earth weep and mourn for her, since no one buys their cargo anymore." Like the kings, these merchants do not mourn because of God but because of Babylon. But like the kings, these merchants are ultimately concerned about themselves, not Babylon. They are sad because no one buys from them anymore.

These merchants supply everything that people sell their souls to buy. These merchants provide the things that people choose to live for instead of living for God. Their cargo is described in 18:12: "cargo of gold, silver, jewels, pearls . . . " These first four items are precious stones and gold and silver. The next four items are fabrics: "fine linen, purple cloth, silk, scarlet cloth," followed by special wood, ivory, and metals: "all kinds of scented wood, all kinds of articles of ivory, all kinds of articles of costly wood, bronze, iron and marble." Next on the list are fragrant spices and ointments: "cinnamon, spice, incense, myrrh, frankincense," followed by food stuff: "wine, oil, fine flour, wheat," and the list is rounded out with animals, transportation, and slaves: "cattle and sheep, horses and chariots, and slaves, that is, human souls."

This list is a summary of the adornments, luxuries, and conveniences that comprise a life of worldliness. These items are all about having your best life now. The merchants used these items to provoke people to selfish indulgence. These items were not used to glorify God, and the people buying what these merchants were selling were not using these things to benefit others. Living for Babylon is all about living for yourself.

We see what it means to live for oneself in 18:14: "The fruit for which your soul longed has gone from you, and all your delicacies and your splendors are lost to you, never to be found again!" The only thing that we can long for that we will never lose is God. Anything that we long for instead of God will be taken from us, and we will never find it again. Anything that we long for without regard for God will be taken from us, and we will never find it again. The only way to keep your life is to lose it. The only way to enjoy delicacies and splendors is to do so for God's glory within the boundaries he has set.

Like the kings, the merchants see the sudden destruction of Babylon. Like the kings they do not come to Babylon's aid but protect themselves by standing far off (18:15). They see that none of Babylon's finery could protect Babylon against God. They see how soon all the finery is turned to dust, and the voice from Heaven describes how they will respond in 18:15–17a:

The merchants of these wares, who gained wealth from her, will stand far off, in fear of her torment, weeping and mourning aloud, "Alas, alas, for the great city that was clothed in fine linen, in purple and scarlet, adorned with gold, jewels, and with pearls! For in a single hour all this wealth has been laid waste."

Men of the Sea (18:17b–19)

The people at the highest levels of society, kings, lament Babylon's fall. The people in the merchant middle class lament Babylon's fall. And now the men of the sea join the lamentation of Babylon's fall in 18:17b–19:

And all shipmasters and seafaring men, sailors and all whose trade is on the sea, stood far off and cried out as they saw the smoke of her burning, "What city was like the great city?" And they threw dust on their heads as they wept and mourned, crying out, "Alas, alas, for the great city where all who had ships at sea grew rich by her wealth! For in a single hour she has been laid waste."

None of these responses have praised God for his justice. None have marveled at God's power to destroy Babylon. None have expressed repentance. None truly loved Babylon, for none moved to help her. All stood far off, and though they lamented Babylon, they were clearly most concerned about what Babylon's fall meant for their own self-interest.

The Righteous Rejoice over Her (18:20)

In contrast to the way the response of the wicked is described in 18:9–19, the righteous are commanded to rejoice in 18:20: "Rejoice over her, O heaven, and you saints and apostles and prophets, for God has given judgment for you against her!" In the end God will vindicate his name and his people by judging Babylon. God's people will rejoice in God. They will celebrate his justice. They will extol his mighty power. They will praise him for his mercy and forgiveness. They will exult in him because he has vindicated them.

When that day comes, what will you be doing? Will you be wailing with those who lived for Babylon, or will you be rejoicing with those who live for God? Will you live for what will be destroyed? Or will you live for God, who alone can satisfy all your longings?

Revelation 18:21–24: The Angel and the Millstone

We read in Jeremiah 51:60–64:

Jeremiah wrote in a book all the disaster that should come upon Babylon, all these words that are written concerning Babylon. And Jeremiah said to

Seraiah: "When you come to Babylon, see that you read all these words, and say, 'O LORD, you have said concerning this place that you will cut it off, so that nothing shall dwell in it, neither man nor beast, and it shall be desolate forever.' When you finish reading this book, tie a stone to it and cast it into the midst of the Euphrates, and say, 'Thus shall Babylon sink, to rise no more, because of the disaster that I am bringing upon her, and they shall become exhausted.'"

The destruction of Babylon that Jeremiah prophesied will be fulfilled by the future destruction of Babylon that John prophesies. We read in 18:21, "Then a mighty angel took up a stone like a great millstone and threw it into the sea, saying, 'So will Babylon the great city be thrown down with violence, and will be found no more.'" We saw "strong" or "mighty" angels in 5:2 and 10:1. It is interesting that the angel in 5:2 was calling for someone to open the seals on the scroll. The second, or perhaps the same, in 10:1 brought that scroll to John for him to eat, just as Ezekiel was to eat the scroll. Now the third angel here in 18:21 enacts a scene much like what Seraiah was to do with Jeremiah's scroll prophesying against Babylon. What John sees will fulfill what Jeremiah prophesied. It also enacts the warning Jesus gave in Matthew 18:6: "whoever causes one of these little ones who believe in me to sin, it would be better for him to have a great millstone fastened around his neck and to be drowned in the depth of the sea."

Notice that this statement that Babylon will be "thrown down" is in the future. This means there is time for Babylon to repent in response to John's message, and there is time for those who believe to come out of her lest they share in her sins and plagues. Babylon will be thrown down when the sixth bowl opens the way for the armies to gather for Armageddon (16:12–16), when the seventh bowl is poured out and the great earthquake splits the city in three (16:18, 19), and when the kings who were her allies strip her naked, eat her flesh, and burn her with fire (17:16). Babylon has abused the nations, and she will be punished for her pride and self-indulgence. Those she abused will not realize that they have been abused but will mourn her demise, while the righteous rejoice (18:9–20).

Revelation 18:22, 23 details all the pleasant things that filled Babylon but will never be enjoyed by her again, beginning with music: "and the sound of harpists and musicians, of flute players and trumpeters, will be heard in you no more." Music should be used to praise God, to enjoy God, and to point people to God. Babylon has abused the refreshing and inspiring gift of music and used it for pride and sensual indulgence. The good gift of music will be taken from Babylon and replaced with the howls of unclean birds and detestable beasts (18:2).

In addition to music, 18:22 says that craftsmanship will be removed from Babylon: "and a craftsman of any craft will be found in you no more." We are capable of art and skillful workmanship because we are like God, the ultimate Creator. The right use of these gifts is to honor him. If we do not honor him with his gifts, he takes them away.

Not only will music and craft be gone from Babylon, we see at the end of 18:22 that "the sound of the mill will be heard in you no more." All production that benefits people by providing them with food will cease.

There will only be darkness with no more relationships, as we see in 18:23a: "and the light of a lamp will shine in you no more, and the voice of the bridegroom and bride will be heard in you no more." Marriage is about the gospel. It is about Jesus and the church. Babylon hates Jesus, rejects him as King, and kills those who preach his gospel. So they have the gift and joy of marriage removed.

Babylon would not be bothered by God, so God will not bother Babylon anymore with his pleasant gifts. God will instead give her what she wants: demons, haunting vultures, and predators. Why does God judge them? The rest of 18:23, 24 explains.

We read at the end of 18:23, "for your merchants were the great ones of the earth, and all nations were deceived by your sorcery." This statement seems to imply that Babylon's great merchants could have been used for good. They could have communicated truth, goodness, beauty, and love for the glory of God. Instead they were used for godless, selfish purposes that rob God of glory and rebel against his truth. They used their power for "sorcery" and deception rather than for the worship of God in truth. Not only that, 18:24 tells us that Babylon actively opposed God's people and his word: "And in her was found the blood of prophets and saints, and of all who have been slain on earth." Murderers of the martyrs, Babylon would not tolerate those who told her what the world was for. She would not extend protection and life to those who championed the true cause and purpose of the universe. She would hear nothing of those who told her how she could have her sins of prostitution forgiven by the blood of Christ. She was so offended by the message of how she could have the stains of her sin washed away that she killed those who told her the good news.

Conclusion

So how does this message affect you? Will you lament when the movie theaters are gone, when the most trendy and popular clothing chains have all closed, and when the pornography industry is shut down once and for all?

Will it make you sad when those who exploit women can no longer enable you to use them for your pleasure? Will it make you sad when all the ways that people take pride in themselves are shown to be bankrupt? Will you lament with the kings, merchants, and men of the sea?

Or are you going to rejoice when God finally brings justice, when he shows his power, and when he vindicates his servants? This is really a question about where your heart is and what you really enjoy. Do you enjoy the world, or do you enjoy God? Do you long to be with God, or would you really rather go to a nice restaurant, the mall, or maybe a football game and enjoy yourself?

Let me ask it another way: do you live for what you were made to live for—God? Or do you live for what you were not made to live for and what will never satisfy you—yourself?

I want to ask the same question in John's terms: will you go to the world's spiritual red-light district to seek your pay-per-pleasure with Babylon the whore? Or will you seek to enjoy the good gifts that God freely gives by thanking him and praising him for those gifts and enjoying them within the boundaries he has set for them?

31

The Harlot and the Bride

REVELATION 19:1–10

ONE OF THE MOST CHARMING CHARACTERS in all of the world's literature is a young lady in Leo Tolstoy's *War and Peace*. Everyone who sees her falls in love with her. Natasha Rostov, the lovely girl's name, is eventually betrothed to the noble and upright Prince Andrey Bolkonski. Because she is young, the marriage is delayed for one year. Natasha is a character who wins the heart of every reader, and readers of *War and Peace* want joy and happiness for her.

Finally Andrey returns to claim his bride. Natasha has waited faithfully for him the whole year, but on the last night she is wooed by a worthless rake named Anatole, who is already married. As I read the story I wanted to warn her; I wanted to shout to her to wait for Andrey! Anatole is a charmer, but it is clear that he will ruin her life. Natasha is completely swept away. She agrees to elope with Anatole, but at the last minute she is rescued from certain destruction. However, Prince Andrey cannot forgive her, and they never marry.

Need

We are all like Natasha—easily dissuaded from what is best for us—and we all need to be convinced that the one who is coming for us is worth the wait so that the seducers who would ruin our lives don't make us unforgivable when the one to whom we are betrothed comes for his bride.

Main Point

This passage contrasts the fall of the harlot with the beauty of the bride so that we will live to be the bride, not the harlot. The harlot is a symbol of the

345

world's idolatry and immorality, while the bride is the symbol of the church. John wants to move his audience to live for the church and not the world, for righteousness and not smut, for Christ and not Satan; so he sets side by side the judgment of the whore and the glory of the bride.

Preview

Revelation 19:1–10 breaks down into three parts. The opening words of 19:1, "I heard what seemed to be the loud voice of a great multitude . . . crying out," are matched almost exactly in 19:6, "I heard what seemed to be the voice of a great multitude . . . crying out." The third section is then marked in 19:9 by the angel speaking to John. Revelation 19:1–5 celebrates God's salvation, 19:6–8 heralds what results from that salvation, and 19:9, 10 comes back from the future moment when God will save and reign to show how John and the angel respond to the announcement of God's future triumph.

19:1–5	Hallelujah, God Saves through Judgment
19:6–8	Hallelujah, God Reigns and the Lamb Takes His Bride
19:9, 10	Blessed Are Those Invited to the Marriage Supper

Context

To this point in Revelation we have seen Jesus and his letters to the churches in chapters 1–3 and the throne of God and the judgments issuing from it in chapters 4–16. The book concludes with the harlot, the King, and the bride in chapters 17–22. Revelation 19:1–10 closes the section on the harlot Babylon. This section began in 17:1–3, and that passage matches the verses that open the section on the bride in 21:9, 10. The end of the section on the harlot, 19:9, 10, is also very similar to the end of the section on the bride in 22:6–9. Between the section on the harlot in 17:1–19:10 and the section on the bride in 21:9–22:9 John describes the King and his kingdom in 19:11–21:8.

Everything that we have seen from 14:1 through what we examine now in 19:1–10 gives us different angles, different perspectives, on the same events. God's pure bride will be saved and married to the Lamb through the judgment of Babylon the whore. The church is personified as a pure bride. The wicked world that stands opposed to God and his purposes is personified as a prostitute. So in 14:4 God's people are figuratively described as "virgins," in contrast to the immorality of the world. Chapter 14 also gives us the imagery of a harvest of the world's deeds, which are figuratively depicted as grapes of wrath (vv. 17–19). Those grapes of wrath are trodden in the winepress of God's wrath (14:19, 20) to produce the wine of the fury of God's wrath (14:10). Chapters 15, 16 then show the outpouring of the bowls that have been filled with "the wrath of God" (15:7). Judgment falls on land and sea, rivers and sun (16:1–9), as well as on the beast's throne (16:10). The Euphrates is dried up, and the rebels gather to Armageddon (16:12–16). God then brings an earthquake that splits Babylon in three, and the cities of the nations fall (16:17–21).

When we move into John's vision of Babylon the whore in chapter 17, this is not a progression forward chronologically. Rather, John sees and gives to his audience a scene that gets at the implications of what Babylon is and how she will fall. The point of depicting Babylon as a prostitute is to get at the way she corrupts and defiles God's good creation. She takes what God has made good and blessed and makes it immoral. She commodifies things that should not be sold, things that are made to be enjoyed within the confines of God's instructions. Babylon sells cheap perversions of God's free gifts. Babylon's consorts destroy her at the end of chapter 17, and this is another way of describing the outpouring of God's wrath on Babylon that we saw in chapter 16. The world that refuses to worship God and to honor Christ as King is a city destroyed by an earthquake, and it is also a prostitute who is brutally murdered by her customers.

Chapter 18 describes reactions to the fall of Babylon. Those who used her lament her fall. For God's people, the fall of Babylon means the exile is over (18:4). Those who used Babylon lose everything they lived for when she falls, but the people of God are called to rejoice over her in 18:20, and that is exactly what we see them do in 19:1–10.

Revelation 19:1–5: Hallelujah, God Saves through Judgment

Babylon is guilty of idolatry and immorality. These are not idle sins. Her idolatry has led her to murder the saints who refuse to participate in that false worship. Her immorality has enabled her to entice the unbelieving world, enslaving the foolish in the worship of what is not God. Does anything have more power among people than religion and sex? Religion is ultimately about knowing God. Idolatry is a corruption of the human impulse to worship. Sex is the sacred union intended for one man and one woman whose marriage relationship is a picture of the relationship between Christ and the church. Sex is the most intimate consummation of that relationship.

Perhaps nothing in existence is more potent and consequential than these two things, religion and sex, both of which are ultimately about God. Babylon has defiled both. Babylon has profaned what God made holy and has taken what should be kept clean and pure and made it dirty and unwhole-some. Proverbs 11:10 says that "when the wicked perish there are shouts of gladness," and Revelation 19:1–8 shows us the shouts of gladness at the fall of Babylon.

As we begin to examine chapter 19, let's remember that John has just described an angel throwing a millstone into the sea and likened it to the future fall of Babylon in 18:21–24. The force at work causing the little ones to stumble (cf. Matthew 18:6) meets her just fate.

John describes the relief that the righteous feel when justice is done and wickedness is removed in 19:1, 2: "After this I heard what seemed to be the loud voice of a great multitude in heaven, crying out, 'Hallelujah! Salvation and glory and power belong to our God, for his judgments are true and just; for he has judged the great prostitute who corrupted the earth with her immorality and has avenged on her the blood of his servants.'" The inhabitants of Heaven respond to Babylon's being thrown down with the word, "Hallelujah!" This word is used four times in this chapter (vv. 1, 3, 4, and 6), and these are the only places it appears in the New Testament. It is simply the transliteration into Greek of a Hebrew term that means "Praise Yahweh."

The "Hallelujah!" in 19:1 is followed by the confession that "Salvation and glory and power belong to our God." Babylon worshiped gods that could not save and killed those who would not go along with her idolatry, but "salvation" belongs to God. Babylon proudly took glory to herself, but "glory" belongs to God alone. Babylon has exercised stolen power in God's world, but "power" belongs to him alone. Babylon's lies will be exposed, and the truth will ring loudly through eternal celebrations of God's "salvation and glory and power."

The first phrase of 19:2 states why "salvation and glory and power" belong to God: "for his judgments are true and just." When God judges, he does not go against reality. His judgments are right. They accord with what is and with what ought to be. There is no lack of evidence. There is no deviation from the standard. There is no prejudice. There is no falsehood. There is no injustice. God's judgments are "true and just." Because of that, "salvation and glory and power" belong to him.

The general statement of truth and justice in the first line of 19:2 is particularized in the second line: "for he has judged the great prostitute who corrupted the earth with her immorality." The prostitute corrupts. God's judgment is "true and just." And those who love righteousness praise God when he gives her what she deserves.

Notice that truth and justice in 19:2 not only means that God judges the prostitute but also that he avenges the martyrs: "and has avenged on her the blood of his servants." Here too we see the whore's immorality and idolatry. Her immorality corrupted the earth. Her idolatry led to God's servants being unjustly slain. Now God justly judges her and avenges "the blood of his servants," just as they prayed he would in 6:9–11. From this we learn that vengeance is not wrong. Unjust vengeance is wrong. Excessive vengeance is wrong. But when God brings vengeance, as we see in 19:2, he visits punishment that accords with his "true and just" judgment. He vindicates truth and those who lived according to truth.

The response to God's triumphant judgment through which salvation comes in 19:1, 2 is seconded in 19:3: "Once more they cried out, 'Hallelujah! The smoke from her goes up forever and ever.'" The first cry of "Hallelujah!" in 19:1, 2 celebrated God's truth and justice in salvation. This second one celebrates the extremity of the harlot's punishment: "The smoke from her goes up forever and ever" (cf. 14:11; 18:9, 18).

Her punishment will never end. Why? Because of the infinite majesty of God, against whom she sinned. The punishment of sin is ultimately about God's word being upheld as justice is visited against sin. Hell lasts forever because God is infinitely great.

This infinite display of rightness wins praise for God from those nearest his throne (cf. 4:4, 6). We read in 19:4, "And the twenty-four elders and the four living creatures fell down and worshiped God who was seated on the throne, saying, 'Amen. Hallelujah!'" Evidently John heard the multitude in Heaven and then saw these heavenly beings worshiping at God's throne. So the multitude in Heaven twice says "Hallelujah!" and then the twenty-four elders and four living creatures agree with an "Amen," adding a "Hallelujah!" of their own.

God deserves all praise, and so as these praises resound from Heaven, we read in 19:5, "And from the throne came a voice saying, 'Praise our God, all you his servants, you who fear him, small and great.'" God's servants in verse 5 are those who "fear him." The fear of God kept them from fearing Babylon and her threats. Now they are called to praise God for his triumph over Babylon.

Have you seen injustice in the world? Have you seen the righteous punished and the wicked rewarded? Have you seen Christians arrested for trying to help people, while those who set out to destroy life are commended? Let me encourage you to trust that God will do justice. God will set all things right. He will avenge his servants and punish the wicked. We can trust him. He is worthy of our praise.

Are you tempted by evil? Lured by immorality? Enticed by idolatry? Look again at the last phrase of 19:3: "The smoke from her goes up forever and ever." Evil, injustice, immorality, and idolatry will only result in regret. If you do not repent and trust in Christ, your regret will last forever. We want these images of God's justice to be sealed to our hearts so that when sin tempts us we see smoke rising from the ruins of Babylon.

Revelation 19:6–8: Hallelujah, God Reigns and the Lamb Takes His Bride

The only differences between 19:1 and 19:6 are:

- 19:1 starts with "After this," while 19:6 starts with "Then."
- 19:1 says the voice is "loud," while 19:6 likens the voice to "the roar of many waters" and "the sound of mighty peals of thunder."
- 19:1 says the voice is "in heaven," while 19:6 does not state a location.

Aside from these differences, the wording of the first half of the two verses is identical. Each statement opens a section in this passage.

The first of these sections, 19:1–5, focuses on the praise of God for the salvation he achieved by judging the great prostitute Babylon. This second section, 19:6–8, focuses on the praise of God for his reign and for the marriage of the Lamb.

We encounter the fourth "Hallelujah!" in the chapter in the middle of 19:6, and then the rest of the verse gives the reason for it: "For the Lord our God the Almighty reigns." Yahweh is praised because he reigns. This means the end of incompetent, unworthy, unqualified government. No more will God's world be troubled by those who cannot rule it. No more will God's world be troubled by those who rebel against his authority, reject his claim on them, refuse to be guided by his wisdom, and trouble those who honor the world's rightful Lord. Now he reigns. Imagine boarding an airplane, having the doors close, and then hearing the pilot announce that as soon as he gets the plane off the ground he's putting his nine-year-old son in the pilot's chair. How relieved would you be if near the end of the flight, after many dips, dives, jerks, and pulls, the pilot announced that he had taken control of the plane? When God begins to reign, the world will finally be ruled as it should be.

The great multitude continues its exclamation in 19:7: "Let us rejoice and exult and give him the glory, for the marriage of the Lamb has come, and his Bride has made herself ready." The multitude joyfully celebrates and honors the Lamb because the day of his wedding has come and his bride is ready.

There is a sense in which God married Israel at Sinai, and then when they were unfaithful to him the prophets indicted the nation as an adulterous wife. God promised to make a new covenant with his people, and Hosea 2:14–23 speaks of that new covenant as a new wedding between Yahweh and his people. Jesus explained that his disciples were not fasting because he, the

Bridegroom, was with them (Matthew 9:14, 15). He told parables about the kingdom of Heaven being like a wedding feast (Matthew 22:1–14) and about being ready for his coming as a bridegroom (Matthew 25:1–13). John the Baptist said that his joy was that of the friend of the bridegroom, which was complete because the bridegroom had come (John 3:29). Paul explained that marriage is about Christ and the church (Ephesians 5:21–33).

This reference to "the marriage of the Lamb" in 19:7 points to the consummation of the new covenant that was inaugurated when Jesus died, rose, and poured out the Spirit. We can scarcely imagine the glory of that wedding day. Never has there been a more worthy bridegroom. Never has a man sacrificed more for his beloved. Never has a man gone to greater lengths, humbled himself more, endured more, or accomplished more in the great task of winning his bride.

Never has a Father more wealthy planned a bigger feast. Never has a more noble Son honored his Father in everything. Never has a man treated his bride-to-be more appropriately. Never has a more powerful pledge, like an engagement ring, been given than the pledge of the Holy Spirit given to this bride. Never has a more glorious residence been prepared as a dwelling place once the bridegroom finally takes his bride.

Great will be the rejoicing. Great will be the exultation. There will be no limit to the glory given to the Father through the Son on that great day.

Never has a bridegroom done more to qualify his beloved to be his bride. Never has a bride needed her bridegroom more.

Never has there been a wedding more significant than this one. Never has a prince with more authority taken a bride with less standing. Never has a bride had her prince die for her, rise from the dead for her, and give to her his own standing before the Father.

Never has a bridegroom loved his bride more. Never has a bride waited as long for her bridegroom. Never has a bride sung more songs to her beloved. Never has there been a wedding with more guests than this one will have. Never has a wedding taken place on a more momentous occasion—the end of the overlapping ages and the ushering in of the kingdom. Never has there been a marriage like this one.

We see in 19:8, "it was granted her to clothe herself with fine linen, bright and pure—for the fine linen is the righteous deeds of the saints." This statement "it was granted her" is a divine passive. God "granted her to clothe herself." Back in 7:14, those clothed in white robes had "washed their robes and made them white in the blood of the Lamb." The fact that it is the marriage of the Lamb in 19:7 brings that connotation in here as well, and added to that is the statement that not only have the stains of misdeeds been washed away by the blood of the Lamb, "righteous deeds" make the "fine linen" shine.

So what do you want? Do you want to buy unsatisfying and perverted imitations of God's gifts from the whore, only to be punished with her forever in anguish and regret, or do you want to be the bride? Isn't it astonishing that such a bridegroom would give himself to us? We don't deserve to have him help us cross the street. And he gave everything. He left Heaven, walked dusty roads, endured the cross, rose from the dead, poured out the Spirit, accomplished redemption for us. It is almost too good to be true. But it *is* true. Wonder of wonders: trust in Jesus and he will come for you on that day.

Is he coming for you? Are you trusting him? If not, what are you hoping for from the future? What is more to be desired than what he offers?

If you are trusting him, he is coming for you. How do we make ourselves "ready," as 19:7 describes? The answer is given in 19:8—with Spirit-wrought righteous deeds through faith. This passage is here so that by the Spirit in faith we will walk in "righteous deeds" that will shine like fine white linen on that day. Contemplating the wedding day that awaits us means meditating on the Bridegroom who is coming for us.

This not only inspires us to do righteousness—it takes all the energy out of evil. Greed turns to generosity because the Bridegroom has met our deepest need and will supply all our wants from his glorious riches. Lust gives way to contented joy in what we have because the Bridegroom offers pleasures more full and free than anything the whore has to offer. Sloth and laziness are turned to zeal for the kingdom because the Bridegroom, King Jesus, summons from us our best and most diligent efforts. Anger and vindictiveness become patient longing for the Bridegroom to enact judgment that is true and just. Envy is replaced by satisfied happiness at the joy of others because we know that the Bridegroom will give us what we need now, and we will lack nothing when he comes. Gluttony is turned to disciplined moderation because the Bridegroom satisfies our cravings. Pride vanishes and we boast only in the cross—the Bridegroom deserves all the glory.

Revelation 19:9, 10: Blessed Are Those Invited to the Marriage Supper

What would life be like if we knew, really knew, that such a bridegroom was coming for us? It would be like what 19:9 says: "And the angel said to me, 'Write this: Blessed are those who are invited to the marriage supper of the Lamb.' And he said to me, 'These are the true words of God.'" The whole book of Revelation was probably read aloud in early Christian worship when John sent it to the seven churches. Those early congregations would have heard in 2:10 that suffering, tribulation, imprisonment, and even martyrdom awaited them. But because they are invited to the marriage supper of the Lamb, they are blessed. Jesus is enough. He is enough in the face of inconvenience. He is enough in the face of cancer. He is enough in the face of persecution. He is enough in the face of imprisonment, and even death. God intends to show his glory by putting his servants through all these things, and when they rejoice because none of this can take Jesus away, people see that Jesus is enough.

Look at what the angel says to John at the end of 19:9: "These are the true words of God." This applies most directly to the blessing that the angel has just stated in the first half of 19:9, but when John puts it in his book, then says at the end of the next verse, 19:10, that "the testimony of Jesus is the spirit of prophecy," these statements take on implications for everything contained in this book. Remember what 1:1 says: "The revelation of Jesus Christ, which God gave him to show to his servants the things that must soon take place." Revelation 1:2 states that John "bore witness to the word of God and to the testimony of Jesus Christ, even to all that he saw." Then 1:3 pronounces a blessing on those who "read," "hear," and "keep what is written" in "this prophecy." Make no mistake about it, John is claiming that Revelation is the word of God and is true: "These are the true words of God" (19:9).

God will judge the harlot, and through that judgment he will save his people (19:1–5). God will reign, and the marriage of the Lamb will come. The bride will be ready, clothed in the fine white linen of "righteous deeds" (19:6–8). Those invited to this feast are blessed. God's word is "true" (19:9). In this uncertain world, what a comfort it is to have the certain word of God.

John finds God's true word and the blessing of being invited to the marriage feast so moving that he wants to worship, as he says in 19:10: "Then I fell down at his [the angel's] feet to worship him, but he said to me, 'You must not do that! I am a fellow servant with you and your brothers who hold to the testimony of Jesus. Worship God.' For the testimony of Jesus is the spirit of prophecy." John seems to forget himself as he sees and hears such awe-inspiring words, and his impulse to worship the glorious being before him is the occasion of a significant revelation: only God is worthy of worship.

The angel refuses to allow John to worship him with a strong prohibition, and then he righteously classes himself as a fellow servant of the one Master. He is a fellow servant with John and John's brothers. Who are John's brothers? Who are those who are invited to the marriage feast of the Lamb? Note what it says in 19:10: "who hold to the testimony of Jesus." If you trust Jesus, you are John's brother. If you trust Jesus, you are a fellow servant with this mighty angel. In chapter 4 God is worshiped. In chapter 5 Jesus is worshiped. Here in 19:10 this mighty angel refuses worship, and another angel refuses worship in 22:8, 9. That Christ receives worship is a profound statement about his status.

Conclusion

What do you stand to lose if you live to be the harlot instead of the bride? You lose freedom, joy, love, intimacy, hope, purity, innocence, and most devastating of all, you lose what you were made for—knowing and worshiping God. You lose the Bridegroom. You lose Jesus.

Our bridegroom is better than Prince Andrey Bolkonski. Prince Andrey could not forgive Natasha, even when she repented with tears. Turn from your sin and go to Jesus. He will take you as his own.

32

The Return of the King

REVELATION 19:11–21

HAVE YOU BEEN TO THE TOMB of the Unknown Soldier at Arlington National Cemetery in Washington, D.C? Perhaps you saw the changing of the guard there? Let me tell you about the men who guard the tomb.

Tomb Guards are between 5'11" and 6'4" tall and have a 34-inch waist. The average tour at the tomb is about a year. Today all the Sentinels are selected from the 1st Battalion of the 3rd U.S. Infantry, known as the Old Guard.

It takes the average Sentinel eight hours to prep his uniform for the next day's work of guarding the tomb. The Guard's gloves are kept wet—year-round in Washington, D.C.—to improve his grip on his rifle. A shank of steel attached to the inside of the face of the heel is built up on each shoe. This allows the Sentinel to click his heels during certain movements.

If you have been to the tomb, you have seen the fluid formal steps down the walk; the Sentinel's hat and bayonet do not bob up and down. As the Guard patrols the Tomb, he takes twenty-one steps, which alludes to the twenty-one-gun salute. On the twenty-first step, the Sentinel stops, then turns and faces the Tomb for twenty-one seconds. Then he turns to face the direction from which he came, changes his weapon to the outside shoulder, counts twenty-one seconds, then steps off for another twenty-one-step walk down the mat. The Sentinel repeats this over and over until he is relieved at the changing of the guard.

The guard is changed every thirty minutes during the summer (April 1 to September 30) and every hour during the winter (October 1 to March 31). During the hours the cemetery is closed, the guard is changed every two hours. At the changing of the guard, all the heel clicks sometimes fall together and sound like one click. The guard change is occasionally done in the "silent" mode (as a sign of devotion to the "Unknowns"). No voice commands—everything is done in relation to the heel clicks and on specific counts.

The Guards at the Tomb of the Unknown Soldier are completely dedicated to their duty of guarding the Tomb. Because of that dedication, the weather does not bother them. In fact, they consider it an honor to stand their watch regardless of the weather. It gets cold, it gets hot, but the Sentinels never budge. And they never allow any effect of cold or heat to be seen by anyone.

The Tomb Guards walk the mat regardless of the threat of severe weather. In the fall of 2003, when Hurricane Isabelle moved through the Washington, D.C. area, the Sentinels continued to walk the mat. Even when the wind knocked over trees, the Tomb Guards stayed at their post and guarded the Tomb.

The Tomb is guarded twenty-four hours a day, seven days a week. In fact, there has been a Sentinel on duty in front of the Tomb every minute of every day since 1937. And the Sentinel does not change the way he guards the Tomb, even at night when there is no one around. The Sentinels do this because they feel that the Unknown Soldiers who are buried in the Tomb deserve the very best they have to give.[1]

Everything about the appearance of the Guards communicates precision, discipline, honor. These soldiers demonstrate extraordinary discipline and commitment to those who have died for our nation. Their commitment is not to a king or an eternal cause, but to unknown men who have given their lives to secure the freedoms and the ideals of our earthly democratic nation.

Need

We Christians don't realize who we are. We too often forget that this world is not our home. We are not earthlings. We seek the city that is to come, which has eternal foundations, whose King is Jesus.

The marching of the Sentinels at the Tomb of the Unknown Soldier is a lot like life. Day after day they do the same thing over and over, just as so many of us walk through the same patterns of life day after day; and just as their repetitious patrol and changing of the guard is endued with enormous nobility and honor, though we are so prone to miss this, our lives too are significant beyond what we realize.

Those Sentinels represent the United States of America; we represent Almighty God. Those Sentinels are the image of American military precision and excellence; as Christians we are being conformed to the image of the risen Christ. We are made and live in the image of God; we are citizens of the kingdom of the Sovereign Lord of the Universe.

Context

We have seen the downfall of Babylon and the announcement that the marriage of the Lamb has come (17:1–19:10), and now in 19:11—21 the King makes his return and routs his enemies.

Main Point and Three Objectives

The purpose of this passage is to highlight the glory of the coming King. It is intended to give hope to suffering Christians by showing them that they have a King who is coming who will triumph over their enemies. Everything in this passage points to the glory of Christ.

In 19:11–21 we see the cavalry that we as Christians will ride in one day. We represent the world's true King. My prayer is that the knowledge that the rightful Lord of the World will return as King and the knowledge of our role in his conquest will do three things for us:

1) Deepen our appreciation of the significance and purpose of our daily lives, mundane though they may seem to us.
2) Increase our propensity toward instant willing obedience to our sovereign King, regardless of time, place, or the possibility of our being caught.
3) Most importantly, stir up in us a longing for our King to come and reign over us. May we be those of whom Paul wrote in 2 Timothy 4:8, those who will receive a "crown of righteousness" because they have "loved his appearing."

Preview

This passage can be divided into three sections marked by the words "I saw" in 19:11, 17, 19. Each section has a unique focus.

19:11–16	The Glory of King Jesus
19:17, 18	Birds Summoned to Celebrate Victory
19:19–21	The Victory of the King

Revelation 19:11–16: The Glory of King Jesus

We read in 19:11, "Then I saw heaven opened, and behold, a white horse! The one sitting on it is called Faithful and True, and in righteousness he judges and makes war." That John saw "heaven opened" (cf. 11:19; 15:5) highlights the fact that our King comes from the right hand of God, where he has taken his seat according to God's command until all his enemies are put under his feet. The subjection of the enemies is what will be depicted here.

That Jesus is seated on "a white horse" proclaims that he comes as the conquering warrior. This was a provocative image in the Roman world in which John wrote. In a culture where emperors and conquering generals rode white horses in triumph, John sees the ultimate conqueror coming in absolute triumph. John then makes seven descriptive statements about the rider on the white horse. The first two are here in 19:11.

First, unlike so many conquerors, the Warrior Messiah is "Faithful and True." Finally the ruler for whom we all long will have arrived. Throughout the Old Testament the nation of Israel was given leaders who were in many ways typological shadows of the coming Royal Messiah, but all these leaders had flaws that made it clear they were not the anticipated one. Moses failed to believe, struck the rock, and didn't enter the land. Matthew's genealogy tells us that David begot Solomon by her who had been the wife of Uriah, reminding us of his great failure. Solomon reigned in messianic splendor, but then his many wives led his heart astray to other gods. In contrast to all these disappointments, Jesus is faithful and true. He will never let us down.

Second, the coming King will judge and make war "in righteousness." No one will question his decisions; no one will doubt the justice of his cause; no one will be able to refute the utter clarity of his motives and purposes. They may rebel against him, but there will be no unrighteousness in him.

Some time back my sweet wife and I watched the movie *Patton*, and I was struck by the complexities and contradictions of one of our national heroes. He got the job done, so we love him. But he was portrayed in the move as a self-seeking, glory-hounding, unrighteous, unfaithful jerk. Whether or not he deserved to be portrayed that way is not the issue; the issue is that there will be no such complexity about the righteousness and faithfulness of King Jesus, the Messiah.

The next three descriptive statements are in 19:12: "His eyes are like a flame of fire, and on his head are many diadems, and he has a name written that no one knows but himself." The third of the seven statements is that "His eyes are like a flame of fire." This tells us that Jesus is absolutely pure and that he sees all things. We are the subjects of this King, and we will give an account to him. There are no compartments of our lives that he does not see. There are no corners of our hearts that his flaming eyes do not search. All things are open and laid bare before the eyes of him with whom we have to do (Hebrews 4:13).

Think of that honor guard in Arlington National Cemetery. The Sentinel does not change the way he guards the Tomb, even at night when there is no one around. The Sentinels do this because they feel that the Unknown Soldiers who are buried in the Tomb deserve the very best they have to give. They are faithful because they think that Unknown Soldiers who gave their lives for freedom deserve it. How much more does the Absolute Monarch of the universe deserve it? Those soldiers died to secure political freedom. We live to honor the one who died to secure spiritual freedom. His sacrifice is far more consequential than that of the Unknown Soldier. And he is not unknown. He is known, and he is always watching, even if it seems that we are going to get away with our sin. Satan lies to you and tells you no one will know what you are tempted to do. Do not entertain that lie. There is no getting away with anything.

Fourth, "on his heads are many diadems." The "many diadems" on his head communicate his absolute authority. There is no dominion, no region, no locality over which he does not reign. He is Lord of all, and he wears the crown of every place. These diadems appear to have been cloth headbands rather than solid crowns,[2] and each diadem would signify a place ruled.

Consider his authority over you. When the King gives an order, however mundane the command may seem, the carrying out of the directive is significant to the servant to the degree that he loves his master. Let me encourage you to think of your job as your calling or your vocation—the word *vocation* is related to the word *calling*, and thinking of what you do as a vocation means that you are doing the task for which God made you. If you conceive of yourself as serving your Master, you will not need preeminence, prosperity, position, promotions, plaudits, or popularity. As we serve him, like the Sentinels at the Tomb of the Unknown Soldier, we do not flinch in the face of sacrifice, hesitate in the presence of adversity, negotiate at the table of the enemy, ponder at the pool of popularity, or meander in the maze of mediocrity.[3] We serve the King.

We find the fifth descriptive statement at the end of 19:12, "he has a name written that no one knows but he himself." This points to the divinity of Christ because it shows that there are aspects of God that we will never know. God is infinite, which means that we will never exhaust him. There are attributes of Jesus in this passage that can be known, and there are aspects of who he is to which we have no access. He is transcendent. He reveals himself to us, but he is ultimately beyond our ability to comprehend.

Sixth, we read in 19:13 that he wears "a robe dipped in blood." This may be a reference to Isaiah 63:1–3, where the robes of the Messiah are splattered with the blood of his enemies. But at this point the battle has not yet taken place. It will happen in 19:20, 21. So it may be preferable to view the blood in which the robe is dipped as a reference to the cross. Either way we can say that Jesus conquered his enemies by shedding his own blood on the cross, and when he returns he will conquer his enemies by shedding their blood. So which conquest will be the one that involves you? If you trust in Jesus, his blood is shed for you. If you rebel against him, refusing to have him as Lord and obey him as King, your blood will be shed for him. I invite you to trust him right now. Let his blood count for you. Live for him. Why would you be among those whose blood he will shed?

The seventh descriptive statement is at the end of 19:13, and it is the third title in the passage. In 19:11 he is called "Faithful and True," in 19:12 "he has a name written that no one knows," and now in 19:13 "the name by which he is called is The Word of God." In the Gospel of John, the reference to Jesus as the Word depicts him as the living revelation of God. Here in Revelation the reference to him as "the Word of God" seems to communicate the authoritative, decisive finality of the judgment he comes to render.

If you have believed in Jesus, if you have placed your faith and hope in him and what he achieved on the cross, the Bible is talking about you in 19:14: "And the armies of heaven, arrayed in fine linen, white and pure, were following him on white horses." That is the cavalry we want to ride in. Look back at 19:7, 8, where "his Bride has made herself ready" and is clothed "with fine linen, bright and pure." The bride is washed clean by the blood of the Lamb and then goes to war with her Beloved.

When you think about who you are, does your place in this cavalry define your identity? The Bible tells us that we are worse than we think we are. When we read about the significance of our sin in the Bible, we realize that it is a lot more heinous than we thought. But the Bible also tells us that if we trust in Jesus, the role we play in God's purposes is more exalted than we would ever expect. Believer in Jesus, one day you will ride a white horse to victory in the cavalry charge led by the risen Christ himself.

My friend Warren Geldmeier recently told me about a comic book he had that had been illustrated by an artist who later became famous. The earlier comic books the artist had done are now very expensive collector's items because of what the artist went on to do later in life. The deeds that we do now in our seemingly insignificant lives are kind of like those early comic books. What we do now is of tremendous significance because of what God is going to make of us in the future.

Let us take up the tasks God has given to us now as those who know that one day we will ride with Jesus. One day we will stand in the heavenly court. Live nobly now. Change diapers with the same sense of significance you would feel if you were preparing the child to be presented before the world's true King. In a sense, that is exactly what you are doing.

Wearing white linen in battle seems like a strange way to dress for war. Perhaps the armies of Heaven wear white because Jesus is the one who will do all the fighting. Note 19:15: "From his mouth comes a sharp sword with which to strike down the nations, and he will rule them with a rod of iron. He will tread the winepress of the fury of the wrath of God the Almighty." Every statement in 19:15 points to the fulfillment of Old Testament prophecy. Isaiah 11:4 says the Messiah will "strike the earth with the rod of his mouth," and in Isaiah 49:2 the servant says that God made his mouth like a sword. Jesus is the fulfillment of these prophecies (cf. also Revelation 1:16; 2:12, 16; 19:21). Ruling with "a rod of iron" means that Psalm 2:9 is fulfilled. The treading of the winepress heralds the fulfillment of Isaiah 63:3. Jesus is the agent of God's judgment, and through this judgment he accomplishes the final deliverance of his people.

Now if Jesus is going to do all the fighting, why are the armies of Heaven there at all? To make the King look good. He redeemed them by his blood, cleansed them, enabled them to do good deeds, fitted them out in fine white linen, put them on majestic white battle stallions, and all their splendor highlights and augments his greatness.

We read in 19:16, "On his robe and on his thigh he has a name written, King of kings and Lord of lords." A statue dating from A.D. 151, some sixty years after the writing of Revelation, has been found in ancient Parthia, and on its thigh it bears the inscription "King of kings."[4] This shows us that John is depicting Jesus in a way that would make sense to his contemporaries. Parthia was particularly feared by Rome because they had defeated Rome in battle. Back in chapter 13 when we saw the beast with seven heads receive a mortal wound that was healed, we noted that John's audience might have seen in that description a reference to the myth of Nero's return. Nero had committed suicide, but it was rumored that he had not died but had gone to Parthia and would lead a Parthian horde back into Rome to reclaim power. Impostors even appeared claiming to be Nero. We noted also that the number of the beast probably points to Nero. Throughout Revelation, Rome and its Imperial Cult is the historical reality behind the persecution of Christians, because Christians refused to participate in its idolatry and immorality. This description of Jesus coming as a conquering King probably would have evoked images of the Parthians, and thus Jesus is presented as the true conqueror whose conquest is aped by the myth of Nero's return. The Parthians rode white horses into battle. Their king wore diadems, and the Romans appear to have eschewed diadems. It appears that John has described Jesus as the ultimate realization of Rome's greatest fear. Jesus, not Nero, will lead a cavalry charge greater than anything Rome has ever seen to seize power.

Jesus, not Nero, and not some beast with a wounded head, rose from the dead. Jesus, not Nero, is worthy of worship. Jesus, not the Parthian king, deserves those many diadems. Jesus, not the Parthian king, is the King of kings. Jesus is Lord!

Everything said to this point in the passage is about the glory of the rider on the white horse. Let me invite you to worship him. See all your hopes realized in him. Plan your life around the future he will bring. Build all your dreams to match what he will do. Pin all your expectations on him. He will not let you down. Sing his praise forever.

Revelation 19:17, 18: Birds Summoned to Celebrate Victory

Having seen and described the rider on the white horse, John writes in 19:17, 18, "Then I saw an angel standing in the sun, and with a loud voice he called to all the birds that fly directly overhead, 'Come, gather for the great supper of God, to eat the flesh of kings, the flesh of captains, the flesh of mighty men, the flesh of horses and their riders, and the flesh of all men, both free and slave, both small and great.'" The description of this angel "standing in the sun" probably means that the physical position of the angel was in the sky either directly in front of or upon the sun. So looking at the angel would be as blinding as looking at the sun itself. This angel makes his proclamation from the skies, "in the sun," and he calls to those who swim the skies, "the birds." He summons the birds to a great feast.

Note that the call for the birds to come happens before the battle, announcing the certainty of the victory. There are two feasts in chapter 19. There was the marriage feast of the Lamb in verse 9, and now there is the great feast of God here in verse 17. The guests at the marriage supper are those who trust Christ, those redeemed from their sins by his blood. The guests at the great feast of God here in 19:17 are the birds, who will feast on God's enemies. Refuse the grace and love and goodness of God, and you deserve to be eaten by great birds of prey. The point of 19:18 is that neither status, influence, nor insignificance will exempt anyone from God's justice. The gospel is a leveler of persons because neither wealth nor status brings anyone closer to God than another—everyone is in need of justification by faith in Christ. The judgment is also a leveler of persons because neither advantage nor disadvantage will affect the justice of God.

If you are not one who by faith in Jesus will ride with him, remember that, as he said, those who are not for him are against him (Matthew 12:30). Not to give him the trust and faith of which he is worthy is to rebel against his authority and goodness. And the rebels will be punished.

Revelation 19:19–21: The Victory of the King

At the pouring out of the sixth bowl in 16:12–16 the way was opened for the assembling of the kings of the whole world for the great day on the field of Armageddon. Then in 17:14 we read that the kings of the earth will make war on the Lamb, and he will conquer them. Revelation 19:19 brings us to the great day of God the Almighty at the Battle of Armageddon. John writes, "And I saw the beast and the kings of the earth with their armies gathered to make war against him who was sitting on the horse and against his army." Satan's fake christ has gathered the armies of the world for the great confrontation with the true Christ and his army. As described in Psalm 2:1–3, "the nations rage," "the peoples plot," and the kings and rulers have set themselves against Yahweh and his Messiah. Theirs is a hopeless cause. They are going to make war on Jesus and the armies of Heaven, but they cannot win.

This is foolishness of the highest order. Do you participate in this folly? Are you living your life to prepare to be part of this kamikaze mission against an Almighty Conqueror? As you plan your days, as you think about what you want from life, as you respond to the circumstances that develop around you, are you embracing the rule of the Sovereign Lord of the Universe or plotting war against him?

The beast, the earth's kings, and their armies want to overcome the Creator and do away with him. They want to set up their own alternative kingdom—as though they could somehow engage a reality where the Creator of reality is not in charge! Theirs is the epitome of mission impossible. If they were to overcome the Creator and King, God himself in the person of Christ, there would be no world left in which they could rule. He is "upholding the universe by the word of his power" (Hebrews 1:3); so if they overcame him, the universe would disintegrate. But he cannot be overcome.

The battle is over in an instant. Note the next verse (19:20): "And the beast was captured, and with it the false prophet who in its presence had done the signs by which he had deceived those who had received the mark of the beast and those who worshiped its image. These two were thrown alive into the lake of fire that burns with sulfur." So two of the three members of the false trinity are captured and thrown into the lake of fire. The third member, Satan himself, will join them in the lake of fire after the millennium (20:10). Here in 19:20, the culprits of chapter 13, the false christ and his false holy spirit, are captured and punished. Then in 19:21 the armies of the beast are defeated: "And the rest were slain by the sword that came from the mouth of him who was sitting on the horse, and all the birds were gorged with their flesh." This is what 19:15 told us would happen to Christ's enemies, and the beasts summoned to the feast in 19:17, 18 eat their fill in 19:21.

Conclusion

Perpetrators of lies and temptations will be justly judged, and those who gave themselves to falsehood will regret what they have done. Don't believe their lies.

Long for Christ's appearing. Obey him with an instant willingness. Your deeds are significant when done unto God. Treasure God. Nothing can do for us what only God can do for us:

- Don't look to *pornography* to satisfy you in ways that only God can. God made beauty not for idolatry but so we would catch a glimpse of his beauty. Worship God, not things in his image.
- Refuse the tendency to rely on all that *money* can do for you in terms of security and prestige and happiness. God gives us money so we can have some conception of his inexhaustible riches and entire self-sufficiency.
- Don't remain in *slothful indulgence* looking for lengthened periods of rest to renew you. God built us so that, as Augustine put it, we have no rest until we rest in him.
- Don't expect other human beings to absolutely satisfy the need you feel for *companionship and love*. God gives us earthly relationships so that we can understand more about love.

The false excitement of sinful pleasure can be likened to the rush of a daring leap off a building fifty stories tall. It will end in destruction. Don't live for a rush that ends in destruction. Live to mount a white horse and ride to victory.

Christ will come on that white horse in glory. On that day even our most mundane actions done by faith in him will take on enormous significance because we will mount white steeds and ride behind the conquering King.

33

The Millennium

REVELATION 20:1–15

I WANT TO TELL YOU about a place called Kanakuk, a Christian sports and adventure camp that I worked at in the summers of my college years. There God gave me a glimpse, I think, of what the millennium will be like. I received a glimpse of the glory of the reign of Christ at Kanakuk Kamp.

No Internet. No television. No radio. No cell phones. No air conditioning. Big hills and broad fields on the shores of a lake in the Ozark Mountains in southern Missouri. Late May to mid-August. Five thousand staff, Christians, mostly college students, athletes all. Fifteen thousand kids between the ages of seven and eighteen. Girls and boys kept separate most of the time. Jet Skis. Zip lines. Ski boats. Spelunking. Camping. Ropes courses. Kayaks. Canoes. Tents. Stargazing. Basketball courts and ballfields. Full days of practice and play, and nights of worship and clean fun at parties where the music is wholesome and nothing unseemly or inappropriate happens. Just being outside at the Kamp with the lake and all the stuff to do takes it close to paradise, and I haven't told you the best part yet.

The best part is the spirit of the place, the attitude that flows out from the Kamp's director. Joe White infuses the staff and washes the whole place clean. Joe has memorized as much or more Scripture as anyone I have ever met, and he obeys the Bible with relentless joy. He is tenaciously optimistic. Negative comments, complaints, and whining have no place at Kanakuk. Remarkably, they are almost nonexistent there. When they happen they are recognizably out of place. Sarcasm and meanness are shocking aberrations. Joe White's obedient faith and contagious joy has produced an atmosphere where the power of righteousness overwhelms evil. I have never been any place like it, before or since.

People with broken lives arrive at Kanakuk, enter into this realm that is led by people who believe, rejoice, obey, and worship, and the happiness and purity of the place is overpowering. Those who are hurt are surrounded by people trusting God and loving them, and the good news of Jesus Christ, believed and lived, transforms, heals, restores, renews.

In my experience, Kanakuk is the closest I've ever been to what I think it will be like to live in the millennium.

Need

We need to have our imaginations ravished by the beauty of holiness, so that we will not be led astray by the ways that Satan perverts beauty with his unholy attractions. We need to have our thoughts about influence taken captive by the power of righteousness, so that the weakness of unrighteous schemes will have no appeal to us. We need to see the usurper thrown down and the true Lord of the world ascend the throne, so that we will live for his kingdom and not that of the impostor.

Main Point

The glory of God will cover the dry lands of this earth like the waters cover the sea when Christ reigns with his resurrected followers in the millennium.

Context

Jesus comes in judgment in 19:11–21, slays his enemies, and throws the beast and the false prophet into the lake of fire (19:20, 21). Then Satan is bound for a thousand years (20:1–3), and during that thousand years resurrected believers reign with Christ on earth (20:4–6). At the end of the thousand years, Satan is released and deceives the nations, led by Gog of the land of Magog, as prophesied in Ezekiel 38, 39, in a final rebellion. Note that in Ezekiel 38, 39 in the latter days Gog attacks the land that has experienced eschatological restoration (cf. especially Ezekiel 38:8, 11, 12).[1] Satan's final rebellion is defeated in 20:7–10, and then 20:11–15 shows the final judgment at the great white throne. Just as the defeat of Gog of Magog in Ezekiel 38, 39 is followed by the description of the new heaven and earth in the form of a cosmic temple in Ezekiel 40—48, so also the defeat of Gog of Magog in 20:7–10 is followed, after the final judgment, by a new heaven and new earth as a cosmic temple in Revelation 21, 22.

Preview

There are four scenes in chapter 20. The text clearly presents them as happening one after another. First Satan is bound in verses 1–3, and then once he is bound, the resurrected followers of Jesus reign for the thousand years of his imprisonment in verses 4–6. At the end of the thousand years, Satan is released and deceives Gog of Magog, and the final rebellion is crushed in verses 7–10. The chapter closes with the final judgment in verses 11–15.

The four scenes of this chapter are as follows:

Revelation 20:1–3   Satan Bound
Revelation 20:4–6   The Millennial Reign
Revelation 20:7–10   Satan Released and the Final Battle
Revelation 20:11–15   The Great White Throne

Revelation 20:1–3: Satan Bound

We read in 20:1, "Then I saw an angel coming down from heaven, holding in his hand the key to the bottomless pit and a great chain." Back in 9:1 an angel fell from Heaven as a star, received a key, and opened the shaft of the abyss, or bottomless pit. The opening of the pit released the scorpion-like locusts who tormented the wicked. This angel in 20:1 comes down from Heaven with the key to the abyss, not to open and release, but to bind and to shut. In verse 1 we see the *implements* that will be used to bind Satan, and in verses 2, 3 we see the *actions* taken to bind him and the *duration* of his imprisonment. The three implements in verse 1 are "the *key*," "the *bottomless pit*," and "a *great chain*."

The angel takes action in 20:2, 3: "And he seized the dragon"—maybe you've heard someone refer to taking a tiger by the tail. Back in 12:3 we read of "a great red dragon, with seven heads and ten horns, and on his heads seven diadems." His tail was so massive that it "swept down a third of the stars of heaven and cast them to the earth" (12:4). Picture the night sky, and try to envision a dragon so large that his tail can sweep a third of the stars down from the heavens. This is a symbolic depiction of the mammoth spiritual draw Satan has to be able to win ranks of angels to his cause. I'm sure he wasn't seized without a fight. Enter into the cosmic drama of this colossal brawl. This scene is the stuff of epic poetry.

We saw in chapter 12 that by his death and resurrection Jesus defanged the serpent, enabling Michael to drive the dragon from the field of Heaven (12:5–11). At that time Satan was thrown to the earth and was given a short time (12:12). Knowing that his time was short, he made war on the woman and her seed (12:13–17). For three and a half years the woman was nourished in the wilderness (12:14), and the two witnesses were able to prophesy (11:3). At the appointed time Satan brought forth a beast from the bottomless pit (11:7; 13:1; 17:8), who killed the two witnesses (11:7), persecuting the church and martyring many for three and a half years (13:5–18). These three-and-a-half-year periods symbolize the protection and persecution of the church from the ascension of Christ to his coming, which we saw in 19:11–21.

So on the basis of Christ's conquest at the cross (12:5–12), and once

Christ has conquered his enemies at his coming (19:19–21), this angelic champion engages in the contest that will close one age and open another. See the shining warrior seize the thrashing serpent, and for all his wrath the dragon cannot break the grip. Not willingly is he subdued. Long he held sway as "the god of this world" (2 Corinthians 4:4), "the prince of the power of the air" (Ephesians 2:2), but now the day of his demise has come.

John heightens the drama of the moment by elaborating on the identity of the one being subdued in 20:2: "And he seized the dragon, that ancient serpent"—this is the serpent who deceived Eve and led Adam into sin, defiling God's good creation. This cursed archfiend has caused more pain and sorrow than words can tell. John continues to identify him: "who is the devil and Satan"—"the devil" is often how the New Testament refers to him. He is also called "Satan" in the New Testament, as well as when he stood to oppose Israel in 1 Chronicles 21:1, when he opposed Job, and when he accused the high priest in Zechariah 3.

After long years and bitter conflicts across two Testaments and all of church history, the enemy of God and his people is finally seized. And he cannot break the angel's hold. Having seized him, we read at the end of 20:2 that the angel "bound him for a thousand years." This is the first of six references to this thousand-year period, all in this chapter (vv. 2, 3, 4, 5, 6, 7).

Some think this binding of Satan for a thousand years happened when Jesus died on the cross, and they think that we are in that thousand-year period right now. In their view chapter 12 described the same thing as we see described in another way here in chapter 20. The differences between chapter 20 and chapter 12 are too significant for me to find that view convincing (see Table 22.1, "Differences in Detail between Revelation 12:7–12 and 20:1–3" in chapter 22 of this commentary). Those who think that we are now in the millennium are called amillennialists, but they do not necessarily think there is no millennium at all, just not one in the future. They hold that we are in the millennium now; so some prefer the label realized or inaugurated millennialism.[2]

Against that perspective, I find the view that the binding of Satan is something that will happen in the future far more compelling. This view holds that the millennium has not happened yet, so we are now in the period *prior to* the thousand years described in this text (thus the label premillennial).[3]

I think an important point about interpreting the Bible can be made here. Sometimes a false dichotomy is introduced when it is said that this is *either* a literal thousand-year period *or* it is only symbolic.[4] I am happy to grant that this is symbolic. One thousand is a perfectly round number and symbolizes a very long time. But the fact that it is symbolic does not mean that it symbolizes the same thing symbolized by other symbolic numbers in Revelation. So when we look at the references to time in Revelation, we find references to unspecified amounts of time, references to time relative to other events, references to units of time, and references to eternity. For example:

- We see an unspecified amount of time when Jesus says in 2:21, "I gave her time to repent." We are not told how much time she had.
- We also find references to time in relationship to other events, such as 1:19's reference to "the things . . . that are to take place after this."
- We find references to units of time, such as hours (e.g., the hour of testing in 3:10), days (ten days of tribulation in 2:10), months (forty-two months in 11:2), and years (a thousand of them in 20:2), and combinations of these (hour, day, month, and year in 9:15).

So 3:10 refers to an "hour of trial." This is a symbolic reference—surely the testing will not end after exactly sixty minutes. But the fact that there are references to years and to eternity means that in relationship to those longer amounts of time, "hour" symbolizes a shorter period of time.

Table 33.1: References to Time in Revelation

Undefined Amounts of Time	
Unspecified	I gave her time to repent: 2:21
	the time for the dead to be judged: 11:18
	a time, times, and half a time: 12:14
Relative Time	
Time of Event Located in Relationship to Other Events	soon: 1:1; 11:14
	near: 1:3
	to take place after this: 1:19
	until I come: 2:25
	until the end: 2:26
	never: 3:5
	how long?: 6:10
	rest a little longer: 6:11
	until we have sealed the servants: 7:3
	no more delay . . . in the days of the [seventh] trumpet: 10:6, 7
	during the days of their prophesying: 11:6
	when they have finished their testimony: 11:7
	after the three and a half days: 11:11
	his time is short: 12:12

	he must remain only a little while: 17:10
	until the words of God are fulfilled: 17:17
	Babylon . . . will be found no more: 18:21
	not deceive the nations any longer, until the thousand years were ended: 20:3
	After that he must be released for a little while: 20:3
	rest of the dead did not come to life until the thousand years were ended: 20:5
	when the thousand years are ended: 20:7

Units of Time	
	hour of trial: 3:10
	silence for about half an hour: 8:1
Hour	at that hour there was a great earthquake: 11:13
	the hour to reap has come: 14:15
	ten kings receive authority for one hour, together with the beast: 17:12 (cf. 17:10)
	in a single hour your judgment has come: 18:10, 17, 19
	for ten days you will have tribulation: 2:10
	day and night: 4:8; 7:15; 12:10; 14:11; 20:10
	no night: 21:25; 22:5
Day (Night)	great day of wrath/the great day of God: 6:17; 16:14
	three and a half days: 11:9, 11
	1,260 days: 12:6
	her plagues will come in a single day: 18:8
Months	five months: 9:5, 10
	forty-two months: 11:2; 13:5
Years	thousand years: 20:2, 3, 4, 5, 6, 7
Combinations	the hour, the day, the month, and the year: 9:15

Eternity	
	Alpha and Omega: 1:8; 21:6; 22:13
	first and last: 1:17; 2:8; 22:13
	beginning and end: 21:6; 22:13
Before and After	is, was, is to come/is and was: 1:4, 8; 11:17; 16:5 (cf. 17:8)
Always	lives forever and ever: 1:18; 4:9, 10; 10:6; 15:7
	might/strength forever and ever: 1:6; 5:13; 7:12
Never Ending	reign forever and ever: 11:15; 22:5
	punished forever and ever: 14:11; 19:3; 20:10
	second death: 2:11; 20:6, 14; 21:8

I think there are also places where Revelation refers to the same period of time in different ways, such as the references to the beast having authority for forty-two months in 13:5, and then 17:12 says he will have authority for one hour. In contrast to an example like that, I don't see any indication in Revelation that this thousand-year period in chapter 20 is to be equated with some other period of time in the book. It seems rather that John distinguishes this thousand-year period from other periods of time in the book, and as we move through the passage we will see how he does this.

So the angel came down with a key and a chain in 20:1 and "seized the dragon" in 20:2, and when verse 2 says that he bound the dragon, it seems he used the "great chain" that he had in verse 1 to do that. The angel completes his task in 20:3: "and threw him into the pit, and shut it and sealed it over him, so that he might not deceive the nations any longer, until the thousand years were ended. After that he must be released for a little while." So the angel uses the *implements* (the key, pit, and chain) in his *actions* against Satan—he seizes

Table 33.2: Revelation's Symbolic Timeline

Daniel's Seventieth Week (Daniel 9:24–27), Church History	Church protected for three and a half years	2:10: for ten days you will have tribulation (cf. 1:9) 11:1, 2: church (temple and altar) protected but the court trampled forty-two months 11:3: two witnesses prophesy for 1,260 days; cf. 11:7, "when they have finished" 12:6: woman flees to the wilderness to a place prepared by God, nourished 1,260 days 12:12: Satan thrown down to earth (12:9), knows his time is short 12:14: woman nourished in her place in the wilderness for a time, times, and half a time
	Beast kills the two witnesses, conquers the saints, has authority for three and a half years	3:10: those who overcome kept from (through) the hour of testing 11:7: when the two witnesses finish their testimony, the beast from the pit makes war, conquers, and kills them (cf. 13:7) 11:9: bodies of the two witnesses lie in the street for three and a half days 13:5: beast has authority for forty-two months 13:6–8: everyone but the elect deceived by the beast 13:7: beast makes war on the saints and conquers them (cf. 11:7) 17:10: the king who has not yet come must remain only a little while 17:12: ten kings will have power with the beast for one hour 17:14: they will make war on the Lamb, and he will conquer them (cf. 16:12–16; Armageddon; 17:12–14; 19:19)
	Christ comes in judgment, Battle of Armageddon	16:14: great day of the wrath of the Lamb (6:16, 17), "great day of God" (16:14) 16:17: "it is done!" 17–19: Babylon's fall, plagues — single day (18:8), judgment — single hour (18:10, 17, 19) 18:21: Babylon no more to be found 19:19: the beast and the kings of the earth (cf. 16:12–16; 17:12–14) make war on Christ 19:20: beast and false prophet thrown into lake of fire 19:21: the rest slain by the sword of his mouth

Millennium	20:2: Satan bound for a thousand years 20:3: Satan unable to deceive the nations until after the thousand years 20:4, 6: Martyrs raised and reign with Christ for a thousand years (cf. 6:9, 10) 11:11: after the three and a half days the two witnesses raised
Short time after the millennium, defeat of Gog and Magog	20:3: Satan to be released for a little while 20:7: Satan released at the end of the thousand years to deceive the nations (20:8) 20:8, 9: Gog and Magog gathered for battle, consumed by fire from Heaven 20:10: Devil thrown into lake of fire where the beast and false prophet were
Final Judgment	20:5: rest of the dead come to life 20:11–13: Great White Throne Judgment; cf. 11:18, time for the dead to be judged 20:14: Death, Hades, and non-elect thrown into lake of fire, second death (cf. 2:11; 20:6; 21:8)
New heaven and new earth	21:3: dwelling of God with man 21:4: former things passed away 21:5: all things made new 21:6: it is done!" 21:25; 22:5: no night 21:9–27: bride, New Jerusalem descend from Heaven; God and the Lamb are the temple 22:14, 15: those who wash their robes are in the city; outside are the unclean

him, binds him with the chain, throws him into the pit, and shuts and seals it, using the key. The rest of 20:3 states the purpose of the action ("so that he might not deceive the nations any longer") as well as its duration ("until the thousand years were ended. After that he must be released for a little while"). Let me say again that acknowledging that this is a symbolic action does not automatically mean that what is symbolized here is the very same thing that was symbolically represented elsewhere in the book.

It has been suggested that "Christ's work of restraining the devil's ability to 'deceive' is not a complete curtailment of all the devil's activities but only a restraint on his deceiving activities."[5] This looks to me like a false dichotomy. It appears that all of the devil's activities are curtailed so that his deception will be restrained. He is chained and shut up in the pit.

Have you ever wondered what life would be like if there were no Tempter? Picture in your mind again the angel whose hands must be large and strong, locking his viselike grip on the ancient serpent, binding him with a chain, hurling him into the pit, shutting it with lock and key, and placing the seal over it. No more satanic deception among the nations. Imagine what life will be like after that happens. John tells us about it in 20:4–6.

Revelation 20:4–6: The Millennial Reign

Adam was commanded by God to exercise dominion, to rule in God's stead (Genesis 1:26–28). Adam was also put in the Garden of Eden "to work it and keep it" (Genesis 2:15), and that is language that the Bible uses elsewhere of what priests do in the tabernacle. Adam was a royal priest. Then God told Israel they would be "a kingdom of priests" (Exodus 19:6). Peter tells Christians they are "a royal priesthood" (1 Peter 2:9), and John wrote in Revelation 1:6 that Jesus has "made us a kingdom, priests to our God and Father." Now that Satan is bound (20:1–3), the reign of the priest-kings begins (cf. 20:6). This angel has done what Adam failed to do—Adam was to guard (keep) the garden. This angel has also done what Israel failed to do when they entered the land—to drive out all its inhabitants. So with Christ slaying his enemies and putting the beast and the false prophet in the lake of fire, and with this angel binding Satan and putting him in a shut and sealed pit for a thousand years, it is as though the land is finally cleansed of the serpent and his seed. Now the glory of God will cover the dry lands of this earth as the waters cover the sea.

We read in 20:4, "Then I saw thrones, and seated on them were those to whom the authority to judge was committed." John sees "thrones," which signify authoritative rule, and he sees people on the thrones who receive authority from God (note the divine passive, "authority to judge was committed"). John tells us more about those seated on the thrones as we continue in verse 4: "Also I saw the souls of those who had been beheaded for the testimony of Jesus and for the word of God." The end of this verse is going to make clear that these are the people reigning from the thrones, but here let's observe that they were physically put to death. These people were beheaded because of the testimony of Jesus and the word of God.

The next phrase of verse 4 tells us that the martyrs in view are those described in chapter 13, where the beast made war on the church. We read in 20:4, ". . . and those who had not worshiped the beast or its image and had not received its mark on their foreheads or their hands." This refers back to what we saw in 13:5–18, where everyone whose name was not written in the Lamb's book of life before the foundation of the world worshiped the beast. Anyone who didn't worship the beast was slain (13:7, 15). Only those who took his mark on their foreheads or hands could buy and sell (13:16–18). So these who were beheaded were faithful to the gospel. This description is not limited to martyrs because Revelation calls all Christians to be faithful unto death and to hold to the word of God and the testimony of Jesus (20:4).[6] Only those whose names were written in the Lamb's book of life refused to worship the beast and its image (13:8). So 20:4 is describing all the elect who refused to worship the beast. They have all been faithful unto death. And then we come to the last phrase of 20:4: "They came to life and reigned with Christ for a thousand years."

Dead people "came to life and reigned with Christ for a thousand years."

Amillennialists claim that this is either regeneration or a coming to life in the presence of God in Heaven.[7] I think that kind of explanation does violence to this text. These are clearly dead people, and these are dead people who were beheaded for the gospel. So their coming to life cannot be describing their regeneration. Look at the phrase in verse 4, "They came to life," which is identified as "the first resurrection" in verse 5, and then immediately preceding that in verse 5 is a reference to "the rest of the dead" coming to life. "The rest of the dead" coming to life after the thousand years is neither regeneration nor an entrance into life in the presence of God in Heaven. It is physical resurrection, and the same is true of the believers coming to life in verse 4. Nor will it work to say that they came to life in the presence of God in Heaven because elsewhere in Revelation we read of people reigning with Christ *on earth*. Compare the last phrase of verse 4 with the last phrase of verse 6:

- 20:4, "They came to life and reigned with him for a thousand years."
- 20:6, ". . . they will be priests of God and of Christ, and they will reign with him for a thousand years."

Now with those two verses in mind look back at 5:10: "and you have made them a kingdom and priests to our God, and they shall reign on the earth."

I submit that the kings and priests who reign with Christ for a thousand years in 20:4–6 are the kings and priests who reign with Christ on earth in 5:10. It is useful also to contrast these statements about reigning for a thousand years here in 20:4, 6 with what we see at the end of 22:5, ". . . they will reign forever and ever."

So I think the most natural reading of 20:4 is to understand it as describing those slain during Satan's war against the church then being resurrected after Christ returns and defeats his enemies, the angel binds Satan, and the thousand-year reign of Christ begins. This picture is substantiated by the description of the coming to life at the end of verse 4 as "resurrection" in 20:5: "The rest of the dead did not come to life until the thousand years were ended. This is the first resurrection." Putting 20:4, 5 together, we see that believers will experience the first resurrection, coming to life and reigning with him for a thousand years. The rest of the dead are not raised until after the thousand-year period.[8]

We have two resurrections envisaged in 20:4, 5. The first is of believers and happens at the beginning of the thousand-year reign of Christ. The second is of the rest of the dead, and it happens at the end of the thousand years. John restates these ideas after he pronounces the fifth of seven benedictions in the book in 20:6: "Blessed and holy is the one who shares in the first resurrection! Over such the second death has no power, but they will be priests of God and of Christ, and they will reign with him for a thousand years" (cf. 1:3; 14:13; 16:15; 19:9; 22:7; 22:14). This reference to "the second death" seems to point to a death that is beyond physical death, and in 20:14 it will be identified as "the lake of fire." The fact that the beast, the false prophet, and Satan will be tormented in the lake of fire "day and night forever" in 20:10 indicates that those who experience this second death never stop dying it.

If you are an unbeliever, if you do not turn from your sins and trust in Christ, you will not receive the blessing just described in 20:6. You will not rise to reign with him. You will not partake in the first resurrection. You will miss seeing the glory of Christ the King. You will not be a priest to God. But if you will repent and trust in Christ, if you will hold to the testimony of Jesus and the word of God, all these blessings and more will be yours. Won't you turn from your sins and trust Jesus today?

If you are a believer in Jesus, 20:4–6 is describing your future. Satan is gone from the scene. Christ is reigning on earth. You will be raised from the dead to sin no more. No satanic deception. No satanic temptation. In the presence of Christ you will do justice and serve as a priest to God. This is what you were made to do. You were created to enjoy God as King in God's land in free obedience to God's law. Uncontaminated. Undefiled. Unsullied. No devil prowling about like a roaring lion. Freedom. Joy. Righteousness.

Is this what you think of when you think of happiness? Oh, how we need to soak ourselves in the Bible so that the Bible will define pleasure for us. Pleasure is not sin. Pleasure is walking with God in unconstrained obedience to him. Pleasure is doing the right thing instinctively. Pleasure is responding with wisdom and justice clothed with a natural, unfeigned humility in the glad enjoyment of God's presence. Pleasure is trusting God and knowing him in all your ways. Can you believe God is going to let us in on this?

Look back at the first sentence in 20:4—the judges on those thrones will administer justice. Look at the second and third sentences of verse 4: those faithful to Christ will be raised from the dead. They will reign with him for a thousand years. A thousand years of resurrection glory doing justice on the earth in the presence of Christ as he reigns as King. The long lives of those early, pre-flood figures such as Methuselah, with his 969 years, will be matched and exceeded by these who rise to reign with Christ.

Revelation 20:7–10: Satan Released and the Final Battle

We see what happens after the thousand years in 20:7: "And when the thousand years are ended, Satan will be released from his prison." This is not an escape but a release. The statement is another divine passive, and we have seen so many of these in Revelation. Let's observe all the ways that John deliberately gives us a sequence of events in this passage. The very things that Satan was doing to the church by deceiving the nations in 13:5–18 are alluded to in 20:4. Thus, when we see him bound in 20:1, 2, then read in 20:3 that he will "not deceive the nations *any longer, until* the thousand years were ended," we see that an activity that Satan was doing throughout church history is brought to an end. The next phrase of 20:3 points to the resumption of his activity after the thousand years ("*After that* he must be released"), and then the final phrase of 20:3 shows that what we are now seeing in 20:7–10 will not last long, "*for a little while*." Along these lines, note that 20:5 states, "The rest of the dead did not come to life *until* the thousand years were ended." Note, too, the first phrase of 20:7, which locates it on this timeline: "And *when* the thousand years are ended . . . " So I submit that the book of Revelation is giving us a timeline. It is a timeline of symbolic events. We can even say it is a symbolic timeline. But as symbolic as the timeline is, and as symbolic as the events are, the fact nevertheless remains that there is a sequence of these symbolic events on this symbolic timeline. The text depicts these events as happening on a timeline in relationship to one another.

First, after the seals are opened in chapters 6—8, chapters 9—16 show the fulfillment of Daniel's seventieth week through the course of church history. Revelation presents Daniel's seventieth week as taking place between Christ's ascension and his return.

At the end of Daniel's seventieth week, Christ comes in judgment and fights the Battle of Armageddon (16:12–16; 17:14; 19:19). At the conclusion of the battle, the beast and the false prophet are thrown into the lake of fire (19:20), and Satan will not join them there until after the thousand years (20:10).

Rather than being thrown into the lake of fire after Armageddon with the beast and the false prophet, Satan is seized, bound, and thrown into the Abyss, which is shut and sealed over him, for a thousand years (20:1–3). He will be released to deceive Gog of Magog into leading a final rebellion after the thousand years (20:7–10).

At the beginning of the thousand years, those who kept the faith are raised from the dead and reign with Christ for a thousand years (20:4–6). The text explicitly calls this "the first resurrection" (20:5), and though it does not explicitly name "the second resurrection," the first part of 20:5 states that "the rest of the dead" are raised after the thousand years. We will see that resurrection in 20:11–15, but before that comes the final rebellion.

So the thousand years end, and Satan is "released" (20:7). We see what he does next in 20:8: "and will come out to deceive the nations that are at the four corners of the earth, Gog and Magog, to gather them for battle; their number is like the sand of the sea." So here is the fulfillment of what Ezekiel prophesied in Ezekiel 38, 39. Deceived by Satan, Gog the king leads the people of Magog up for the final assault on the world's true King. Other enemy armies in the Bible have been likened to "the sand of the sea" (see especially Joshua 11:4; Judges 7:12), and their defeat points to the defeat of Gog and the people of Magog.

They wage their hopeless campaign that ends in fire and shame (20:9): "And they marched up over the broad plain of the earth and surrounded the camp of the saints and the beloved city, but fire came down from heaven and consumed them." God delivered Elijah in this way in 2 Kings 1, the two witnesses this way in 11:5, and now all the saints are delivered by fire from Heaven.

We read of Satan's end in 20:10: "and the devil who had deceived them was thrown into the lake of fire and sulfur where the beast and false prophet were, and they will be tormented day and night forever and ever." Amillennialists argue that the battle in 20:7–10 is another description of the battle in 19:17–21,[9] but the details are simply too different for that to be the case. At the end of the battle in 19:17–21, the beast and false prophet are thrown into the lake of fire (19:20), and then Satan is bound for a thousand years (20:1–3). At the end of the battle in 20:7–10, Satan, having been released from his thousand-year imprisonment (20:3, 7), is thrown into the lake of fire where the beast and false prophet already were (20:10). Notice how clear this verse is that they are neither pardoned nor annihilated: "they will be tormented day and night forever and ever" (20:10). They committed an infinitely heinous crime, so their punishment will be infinite.

Let me invite you to consider again the futility of rebelling against God, whether in big things or small. If you refuse to repent of your sins and trust in Christ, you will not escape. Your rebellion is futile. You will either repent and trust Jesus and be saved, or you will be destroyed. Concerning those of us who have repented and know the good we ought to do and hesitate to do it, our small-scale rebellion is futile too. So if the Bible tells us to do everything without grumbling or complaining (Philippians 2:14), our choices are: obey and rejoice in the Lord and enjoy his blessing; or rebel, complain, grumble, and be miserable. We will not escape. If he calls us to take up the cross, lay down our lives, pursue the greatness that comes from serving others, and store up treasure in Heaven, we can either enjoy the satisfaction of walking with God in obedience, or refuse to obey and suffer the pangs of conscience and the consequences that come with our sin. Rebellion against God is futile, whether you're trying to dethrone Christ at the last battle or just trying to get away with a little self-indulgence. On a small scale or large, all self-indulgence is the attempt to dethrone Christ. You will not succeed.

Revelation 20:11–15: The Great White Throne

After Armageddon at the end of chapter 19, after the binding of Satan for a thousand years, during which time resurrected saints rule with Christ, after Satan is released to deceive Gog of Magog, and after the final rebellion is put down, we read of the final judgment in 20:11–15. This scene is reminiscent of Daniel 7:9, 10, where the Ancient of Days takes his seat on his throne, and "the court sat in judgment, and the books were opened."

We read in 20:11, "Then I saw a great white throne and him who was seated on it. From his presence earth and sky fled away, and no place was found for them." We know what a throne is, but it is difficult for us to imagine the earth and sky fleeing. Their flight has been promised in texts that prophesied that the Lord would once more shake heavens and earth, sea and dry land (Haggai 2:6; Hebrews 12:26–28), and the removal of the skies, mountains, and islands has been anticipated in 6:14 and 16:20. They will be replaced with the new heaven and new earth in 21:1.[10] I am not sure where the throne is to be envisioned with earth and sky having fled, but God takes his seat, and heavens and earth flee.

We read of the second resurrection (cf. 20:5) and the final judgment in 20:12, 13,

> And I saw the dead, great and small, standing before the throne, and books were opened. Then another book was opened, which is the book of life. And the dead were judged by what was written in the books, according to what they had done. And the sea gave up the dead who were in it, Death and Hades gave up the dead who were in them, and they were judged, each one of them, according to what they had done.

All the dead are raised—significant or not, whether they died at sea or were hidden in Hades. The books are opened, including the book of life, and since people are judged by what was written in the books according to what they had done, it appears that the books may contain a record of deeds. Perhaps the Bible, with its standard of righteousness, is among these books. No evidence is lacking. Just judgment is rendered. Elsewhere in Revelation those whose names are written in the Lamb's book of life from the foundation of the world remain faithful to God and Christ (13:8; 17:8); so the names of the elect are there. They are justified by their faith in Christ, which is evidenced by their deeds.

This is what you face: resurrection, the opening of the books, and judgment according to what is written in them. How are you going to fare on that day? Is your name written in the Lamb's book of life? Are you living according to what is written in the Bible? You will be judged according to what you do: will you be justified because you trusted in Christ and repented of your sin, or will you be condemned because you refused to follow Christ and instead followed your sin?

Satan has already been thrown into the lake of fire in 20:10. I point that out because Paul says in 1 Corinthians 15:26, "The last enemy to be destroyed is death." This fits with what we now see in 20:14: "Then Death and Hades were thrown into the lake of fire. This is the second death, the lake of fire." Death and Hades are personified here, and the fact that they themselves are thrown into the lake of fire seems to mean that the experience of death, and the holding place of the dead, Hades, are both done away with in the lake of fire. I submit, then, that this second death in the lake of fire is not a place where one ceases to exist. Rather, Death and Hades themselves are in the lake of fire, which seems to mean that this second death has more to do with being separated from God and life in him than it has to do with the cessation of thought, experience, pain, and sorrow. So when we read in 20:15, "And if anyone's name was not found written in the book of life, he was thrown into the lake of fire," we should not conclude that they are going to be annihilated. Rather, death itself has been swallowed up by the lake of fire. Death, the last enemy, is defeated. It is no refuge for those suffering "day and night forever and ever" (20:10)—that is, torment with Satan, the beast, and the false prophet.

Conclusion

God declared that he would fill the earth with his glory in Numbers 14:21. Habakkuk 2:14 says "the earth will be filled with the knowledge of the glory of the LORD as the waters cover the sea." In Psalm 72:19 David prays that God would do this through the agency of his seed, the Messiah. It is true that even now, as disciples are made in all nations, the glory of God is expanding across the world. Revelation 20 teaches that after the Battle of Armageddon, the beast and false prophet will be thrown into the lake of fire, Satan will be imprisoned, and for a thousand years Jesus will reign with his resurrected followers. They will cover the earth with the knowledge of the glory of God in a way that brings maximal fulfillment to every promise in the Bible.

This is our hope for the future, and we are seeking to experience as much of it in the present as we possibly can.

34

A New Heaven
and a New Earth

REVELATION 21:1–8

"AND THEY LIVED HAPPILY EVER AFTER." The stories end that way, and we might be tempted to think that they end that way because there is nothing interesting left to say—no more drama, no more tension, no more threat, no more excitement. My friend Denny Burk had prayed a beautiful prayer during our wedding ceremony, and the morning after the wedding I sat at the kitchen table, reading that prayer. Before long I was weeping. I think it was a kind of emotional catharsis. Before the wedding I was amazed that I might get to be Jill's husband (I'm still amazed by it!), and I couldn't wait for it to happen. Now I was overwhelmed that it had really come true.

To be honest, I think I wondered if there was anything else to look forward to in life. The best day of my life had come and gone. Was there anything left to long for in life? I was too shortsighted to see that life with Jill was going to be even better than the wedding day itself and that there were all sorts of things to look forward to, from doing things together to having children to walking life's pathways and enjoying each other's company. Just being with her is a blessing unto itself.

Need

Perhaps when you think about what will happen in the new heaven and new earth, you wonder if there will be anything else to look forward to. Perhaps you wonder if all the suspense, all the drama, all the tension will be gone. To think about the new heaven and new earth as though there might not be sufficient contrast to make it interesting would be as foolish as a single man being worried that after the wedding day there is nothing left to which to look forward.

Main Point

We look forward to a new heaven and new earth where we will live in God's presence, experiencing his mercy, satisfied by his pleasures, aware of his justice forever.

Context

We have seen the fall of the harlot in 17:1–19:10, and we are now at the end of this section on the King in 19:11–21:8. We have seen the King return (19:11–21), reign for a thousand years (20:1–6), and put down a final rebellion (20:7–10), and after the last judgment (20:11–15) the King and his bride enter into the new heaven and new earth (21:1–8). The final section of the book will be on the bride (21:9–22:9) and then the conclusion of the whole book (22:10–21).

Preview

Revelation 21:1–8 falls into two parts:

21:1–4   The Former Things Have Passed Away
21:5–8   "I Am Making All Things New"

This passage is all about the fulfillment of God's Old Testament promises and the completion of the story of the world. The story of the world is not a tragedy that ends in death and shame but a comedy that ends in cosmic renewal and the marriage of the Lamb and his bride. The new exodus is finally consummated, the return from exile completed, and God tabernacles among his people.

Revelation 21:1–4: The Former Things Have Passed Away

As we begin to consider these first four verses of chapter 21, note that in verse 1 "the first heaven and the first earth had passed away," and then at the end of verse 4, "the former things have passed away." These two statements bracket 21:1–4 and indicate that their main thrust is that the old is gone. And then the next section, 21:5–8, opens with God asserting, "I am making all things new." So we could summarize these eight verses with Paul's phrase, "The old has passed away; the new has come" (2 Corinthians 5:17). Revelation 21:1, 2 will tell us about the new heaven and earth and the holy city; then verses 3, 4 describe life there when the old has gone and the new has come.

New Heaven, New Earth, Holy City

John wrote in 20:11, "Then I saw a great white throne and him who was seated on it. From his presence earth and sky fled away, and no place was found for them." God filled the first heaven and earth with his glory while the Messiah reigned in the millennium, and earth and sky do not return after they flee his presence at the great white throne judgment. Instead John tells us in 21:1, "Then I saw a new heaven and a new earth, for the first heaven and the first earth had passed away, and the sea was no more." This fulfills what the Lord promised in Isaiah 65:17: "For behold, I create new heavens and a new earth, and the former things shall not be remembered or come into mind" (cf. Isaiah 66:22). The first heaven and earth apparently passed away, then, when they fled God's presence, and whereas the spheres of the first creation were the heavens and the earth and the waters of the deep (cf. Genesis 1:1; Exodus 20:4), in the new creation there is no sea. The first audience of Revelation would have heard of the beast rising from the sea back in 13:1, which probably confirmed ideas of the sea as the great dark unknown from which evil comes. These ideas can also be seen in the beasts from the sea in Daniel 7:3 and in the later chapters of Job, where Leviathan, the great beast of the sea, seems to symbolize Satan (cf. Job 41:1–34). Satan has now been thrown into the lake of fire (20:10), and in the new heaven and earth there is no sea from which evil will arise to infiltrate this pristine and pure new heaven and new earth.

Verse 1 gives us the wide-angle view of the new heaven and earth, and now 21:2 seems to focus in on the new city: "And I saw the holy city, new Jerusalem, coming down out of heaven from God, prepared as a bride adorned for her husband." Here John describes the fulfillment of Isaiah 52:1, where Jerusalem, the holy city, is called to put on beautiful garments, and it also fulfills Isaiah 61:10, where the redeemed are likened to a bride who "adorns herself with her jewels." These verses tell us that brides in the ancient world, like brides where marriage is valued today, looked their best on their wedding day. We also see this from the lavish descriptions of the bride's beauty in the Song of Songs, in the description of the bride in Psalm 45:13, and in the preparations the king provided in the book of Esther. I am always surprised by how much time brides devote to their hair and makeup on their wedding day, but the result is that she will look her best for her husband. And so it is with the shining city that descends from God in Heaven.

Have you been hurt by some form of impurity? Who hasn't, right? Look at 21:1, 2 and be encouraged. Trust Christ and hope for the glory of the purity of the cleanness of the new heaven and new earth and the holy city. If you will trust him, no defilement awaits you. No shameful snares. No dirty traps or miry bog with an attractive exterior. It will be pure, clean, holy, new, and there will be no sea from which serpents can rise.

I have heard stories of wicked things people have done to missionaries such as people forced to ingest human excrement or women being violated. The unassailable purity of the new heaven and new earth can provide *hope* to sustain you through such horrors, and *believing* that God will do this can heal you from whatever you may experience.

God with Men

Why is this holy *city* in the new *creation* likened to a *bride*? The answer seems to be given in 21:3: "And I heard a loud voice from the throne saying, 'Behold, the dwelling place of God is with man. He will dwell with them, and they will be his people, and God himself will be with them as their God.'" So this new Jerusalem is a *city* because God will dwell there, and it seems to be likened to a *bride* because God will be in covenant with his people who dwell with him there. The language, "they will be his people, and God himself will be with them as their God" recalls covenantal language elsewhere in the Bible, especially in Jeremiah and Ezekiel (cf. Genesis 17:7, 8; Exodus 6:7; 29:45; Leviticus 26:12; Jeremiah 7:23; 11:4; 24:7; 30:22; 31:1, 33; 32:38; Ezekiel 11:20; 34:24; 36:28; 37:23, 27; Zechariah 8:8; 2 Corinthians 6:16; Hebrews 1:5; 8:10; Revelation 21:3, 7). So it seems that the most fundamental and intimate of covenantal relationships between human beings, marriage, exists to communicate the kind of relationship God will enjoy with his people (cf. Ephesians 5:21–33).

Revelation 21:3 describes the "tabernacle" of God and speaks of God "tabernacling" with man. The Lord promised to dwell in the midst of Zion in Zechariah 2:10 (cf. 2:14 LXX). This means that in the new creation in the holy city when God enters into the new marriage covenant with his bride, what was aimed at in Eden, in the tabernacle, in the temple, and in the church will finally be realized. God will dwell with his people. In a new cosmos, in a holy city, with no sea from which an evil snake might arise, God will dwell with his people in intimate, covenant relationship.

Can you imagine the glory of this? All the stain and smudge and smear of the old creation gone and replaced by a new heaven and earth. A holy city that has never been defiled and never will be contaminated by anything evil or unclean, in which righteousness dwells as the presence of God tabernacles with man.

Revelation 21:4 describes what life will be like in the clean land in the presence of God: "He will wipe away every tear from their eyes, and death shall be no more, neither shall there be mourning, nor crying, nor pain anymore, for the former things have passed away." This fulfills what Isaiah prophesied in Isaiah 25:8: "He will swallow up death forever; and the Lord GOD will wipe away tears from all faces." It fulfills Isaiah 35:10 (". . . sorrow and sighing shall flee away"; cf. Isaiah 51:11) and Isaiah 65:19 ("no more shall be heard in it the sound of weeping and the cry of distress"). The upshot of 21:4 is that God will remove all the ill effects of sin and will guarantee that sin will never again result in death, disqualification, or disaster. Death is in the lake of fire and will not enter the new heaven and new earth (20:14). Verse 3 says that God will dwell with his people, and then verse 4 opens with the declaration that he will comfort them by wiping away all their tears. The rest of verse 4 proclaims that God's presence guarantees that there will be no more sin, which causes death and mourning and crying and pain. Revelation 21:4 teaches that God will comfort his people and remove the sorrows of sins past, and God will protect his people such that never again will they experience what results from sin.

Revelation 21:4 says that "the former things have passed away," and then in 21:5 the Lord declares that he is "making all things new." This fulfills what the Lord declared in Isaiah 43:18, 19: "Remember not the former things, nor consider the things of old. Behold, I am doing a new thing."

Believer in Jesus, do you feel some great tension in your life? Is there a massive sorrow in your heart that results from some sin or some disaster or some disappointment? Let me invite you to look again at 21:3, 4 and see there that God is going to dwell with you and comfort you. Find in that hope the resolution to all tension, the comfort for all sorrow, the healing from every disaster, and the consolation that swallows up every disappointment. God is greater than all your pain.

If you are not a believer in Jesus, let me invite you to try to imagine something better than what this passage offers you. I don't think you can come up with anything that would be superior to this. What could you desire that would be better than what this passage describes? A new heaven and earth, a holy city, the presence of God, comfort for all sorrow, and protection from any future pain. What more could you want? Is what draws you away from God really better than this?

Revelation 21:5–8: "I Am Making All Things New"

God makes three statements in 21:5–8. The first two statements are in verse 5, and the third spans verses 6–8. The first of these three is a statement of what God is doing; the second is a command to write; and the third is a statement of who God is and what he promises to both the righteous and the unrighteous. Revelation 21:1–4 declares that the old has passed away, showing what life will be like as God dwells with his people and comforts and protects them in a new heaven and new earth with its holy city. Revelation 21:5–8 sketches the new state of affairs that God brings about, insisting on his truthfulness and identity as he announces rewards for the righteous and consequences for the wicked.

The first of these three statements that God makes is in 21:5: "And he who was seated on the throne said, 'Behold, I am making all things new.'" Have you noticed how even when old things are renovated they look old and how new things have a discernible freshness to them? Everything is going to be made new. Nothing in God's new creation will have the look of something old and dilapidated. Ecclesiastes 1:9 says, ". . . there is nothing new under the sun," and of this earth that is true. But in the new heaven and new earth God will make all things new. Ecclesiastes 1:15 says, "What is crooked cannot be made straight, and what is lacking cannot be counted." But when God makes all things new, there will be nothing bent that needs to be straightened and nothing lacking.

The rest of 21:5 has the second of these three statements from God: "Also he said, 'Write this down, for these words are trustworthy and true.'" Here God asserts his faithfulness. Every verse in 21:1–8 depicts the fulfillment of something promised in the Old Testament. God keeps his word. He will do what he says, and because he is faithful and true, he commissions John to write. By recording this, John shows us that he wrote this book because God told him to write this book. The idea here is that this is written down for the day when these things come to pass. On that day the words recorded in the book will be seen to be true. The Bible claims to be God's revelation of himself to us. When we believe the Bible to be God's Word, we are believing what it tells us about itself. In addition to believing what it tells us about itself, the Holy Spirit bears witness that these things are so and confirms the Bible's claims.

God's third statement begins in verse 6 and continues through verse 8. Let's look at this phrase by phrase. Note how 21:6 begins: "And he said to me . . . " The addition of "to me" continues the emphasis on direct revelation from God that John is receiving. Verse 6 continues, "It is done!" God announces that it is done—the making of all things new described in this passage—before it happens. God can do this because of what he said to John at the end of verse 5: "these words are trustworthy and true." So God declares "It is done!" because he will do it. In addition to his faithfulness to his word,

God asserts his eternality in the next phrase of verse 6: "I am the Alpha and the Omega, the beginning and the end." This is a twofold statement that God is the first and the last. Alpha is the first letter of the Greek alphabet and omega the last. If God is already the end, then he knows what will happen, so he can say what will be done. This statement asserts his unique identity as the everlasting God. The remainder of what God says here will deal with rewards and punishments.

The last phrase of 21:6 is a promise: "To the thirsty I will give from the spring of the water of life without payment." This fulfills the call in Isaiah 55:1 to the thirsty who have no money to come and drink freely. The promise in 21:6 is designed to make us thirst for the water of life more than we thirst for anything else in life. For what do you thirst? Do you long to drink deeply from "the spring of the water of life"? What is this spring? In 22:1 we read of "the river of the water of life, bright as crystal, flowing from the throne of God and of the Lamb" (cf. Zechariah 14:8). This seems to be the spring in view in 21:6, from which the water of life flows. So I think this is a figurative way of describing being satisfied in God, who called himself "the fountain of living waters" in Jeremiah 2:13. There is a river of delights that flows from God. Do you want to drink from that river? Do you thirst for God? Do you love his justice and his mercy? Not to love God's justice is to celebrate corruption. Not to love God's mercy is to fail to love the most beautiful and astonishing reality that God has created. Is there anything you wouldn't give to gain the ability to drink from that well? There is no monetary price to buy this. No amount of money will get you a drink from this water. The only thing that qualifies you for a drink is thirsting for it. Thirsting for it, though, means thirsting for God. If you thirst for other things, you don't thirst for this, as will become plain in verse 8.

God continues to speak in 21:7: "The one who conquers will have this heritage." What heritage? We might render this phrase, "The one who conquers will inherit these things" (cf. NASB). The inheritance promised here is the inheritance that belongs to sons of God, as the rest of verse 7 states: "and I will be his God and he will be my son." The sons of God are heirs of the world, as Paul describes Abraham and his offspring (cf. Romans 4:11–16). The sons of the King are exempt from taxation, as Jesus explained to Peter (Matthew 17:24–27). This is why 21:6 says that God will give the right to drink "from the spring of the water of life *without payment*," and then verse 7 speaks of what those who overcome will inherit. Those who are united to Christ by faith are heirs according to promise (Galatians 3:26–29). If you trust in Jesus and thirst for God more than you thirst for anything else, everything promised in this book is yours. As Paul said to the Corinthians, "all things are yours, whether Paul or Apollos or Cephas or the world or life or death or the present or the future—all are yours, and you are Christ's, and Christ is God's" (1 Corinthians 3:21–23). If you trust in Christ and thirst for God, he will be your God—your provider, protector, savior, and defender—and you will be his son, an heir of all that is his.

But if God is not what you worship, if you thirst for things other than him, your life will show it. If you do not trust Christ and thirst for God, 21:8 is talking about you: "But as for the cowardly, the faithless, the detestable, as for murderers, the sexually immoral, sorcerers, idolaters, and all liars, their portion will be in the lake that burns with fire and sulfur, which is the second death." Rather than bold self-abandon for God's glory, you will be a coward. Rather than steadfast faith you will not believe, and you will be unfaithful. Rather than being holy and pleasing to God you will be "detestable." Rather than laying down your life for others you will kill them or use them to get what you want. Rather than regulating your sexuality according to the Bible you will be "sexually immoral." Rather than worshiping God as the all-powerful you will make use of sorcery and witchcraft in an attempt to manipulate the world. Rather than worshiping the Creator you will worship created things. Rather than living according to the truth you will live out and speak lies. And you will go where you belong, where you will get what you deserve—the lake of fire, the second death.

The location of this lake of fire in 21:8 is not fully exposited, but it clearly continues to exist in the new heaven and new earth. This fulfills the scene depicted in the new heavens and new earth in Isaiah 66:22–24, where we read of the rebels whose "worm shall not die, their fire shall not be quenched, and they shall be an abhorrence to all flesh" (v. 24).

If you do not love God, you will not love righteousness. Instead of loving God and understanding the truth and embracing righteousness, you will reject righteousness, believe lies, and hate God. You will be justly punished in the lake of fire with the other rebels—Satan, the beast, the false prophet, and the rest of the damned.

God is more satisfying than anything else in existence, and we should thirst for him. If we trust Christ and thirst for him, he will give us the river of his living water to quench our thirst. If we do not, he will punish our unrighteousness and give us what we deserve.

Conclusion

Are you bothered by the so-called problem of evil? Have you asked yourself what would justify human history? What would make this world and everything that has been done in it worth creating? If God is omniscient, then he knew everything that would happen in the world that he created when he started the project. What could possibly warrant all the pain, death, disease, rebellion, wickedness, and sorrow that has happened in this world? Babies die. People get AIDS and cancer. Murderers do awful things. People are enslaved to sins that ruin their lives. Dictators murder their citizens, and genocides take place. What would justify human history? Why would God create a world where all this would take place?

Why would God create a world where people rebel against him? A world where people would crucify his Son. A world where children reject the teaching of their parents and refuse to believe the gospel their parents believe. What would cause God to allow all this?

We may never fully understand what God has done in this world, but 21:1–8 shows us that God will make a new heaven and new earth that is pure, that, unlike the first one, will never be defiled. He will comfort those who trust him, wiping away every tear, protecting them from all sin, dwelling in their midst, satisfying their thirst, relating to them as a bridegroom in covenant, as a father to a beloved son, as a faithful God in covenant with his people. And God's people will know him. They will know the glory of his justice and the glory of his mercy, and they will perceive these things in the salvation that comes through judgment. In studying Revelation, we pass through the final judgment in 20:11–15 on our way to the new heaven and new earth, in which righteousness dwells. God created the world so that he could make known his justice and his mercy. The justice God will demonstrate against the wicked is on display in the new heaven and new earth in his wrath on those who burn in the second death of the lake of fire in 21:8. For all eternity God's justice will be on display so that the redeemed who enjoy God's mercy will continue to feel the mercy they have received.

35

The New Jerusalem

REVELATION 21:9–27

FORT KNOX IS FAMOUS FOR being the stronghold where America's gold is held. It is thought to be an impregnable fortress. The United States Department of the Treasury has held the nation's deposit of gold bullion there since 1937. Gold bullion is 99.9 percent pure gold in bulk form, such as bars. It is not possible for humans to extract 100 percent pure gold.[1] As an interesting side note, all the gold that has ever been mined has an estimated value of just under six trillion dollars.[2]

The gold vault is lined with granite walls and a blast-proof door that weighs twenty-two tons. People cannot be trusted, so "No single person is entrusted with the entire combination to the vault. Ten members of the Depository staff must dial separate combinations known only to them. Beyond the main vault door, smaller internal cells provide further protection."[3] Several fences surround the facility, and armed guards are present. Fort Knox holds 5,050 tons of gold, worth roughly 173 billion dollars.

"All of the gold in the depository, if pure, could form a cube 19.7 feet (6 m) on a side—a volume of 216 m^3. In comparison, all the gold ever mined in the world would form a cube 64.3 feet (19.6 m) on a side, with a volume of approximately 7500 m^3."[4]

The Fort Knox Bullion Depository is closed to visitors. No tours are allowed.[5]

Gold isn't the only thing in this world that can be stolen. Three or four years ago, the copper downspouts attached to the gutters at the church I pastor (Kenwood Baptist Church) were stolen. I'm told it's a good thing that our heating and air conditioning units are on the roof because churches that have them on the ground have had them stolen. We have bars on some of the windows at our church because people have broken in to steal things.

What kind of world is this where people will steal copper downspouts from a church for the money they will get by recycling the copper?

Need

We need to see how dangerous it is to set our hearts on treasure here on earth, where thieves break in and steal, and where moth and rust destroy (Matthew 6:19). We also need to be transformed so that we live like we believe that God is able to provide. What would your life be like if you knew you were heir to more gold than Fort Knox could ever hold? What would your life be like if you knew that your Father was so wealthy that he will build a city that is 1,500 miles long, 1,500 miles wide, and 1,500 miles high, all of pure gold like clean, transparent glass? What would life be like if there was something so much more valuable to you than gold with which you could pave the streets? Let me invite you to contemplate the incalculable worth of the splendor of the glory of God shining out from his very presence.

Main Point

The treasure in the new heaven and new earth is God. Look at how casually what is treasured by sinful hearts is used in the new heaven and new earth. They take the largest pearls in the world and make them into gates; then they leave the gates open, even though the city is made of pure gold; and they have the audacity to take all that jasper and build it into a wall, all that gold and use it to pave the streets. All this shows that the real treasure of the new heaven and new earth is God himself.

Context

We have seen the fall of the harlot (17:1–19:10) and the return of the King and his millennial reign giving way to the new heaven and new earth (19:11–21:8), and now we move into the section that focuses on the bride of the Lamb (21:9–22:9). In 21:9–27 the focus is on the temple-city, and then in 22:1–5 it shifts to the Edenic aspects of that city.

Preview

We will see that God is the great treasure of Heaven in each of the three sections of 21:9–27.

21:9–14	The Descent of the Edenic Temple-City
21:15–21	The City's Measurements and Materials
21:22–27	God and the Lamb Are Its Temple

Revelation 21:9–14: The Descent of the Edenic Temple-City

The language in 21:9, 10, which opens the section on the bride, matches the language in 17:1–3, which opens the section on the harlot. These parallel phrases invite us to learn from the contrast between the harlot's outcome and the bride's glory. Just as "one of the seven angels who had the seven bowls" full of the seven last plagues invited John, saying, "Come, I will show you the judgment of the great prostitute" in 17:1, so now one of those angels invites John, saying, "Come, I will show you the Bride, the wife of the Lamb" in 21:9. And just as the angel carried John away in the Spirit and showed him the harlot in 17:3, so in 21:10 John writes, "And he carried me away in the Spirit." Back in 17:3 the angel carried John "into a wilderness" where he saw the whore and the blasphemous beast. Now the angel carries John "to a great, high mountain, and showed [him] the holy city Jerusalem coming down out of heaven from God, having the glory of God, its radiance like a most rare jewel, like a jasper, clear as crystal" (21:10b, 11). Unlike Babylon's now worthless "gold and jewels and pearls" in 17:4 and her wasted "luxury" in 18:7, the glory of the holy city will never fade.

John sees "a great, high mountain" because God promised to make "the mountain of the house of the LORD . . . the highest of the mountains" (Isaiah 2:2). Just as Ezekiel was supernaturally transported to "a very high mountain" where he saw the new temple (Ezekiel 40:2), so John is "carried . . . in the Spirit to a great, high mountain" (21:10). John sees a city (cf. Ezekiel 40:1, 2) that seems itself to be a light-giving body; it radiates like a semi-translucent jasper that shines like crystal (21:10, 11). The city is like God—shining with his own radiant glory. The city looks like God and has his glory because of its conformity to his character. This is very different from the harlot in chapter 17, whose immorality and idolatry resulted in abominable practices that result in the wrath of God (vv. 1, 5, 6). Just as the harlot was a symbol of Babylon, so now "the Bride" in 21:9 is identified as the new Jerusalem in 21:10.

Where is your home, Babylon or Jerusalem? Maybe you know that you belong to Babylon, and you're afraid of the destruction coming upon you. I call you to repentance. I call you to flee the wrath to come. I call you to forsake the abominations of Babylon the great whore. Turn from the idolatry and immorality she uses to enslave you. Trust in Jesus who is mighty to save you.

Maybe you know that Jerusalem is your happy home. Are you conducting yourself like the pure bride of the Lamb, or are you harboring hopes of enjoying Babylon at every opportunity? Let us pursue "holiness without which no one will see the Lord" (Hebrews 12:14).

John describes the wall, gates, and foundations of the wall of the city in 21:12–14:

> It had a great, high wall, with twelve gates, and at the gates twelve angels, and on the gates the names of the twelve tribes of the sons of Israel were inscribed—on the east three gates, on the north three gates, on the south three gates, and on the west three gates. And the wall of the city had twelve foundations, and on them were the twelve names of the twelve apostles of the Lamb.

This city is similar to the camp of Israel, where the twelve tribes of Israel were encamped around the tabernacle, with three tribes on each side, north, south, east, and west. The fact that there are angels at the gates seems to recall key angelic figures seen in the Old Testament: the cherubim guarding the way to the tree of life in Genesis 3:24, the angel with a drawn sword encountered by Balaam as he approached the camp of Israel (Numbers 22:22–35), and the man with a drawn sword Joshua encountered as the people prepared to enter the promised land (Joshua 5:13–15). These angels at the gates in 21:12 indicate that those who enter the holy city will be entering the fulfillment of the Garden of Eden, thus also fulfilling the purpose of the tabernacle, the temple, and the promised land.

The fact that the names of the twelve tribes of Israel are inscribed on the gates (21:12), with the names of the twelve apostles of the Lamb on the foundations of the wall (21:14), means that all the people of God in the Old and New Covenants will enjoy life in the presence of God in this new Edenic temple-city that descends from God in Heaven.

We can take comfort in those walls. They provide protection and healthy boundaries. The twelve gates are guarded by twelve angels (21:12), another indication that never again will anyone succeed in despoiling God's place or God's people. God's new creation will be undefiled and protected.

Do you know what guarantees this? God does. He promised in Zechariah 1:16, "Therefore, thus says the LORD, I have returned to Jerusalem with mercy; my house shall be built in it, declares the LORD of hosts, and the measuring line shall be stretched out over Jerusalem." And then he promised in Zechariah 2:5, "And I will be to her a wall of fire all around, declares the LORD, and I will be the glory in her midst." This city is radiant with the glory of God. This city is strong and secure because God is in her midst. What we want about this city is God, and by trusting in Jesus and walking in his Word by the power of the Spirit, wonder of wonders, we are God's temple now. So in our experience of God's presence mediated to us by our faith in Christ as the Spirit works through the Word in our lives, we have now what will be the best thing about the new heaven and new earth—the covenant presence of God to bless us and be with us. We look forward to the day when our awareness of that reality and our access to God will be unbroken and unhindered by sin and shortsightedness, when we dwell in God's presence in the Edenic temple-city.

Revelation 21:15–21: The City's Measurements and Materials

John describes the measurements of the city and the materials of which it is made in 21:15–21. The angel measures the city in 21:15, 16 and the wall in 21:17. John states what the wall and city are made of in 21:18, then describes the foundations of the wall in 21:19, 20 before concluding with the gates and the street in 21:21.

The measuring begins in 21:15, where John writes, "And the one who spoke with me had a measuring rod of gold to measure the city and its gates and walls." What John sees here fulfills Ezekiel's vision of "a man whose appearance was like bronze, with a linen cord and a measuring reed in his hand" (Ezekiel 40:3) who gives Ezekiel a guided tour of a restored temple in Ezekiel 40—48. The new temple that Ezekiel described symbolizes the new heavens and new earth. God is going to dwell there; so it is as though the whole place is the Holy of Holies.

Our cue to the significance of the act of measuring is in the depiction of the fulfillment of Ezekiel 40, and John writes in 21:16, "The city lies four-square, its length the same as its width. And he measured the city with his rod, 12,000 stadia. Its length and width and height are equal." So the city is a perfect cube, just as the Holy of Holies was a perfect cube. The city is the Holy of Holies because this is the perfectly ordered place in which God is present.

There are various estimates, but these 12,000 stadia appear to be about 1,500 miles.[6] The area of this perfect cube appears to be "the approximate size of the then known Hellenistic world."[7] Thus, it seems that John is saying that the whole world is going to become the Holy of Holies, the place where God dwells.

We see the measure of the wall in 21:17: "He also measured its wall, 144 cubits by human measurement, which is also an angel's measurement." Some interpreters think that the reference to the human measurement being also an angel's measurement simply means that the angel used a measurement that all people would recognize.[8] Another view is that the mention of human and angelic measurement is intended to point us to the heavenly meaning beyond the earthly picture.[9] The book of Revelation uses earthly images to describe heavenly realities.

We are told in 21:17 that the wall measures "144 cubits." If these 144 cubits refer to the height of the wall, the wall would be just over 200 feet high. A wall as high as a twenty-story building would be "a great, high wall" (21:12) even today, but it is hardly proportional to the height of the city, which 21:16 indicates will be 12,000 stadia, or 1,500 miles. Some suggest that "144 cubits" refers to the wall's thickness, but even then a wall that is 1,500 miles high would need to be thicker than 200 feet. So this is probably not a literal description. It is meant to be overwhelming in proportion, and it is, but we're not intended to try to make it into a blueprint. The 144 cubits of the wall is a multiple of 12, as also the 12,000 stadia are, and these multiples of 12 probably point to completion, wholeness. The temple-city is presented in symbolic measurements that point to the whole of reality becoming the dwelling place of God. And yet there will be an "outside," where the wicked are (22:15).

John said the radiance of the city was like jasper in 21:11, and we see why in the first half of 21:18: "The wall was built of jasper." Think of the wealth of resources necessary to build a wall of jasper. There is no end of this supply. And then we see another indication that the whole place is the Holy of Holies in the second half of 21:18: "the city was pure gold, clear as glass." Everything in the Holy of Holies was overlaid with gold (cf. Exodus 25). The precious material corresponds to the sanctity of the place.

Paul spoke of the church being "a holy temple" that is being "built on the foundation of the apostles and prophets" in Ephesians 2:20, 21, which itself interprets Jesus' telling Peter he was the rock on which the church would be built (Matthew 16:18). This matches John's description of the names of the apostles being on the foundations of the wall in 21:14, and we read more about the foundations in 21:19, 20:

> The foundations of the wall of the city were adorned with every kind of jewel. The first was jasper, the second sapphire, the third agate, the fourth emerald, the fifth onyx, the sixth carnelian, the seventh chrysolite, the eighth beryl, the ninth topaz, the tenth chrysoprase, the eleventh jacinth, the twelfth amethyst.

These precious stones were set in four rows of three on the high priest's breastplate (Exodus 28:17–20), and they are also associated with the Garden of Eden (Ezekiel 28:13, 14; cf. Genesis 2:12). Solomon also laid the foundation of the temple with precious stones (1 Kings 5:17; 7:9, 10). What John describes in 21:18–20 fulfills what Isaiah prophesied in Isaiah 54:11, 12:

> O afflicted one, storm-tossed and not comforted, behold, I will set your stones in antimony, and lay your foundations with sapphires. I will make

your pinnacles of agate [ESV margin, jasper], your gates of carbuncles, and
all your wall of precious stones.

It seems that these precious stones reflect the beauty of God himself—
rare, valuable, radiating light in many-hued splendor. So God's glory is
reflected in Eden, in the tabernacle, and in the high priest's vestments, and it
will be supremely displayed in the new Jerusalem that comes down from God,
having his glory (21:11), as the foundations of the wall are adorned with these
stones that shine with the beauty of God.

John describes the gates and the streets in 21:21: "And the twelve gates
were twelve pearls, each of the gates made of a single pearl, and the street of
the city was pure gold, transparent as glass." Can you imagine twelve massive
pearls, each large enough to be made into a gate? Such gates would be price-
less, and beautiful, and in this holy city they are safe from vandalism and theft.

John wrote in 21:18 that "the city was pure gold, clear as glass," and now
we see in 21:21 that "the street of the city was pure gold, transparent as glass."
All these precious stones and metals are shouting limitless wealth. This city,
like this world that we all get to live in, has resources that can scarcely be
imagined. Notice that in both verses 18 and 21 the gold is called "pure" and
likened to "transparent," clean glass. This gold has a quality and purity superior to the gold in Fort Knox, but it isn't locked away in a vault. Rather, God
uses it to pave the streets! We can think of Moses being instructed to remove
his sandals because the ground was holy where God appeared to him (Exodus
3:5), and this picture of streets paved with pure gold that is transparent like
clean glass points to the ultimate holy ground. The people who walk these
streets are going to have clean feet because of the blood of Christ. The inhabitants of this city will be holy, and the streets of gold will never be smudged
with dirty feet because there won't be any dirty feet there. They have all been
washed by the servant who "loved them to the end" (cf. John 13:1–20).

Revelation 21:22–27: God and the Lamb Are Its Temple

Jesus told the Jews that if they destroyed "this temple," he would rebuild it
in three days. He was talking about "the temple of his body" (John 2:17–22).
Then Jesus told the disciples in John 14 that he was going to prepare a place
for them, a new temple in which they would be with him and the Father (John
14:2, 3). John describes the fulfillment of what Jesus promised in 21:22: "And
I saw no temple in the city, for its temple is the Lord God the Almighty and the
Lamb." God and the Lamb are the temple. This means that whereas formerly
there was a structure, a tent or a building, that was holy because God was
there, now the structure is the whole of reality. The temple is the new heaven

and new earth. Just as the temple was formerly the holy place in the midst of the wider world, now God and the Lamb are what the temple was: they are the holy in the midst of the world, and there is not a particular building that is the temple because the world itself has become the temple. This is what the Old Testament prophesied in passages such as Zechariah 14:20, 21.

John elaborates on the statement in 21:3 that God will "dwell" with man with the statement in 21:22 that God and the Lamb are the temple and adds in 21:23, "And the city has no need of sun or moon to shine on it, for the glory of God gives it light, and its lamp is the Lamb." This fulfills what God promised in Isaiah 60:19, 20:

> The sun shall be no more your light by day, nor for brightness shall the moon give you light; but the LORD will be your everlasting light, and your God will be your glory. Your sun shall no more go down, nor your moon withdraw itself; for the LORD will be your everlasting light, and your days of mourning shall be ended.

Have you ever taken a candle or a flashlight outside on a clear, sunny day? You can barely see the light of the candle or flashlight at all. The glory of God and the lamp of the Lamb will so outshine the sun and the moon that the lights of the heavens will no longer be necessary.

The temple in Jerusalem was the focal point of pilgrimage, and the sun is the light by which people see, by which they walk and work. In the new city sun and temple are replaced by God and the Lamb, with the result that John writes in 21:24, "By its light will the nations walk, and the kings of the earth will bring their glory into it." In this world the nations walk by the light of the sun, but in the new heaven and earth the nations will walk by the light of the glory of God. "By *its* light" refers to the light of God's glory, and it seems that the "it" at the end of the verse also refers back to God's glory: "the kings of the earth will bring their glory into it." The idea is that life will be conducted by the light of the glory of God, and those who rule on earth will bring their glory to God's glory. Some think that the kings of the earth in view here are formerly rebellious kings who were converted at the coming of Christ. That may be so, but it seems more natural to see this as describing either those who reign during the millennium of 20:4—resurrected martyrs—or those who reign in the new heaven and earth. Those who rule on earth will live by God's glory, and they will add their glory to God's glory. There will be no more false pride, vainglory, or idolatry, which attributes to idols what belongs to God.

The description of the city continues in 21:25: "and its gates will never be shut by day—and there will be no night there." The New Testament refers in several places to thieves that come at night (Matthew 24:43; 1 Thessalonians

5:2), and the whole point of a gate is to protect what is inside. The fact that the "gates will never be shut by day" means that no one is going to attack these walls, and the addition of the statement that "there will be no night" means that thieves will never have an hour of darkness in which to steal, kill, and destroy. This is a city of phenomenal wealth, but the wicked are in the lake of fire (20:15) and can never enter the city (21:27; 22:15).

The inhabitants of this city are so satisfied in God that they will never be tempted to steal. They will enjoy the beauty of the place in ways that glorify God, as we see in 21:26, 27: "They will bring into it the glory and the honor of the nations. But nothing unclean will ever enter it, nor anyone who does what is detestable or false, but only those who are written in the Lamb's book of life." John says in 21:26 that Isaiah 60:5 will be fulfilled: "the wealth of the nations shall come to you." In 21:27 Isaiah 35:8 is fulfilled: "the unclean shall not pass over it," along with Isaiah 52:1 ("there shall no more come into you the uncircumcised and the unclean") and Zechariah 14:21 ("there shall no longer be a trader [ESV margin, Canaanite] in the house of the LORD of hosts on that day"). Only the elect, whose names "are written in the Lamb's book of life" (21:27), will be there. The elect will not worship the beast (13:8; 17:8), and they alone will enter the city.

God wrote these people's names in the Lamb's book of life before the foundation of the world. It is not unfair of God to write down some names and not others. He is God. He shows mercy to whom he pleases (Exodus 33:19). He does not owe mercy to anyone. He has chosen to guarantee that some will be faithful to him, and the rest he allows to make their own choice. They choose to worship the beast and suffer the consequences. But it is not as though those whose names are written in the Lamb's book of life do not get the same choice. God so works that they are born again, and as a result they have the ability to see God's hidden kingdom. Because of that, they choose to resist the beast. They choose, and God chose them. Humans are responsible, and God is sovereign.

Conclusion

Imagine that you were born into a miserable situation—no family, no future, no hope. A father you did not know and never would have met sets his love on you. He makes elaborate plans to redeem you for himself, make you part of his family, and give you hope and a future. The price for your redemption is shocking, but this father who has decided to adopt you doesn't even flinch.

At a cost to himself that you cannot fathom, a price that you will not understand until your own faculties have matured, he ransoms your life. The redemption entails a journey of a distance we have no categories for comprehending, a sacrifice that risks everything, suffers, dies, and rises from the dead, and in the triumphant resurrection your life is secured. He has bought you back, and he will fetch you home.

He puts his name on you, and he has promised to bring you into his home where you will permanently live in his presence. While you await the finalization of the adoption process, he gives you a down payment that can never be revoked, sealing the arrangement irrevocably. What Josh and Jenn have done parallels so beautifully what our Father has done. We have been adopted. The Father who has redeemed us and made us part of his family shows us in this passage what we will inherit, the place where we will live with him. If we believe this, let us live like the children of such a Father.

36

They Will See His Face

REVELATION 22:1–9

IMAGINE THE ANGUISH YOU WOULD FEEL if this scenario were your story: you built a home for your children, planted a vineyard in the surrounding fields, provided everything that your children would need to live and be happy, but despite all that, one of your children kills his brother. Then another one of your children takes grapes from the vineyard, makes strong wine, and gets himself good and drunk. To your astonishment the bedrooms you built for your children's safety and protection become dens of adultery and smut. The children continue to kill each other, steal from each other, and lie to one another, and as things get worse and worse they begin to proclaim that they have no father. They have the gall to assert that you, the builder of the house in which they live, the one who fathered them and gave them life, do not exist at all. Imagine the pain of having your own children defile your home, declare that they have no father, and shout that they hate you.

God created this world as a cosmic temple. Contrast the holiness and cleanliness required of the priests who enter the temple with the abominable filth that humans have spread all over this planet that God made to display his glory. Even those of us who trust in Jesus and try to live by the Bible fall miserably short of the glory of God's holiness. What would you do if you were God? How would you react to the ruination of the house you built, the misuse of the gifts you gave, and the defiling of the masterpiece—the crown of all creation—the human body and person?

Our God and Father has initiated a cosmic rescue operation. His plan is to save through judgment, to show justice and mercy, and then to bring those he saves into a new heaven and new earth.

Need

Do you want to know how things are going to turn out? Do you want to know what the future holds? Do you wonder whether there is any hope, any resolution, any restoration?

If there is something that makes trusting Jesus and being faithful to the Bible worth persevering through the worst thing that could possibly happen to us, we need to know what it is, right? If there is something that will bring cleansing from all defilement, healing from every wound, the satisfaction of every longing, and an intimacy that will swallow up every alienation, we need to know about that, right?

Main Point

Revelation 22:1–9 declares that God is going to keep his word and return those who trust him to a new and better Garden of Eden.

Context

We saw the temple-city descend from God, full of his glory, in 21:9–27, and now in 22:1–9 we will see that the temple-city is a new and better Eden. God will heal every hurt, and those who trust him will see his face. They will enjoy his presence. After this passage the book closes in 22:10–21.

Preview

Revelation 22:1–9 falls into two parts:

22:1–5   The River, the Tree, and the Presence
22:6–9   Keep the Words

Revelation 22:1–5: The River, the Tree, and the Presence

There is no break in the action between the end of chapter 21 and what we see in chapter 22. John has been describing the new Jerusalem in chapter 21, and the description continues in chapter 22, focusing on Edenic aspects of the temple-city. We read in 22:1, "Then the angel showed me the river of the water of life, bright as crystal, flowing from the throne of God and of the Lamb." This matches the river that "flowed out of Eden to water the garden" in Genesis 2:10. There was and is no river flowing in the literal city of Jerusalem, but Ezekiel saw water issuing from the temple in Ezekiel 47:1. Psalm 46:4 says, "There is a river whose streams make glad the city of God," and Zechariah 14:8 promises that "living waters shall flow out from Jerusalem." Jesus offered "living water" to the woman at the well in John 4:10–14 (cf.

John 7:37–39). All this is fulfilled in 22:1 by "the river of the water of life . . . flowing from the throne of God and the Lamb."

Even in our sanitized world where water comes from a treatment plant through dependable pipes and faucets that we turn on and off at a whim, we cannot live without water. John described this scene for an ancient audience whose water came from rivers, streams, rainfalls, and wells. A poisoned well in the ancient world meant that people were going to die, as did a drought. So this description of "the river of the water of life, bright as crystal" in 22:1 points to God's providing a basic need that enables survival. But it isn't merely survival, this is a *river*—the supply is abundant, and the "water of life" in this river is "bright as crystal"—so it is both beautiful and pure. This fulfills Ezekiel's vision of a river flowing from the temple that makes the seawater fresh and gives life to all kinds of fish (Ezekiel 47:8–10).

We read in 22:2 that this water flows "through the middle of the street of the city." So it seems that the street is a wide boulevard with a river running through its center. Verse 2 continues by moving from "the water of life" to "the tree of life": ". . . also, on either side of the river, the tree of life with its twelve kinds of fruit, yielding its fruit each month. The leaves of the tree were for the healing of the nations." The river fulfilled Ezekiel's prophecy, and the tree does the same. We read in Ezekiel 47:12, "And on the banks, on both sides of the river, there will grow all kinds of trees for food. Their leaves will not wither, nor their fruit fail, but they will bear fresh fruit every month, because the water for them flows from the sanctuary. Their fruit will be for food, and their leaves for healing."

Ezekiel 47:12 describes trees planted by streams of water whose leaves do not wither and whose fruit does not fail. This is an unmistakable allusion to Psalm 1. When we put these texts together, we see that those who do what Psalm 1 commends—delighting in the Law of the Lord and meditating on it day and night—become like the new heaven and new earth, where the river of living water makes the soil rich for the tree of life whose leaves do not wither. Those who delight in the Bible and meditate on it day and night are like the tree of life. Their leaves don't wither, and all they do prospers. Is that what your life is like? Do you want your life to be that way? Give your brain Bible! Meditate on it day and night. Delight yourself in it.

Just as we cannot live without water, we cannot live without food. So just as there is a "river of the water of life" in 22:1, there is a "tree of life" in 22:2. There is a glorious variety in the fruit of this tree: "twelve kinds of fruit." I have never seen a tree that produces twelve kinds of fruit, nor have I seen a tree that bears fruit every month of the year. But this tree does just that, "yielding its fruit each month." And the river does not limit access to this tree because the tree is "on either side of the river." The fruit is abundant, accessible, constant, and of stunning variety.

As "the river of the water of life" matches the river flowing out of Eden in Genesis 2:10, this "tree of life" matches "the tree of life . . . in the midst of the garden" in Genesis 2:9. The river and the tree are about food and water, and they signal a return to a new and better Garden of Eden.

The last phrase of 22:2 tells us that when the redeemed enjoy the new and better Eden, old hurts will be healed. The nationalism, the racism, the acrimony, the bitterness, and the long history of warfare will be healed. The nations will be healed by the leaves of the tree of life. The redeemed of every tribe will enjoy the crystal-clear water of life, the twelve fruits of "the tree of life," and "healing." Revelation 22:1, 2 corresponds to and goes beyond what we see of the Garden of Eden in Genesis 2:9, 10.

Table 36.1: The New and Better Eden

Genesis	Revelation	Ways the New Garden Is Better
Genesis 2:10: "A river flowed out of Eden to water the garden"	Revelation 22:1: "the river of the water of life, bright as crystal, flowing from the throne of God and of the Lamb"	• Living water • "Bright as crystal" • "Flowing from the throne of God and of the Lamb"
Genesis 2:9: "The tree of life was in the midst of the garden"	Revelation 22:2: "on either side of the river, the tree of life with its twelve kinds of fruit, yielding its fruit each month. The leaves of the tree were for the healing of the nations"	• The tree is on both sides of the river • "Twelve kinds of fruit" (Ezekiel 47:12) • Continual production • "Healing"

All around us people are doing things that they foolishly think will prove to be shortcuts back to the Garden of Eden. There is only one way back to Eden: trusting Christ and obeying the Bible. Those things that look like shortcuts are nothing but broad paths and easy roads that lead to destruction.

Do you want to drink from that river? Do you want to eat of that tree? Do you want the healing of its leaves? You can't earn it. There is nothing you could ever do to merit access to this fruit. You've already blown it, and there's no undoing what you've done to disqualify yourself from the presence of God. He's holy—you're not. You can't undo the ways you've been unholy. Your only hope is Jesus. When he died, he took the penalty for your unholy deeds. If you trust him, his righteous life will count for you. If you trust Jesus, the river and the tree will be yours to enjoy.

Revelation 22:3 says, "No longer will there be anything accursed."

Disobedience resulted in God's curse in Genesis 3. This first phrase of 22:3 declares that God has dealt with our disobedience. The curse has fallen. Judgment has been done. God has worked a righteous cleansing in those who have believed in Jesus Christ, and disobedience will never again result in a curse. This also means that never again will the fellowship between God and his people be interrupted, as the next phrase of verse 3 makes plain: "but the throne of God and of the Lamb will be in it." There will be no curse in the clean and holy realm where God dwells. Rather than disobeying and bringing down curses, we read in the last phrase of 22:3, "and his servants will worship him." God redeemed Israel from Egypt so they could serve him, but as soon as they were freed they began to rebel against him. The fulfillment of the exodus being described here in Revelation will have a very different outcome. God redeemed his people so they would serve him, and 22:3 tells us they will do just that.

In the last phrase of 22:3 the pronouns "his" and "him" are both singular, and they point back to "God" and "the Lamb" in the previous phrase in verse 3. So you have two persons, God and the Lamb, referred to by the singular pronouns "his" and "him" in verse 3, and verse 4 continues by referring to "his face" and "his name." Each of these singular pronouns refers to God *and* the Lamb. There are two persons, but the pronoun is singular. This is because of what Jesus declared in John 10:30: "I and the Father are one" (cf. also Revelation 11:15). It would take the church some time to sort out what the unity of being and nature within a plurality of personhood does and does not entail, but the New Testament clearly teaches that the Father and Jesus are two persons who share one nature. They are two, and they are one. John's understanding of this reality is reflected in his grammar; the singular pronouns refer to two persons—God and the Lamb.

Of course, the Holy Spirit is also God. They are three, and they are one. Worship the Triune God. Worship him for the unity in diversity. Worship him because he is beyond your understanding. Praise him that he is above you. Know God, and lose yourself in the wonder of who he is!

In this city whose wall is made of jasper, whose gates are twelve massive pearls, whose street is of pure gold, the inhabitants worship the Creator rather than created things. All the disorder at work in this world is finally set right. The wealth of the city, the pure water of life, the twelvefold fruit of the tree of life, and the nation-healing leaves all point to the One who made these things. Rather than becoming idols, these things spur the servants of God to worship the One who is worthy, God himself.

God is the best thing about this new and better Eden, and John teaches that reality even in the way that he organizes what he has to say about this

Edenic temple-city. He has saved the best for last. The last thing that John describes in 22:4, 5 will be the best part of being there: "They will see his face, and his name will be on their foreheads. And night will be no more. They will need no light of lamp or sun, for the Lord God will be their light, and they will reign forever and ever." The Lord said to Moses in Exodus 33:20, "you cannot see my face, for man shall not see me and live," and John declares in John 1:18, "No one has ever seen God." I take this to mean that when Numbers 12:8 describes the Lord speaking with Moses "mouth to mouth" and when Deuteronomy 34:10 describes the Lord knowing Moses "face to face," these are figurative ways of describing the exceptionally revelatory way in which Moses knew God. Still, Moses did not see God's face.

But 22:4 says that those whose names are written in the Lamb's book of life (see 21:27) will see God's face. This is a renewal of walking with God in the cool of the day and then some. This is access to God like no one has ever known. God created people to know him, and when his purposes come to fruition, we who trust Christ will indeed know him. Those who trust in Jesus "will see his face." This is a heretofore unexperienced intimacy with God. It is more than we could handle in our present state. It goes beyond our wildest dreams. Most of us will never see the face of this country's top general, the Chief Justice, or the President. But this text is telling us that everyone who trusts in Christ will see God's face.

The next words about God's name being on the foreheads of those who inhabit the shining city point to God's character and glory shining out from all they think, say, and do. The very character of God will be evident in the lives of those who live in the holy city Jerusalem.

We saw in 21:25 that there will be "no night there" and in 21:23 that the sun will not be needed, and it seems that these ideas are repeated in 22:5 to say that there will be no place that is not continually made bright by the light of God's glory. The statement that "the Lord God will be their light" in 22:5, hard on the heels of the statement that "they will see his face" in 22:4, means that no place will ever lack the light of God's glorious presence. There will be an ongoing, all-enlightening enjoyment of the radiance emanating from the one we worship. This seems to be reinforced by the final statement in 22:5 that those who see God's face "will reign forever and ever." God's "*servants*"—so described in 22:3—will "*reign*"—as described in 22:5—as they "*worship*" (22:3) and live out God's character, which is what having God's name "on their foreheads" (22:4) entails. The servants will reign as they worship and reflect God's character. What could be better than reigning by serving, worshiping by living out the character of God himself?

John saved the best thing about the Edenic temple-city for last. It is better than walls of jasper whose foundations are twelve precious stones, better than gates of pearl and a street of gold, better than a river of the water of life and a tree of life whose leaves heal the nations. It is better than all that. It is the best of all. What makes all the rest meaningful? The presence of God.

Is this the way that you think about Heaven? If you found out that God and Jesus weren't going to be in Heaven, but the street would still be gold and the gates pearl and the walls jasper and the water living and the tree's leaves healing, and all your dearly departed there, but Jesus and the Father would not be there, would you still want to go? If you hesitate at all, please recognize that Heaven without Jesus and the Father would be nothing less than a gold-plated Hell. Jesus and the Father are Heaven. And that is no less true now than it will be then.

Maybe you are worried about expanding government control and rising taxes. Maybe you are worried about the loss of religious liberty in this country. Let me encourage you: if you have been born again, no one can undo the new life God has wrought in you. If you trust in Jesus, no one can make you stop believing in him. If the Holy Spirit lives in you, no one can take him away. If others take all your money and use it to persecute Christians, even imprisoning and martyring some, they cannot take from you the hope that Jesus will come. Jesus will judge. Jesus will do righteousness. Jesus will come for his bride. God will grant access to the Edenic temple-city of the new heaven and new earth, and all who have called on the name of the Lord will see God's face. The best thing about your life then—namely, God—is the best thing about your life now. No one can take God's love from you. No one can remove the fact that God did not spare Jesus, that God has accomplished his elaborate plan to redeem his children.

Do you live that way? Does your study of the Bible reflect these realities? Do you pray like God is the best part of your life? Do your desires show it to be so? Pray that God would make it so right now. Pray that God would help you to know him as the best part of your life. He is. So pray that he would make you feel it and know it and live like it. Oh, that the Lord might transform us with the truth that he is the best thing about our life now and the life to come. Jesus said, "This is eternal life, that they may know you, the only true God, and Jesus Christ whom you have sent" (John 17:3).

Revelation 22:6–9: Keep the Words

In 22:6–9 John uses some phrases that punctuate the end of this section of the book and others that reach all the way back to the opening of the whole of this apocalyptic prophecy in the form of a circular letter. In verses 7 and 9 he refers to keeping the words of this book; so it seems he is calling his audience to hear and heed now that he has reached the end.

John is tying things up. Near the beginning of the vision of the new heaven and earth, in 21:5, the one seated on the throne told John to write because "these words are trustworthy and true." Now as we reach the end of this vision of the new heaven and earth, we read in 22:6, "And he said to me, 'These words are trustworthy and true. And the Lord, the God of the spirits of the prophets, has sent his angel to show his servants what must soon take place.'" It is difficult to know who spoke these words. They are the same words spoken by the one seated on the throne in 21:5, but in 21:9, 15 an angel is speaking to John. Right after this statement in 22:6, Jesus speaks in 22:7. Though we are not sure exactly who has spoken, 22:6 clearly indicates that the ultimate source of the message is God himself. And the reference to God sending his angel to show his servants what must soon take place in 22:6 recalls the same language that opened the whole book in 1:1.

Then Jesus speaks in 22:7: "And behold, I am coming soon. Blessed is the one who keeps the words of the prophecy of this book." We can be sure that this is Jesus speaking because he is the one who said, "I am coming soon" every other time that phrase appears in Revelation (2:16; 3:11; 22:12, 20). The blessing that Jesus speaks in 22:7 on those who "keep the words of the prophecy of this book" also points back to the book's opening, where the same blessing was stated in 1:3.

In 22:8, 9 John uses phrases that match the ending of the section on the harlot in 19:9, 10.

> I, John, am the one who heard and saw these things. And when I heard and saw them, I fell down to worship at the feet of the angel who showed them to me, but he said to me, "You must not do that! I am a fellow servant with you and your brothers the prophets, and with those who keep the words of this book. Worship God."

So John has signaled that 22:6–9 ends the vision of the new heaven and earth by using the phrase, "These words are trustworthy and true" from the beginning of the vision of the new heaven and earth in 21:5. He has signaled that just as 19:9, 10 ends the section on the harlot that began in 17:1, so also 22:8, 9 ends the section on the bride that began in 21:9, 10, which means that we are at the end of the whole section of Revelation that begins in chapter 17 and continues through 22:9. And in the statements in 22:6, 7 John reaches all the way back to 1:1–3 to show that we have come to the end of the whole project.

Notice the heavy emphasis in 22:6–9 on the importance of these words.

They are called "trustworthy and true" in verse 6. The chain of revelation is also alluded to in 22:6—the information comes from God, who sent his angel to reveal these things to his servants. Then Jesus ratifies the message by saying he is coming soon and by blessing those who keep "the *words* of the *prophecy* of this *book*" in 22:7. Then John signs his name in 22:8. He insists that he is the one who "heard and saw" all this. This book is firsthand, eyewitness testimony. And if that were not enough, the angel insists in 22:9 that he serves with "those who keep the words of this book."

If the governor of your state sent you an email that he was going to drop by your home, would you mow the lawn, tidy up the house, and have refreshments ready for his arrival? What if the President of the United States sent his chief of staff to your city, who then sent a member of the Secret Service to your home to tell you that the President himself was coming soon? This book of Revelation is far more important and eventful than any email, and the book of Revelation was communicated to one whose testimony is more to be trusted than that of the President's chief of staff. It was also sent through an angel whose powers are far superior to that of a Secret Service agent. And the one who is to come is unspeakably greater than some governor or president. He is King of kings and Lord of lords. He has given his word to us. Our allegiance is to him.

Heed the words of this book. Worship God. Get this blessing for yourself. Be a student of the Bible. Read it. Memorize it. Hide it in your heart. Meditate on it. Do not let it depart from your mouth.

Conclusion

Won't you live in the land watered by the river of life? Won't you live to eat of the tree whose leaves are for the healing of the nations? Won't you commit yourself to being one who will see God's face, bear his name on your forehead, and reign forever? Won't you turn from your sin and trust in Christ?

Won't you trust the testimony of John the eyewitness? Won't you believe that the words of the book of Revelation are trustworthy and true? Won't you enjoy the blessing on those who keep the words of the prophecy of the book of Revelation? Won't you worship this God who is worthy of all praise?

> This the book that tells the story
> Of the Lord and all his glory
> The world's Creator, strong and free
> Ever One, ever Three
>
> He made the world and made it good
> His image placed in Eden's wood

Rebellion there wrought sin and death
Loss of life, end of breath

But when the Lord there cursed the snake
A solemn promise he did make
The woman's seed would crush his head
On evil he would tread

From Eden then there was exile
Because God's presence they defiled
And in the story of this book
We read of all it took

To raise man up and set him free
In God's presence again to be
God's mercy here is on display
And so to you I say

Behold the book of hope and life
It sings of Christ and how through strife
He did indeed on evil tread
Dying, he crushed Satan's head

Then rose again to justify
All those who on him do rely
For he alone this work can do
He alone can save you

And so this book to you I give
Hoping and praying you will live
By faith in promises made here
Trust replacing all your fear

So take this book, my friend, and read
Its pages will meet every need
And we will sing the praise of Christ
Who by his death gives life

James M. Hamilton Jr.
November 15, 2008

37

Come, Lord Jesus!

REVELATION 22:10–21

FRODO AND THE FELLOWSHIP OF THE RING had set off from Rivendell on the great quest to destroy Sauron's ring. Providence forced them to pass through the Mines of Moria, and there at the bridge of Khazad-dûm Gandalf faced the Balrog. He gave his life so that the other members of the Fellowship might live. The members of the Fellowship believed Gandalf the Grey to be dead, and apparently he was. He was sent back, however, from the dead with even greater power as Gandalf the White. Though raised from the dead, it was only when he returned to them that the other members of the Fellowship were helped by him.[1]

Tolkien's story has obvious parallels with the true story of the world, in which Jesus gave his life for his people, then rose from the dead.[2] We read in Acts 1:3 that Jesus gave many convincing proofs that he was alive over the course of forty days. Jesus promised his disciples that he would return to accomplish their final deliverance (John 14:2, 3), and when he ascended into Heaven two angelic figures declared that he would return just the way the disciples saw him go (Acts 1:10, 11).

Jesus accomplished salvation by his death and resurrection, and his resurrection guarantees his return. He is greater than Gandalf the Grey, and he will defeat the world's Adversary and bring about the new age. He now waits at the right hand of the Father in resurrection glory, and from thence he shall come to judge the quick and the dead.

The resurrection guarantees the return.

Need

Will God accomplish his purposes? Has Satan been defeated, and if so, will he be dislodged? If his hold on the world is going to be broken, when will that be? When will the tears be wiped away? When will the dead be raised? When will the broken be healed and the old made new?

Main Point

Revelation 22:10–21 teaches that Jesus is coming to judge the wicked and to save those who love him, who are eager for his arrival.

Context

Jesus appears to John in resurrection glory in Revelation 1 and then calls the churches to faithfulness in chapters 2, 3, promising them the rewards we have seen him give in chapters 20—22. We saw the throne and the judgments in chapters 4—16. In chapter 4 John was called up into the heavenly throne room, where he saw God worshiped. Then the slain Lamb, risen from the dead, took the scroll from the Father in chapter 5, and as he unsealed the scroll, the judgments fell in chapters 6—16—the breaking of the seals, the blowing of the trumpets, and the outpouring of the bowls. Then in chapters 17—22 John saw the harlot, the King, and the bride. Babylon the harlot was destroyed in chapters 17, 18, the King returned and set up his thousand-year kingdom in chapters 19, 20, and then he and his bride entered the new heaven and earth in chapters 21, 22.

Just as the whole book was introduced in 1:1–8, so the whole book is concluded in 22:10–21. We have come to the end of the book of Revelation, the last words of the whole Bible. What is the last thing God says to his people? We have it in this passage.

Preview

This passage falls into three parts:

22:10–17	Don't Seal the Book Because Jesus Is Coming
22:18–20	Don't Change the Book Because Jesus Is Coming
22:21	The Grace

In the first section, 22:10–17, Jesus tells John not to seal the book in verse 10 and that he is coming soon in verse 12, and the Spirit and the bride respond by calling Jesus to "Come" in verse 17. In the second section Jesus gives a warning not to alter the contents of the book in verse 18 and states that he is coming soon in the first part of verse 20, and at the end of verse 20

John responds by calling Jesus to "Come." So these two main sections of this passage have these three parts: Jesus makes a statement about the book of Revelation and announces that he is coming soon, and then those who love him respond by calling him to come.

Revelation 22:10–17: Don't Seal the Book Because Jesus Is Coming

John has seen the Edenic temple-city in Revelation 21:9–22:5. Then in 22:6–9 there was a blessing on those who "keep the words of the prophecy of this book" (v. 7), and then the angel said he was a fellow servant with those "who keep the words of this book" (v. 9). John now writes in 22:10, "And he said to me, 'Do not seal up the words of the prophecy of this book, for the time is near.'" The angel who has just spoken to John in 22:9 is the speaker here, and what he says to John is in direct contrast to what was spoken to Daniel. Daniel was told, "But you, Daniel, shut up the words and seal the book until the time of the end" (Daniel 12:4),[3] but now that "the time is near" in 22:10, John is instructed not to seal the book. In Daniel 12:8, 9 Daniel asks what the outcome of the things that he has seen will be, and he is told to seal the message because it pertains to the time of the end. The situation in Revelation is that the end has come, so the message is unsealed. This whole book of Revelation shows us Jesus Christ, and it is given from God through Jesus via the angel to John so that God's servants will know what will soon take place (1:1–3; 22:6, 16). As these events have been unveiled, we have seen Jesus open the seals on the scroll that details the end of history in chapters 5, 6, and we also saw John commanded to seal up and not write down what the seven thunders said back in 10:4. Thus, when John is commanded not to seal the words of the book because the time is near in 22:10, we see that this means that the future has been unveiled in this book, and it is to be made known and not kept secret.

With the future unveiled and unsealed, 22:11 gives a surprising set of commands: "Let the evildoer still do evil, and the filthy still be filthy, and the righteous still do right, and the holy still be holy." Notice that these "Let the" statements are imperatives, not indicatives. They are commands to act a certain way, not statements about how people are acting. In a surprising and paradoxical way, this command for people to act according to their nature establishes human responsibility. Reality has been made known, and now in light of reality, people are commanded to do *what they want to do* on the basis of *who they are*.

Evil people want to do evil. Filthy people want to be filthy. In the same way, righteous people want to do right, and holy people want to be holy. So in this book of Revelation, the way that God will save and judge is made known, and then it is as though the angel says to the audience, do what you want to do!

Are you a believer in Jesus? The last two statements in 22:11 apply to you because you are "holy" and "righteous." "Do [what is] right." "Be holy." Why? Because of what is unsealed and unveiled in this Revelation.

Are you an unbeliever? Have you decided that you are going to do it your way? Are you thinking that you don't want to repent of your sins, don't want to be identified as a Christian, and don't want to be in church to hear the Bible taught on a regular basis? The first two commands of 22:11 are for you—you are "evil" and "filthy," and you are commanded to keep right on doing evil and filth. Why would the Bible command you to do that?

I think these commands are given here to scare us into changing our ways. This book shows that God is going to judge evil people and exclude them from his presence because they are filthy, and now the evil and filthy are commanded to keep right on doing what they want to do. But this command is meant to force us to realize that if we are vile, evil, filthy, and unrepentant, God is going to display the glory of his justice upon us. This command is given to us to force us to recognize what awaits us and to push us to repent.

God wants you to repent. If you will look at your life, you will see a lot of evidence that God has been wooing you to himself. If you are an unbeliever, you are unbelieving precisely because you have been refusing to repent of your sin and trust in Jesus.

Imagine being at the Grand Canyon and having a tour guide take you to some massive precipice. You look over the edge and realize that the drop is so deep it makes you dizzy. Then the tour guide says, "Let the self-assertive fool who wants to destroy himself disregard caution, ignore my instructions, and go over the edge." Is that what the tour guide wants you to do?

No! He wants you to take care. He wants you to heed his warning. He wants you to realize that if you disregard what he says, your life is over.

God wants you to repent. God gives you this command not because he wants you to keep doing what is evil and filthy but because he wants you to realize that is what you are doing. He wants you to know for certain that there is a difference between what is evil and what is right, between what is filthy and what is holy. He wants you to perceive that difference, recognize that you are evil, feel your inability to change yourself, and cry out to him for help. He wants you to be desperate. You are wretched, and he wants you to realize it.

God wants you to cry out to him to make you want to be holy, want to be right, so that you will do what is holy and right. If you know today that you are not turning from your sin and trusting in Jesus, if you know that your deeds are evil and filthy, won't you cry out to God? Won't you call on the name of the Lord Jesus? Because of the death and resurrection of Jesus, you can be saved. If you will trust in Jesus, God will make you holy.

You will find that where you used to love sin, you love doing what is right. Where you used to be at enmity with God, you have been reconciled. Where you formerly hated God and the Bible, you now love God, praise Jesus, and are hungry to know the Bible. Why would you perish? Won't you repent and trust in Jesus?

The truth has been unsealed in 22:10, a response to the truth is commanded in 22:11, and now in 22:12, 13 Jesus punctuates the message by announcing that he is coming to judge, underscoring that announcement with his own declaration of who he is. Jesus says, "Behold, I am coming soon, bringing my recompense with me, to repay everyone for what he has done. I am the Alpha and the Omega, the first and the last, the beginning and the end." Jesus is coming, and he is going to hold people personally responsible for what they have done. No one will have any excuse about the devil making them do it, about God making them into some robotic evildoer, or about their DNA dictating that they would behave in certain ways and not others.

We all know that we do what we want to do. We all know that we are responsible for what we do. We all know that God will call us to account. Jesus announces here in 22:12 that he is going to recompense people according to their actions. And then in 22:13 he states three times that he is the eternal God, one with the Father from everlasting to everlasting. He started everything, and he will finish everything. No one will outlast him. No one will escape him. No one will have an excuse based on a preexisting condition of which he is unaware. Jesus has all the evidence because he has always been. He will judge justly.

So 22:10–13 has called for the message to be unsealed and unleashed and commanded one of two possible responses to the message, and Jesus has announced that he will come to judge, declaring his eternal nature.

Revelation 22:14, 15 states the only two possible outcomes. These are the only two ways that people will be recompensed for what they have done. John writes, "Blessed are those who wash their robes, so that they may have the right to the tree of life and that they may enter the city by the gates. Outside are the dogs and sorcerers and the sexually immoral and murderers and idolaters, and everyone who loves and practices falsehood."

The first part of 22:14 is the last of seven benedictions in Revelation (cf. 1:3; 14:13; 16:15; 19:9; 20:6; 22:7). Do you see what it implies? It implies that all humans have a dirty robe, and it declares that those who "wash their robes" are "blessed." Back in 7:14 the redeemed are identified as those who "have washed their robes and made them white in the blood of the Lamb."

This is a figurative way of saying that these people are saved because they trust in the death and resurrection of Jesus Christ. The "robes" are the way you have clothed yourself by your actions. We all have dirty robes. We have all done what is evil and filthy. The only people who will have clean robes are those who wash their robes in the blood of Jesus. Jesus died to pay the penalty for sin. Does his death count for you, or will you pay that penalty yourself? How do you wash your robe in the blood of Jesus? Trust him. Turn away from all the things you have done that are filthy and put your hope in Jesus. He is mighty to save. He can make your robe clean.

Look at the two things those blessed people who "wash their robes" in the blood of Jesus get to do in the rest of 22:14: they get to eat of "the tree of life," and they get to "enter the city by the gates." This means they get to enter the presence of God and enjoy his good gifts.

Do you remember who was first given authority over the tree of life? God blessed Adam and Eve and gave them access to all trees except "the tree of the knowledge of good and evil" (Genesis 1:28; 2:16, 17). When they sinned by eating from that tree (3:6), God denied them access to the tree of life (3:24). The path to authority over the tree of life is the path of obedience, and the path of obedience is the one that allows God to define good and evil. Those who obey the gospel, washing their robes in the blood of the Lamb, have allowed God to show them what good and evil are, and they are like new and better Adams in a new and better Eden with authority over a new and better tree of life.

In contrast, 22:15 tells us about those who have dirty robes and refuse to turn to Christ for cleansing. These people are called "dogs" because they act like dogs. They roll in filth, they stink, and they cannot cleanse themselves. Rather than submit to God and serve him, they try to control the world through sorcery. Rather than relish the pure joys of marital intimacy, they are "sexually immoral." Rather than love people, they are "murderers." Rather than worship God alone, they are "idolaters." Rather than live in accordance with and speak the truth, they "love and practice falsehood." Rather than drink deeply of the water of life, they slurp the slime of death.

Which outcome will be yours? Will you wallow in filth and stench? Or will you go to Christ for cleansing? Will you have the curse of being banished from God's presence outside the gates of the city? Or will you have the blessing of a clean robe that you can wear as you enter the city by the gates to feast on the fruit of the tree of life in the presence of the King?

Just as Jesus punctuated the command to respond to the unsealed book (22:10, 11) by saying he was coming soon and announcing his identity in 22:12, 13, so also he punctuates the description of the two outcomes (22:14,

15) in 22:16: "I, Jesus, have sent my angel to testify to you about these things for the churches. I am the root and the descendant of David, the bright morning star." Notice how similar the first part of 22:16 is to what was said of God the Father in 22:6: "And the Lord, the God of the spirits of the prophets, has sent his angel to show his servants what must soon take place." Both the Father and Jesus are sending their angel to testify and reveal. Together they do what only God can do. No one else does what the Father and Jesus do.

We saw one throne shared by Father and Son in 22:3—"the throne of God and of the Lamb." We saw singular references ("him," "his face," "his name") to God and the Lamb in 22:3, 4. And now we see the Father doing the sending in 22:6 and Jesus doing the sending in 22:16. Behold the mystery of the Trinity!

So this first phrase of 22:16 identifies Jesus with God in that like the Father he sends his angel to testify, and the rest of 22:16 identifies Jesus as man, the prophesied son of David. He is the root prophesied in Isaiah 11:1. He is the offspring of David prophesied in 2 Samuel 7:12–14. He is the star prophesied in Numbers 24:17. He is God, and he is man, lion and lamb, slain and risen, conqueror and peacemaker, reigning and returning, servant and king, creator and consummator. He is Lord.

How do you react to that proclamation? Do you resent it? Do you feel a certain disdain for all this? Or does your heart sing? Look at how the bride and the Spirit respond in the first part of 22:17: "The Spirit and the Bride say, 'Come.' And let the one who hears say, 'Come.'" The Holy Spirit and the church together respond to the announcement that Jesus is coming with the eager longing that he indeed come! John *commands* his audience to join with the Spirit and the church in calling on the Lord Jesus to come. I urge you to obey that command. Cease your resistance to the coming King. Repent of your vain attempts to serve yourself. Join the Spirit and the church in calling Jesus to come.

Maybe you want to do just that, but you're not sure what to do. John tells you what to do in the rest of 22:17: "And let the one who is thirsty come; let the one who desires take the water of life without price." Are you thirsty? Come to Jesus. Do you want the water of life? Come to Jesus. John calls you to come and drink. Drink deeply of Jesus. Satisfy your thirst on the living water that flows from his throne. Where do you get this living water? From Jesus. How do you taste what you cannot see? Put the words of the Scripture in your mouth. Say them over and over. Ingest them. Think on them until you understand their meaning. And then trust the one who inspired the message, even if the world and Satan and your flesh give you reasons to doubt him. Believe the Bible and drink deeply of this living water.

In 22:10–17 we see that the book is unsealed. God's truth is unleashed on the world. We see that a response to God's truth is commanded—embrace it or be filthy. That command is supported by an announcement from Jesus that he is coming and that he is eternal. Then we see the two outcomes: clean robes and the tree of life in God's presence, or rebellion and banishment from God's presence. Then Jesus announces himself as God and man, and the Spirit and the church call for him to come. John then invites those who hear, who thirst, to come and drink of Jesus.

The unsealed book says Jesus is coming to judge, and those who love him call for him to come. Are you welcoming him or resisting him right now?

Revelation 22:18–20: Don't Change the Book Because Jesus Is Coming

In 22:7 Jesus blessed those who keep "the words of the prophecy of this book." Then in 22:9 the angel identified himself as a fellow servant with "those who keep the words of this book." Then in 22:10 the angel told John, "Do not seal up the words of the prophecy of this book," which means that we keep the words by setting them free to have their way in our lives. And now in 22:18, 19 John writes, "I warn everyone who hears the words of the prophecy of this book: if anyone adds to them, God will add to him the plagues described in this book, and if anyone takes away from the words of the book of this prophecy, God will take away his share in the tree of life and in the holy city, which are described in this book." We must not add to or take away from the words of the book of Revelation. This means that anyone who alters the contents of the book by adding to them or subtracting from them faces judgment.

Those who undertake to explain the contents of the book are neither adding to nor taking from but expositing. They are to be advancing the message of the book, not hindering or hiding or altering its message. James 3:1 says teachers face stricter judgment, but teaching is not adding to or taking from the words because teaching seeks to set the words free so that people will hear and heed them. Rather, taking from and adding to the book of Revelation means altering the message to suit one's own ends. Taking from and adding to the words puts the one who takes and adds in the place of God. To do this may seem humble in the eyes of worldly people, just as worldly people may think it arrogant to announce that God has spoken. But taking from and adding to the words of God acts out a heinous arrogance toward him. The righteous will recognize such arrogance, and the righteous will see the humility in the hearts of those who understand that God's Word binds the conscience. Notice how the punishment of those who take from or add to the Word fits the crime: those who add to the book have its plagues added to them; those who take from the book have their access to the tree taken from them. Be humble toward God. Tremble at his word. Unleash it.

Once again Jesus validates this teaching with the announcement that he is coming in 22:20: "He who testifies to these things says, 'Surely I am coming soon.'" And once again those who love Jesus eagerly welcome him, as John responds, "Amen. Come, Lord Jesus!" So there is a pattern in 22:10–17: a statement about "the words of the prophecy of this book," attested by the declaration from Jesus that he is coming, accompanied by the rewards and consequences he brings, and responded to by those who love Jesus as they call him to "Come." This pattern is repeated in short form in 22:18–20: a statement about "the words of the prophecy of this book," accompanied by a warning of the consequences of refusing any part of it, attested by the declaration from Jesus that he is coming, which is responded to by John calling Jesus to "Come."

Revelation 22:21: The Grace

What do we need between now and the time when Jesus comes? John tells us in the last verse of his book. In 22:21 he writes, "The grace of the Lord Jesus be with all. Amen." This is what we need to walk in Christlikeness. This is what we need to hold fast the Word of God and the testimony of Jesus. This is what we need to resist the temptations of the harlot and the onslaught of the beast. This is what we need to have the resolve to test false teachers, to stand against the synagogue of Satan, to reject the teaching of the Nicolaitans, and to cast out Jezebel. We need the grace of Jesus. He was faithful unto death, and God raised him from the dead. We must follow him in faithfulness, and we need his grace to do so. Jesus was raised by the glory of the Father, and if we follow in his footsteps by grace through faith, we too will be raised to reign with him.

Conclusion

Will God accomplish his purposes? Has Satan been defeated, and if so, will he be dislodged? If his hold on the world is going to be broken, when will that be? When will the tears be wiped away? When will the dead be raised? When will the broken be healed and the old made new?

Does it look like God's word will be kept? Or does it look to you like all things will go on as they always have? Let me invite you to consider what a crushing defeat the crucifixion *looked like* on the Friday it happened and the Saturday that followed. If anything would prove that Jesus was not the Messiah, his dying nailed to a Roman cross would. He was dead. Buried.

And from the ashes a fire was woken.
A light from the shadows did spring.
Renewed was the body once broken.
The crownless again shall be King![4]

- From death came life.
- From defeat came victory.
- From darkness came light.
- From despair came hope.
- From judgment came salvation.
- From shame came glory.
- Through Satan's machinations God's purpose was fulfilled.
- By the wicked deeds of men God accomplished his ordained plan.
- From the breaking came healing.
- From the defiling of the Holy One comes cleansing.
- Because he was forsaken of God, Jesus Christ can promise his own
  that he will never leave them.
- Because he rose, we know that he will come again.

Does it look to you like he will not come again? It looked like his project had failed when they placed him in the tomb. Does it look to you like he will not triumph? It has seemed that way before. Does it look to you like the wicked will not be judged, like evil will hold the field, like sin cannot be overcome, like the world cannot be made new? Perhaps, but God wants to pull off dramatic reversals that are beyond anything we can imagine. When Jesus comes again, his enemies will be as surprised as the wicked were to find the tomb empty. When Jesus comes again for his own, his coming will be as startling and rejuvenating, as thrilling and heartening, as enlivening and reassuring as was his resurrection from the dead.

Soli Deo Gloria!

Notes

Preface

1. Available online: http://involve.9marks.org/site/DocServer/9MarksDoc_Application_Grid.pdf?docID=841; accessed May 31, 2011.

Chapter One: The Revelation of the Glory of God's Justice and Mercy

1. See James M. Hamilton Jr., "The Glory of God in Salvation through Judgment: The Centre of Biblical Theology?" *Tyndale Bulletin* 57.1 (2006), pp. 57–84, and *God's Glory in Salvation through Judgment: A Biblical Theology* (Wheaton: Crossway, 2010).

2. Richard Bauckham, *The Climax of Prophecy: Studies on the Book of Revelation* (London: T & T Clark, 1993), p. xi.

3. This is Mark Dever's phrase, which he used to describe the overview sermons he did on each book of the Bible. These are now published as *Promises Made: The Message of the Old Testament* (Wheaton: Crossway, 2006) and *Promises Kept: The Message of the New Testament* (Wheaton: Crossway, 2005).

4. Cf. C. H. H. Scobie, *The Ways of Our God: An Approach to Biblical Theology* (Grand Rapids: Eerdmans, 2003), pp. 166, 178, 179.

5. On "The Nature of Apocalyptic" literature, see Roger Beckwith, *The Old Testament Canon of the New Testament Church and Its Background in Early Judaism* (Grand Rapids: Eerdmans, 1985), pp. 344, 345.

6. Bauckham, *Climax of Prophecy*, p. 9.

7. Richard Bauckham, *The Theology of the Book of Revelation*, New Testament Theology (Cambridge: Cambridge University Press, 1993), p. 2.

8. I read it aloud at one sitting recently, and it took me one hour and thirteen minutes.

9. See further the discussion on Revelation 2, 3 in Chapter 4 of this book.

10. Bauckham, *Climax of Prophecy*, p. 3. Bauckham holds that the body of Revelation is a single visionary experience.

11. Ibid., p. 4.

12. For a study of the way God dwells in the tabernacle and temple in the Old Testament, then indwells his people in the New Testament, see my book *God's Indwelling Presence: The Holy Spirit in the Old and New Testaments*, NACSBT (Nashville: Broadman and Holman, 2006).

Chapter Two: The Blessing of the Revelation of Jesus Christ

1. Suetonius, "Domitian," VIII.I.3, in *Lives of the Caesars*, trans. J. C. Rolfe, rev. ed. Loeb Classical Library, Vol. 38 (Cambridge, MA: Harvard University Press, 1997), p. 323.

2. Ibid., VIII.II.3, p. 325.

3. Ibid., VIII.VIII.4, p. 337.

4. Ibid., VIII.X.2, p. 341.

5. Ibid., VIII.XXII, p. 363.

6. Ibid., VIII.XVI.2, p. 355.

7. Ibid., VIII.XVIII, p. 359.

8. Ibid., VIII.XIII.2, p. 349.

9. Irenaeus, *Against Heresies*, V.XXX.3 in *The Ante-Nicene Fathers*, Alexander Roberts and James Donaldson, ed., 1885–1887, 10 volumes (reprint Peabody, MA: Hendrickson, 1994), 1:559, 560. For discussion of other possibilities as to the date of Revelation, see D. A. Carson and Douglas J. Moo, *An Introduction to the New Testament*, 2nd ed. (Grand Rapids: Zondervan, 2005), pp. 707–712.

10. See also the comments on the apocalyptic and prophetic genres in chapter 1 of this book on Revelation 1—22.

11. See the comparison of the 1963 and 2000 versions of the Baptist Faith and Message with commentary on Article 1, "The Scriptures," at http://www.precious heart.net/religious%20freedom/Baptist-Faith-Message-comp.pdf; accessed May 7, 2008.

12. See the Chicago Statement on Biblical Inerrancy, available many places online, for instance: http://www.bible-researcher.com/chicago1.html; accessed May 7, 2008.

13. All quotations of the Apostolic Fathers come from *The Apostolic Fathers*, 3rd ed., ed. and trans. Michael W. Holmes (Grand Rapids: Baker, 2007).

14. This is, of course, disputed. See the convincing discussions in favor of John the Apostle as the author of Revelation in Carson and Moo, *An Introduction to the New Testament*, pp. 700–707; Grant R. Osborne, *Revelation*, Baker Exegetical Commentary on the New Testament (Grand Rapids: Baker, 2002), pp. 2–6.

15. On the value of eyewitness testimony in the ancient world, see Richard Bauckham, *Jesus and the Eyewitnesses: The Gospels as Eyewitness Testimony* (Grand Rapids: Eerdmans, 2006), pp. 8–11.

16. See the comments on the churches in chapter 3 of this commentary, in the discussion on Revelation 1:11, and in chapter 4 in the discussion on Revelation 2—3.

17. See the fascinating discussion in Richard Bauckham, *The Theology of the Book of Revelation*, New Testament Theology (Cambridge: Cambridge University Press, 1993), pp. 109–125.

18. See further J. I. Packer and Mark Dever, *In My Place Condemned He Stood: Celebrating the Glory of the Atonement* (Wheaton: Crossway, 2008).

19. Suetonius, "Domitian," VIII.XIV, p. 349.

Chapter Three: John's Vision of the Risen Christ

1. Richard Bauckham, *The Theology of the Book of Revelation*, New Testament Theology (Cambridge: Cambridge University Press, 1993), pp. 1, 2.

2. Patmos is thirty-seven miles southwest of Miletus, which is the harbor town of Ephesus. The island is ten miles long and six miles wide.

3. Cf. Eusebius, *Ecclesiastical History*, 3.17–20: "At this time [under Domitian, ca. A.D. 95], the story goes, the Apostle and Evangelist John was still alive, and was condemned to live in the island of Patmos for his witness to the divine word. . . . After Domitian had reigned fifteen years, Nerva succeeded. The sentences of Domitian were annulled, and the Roman Senate decreed the return of those who had been unjustly banished. . . . At that time, too, the story of the ancient Christians relates that the Apostle John, after his banishment to the island, took up his abode at Ephesus."

4. Beale, citing many texts, states, "The phrase ['the word of God/the Lord'] refers typically elsewhere in the NT to the gospel traditions of Jesus' words and acts," G. K. Beale, *The Book of Revelation*, New International Greek Testament Commentary (Grand Rapids: Eerdmans, 1999), p. 202.

5. Richard Bauckham, *The Climax of Prophecy: Studies on the Book of Revelation* (New York: T & T Clark, 1993), pp. 3, 4.

6. Grant R. Osborne, *Revelation*, Baker Exegetical Commentary on the New Testament (Grand Rapids: Baker, 2002), p. 85.

7. Colin J. Hemer, *The Letters to the Seven Churches of Asia: In Their Local Setting* (Grand Rapids: Eerdmans, 2001 [1986]), p. 15.

8. Osborne, *Revelation*, p. 85.

9. Osborne notes that John is commanded to write twelve times in Revelation, here at 1:11, seven times in the letters to the churches (2, 3), and in 1:19; 14:13; 19:9; 21:5 (ibid., p. 84).

10. First Maccabees 1:21 may indicate that there was only one lampstand in the second temple. So Barry G. Webb, *The Message of Zechariah*, The Bible Speaks Today (Downers Grove, IL: InterVarsity, 2003), p. 91 n. 143.

11. I think that the events narrated in Revelation 1 fulfill those recounted in Zechariah 4, but I also think it is possible to regard what John has written as an interpretation of Zechariah 4, taking nothing away from the reality of John's visionary experience: John's mind was shaped by the literary forms of the Old Testament, so he probably interpreted his vision of Jesus through the lens of Zechariah 4. His account of what he saw was probably also influenced by the language of the Old Testament, such that as he records what he saw, he is offering an account of an event that both fulfills what is in the Old Testament and at the same time interprets the Old Testament text, shedding new light on the original meaning of the Old Testament text.

12. Cf. Joyce G. Baldwin, *Haggai, Zechariah, Malachi*, TOTC (Downers Grove, IL: InterVarsity, 1972), pp. 118–124. Baldwin suggests that the lampstand points not only to the temple but to "the Jewish community," and she refers to "the church of both Old and New Testament times" (p. 124). It seems anachronistic to refer to the "church" of Old Testament times. I have argued that under the old covenant the temple was indwelt by the Holy Spirit, whereas under the new covenant God's people are his temple, and believers are indwelt by the Spirit. See James M. Hamilton Jr., *God's Indwelling Presence: The Holy Spirit in the Old and New Testaments*, NACSBT (Nashville: Broadman and Holman, 2006). Beale (*Revelation*, pp. 207, 208) cites a number of extrabiblical texts that interpret the lampstand as pointing not only to the temple but to the people, and this fits with the "spiritualization" of the temple seen also at Qumran, where the covenanters seem to have understood their community as replacing the corrupt temple in Jerusalem (e.g., 1QS 9:6). I see this as a development taking place after the close of the Old Testament canon and probably not intrinsic to the Old Testament itself. Within the Old Testament, the temple is viewed as the dwelling of God, the place where he has set his name. God's Spirit does leave the temple before it is destroyed (Ezekiel 8—11), but at the rebuilding of the temple it seems that the Lord promised to reinhabit the rebuilt temple (cf. Haggai 2:3–5).

13. So Webb, *Zechariah*, p. 93, and Baldwin, *Haggai, Zechariah, Malachi*, p. 124.

14. Beale, *Revelation*, pp. 208, 209.

15. Similarly Beale, *Revelation*, p. 209. Osborne states that "the tendency to utilize OT descriptions of God for Jesus" is "characteristic of the Apocalypse" (*Revelation*, p. 90).

16. On this see Mark E. Dever, *The Gospel and Personal Evangelism* (Wheaton: Crossway, 2007), pp. 69–71, where Dever explodes the idea that sharing the gospel involves imposing our opinions on others. It is no imposition of personal opinion to state facts.

17. Beale, *Revelation*, pp. 209, 210; Osborne, *Revelation*, p. 91. Alternatively, Cameron Jungels writes, "For centuries bronze was the metal of choice for weaponry and tools. Eventually it gave way to iron. Since bronze was not the choicest of metals, here it probably is used to communicate its strength as used in weapons of warfare, especially since it is describing the feet of Jesus. In other words Jesus' powerful feet will trample on and defeat his foes" (private correspondence, December 11, 2010).

18. For "loosing" and "binding" with reference to the forgiveness of sins, see Matthew 16:18, 19; 18:15–18; John 20:22, 23.

Chapter Four: The Risen Christ to the Seven Churches

1. See lines 57, 58 in the Muratorian Canon, as numbered in *New Testament Apocrypha*, 2 vols., ed. Wilhelm Schneemelcher, trans. R. McL. Wilson (Louisville: Westminster John Knox, 1991), 1:36. The Muratorian Canon is an eighth-century manuscript named for L. A. Muratori (1672–1750), who found this annotated catalogue of the writings of the New Testament and published it in 1740. It seems to have originated in Rome in about A.D. 200 (cf. ibid., p. 34).

2. So also Richard Bauckham, *The Theology of the Book of Revelation*, New Testament Theology (Cambridge: Cambridge University Press, 1993), p. 16; David E. Aune, *Revelation 1–5*, Word Biblical Commentary (Nashville: Thomas Nelson, 1997), p. 119.

3. Having arrived at this position independently, I was glad to find it confirmed and clarified in G. K. Beale, *The Book of Revelation*, New International Greek Testament Commentary (Grand Rapids: Eerdmans, 1999), pp. 226, 227.

4. Cf. Beale's reflections, *Revelation*, pp. 226, 227.

5. For more discussion of the Holy Spirit's role in regeneration, see my book *God's Indwelling Presence: The Holy Spirit in the Old and New Testaments*, NACSBT (Nashville: Broadman and Holman, 2006).

6. Gregory A. Wills, *Democratic Religion: Freedom, Authority, and Church Discipline in the Baptist South 1785–1900* (New York: Oxford, 1997), p. 42.

Chapter Five: First Love

1. For more detail, see the chapters on each letter and the chapter that overviews the seven letters as a whole.

2. Cf. C. E. Arnold, "Centers of Christianity," in *Dictionary of the Later New Testament and Its Development*, pp. 146, 147 (pp. 144–152). Ignatius also wrote a letter to the church in Ephesus early in the second century.

3. See B. B. Blue, "Architecture, Early Church," in ibid., pp. 92, 93 (pp. 91–95).

4. This string of positive characteristics is not evident in all English translations, but this is how the Greek text is structured.

5. The word *apostle* is used in two ways in the New Testament. On the one hand, it refers to that closed circle of men who saw the risen Lord Jesus and were commissioned by Jesus. This closed circle included the twelve disciples, which came to include Matthias (Acts 1:15–26), Paul and Barnabas (Acts 14:14; 1 Corinthians 9:1; 15:8, 9), and the Lord's brothers—James (1 Corinthians 15:7) and possibly Jude. On the other hand, the word *apostle* can be used to refer to "messengers" of the churches and the "brothers" (2 Corinthians 8:23). Epaphroditus (Philippians 2:25) and possibly Andronicus and Junia (Romans 16:7) are referred to as "apostles" in this sense.

6. See also Shepherd of Hermas, *Mandate* 11.12; *Didache* 11:6, 9; 12:1–4, and David E. Aune, *Revelation 1–5*, Word Biblical Commentary (Nashville: Thomas Nelson, 1997), p. 155.

7. Aune, *Revelation 1–5*, p. 147.

8. Ibid., p. 150.

Chapter Six: Faithful unto Death

1. See Oskar Skarsaune, *In the Shadow of the Temple: Jewish Influences on Early Christianity* (Downers Grove, IL: InterVarsity, 2002), pp. 235, 236.

2. Eusebius, *Ecclesiastical History*, 5.1.18–19, Loeb Classical Library, 153:415.

3. Eusebius, *Ecclesiastical History*, 5.1.55–56, Loeb Classical Library, 153:433–435.

4. Colin J. Hemer, *The Letters to the Seven Churches of Asia in Their Local Setting* (Grand Rapids: Eerdmans, 2001 [1986]), p. 67; see also David E. Aune, *Revelation 1–5*, Word Biblical Commentary (Nashville: Thomas Nelson, 1997), pp. 162, 176.

5. I take this kind of language to reflect the division of humanity into the two camps described in Genesis 3:15—the seed of the woman and the seed of the serpent. For discussion see my essay, "The Skull Crushing Seed of the Woman: Inner-Biblical Interpretation of Genesis 3:15," *SBJT*, 10.2 (2006), pp. 32, 33 (30–54), available online: http://www.jamesmhamilton.org/renown/wp-content/uploads/2008/04/hamilton_sbjt_10-2.pdf. Similarly, having summarized parallel ideas in the Qumran scrolls and extrabiblical Jewish literature, Aune (*Revelation 1–5*, p. 165) writes, "This may reflect a cosmological dualism that divides the world of humanity into two separate and hostile camps, with Christians by implication belonging to the 'synagogue of the Lord.'"

6. Quoted by Michael Haykin on his blog, "Historia Ecclesiastica," http://www.andrewfullercenter.org/index.php/2008/09/doddridge-more-afraid-of-doing-wrong-than-of-dying/ (accessed September 22, 2008).

7. See the full biography by Diarmaid MacCulloch, *Thomas Cranmer: A Life* (New Haven, CT: Yale, 1996).

8. Ibid., pp. 583, 584.

9. Ibid., pp. 586, 587.

10. Ibid., p. 587.

11. Ibid., p. 588.

12. Ibid., p. 594.

13. Ibid., p. 600.

14. Ibid.

15. Ibid., pp. 601–603.

16. Ibid., p. 603.

17. Ibid.

18. Ibid.

Chapter Seven: Repent of Nicolaitan Teaching

1. Whereas many of the pronouns and verb forms are addressed to the angel of the particular church, here it is clear by the plural "among you" that the whole church is being addressed (cf. 2:20, 24 [2x], 25). I owe this observation to David E. Aune, *Revelation 1–5*, Word Biblical Commentary (Nashville: Thomas Nelson, 1997), p. 207.

2. Colin J. Hemer, *The Letters to the Seven Churches of Asia in Their Local Setting* (Grand Rapids: Eerdmans, 2001 [1986]), p. 82.

3. Aune, *Revelation 1–5*, p. 194, cf. p. 182.

4. Hemer, *The Letters to the Seven Churches*, pp. 82–85.

5. S. R. F. Price, *Rituals and Power: The Roman Imperial Cult in Asia Minor* (New York: Cambridge University Press, 1984), p. 1. See the "fragments of a marble pedestal from Pergamum" bearing the inscription, "The Emperor, Caesar, son of a god, the god Augustus, of every land and sea the overseer" cited, with a drawing of the pedestal, by Adolf Deissmann, *Light from the Ancient East*, trans. Lionel R. M. Strachan (Grand Rapids: Baker, 1978 [1927]), p. 347.

6. For explanations of what eating food offered to idols entailed, see Aune, *Revelation 1–5*, pp. 186, 191–194.

Chapter Eight: King Jesus versus Jezebel

1. Joseph J. Ellis, *Founding Brothers: The Revolutionary Generation* (New York: Vintage, 2002), p. 132.

2. David E. Aune, *Revelation 1–5*, Word Biblical Commentary (Nashville: Thomas Nelson, 1997), pp. 201, 202, citing J. Reynolds, *Aphrodisias and Rome* (London: Society for the Promotion of Roman Studies, 1982) document 12, line 1, p. 101.

3. So Colin J. Hemer, *The Letters to the Seven Churches of Asia in Their Local Setting* (Grand Rapids: Eerdmans, 2001 [1986]), p. 121.

4. Aune (*Revelation 1–5*, p. 206) notes that 2:23 alludes to Jeremiah 17:10.

5. Aune helpfully sets the Greek text of 2:26b, 27 next to the Greek translation of Psalm 2:8, 9 to highlight the many points of contact between the two passages (*Revelation 1–5*, p. 209).

6. The fact that Numbers 24:17 and Psalm 2:7–9 are often cited in Biblical and extrabiblical literature with reference to the messianic hope seems to strengthen the conclusion that Numbers 24:17 informs the promise made in Revelation 2:28.

Chapter Nine: Wake Up!

1. Colin J. Hemer, *The Letters to the Seven Churches of Asia in Their Local Setting* (Grand Rapids: Eerdmans, 2001 [1986]), p. 133.

2. Herodotus, *The Persian War*, 1.84, trans. George Rawlinson, The Modern Library, 1942, available online: http://mcadams.posc.mu.edu/txt/ah/Herodotus/Herodotus1.html; accessed October 3, 2008, emphasis mine.

3. Polybius, *Histories*, 7.15–18, trans. W. R. Paton, Loeb Classical Library, English text available online: http://penelope.uchicago.edu/Thayer/E/Roman/Texts/Polybius/7*.html; accessed October 3, 2008.

4. The connection in 5:6 between the "seven spirits of God" and the "seven eyes" seems to be informed by John's understanding of Zechariah 4, esp. vv. 2–10.

See further Richard Bauckham, *The Theology of the Book of Revelation*, New Testament Theology (Cambridge: Cambridge University Press, 1993), pp. 110, 111.

5. David E. Aune, *Revelation 1–5*, Word Biblical Commentary (Nashville: Thomas Nelson, 1997), p. 218.

6. This might be what is happening in Sardis, but Grant Osborne rightly notes that "there is no corroborative evidence of Jewish attacks against the Sardian Christians in the text, as there is in the letters to Smyrna and Philadelphia. Therefore, it must remain conjectural." Grant R. Osborne, *Revelation*, Baker Exegetical Commentary on the New Testament (Grand Rapids: Baker, 2002), p. 180 n. 15.

7. See Hemer, *The Letters to the Seven Churches*, p. 149.

8. See ibid., pp. 149, 151.

9. Aune, *Revelation 1–5*, p. 221.

Chapter Ten: An Open Door No One Can Shut

1. For this information on Charles Simeon I am mainly dependent upon John Piper, "Brothers, We Must Not Mind a Little Suffering: Meditations on the Life of Charles Simeon," delivered at the 1989 Bethlehem Conference for Pastors, available online: http://www.desiringgod.org/ResourceLibrary/Biographies/1460_Broth ers_We_Must_Not_Mind_a_Little_Suffering/; accessed October 6, 2008. See also Handley Moule, *Charles Simeon: Pastor of a Generation* (Fearn, Ross-shire, UK: Christian Focus, 1997 [1892]).

2. See further the "Context" section of each study on the individual seven letters, as well as the study that overviews the seven letters as a whole.

3. See the study on the letter to the church at Smyrna.

4. See the exchange between Douglas J. Moo and Gleason L. Archer Jr. in *Three Views on the Rapture: Pre-, Mid-, or Post-Tribulational?* (Grand Rapids: Zondervan, 1996 [1984]), pp. 196–198, 218–221.

Chapter Eleven: I Will Spit You out of My Mouth

1. Colin J. Hemer, *The Letters to the Seven Churches of Asia in Their Local Setting* (Grand Rapids: Eerdmans, 2001 [1986]), pp. 186, 187.

2. Ibid., p. 188.

3. Ibid., pp. 188, 189.

4. Ibid., pp. 191–196, 208.

5. Ibid., pp. 196–199, 208.

6. Ibid., pp. 200, 208.

7. Ibid., p. 202, citing Plutarch, *Sulla* 25.2.

8. For discussion, see ibid., pp. 186–191.

9. John Piper, *Don't Waste Your Life* (Wheaton: Crossway, 2007), p. 12.

Chapter Twelve: The Throne Room Vision

1. Ezekiel 1:10: "As for the likeness of their faces, each had a human face. The four had the face of a lion on the right side, the four had the face of an ox on the left side, and the four had the face of an eagle."

Chapter Thirteen: The One Seated on the Throne

1. Similarly G. K. Beale, *The Book of Revelation*, New International Greek Testament Commentary (Grand Rapids: Eerdmans, 1999), p. 332: ". . . the main point

of the vision and of the whole chapter: God is to be glorified because of his holiness and sovereignty" (italics removed).

2. For the story of what has taken place at Southern, see Gregory A. Wills, *Southern Baptist Theological Seminary, 1859–2009* (Oxford: Oxford University Press, 2009).

3. See, e.g., Grant R. Osborne, *Revelation*, Baker Exegetical Commentary on the New Testament (Grand Rapids: Baker, 2002), pp. 228, 229.

4. See the study on Revelation 3:1–6.

5. For further discussion of these living creatures, see Beale, *Revelation*, pp. 328–331.

6. For further comments on 4:9–11, see the study on chapters 4–5.

Chapter Fourteen: The Lamb Standing as Though Slain

1. Cf. G. K. Beale, *The Book of Revelation*, New International Greek Testament Commentary (Grand Rapids: Eerdmans, 1999), p. 365: "The glory of God and the Lamb, which is grounded in their sovereignty, is the main point of the ch. 5 vision, as well as the vision in ch. 4" (italics removed).

2. For a summary of other possibilities regarding the scroll and its contents, arguing for the view taken here, see Grant R. Osborne, *Revelation*, Baker Exegetical Commentary on the New Testament (Grand Rapids: Baker, 2002), pp. 248–250.

3. See Edmund Spenser's poem *The Faerie Queene*.

4. See especially the discussion in Peter G. Bolt, *The Cross from a Distance: The Atonement in Mark's Gospel*, NSBT (Downers Grove: InterVarsity, 2004), pp. 71–75.

5. Available online: http://www.tenth.org/fileadmin/files_for_download/Pdf_ar ticles/000507_JMB.pdf; accessed January 20, 2009.

Chapter Fifteen: God's Plan to Save and Judge

1. Eusebius, *Ecclesiastical History* 6.7, Loeb Classical Library, 265, p. 29.

2. "China: Pastor Sent to Labor Camp," The Voice of the Martyrs website, http://www.persecution.com/public/newsroom.aspx?story_ID=MTYw; accessed 2009.

3. "China: Persecution Increases," The Voice of the Martyrs website, http://www.persecution.com/public/newsroom.aspx?story_ID=MTU4; accessed 2009.

4. "Pakistan: Christian Homes Burned," The Voice of the Martyrs website, http://www.persecution.com/public/newsroom.aspx?story_ID=MTU2; accessed 2009.

5. Eusebius, *Hist. Eccl.* 6.41, Loeb Classical Library, 265, p. 103.

6. Ibid., p. 107.

7. Though I usually quote the ESV, here I believe the NASB has superior renderings. In particular, the NASB is right to join the "seven weeks and sixty-two weeks" in Daniel 9:25, against the accentuation of the Masoretic Text (which the ESV follows to arrive at its rendering, "seven weeks. Then for sixty-two weeks"). This rendering is superior in that it matches the visions in Daniel 2, 7, 8, which prophesy of what will take place between Daniel's time and the time of the Messiah.

8. See Bob Pickle's Table of Sabbatical Years available online: http://www.pick le-publishing.com/papers/sabbatical-years-table.htm#164; accessed July 25, 2009. I wish to thank Professor Peter J. Gentry for drawing my attention to this resource.

9. I am grateful for Dr. Gentry's interaction on this point, and I wish to point out that he takes "the prince who is to come" in 9:26 to be the Messiah described in 9:25,

whereas I remain convinced that "the prince who is to come" in 9:26 is a different figure, the Antichrist, because it seems to me to fit more naturally with Daniel 11:31; 12:11; Matthew 24:15/Mark 13:14.

Chapter Sixteen: The Seals on the Scroll

1. Epistle to Diognetus, 7:7.

2. Available online: http://www.sunnewsonline.com/webpages/news/national/2009/aug/06/national-06–08–2009–01.htm; accessed August 8, 2009.

Chapter Seventeen: The Sealing of the Servants of God

1. See further G. K. Beale, *The Book of Revelation*, New International Greek Testament Commentary (Grand Rapids: Eerdmans, 1999), p. 406.

2. For further discussion, see Grant R. Osborne, *Revelation*, Baker Exegetical Commentary on the New Testament (Grand Rapids: Baker, 2002), pp. 313–315.

3. See the discussion in Richard Bauckham, *The Climax of Prophecy: Studies on the Book of Revelation* (Edinburgh: T&T Clark, 1993), p. 217.

4. This interpretation was explained to me in private conversation with Professor Thomas R. Schreiner. See also ibid., p. 215.

5. Cf. also 1 Maccabees 9:27, "and there was great tribulation in Israel, such as had not been from the day when there was not a prophet among them" (applying Daniel 12:1 to the events in the second century B.C.).

Chapter Eighteen: Trumpeting the End of the World

1. In this case the *kai* between "hail" and "fire" might be an "epexegetical *kai*," resulting in the translation, "hail, even fire."

2. For my view on the chiastic structure of the whole book of Revelation, see the chapter in this book on Revelation 6—16.

3. D. A. Carson, *Memoirs of an Ordinary Pastor: The Life and Reflections of Tom Carson* (Wheaton: Crossway, 2008), p. 72.

Chapter Nineteen: The Unimagined Horrors of God's Judgment

1. J. R. R. Tolkien, *The Return of the King*, 2nd ed. (Boston: Houghton Mifflin, 1993 [1965]), p. 97.

2. Grant R. Osborne, *Revelation*, Baker Exegetical Commentary on the New Testament (Grand Rapids: Baker, 2002), p. 373.

Chapter Twenty: Eat This Scroll (and Prophesy the History of the Future)

1. *American V: A Hundred Highways*, American Recordings, 2006.

2. Richard Bauckham, *The Theology of the Book of Revelation*, New Testament Theology (New York: Cambridge University Press, 1993), pp. 82, 83.

3. Cf. also Jeremiah 15:16, "Your words were found, and I ate them, and your words became to me a joy and the delight of my heart, for I am called by your name, O LORD, God of hosts."

Chapter Twenty-one: Bearing Witness 'til Kingdom Come

1. John G. Paton, *John G. Paton: Missionary to the New Hebrides*, ed. James Paton (Edinburgh: The Banner of Truth Trust, 2002 [1889]), pp. 55, 56.

2. See T. Desmond Alexander, *From Eden to the New Jerusalem: Exploring God's Plan for Life on Earth* (Nottingham, UK: Inter-Varsity Press, 2008), and G. K. Beale, *The Temple and the Church's Mission: A Biblical Theology of the Dwelling Place of God* (Downers Grove, IL: InterVarsity, 2004).

3. Harold W. Hoehner, "Daniel's Seventy Weeks and New Testament Chronology," *Bibliotheca Sacra* 46 (1975): pp. 47–65. Similarly Gleason L. Archer, "Daniel," in *The Expositor's Bible Commentary*, ed. Frank E. Gaebelein, Vol. 7 (Grand Rapids: Zondervan, 1985), p. 26.

4. For all the references to this three-and-a-half-year period in Daniel and Revelation, see Table 15.4 in the chapter on Revelation 6—16.

5. Cf. a similar suggestion of prophetic foreshortening, but coming to different conclusions, in Roger T. Beckwith, *Calendar and Chronology, Jewish and Christian: Biblical, Intertestamental and Patristic Studies*, Arbeiten zur Geschichte des antiken Judentums und des Urchristentums (Leiden: E.J. Brill, 1996), pp. 308, 309.

6. Ibid., p. 309.

7. Meredith G. Kline, "The Covenant of the Seventieth Week," in *The Law and the Prophets: Old Testament Studies in Honor of Oswald T. Allis*, ed. J. H. Skilton (Phillipsburg, NJ: Presbyterian and Reformed), pp. 452–469; http://www.moner gism.com/Kline,%20Meredith%20-%20The%20Covenant%20of%20the%20Sev entieth%20Week%20%28Daniel%209%29.pdf. So also Kim Riddlebarger, *A Case for Amillennialism: Understanding the End Times* (Grand Rapids: Baker, 2003), pp. 154–156.

8. Archer, "Daniel," in *The Expositor's Bible Commentary*, pp. 113, 116, 117.

Chapter Twenty-two: The Seed of the Woman Conquers the Serpent

1. Grant R. Osborne, *Revelation*, Baker Exegetical Commentary on the New Testament (Grand Rapids: Baker, 2002), p. 461. See also Daniel 11:32.

2. G. K. Beale, *The Book of Revelation: A Commentary on the Greek Text*, New International Greek Testament Commentary (Grand Rapids: Eerdmans, 1999), p. 639.

3. See the literature cited in Table 21.2 in Chapter 21.

4. For a table that lays out these positions, see Table 21.2, "Interpretations of Daniel's Seventieth Week," in Chapter 21. If I am incorrect in my interpretation of Daniel 9, and if the covenant that is confirmed for the many in Daniel 9:27 refers to the cross of Christ, then Beckwith's view or the view typically embraced by amillennialists would seem most likely correct (though they would still be wrong on the millennium!). At this point it seems to me that the ending of sacrifice and the desolating abomination in Daniel 9:27 should be read as negative things (rather than the positive death of Christ on the cross and the destruction of Jerusalem in A.D. 70) paralleling the similar descriptions in Daniel 8:11–13; 11:31; 12:11. That is, because of the parallels between Daniel 9:27 and 8:11–13, 11:31, and 12:11, I am not at present convinced that the covenant confirmed for the many in 9:27 refers to the death of Christ on the cross.

5. Russell D. Moore, *Adopted for Life: The Priority of Adoption for Christian Families and Churches* (Wheaton: Crossway, 2009), pp. 59–84.

Chapter Twenty-three: The Beast

1. Suetonius, *The Life of Nero*, 40.

2. This whole discussion is dependent upon the essay "Nero and the Beast," in Richard Bauckham, *The Climax of Prophecy: Studies on the Book of Revelation* (Edinburgh: T&T Clark, 1993), esp. pp. 407–452. Bauckham provides a quotation from Philostratus, *The Life of Apollonius of Tyana*, Christopher P. Jones, ed., 4.38, in which Nero is referred to as a beast (410). See also R. H. Charles, *A Critical and Exegetical Commentary on the Revelation of St. John*, International Critical Commentary, Vol. 2 (Edinburgh: T & T Clark, 1920), pp. 80, 81.

3. Bauckham, *The Climax of Prophecy*, p. 408.

4. Compare also Daniel 7:2b, "the four winds of heaven were stirring up the great sea," and Revelation 7:1's description of the four angels "holding back the four winds of the earth, that no wind might blow on earth or sea. . . ."

5. Cf. especially the description of the Lamb "standing, as though it had been slain" in 5:6 with the description of the beast's head as though slain in 13:3.

Chapter Twenty-four: The False Prophet

1. See Table 15.1, "The Chiastic Structure of Revelation."

2. See also the similarity of the phrases in the Greek of Revelation 10:1 and 13:1.

3. Richard Bauckham, *The Climax of Prophecy: Studies on the Book of Revelation* (Edinburgh: T&T Clark, 1993), p. 387.

4. Ibid., pp. 388, 389.

Chapter Twenty-five: The Song of the Redeemed

1. James Joyce, *A Portrait of the Artist as a Young Man* (New York: B. W. Huebsch, 1916), pp. 152, 153. I wish to thank Travis Cardwell for bringing this quotation to my attention.

2. Ibid., pp. 151, 152.

Chapter Twenty-six: The Harvest of the Earth

1. Antonio James is the subject of the first chapter of the book about Burl Cain's work at Angola prison by Dennis Shere, *Cain's Redemption: A Story of Hope and Transformation in America's Bloodiest Prison* (Chicago: Northfield, 2005), pp. 19–27, quotes on pp. 22, 26.

2. G. K. Beale, *The Book of Revelation: A Commentary on the Greek Text*, New International Greek Testament Commentary (Grand Rapids: Eerdmans, 1999), pp. 776–778.

3. Grant R. Osborne, *Revelation*, Baker Exegetical Commentary on the New Testament (Grand Rapids: Baker, 2002), pp. 551–553.

4. Eugene Tanniehill's story is told in the story of Burl Cain's work as warden of Angola prison in Shere, *Cain's Redemption*, pp. 83–94.

Chapter Twenty-seven: Seven Angels with Seven Plagues

1. "Medal of Honor," http://en.wikipedia.org/wiki/Medal_of_Honor; accessed April 4, 2011.

2. Lecrae, "Don't Waste Your Life," from the album *Rebel*, Central South District, 2008.

Chapter Twenty-eight: The Seven Bowls of Wrath

1. The ESV wrongly gives the impression that the water became "like blood," but "like" compares the blood to that of a corpse, not to the blood itself.

2. Grant R. Osborne, *Revelation*, Baker Exegetical Commentary on the New Testament (Grand Rapids: Baker, 2002), p. 581; G. K. Beale, *The Book of Revelation: A Commentary on the Greek Text*, New International Greek Testament Commentary (Grand Rapids: Eerdmans, 1999), p. 817.

Chapter Twenty-nine: The Harlot and the Beast

1. See Gregory K. Beale, "The Danielic Background for Revelation 13:18 and 17:9," *Tyndale Bulletin* 31 (1980): 163–170.

Chapter Thirty-two: The Return of the King

1. This information on the Sentinels is from http://www.tombguard.org/FAQ.html and http://www.tombguard.org/general.html; accessed June 5, 2004.

2. David Andrew Thomas, *Revelation 19 in Historical and Mythological Context*, Studies in Biblical Literature (New York: Peter Lang, 2008), p. 19.

3. This language comes from a document that was given to me when I was in college called "The Fellowship of the Unashamed"; available online: http://www.godswork.org/inspiration6.htm; accessed April 27, 2011.

4. Thomas, *Revelation 19 in Historical and Mythological Context*, p. 140. The historical information on Parthia here depends heavily on Thomas's study.

Chapter Thirty-three: The Millennium

1. Cf. Emil Schürer, *The History of the Jewish People in the Age of Jesus Christ (175 B.C.–A.D. 135)*, ed. Geza Vermes, Fergus Millar, and Matthew Black, Vol. 2 (Edinburgh: T. & T. Clark, 1973), p. 536: "Often, however, the glory of the messianic kingdom is not regarded as final and supreme. An even higher heavenly bliss is looked for, with the result that only a limited duration is ascribed to the rule of the Messiah, the length of which is fully debated in the Talmud."

2. G. K. Beale, *The Book of Revelation: A Commentary on the Greek Text*, New International Greek Testament Commentary (Grand Rapids: Eerdmans, 1999), p. 973.

3. Richard Bauckham agrees that the book of Revelation teaches the premillennial perspective, but he does not think we should expect the millennium to happen. He writes, "Thus John has taken from the Jewish apocalyptic tradition the notion of a temporary messianic reign on earth before the last judgment and the new creation (cf. 2 Bar. 40:3; 4 Ezra 7:28–9; b.Sanh. 99a), but he has characteristically made something different of it. He has used it to depict an essential aspect of his concept of the victory of the martyrs over the beast. . . . The millennium becomes incomprehensible once we take the image literally. But there is no more need to take it literally than to suppose that the sequences of judgments (the seal openings, the trumpets, the bows) are literal predictions. John no doubt expected there to be judgments, but his descriptions of them are imaginative schemes designed to depict the meaning of the judgments. John expected the martyrs to be vindicated, but the millennium depicts the meaning, rather than predicting the manner of their vindication." Richard Bauckham, *The Theology of the Book of Revelation*, New Testament Theology (New York: Cambridge University Press, 1993), p. 108.

4. The conclusion that millennial expectation is somehow out of step with the genre of apocalyptic literature or Jewish expectation is unwarranted. Emil Schürer writes, "the moment of [the Messiah's] coming was again reckoned variously, according to whether the days of the Messiah were identified with the future עוֹלָם or the present one." Schürer, *The History of the Jewish People in the Age of Jesus Christ*, Vol. 2, p. 523.

5. Beale, *Revelation*, p. 986.

6. See the discussion in Grant R. Osborne, *Revelation*, Baker Exegetical Commentary on the New Testament (Grand Rapids: Baker, 2002), pp. 703–706.

7. Beale, *Revelation*, pp. 1003–1015.

8. Cf. N. T. Wright, *The Resurrection of the Son of God*, Vol. 3, Christian Origins and the Question of God (Minneapolis: Fortress, 2003), pp. 474, 475: "to use the word 'resurrection' to *refer to* death in an attempt to invest it with a new meaning seems to me to strain usage well beyond breaking point. In addition, verse 4 seems to envisage two stages; first, the martyrs are killed; then, at a later stage, they come to life. Collapsing these two into one . . . seems implausible. This does not mean, of course, that we are thereby projected into a premillennial literalism. Rather, it seems likely that we are faced here with a radical innovation: a use of the word 'resurrection' to mean a coming-to-life in a sense other than, and prior to, that of the final bodily raising. . . . I regard the use of the word 'spiritual' to mean 'non-bodily' as misleading; and we should note carefully that in 20.4 the souls 'came to life'. This implies that they were formerly 'dead souls' (still existing souls, but in a state of death), and that they entered a new, second stage of post-mortem existence, a form of new life. For them, it seems, the journey to the ultimate destination is a *three* step progression after death: first, a state of being 'dead souls'; second, whatever is meant by the 'first resurrection'; third, the implied 'second' or 'final' resurrection described (though not with that phrase) in chapters 21 and 22." Wright is convincing on the point that using the word "resurrection" to refer to death strains the usage beyond the breaking point, but he is not convincing in his assertion that the instance of the word in Revelation 20:5 is a radical linguistic innovation.

9. Beale, *Revelation*, p. 976.

10. See Schürer, *The History of the Jewish People in the Age of Jesus Christ (175 B.C.–A.D. 135)*, p. 537: "wherever the messianic kingdom is envisaged as one of temporary duration, the end of this time is expected to be marked by another renewal of the world and the last judgment."

Chapter Thirty-five: The New Jerusalem

1. "Precious Metal," http://en.wikipedia.org/wiki/Gold_bullion#Bullion; accessed March 13, 2010.

2. "Gold," http://en.wikipedia.org/wiki/Gold; accessed March 13, 2010.

3. "United States Bullion Depository," http://en.wikipedia.org/wiki/United_States_Bullion_Depository; accessed March 13, 2010.

4. Ibid.

5. See http://www.treasury.gov/resource-center/faqs/About-Treasury/Pages/tours.aspx; accessed March 13, 2010.

6. Grant R. Osborne, *Revelation*, Baker Exegetical Commentary on the New Testament (Grand Rapids: Baker, 2002), p. 752.

7. G. K. Beale, *The Book of Revelation: A Commentary on the Greek Text*, New International Greek Testament Commentary (Grand Rapids: Eerdmans, 1999), p. 1074.

8. Osborne, *Revelation*, p. 754.

9. Beale, *The Book of Revelation*, p. 1077.

Chapter Thirty-seven: Come, Lord Jesus!

1. See J. R. R. Tolkien, *The Fellowship of the Ring* and *The Two Towers*.

2. This sermon was preached at Kenwood Baptist Church in Louisville, Kentucky on April 4, 2010, Easter Sunday.

3. This is just one of several points of contact between Revelation and Daniel 12. Others include: the deliverance of those whose names are written in the book (Daniel 12:1; cf. Revelation 13:8; 17:8; 21:27); resurrection of the righteous and the wicked (Daniel 12:2; Revelation 20:4, 5, 12–15); and the references to three-and-a-half-year periods (Daniel 12:7, 11; Revelation 11:3; 12:14, see also Table 15.4).

4. This is an adaptation of a poem J. R. R. Tolkien put on the lips of Bilbo Baggins for Strider, Aragorn, son of Arathorn in *The Lord of the Rings*.

Scripture Index

General Index

Index of Sermon Illustrations

words, "Well done, good and faithful
servant," 302

Second coming of Christ
If we had known 9/11 was coming, we
would have warned everyone we
could; it should be the same with
Christ's return, 17, 26
Lost, unsure how to find his parents, a
note from the author's father encourages him and promises the father's
return; and Christ will come back for
us, 221–222, 230
If we knew the governor of our state or
the President of the United States was
coming to visit us, we would make
elaborate preparations to appear before
him; how much more should we do so
regarding the future return of Christ,
409

Sovereignty of God
Months before his death from cancer,
pastor James Montgomery Boice
told his congregation that if we could
change what God is doing in our life,
we would make things worse—a good
God is in control, 160
Sometimes it seems as if God is choosing
inferior players for a pickup basketball
game, but his team wins every time,
249
We would probably panic if an airline
pilot let his nine-year-old son fly the
plane; in contrast, when God begins
his rule on the earth, all will be well,
350

Spiritual warfare
As Sardis was twice captured at the point
of its supposed greatest strength, so
we too must remain ever vigilant,
103–104
The Nazgûl, the "Black Riders" in Tolkien's The Lord of the Rings, illustrate
our spiritual enemies, 209

Formidable spiritual enemies can be defeated as God's servants courageously
fight against them, 218–219
Even after his suicide, some believed
Nero would return with a victorious
army, a picture of the beast in a future
day, 257, 361

Temptation
The Knight of the Redcrosse, in Spenser's
The Faerie Queen, learns that the
beautiful lady luring him is a witch in
disguise, 85
The rush felt when leaping off a fifty-
story building illustrates the false
excitement of sinful pleasure, 364

Transformation
Antonio James, a murderer on Death Row,
comes to Christ and asks the family of
his victim to forgive him, 291
Now known as the Bishop of Angola Prison, Eugene Tanniehill came to Christ
while serving a life sentence and has
won many others to Christ, 299

True wealth
The spiritual wealth of followers of Christ
contrasts with the material wealth of
the world, as illustrated by a passenger
on the *Titanic* having nothing but a
lifeboat while others have jewels and
much money but no lifeboat, 78
We have so much more in Christ than
Jews had in the synagogue, 118
Fort Knox contains unimaginable amounts
of gold, but our heavenly treasures are
worth so much more, 391–392

Victory
Achilles, thought to be immortal, died
because of his one weakness, but followers of Christ truly are invulnerable,
187
Formidable spiritual enemies can be defeated as God's servants courageously
fight against them, 218–219